HUMAN ENVIRONMENTS
A CROSS-CULTURAL ENCYCLOPEDIA

ENCYCLOPEDIAS OF THE HUMAN EXPERIENCE

David Levinson, Series Editor

HUMAN ENVIRONMENTS
A CROSS-CULTURAL ENCYCLOPEDIA

David Levinson

ABC-CLIO
Santa Barbara, California
Denver, Colorado
Oxford, England

Library of Congress Cataloging-in-Publication Data

Levinson, David, 1947–
    Human environments : a cross-cultural encyclopedia / David Levinson
        p.   cm. — (Encyclopedias of the human experience)
    Includes bibliographical references and index.
    1. Human ecology—Encyclopedias.
    I. Title   II. Series.
GF4.L49   1995   304.2'03—dc20   95-39798

ISBN 0-87436-784-0 (alk. paper)

02 01 00 99 98 97 96 95   10 9 8 7 6 5 4 3 2 1 (hc)

ABC-CLIO, Inc.
130 Cremona Drive, P.O. Box 1911
Santa Barbara, California 93116-1911

This book is printed on acid-free paper ∞.
Manufactured in the United States of America

Contents

Contents

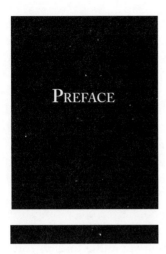

Human beings live in, are influenced by, and influence four types of environments: the physical, the biological, the sociocultural, and the supernatural. The physical environment includes the climate, weather, landforms, and natural resources including plants. The biological environment includes nonhuman organisms such as animals, fish, insects, bacteria, and viruses. The sociocultural environment is composed of members of one's own culture and other cultures and the relationship between and among individuals and groups. The supernatural environment is composed of beliefs about the supernatural world and the forces that inhabit it. This volume is about the physical environment and, more specifically, about the relationships between humans and their physical environments around the world. At the same time, however, the biological, sociocultural, and supernatural environments are not ignored because in all cultures an interrelationship exists among these four environments. I stress, with numerous examples from cultures around the world, that the Western model of the world that rigidly distinguishes among these four environments is not the model of the universe typical of most cultures. Rather, in many cultures no clear distinction is made between these four environments; instead, they are viewed as integrated components of a whole. And in many cultures, people believe that an understanding of any one type of environment depends on an understanding of the others. Thus, throughout the volume the reader will find descriptions of how cultures organize themselves economically, socially, and politically to exploit their physical and biological environments and descriptions of how cultures routinely call on the supernatural when interacting with their physical environment. Conversely, the reader will also learn how the physical environment shapes peoples' beliefs about the supernatural world and limits and provides opportunities for various forms of social organization and interaction.

Humans inhabit six general types of ecosystems and a variety of bioregions, or ecological zones, within each of these systems.

1. Desert or dry lands that receive less than 10 inches of rain per year; sandy or rocky soil; vegetation mainly in the form of shrubs and grasses; and few or no trees

2. Tropical rainforests that have much rainfall; a warm to hot, humid climate; green vegetation throughout the year; a great variety of flora and fauna; and soil that is of low fertility and subject to erosion

3. Boreal forests that have long, cold winters and short summers; numerous coniferous trees; and relatively few deciduous trees

4. Grasslands that have a semiarid climate and are covered by grasses or grasslike plants such as prairies, steppes, and savannas

5. Temperate deciduous forests that have moderate temperatures; distinct seasons; rainfall from 30–60 inches per year; and a mix of vegetation types such as coniferous and deciduous trees, shrubs, and grasses

6. Tundra, the ecosystem found in Arctic regions, that has wet soil; permafrost beneath the soil; and short plants such as grasses, lichens, and sedges

Humans, of course, do not live in marine or freshwater environments although they do exploit these environments for food, travel, and other purposes. In addition to these six major types of ecosystems based on climate and vegetation, humans also live in regions defined by elevation such as mountains, on islands, and in locales defined by the availability of water such as river valleys and deltas. In this volume the reader will find information about the human-environment relationship in all of these different environments as well as in numerous localized ecosystems within these general environmental regions.

The information in this volume pertains mainly to people in some 150 traditional, non-industrialized cultures. Such a focus is especially valuable for a survey of human-environment relationships because people in these cultures are in regular and close contact with their physical environments. For many of these cultures, survival requires careful and efficient use of their environment to obtain sufficient food, shelter, clothing, and other necessities of life. For these cultures, most information provided here pertains to customary beliefs, ideas, and behaviors—that is, the way of life typical of a culture or society—rather than to specific behaviors of individuals.

Five general subject areas relevant to the culture-environment relationship are covered by the entries in this volume. First are general environmental adaptations that to some extent are a concern in all cultures, such as the annual subsistence cycle, mobility-sedentism, settlement patterns, and dwelling style and form. Second are specific subsistence systems used to collect or produce food such as hunting and gathering, fishing, and agriculture. Third are conceptualizations of, beliefs about, and attempts to control or influence key features of the environment such as the components of the universe, sun and moon, space, color, time, fire, wind, seasonal changes, distance, and the weather. Fourth are beliefs about and efforts to control specific environmental events such as storms, thunder and lightning, and food shortages. And fifth are general concepts about the environment used in the environmental and social sciences as applied to non-Western peoples; these are discussed in articles including "Tragedy of the Commons," "Carrying Capacity," "Built Environments," "Environmental Ethics," and "Environmental Disasters." Taken as a group, the entries in this volume point to both the commonalities across cultures that people experience in interacting with their environments and highlight the enormous variation displayed across cultures in developing, inventing, discovering, and applying mechanisms that mediate the human-environmental relationship.

In closing, I want to thank my wife, Karen Christensen, for sharing many thoughts about the environment and also much reference material from her personal library. I also want to thank Patricia Andreucci for her help in finding and acquiring various materials.

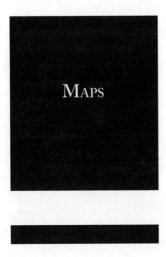

MAPS

The following maps show approximate locations
of the cultures mentioned in the text.

Africa and the Middle East

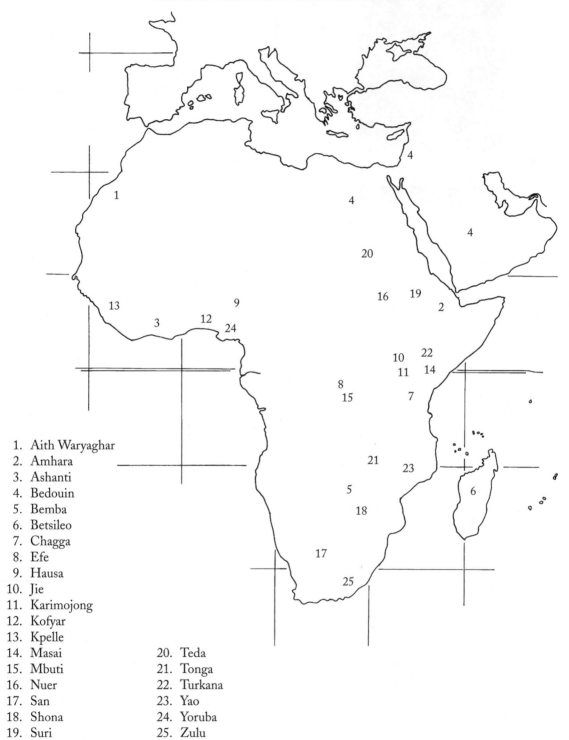

1. Aith Waryaghar
2. Amhara
3. Ashanti
4. Bedouin
5. Bemba
6. Betsileo
7. Chagga
8. Efe
9. Hausa
10. Jie
11. Karimojong
12. Kofyar
13. Kpelle
14. Masai
15. Mbuti
16. Nuer
17. San
18. Shona
19. Suri
20. Teda
21. Tonga
22. Turkana
23. Yao
24. Yoruba
25. Zulu

Central and South America

1. Ache
2. Aymara
3. Aztec
4. Garifuna
5. Haitians
6. Inca
7. Jamaicans
8. Maya
9. Mundurucu
10. Quechua
11. Siriono
12. Toba
13. Tzeltal
14. Warao
15. Yaghan
16. Yanomamö
17. Zapotec

Europe and Asia

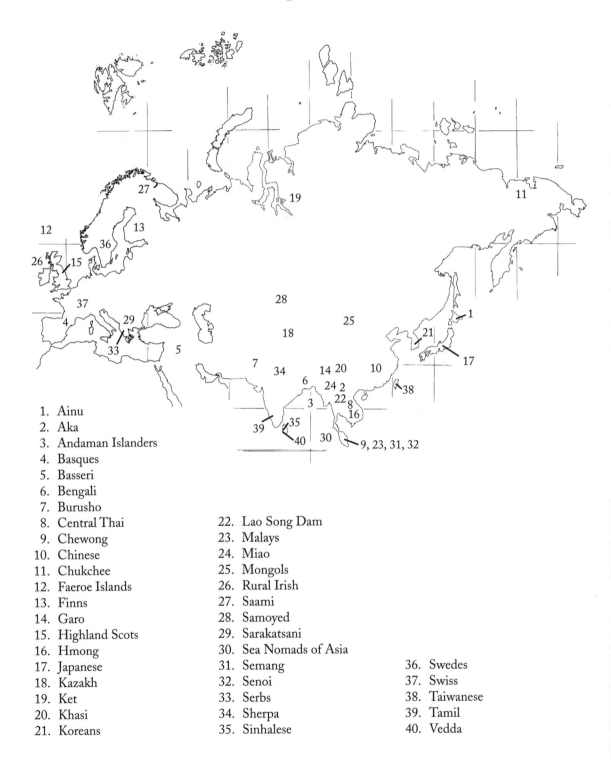

1. Ainu
2. Aka
3. Andaman Islanders
4. Basques
5. Basseri
6. Bengali
7. Burusho
8. Central Thai
9. Chewong
10. Chinese
11. Chukchee
12. Faeroe Islands
13. Finns
14. Garo
15. Highland Scots
16. Hmong
17. Japanese
18. Kazakh
19. Ket
20. Khasi
21. Koreans

22. Lao Song Dam
23. Malays
24. Miao
25. Mongols
26. Rural Irish
27. Saami
28. Samoyed
29. Sarakatsani
30. Sea Nomads of Asia
31. Semang
32. Senoi
33. Serbs
34. Sherpa
35. Sinhalese

36. Swedes
37. Swiss
38. Taiwanese
39. Tamil
40. Vedda

North America

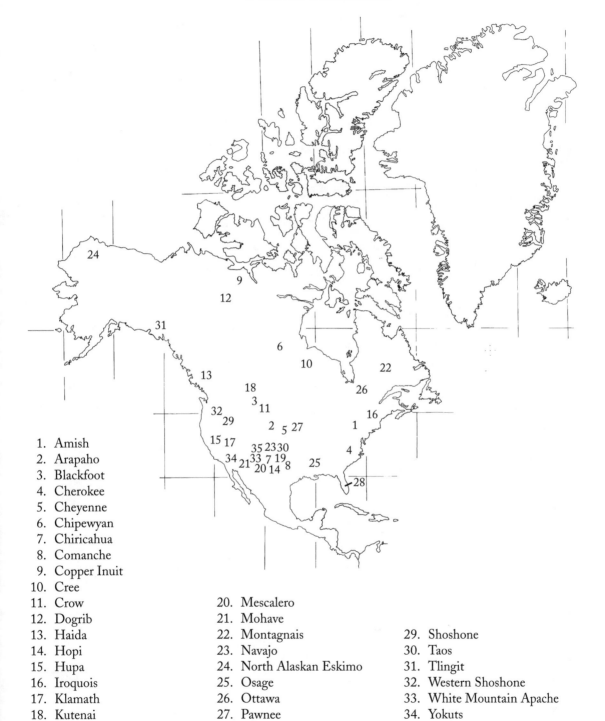

1. Amish
2. Arapaho
3. Blackfoot
4. Cherokee
5. Cheyenne
6. Chipewyan
7. Chiricahua
8. Comanche
9. Copper Inuit
10. Cree
11. Crow
12. Dogrib
13. Haida
14. Hopi
15. Hupa
16. Iroquois
17. Klamath
18. Kutenai
19. Laguna

20. Mescalero
21. Mohave
22. Montagnais
23. Navajo
24. North Alaskan Eskimo
25. Osage
26. Ottawa
27. Pawnee
28. Seminole

29. Shoshone
30. Taos
31. Tlingit
32. Western Shoshone
33. White Mountain Apache
34. Yokuts
35. Zuni

Oceania

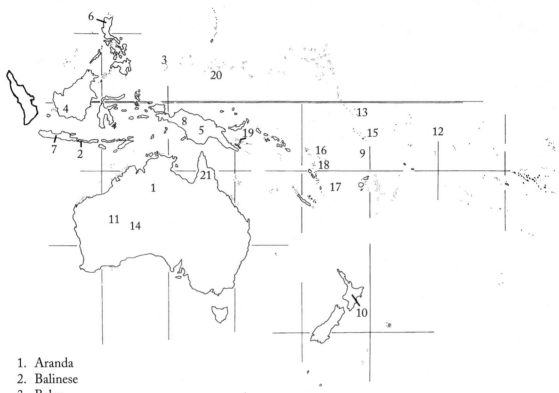

1. Aranda
2. Balinese
3. Belau
4. Dyaks
5. Enga
6. Ifugao
7. Javanese
8. Kapauku
9. Mangaia
10. Maori
11. Mardudjara
12. Marquesas Islanders
13. Nauru
14. Ngatajara
15. Romonum Islanders
16. Samoans
17. Tikopia
18. Tonga
19. Trobriands
20. Trukese
21. Wik Mungkan

HUMAN ENVIRONMENTS

A CROSS-CULTURAL ENCYCLOPEDIA

ing systems" rather than agriculture or agrarian societies. A farming system is any type of human organization (family, community, corporation, collective, or kinship group) "engaged in agricultural production as it is wedded in a social, political, economic, and environmental context" (Turner and Brush 1987:13).

The major subsystems that both make up and influence farming systems are human, environmental, and genetic. The human subsystem includes factors such as rules governing land ownership and use, labor relations, population size and density, human discoveries and innovations, relations between different social and economic units, consumption patterns, distribution, and politics. The environmental subsystem includes the climate, seasonal variation, soil quality, water availability, insects, predators, and diseases. The genetic subsystem includes population dynamics, reproduction patterns, and the genetically determined features of plants and animals.

Farming systems found across cultures can be classified into three broad groups, based on three criteria: (1) output intensity—yield per unit and time; (2) technological type—labor input per unit and the degree of reliance on irrigation, fertilizers, pesticides, and mechanization; and (3) production type—agricultural products consumed by the farmer or in the local community or exported for sale. The three types of farming systems are the paleotechnic, mixed-technic, and neotechnic. Paleotechnic, or consumption, systems are basically horticultural systems or low output operations that rely on human labor and in which the farmer keeps all or nearly all of the product for his own use. Neotechnic systems are the opposite; they rely on fossil-fuel energy to produce vegetable and animal products that are sold outside the local community. Mixed-technic systems combine elements of the other two types and generally are characterized by farmers keeping a small portion of what they grow for their own use and selling the rest both within and outside the local community.

Agriculture Agriculture is a subsistence system characterized by the use of domesticated plants and animals to produce food for consumption or sale. Nearly all people in the world today live on food produced by agriculture. In modern industrialized nations, people mainly eat food that is grown by others and purchased in the marketplace. In traditional societies, primarily in the Southern Hemisphere, people consume food they grow themselves or that they acquire through purchase or trade in local or regional markets. Approximately 50 percent of the world's population is engaged in agricultural work, with most farmers found in societies in China, South Asia, Southeast Asia, and Africa. Although agricultural operations in industrialized nations yield vast quantities of food, only a small percentage of the populations of these nations (about 2 percent in the United States, for example) are directly involved in agriculture. Because agriculture is a very complex human activity and because of the very broad range of types of agriculture found across cultures, scientists now generally speak of "farm-

Neotechnic farming systems, also called energy intensive systems, are the dominant type (in number, size, output, and consumption of energy and natural resources) in modern nations such as the United States. Energy intensive agriculture developed in the mid- to late-nineteenth century when mechanized farming powered by fossil-fuel energy (first steam from coal and then gasoline) began replacing human and animal energy. Although mechanized farming alone does not produce a higher yield per acre, the use of gasoline-powered tractors, combines, threshers, and other equipment meant that much less labor was needed to farm much larger areas of land. During the 1930s, the development of scientific genetic plant and animal engineering replaced earlier trial-and-error methods. As a result, more adaptive and more marketable plants and livestock could be raised. The development of chemical fertilizers, pesticides, and herbicides for plants and specialized diets and antibiotics for animals completed the evolution from human-and-animal-based to energy intensive farming. The current manifestation of energy intensive farming is agribusiness, which involves the intensive use of specialized technology and fossil-fuel energy to raise, market, and distribute domesticated animals and their products (such as eggs and milk, cereals, fruits, and vegetables) to large urban and suburban markets. Agribusiness often involves very large farms, absentee owners, managers whose expertise is in business management and marketing, and a profit motive. Small farmers involved in energy intensive farming often consume little of what they grow themselves, and often find it more economically beneficial to sell what they grow and to purchase and store food, often in processed form, grown by others.

By about 2,000 years ago, virtually all plants that are now domesticated were already domesticated. Since then, no important new plant species have been domesticated for agricultural use. Instead, human effort has been devoted to re-fining and selecting existing varieties to best meet local conditions. Varieties are selected or bred to be resistant to certain diseases or insects, to tolerate drought conditions, to produce during a short growing season, to be easier to harvest, and to produce a greater quantity of edible material. Thus, domesticated varieties of a plant differ greatly from wild varieties—they are larger, have fewer seeds, mature faster, grow more quickly, and compete more successfully with wild plants such as trees, grasses, and weeds. One major manifestation of the effort by humans to control agriculture has been the diffusion of domesticates from one region to another—for example, potatoes from South America to North America and Europe and cassava from South America to Africa. This diffusion also extends to the use of foods grown in one region in another region—for example, tobacco grown in North America, sugar cane grown on Caribbean islands, and tea grown in South Asia being used in Europe. The major domesticated plants grown around the world today include grains such as wheat, rice, millet, sorghum, oats, rye, barley, and corn (maize); fruits such as plums, dates, figs, bananas, olives, grapes, and apples; sugar cane; root crops and tubers such as yams, taro, cassava, and potatoes; legumes such as beans, peas, and vetch; and a wide variety of vegetables.

The Evolution of Agriculture

For nearly all of the 3 million or more years that humans and their ancestors have lived on the earth, they have subsisted by means other than agriculture. Agriculture first appeared about 10,000 years ago, with the domestication of plants and animals in the Near East and independently in the millennia that followed in Southeast Asia (6800 B.C.), Peru (5600 B.C.), Mexico (5000 B.C.), China (5000 B.C.), and sub-Saharan Africa (3000 B.C.). It is not yet known why peoples around the world who previously subsisted by hunting, gathering, and fishing switched to agriculture. One factor may have

Farmer plowing his field in India

been a change in the climate to a regular annual cycle of dry and wet seasons that forced people to grow food to sustain them through the dry season when wild food sources were unreliable. Another factor was population pressure. By about 12,000 B.C., the world was relatively heavily populated with hunter-gatherers. People were forced to begin growing their own food to compensate for food shortages caused by over-population and overexploitation of natural food resources. And, at least in the Old World, food produced through agriculture allowed for population expansion and greater reliance on agriculture as well as migration. Hunter-gatherers would have been outnumbered by those living in larger, settled agricultural groups; therefore, the settlements of the latter would have very likely expanded into new territory at the expense of the former.

Although agriculture developed in both the Old and New Worlds, the farming systems differed. In the Old World, domesticated animals played a key role in farming, while they were unimportant in the New World. In the Old World, the domestication of animals accompanied, and in some regions perhaps preceded, the domestication of plants. Domesticated animals were important for agriculture because their manure provided a reliable and rich form of fertilizer that enabled farmers to maintain or even improve the soil fertility from year to year. Thus, with a steady supply of food from the same or ever expanding fields, Old World farmers were able to live in permanent settlements near their fields, while the settlements themselves expanded over time as soil fertility was improved. Farmers in the New World did not use domesticated animals and as a result had no equally reliable means of maintaining or improving soil fertility. Instead, they farmed in river-fed valleys or along riverbanks where silt deposits enriched the soil, built their fields near natural sources of minerals that would wash down into the fields, or farmed on ash fields or near runoffs from these fields. Because these sources of soil nutrients were less reliable than manure, most New World settlements were smaller and less permanent than those in the Old World.

Varieties of Farming Systems

Across cultures, and even within a single society, great variation exists in the crops grown and the specific farming approaches and methods used. The following examples of nonenergy intensive farming systems across five cultures and one energy intensive system point to some of this variation. These examples also indicate simi-

larities across cultures including multicropping; crop rotation; use of natural fertilizers; cooperation among members of the farming community; and a willingness to combine traditional strategies and methods with new innovations such as irrigation systems, new seed varieties, and chemical fertilizers and pesticides.

A substantial percentage of the world's population lives in rural villages in East Asia, Southeast Asia, and South Asia. They grow wet rice as their staple food. In most communities, home vegetable gardens are kept. Other cereals such as millet are also grown, while in some regions still feeling the effects of Western colonialism, sugar cane, tea, tobacco, and other cash crops are grown for sale. Wet rice farming is labor- and land-intensive; many of the steps do not lend themselves to mechanized farming—even oxen are not always helpful. For example,

Sugar cane is a major crop on plantations in tropical regions, such as this one in the French Antilles in the Caribbean.

wet rice farming in Java, which is often done on irrigated, terraced fields, requires successful completion of the following sequence of tasks.

1. Select and store seeds at the end of the harvest season

2. Germinate seeds

3. Prepare the seed beds in the rice fields

4. Spread the seeds and keep shoots covered with water

5. Spread fertilizer

6. Prepare the soil by flooding, hoeing, plowing, harrowing, and weeding to create surface of smooth mud covered by a thin layer of water

7. Transplant shoots from the seed beds to the fields

8. Weed and fertilize the fields

9. Harvest

This general pattern of wet rice farming has persisted over large areas of Asia for thousands of years. Because of the relatively large quantities of food produced, this system can support large rural populations on the same land for generations.

The Kofyar of northern Nigeria, who number about 80,000, practice intensive agriculture on cleared land near their homesteads supplemented by slash-and-burn horticulture on fields further from home. Using iron hoes, axes, and food processing equipment, the Kofyar grow cowpeas, millet, yams, acha, corn, pumpkins, sorghum, rice, beans, groundnuts, and other crops. In addition, each farmer keeps goats in stone corrals and huts and chickens. The goat manure and compost that form in the corrals are used as fertilizer to keep the soil rich despite regular use during the agricultural cycle that runs from March or April to December. In addition to manure and compost, the soil is enriched with ash hauled from the kitchen fires; by intercropping nitrogen-fixing cowpeas with the millet and

sorghum (the staple crops); through crop rotation; and with the manure from cattle of the neighboring Fulani, who the Kofyar encourage to camp on their fallow fields. In addition to maintaining soil fertility, the Kofyar must also manage their water supply; most of the rain falls during the six-month rainy season each year. Fields are terraced and supported by stone walls; a maintained system of trenches and storage holes controls erosion and runoff. Through this combination of techniques, the Kofyar keep their soil fertile from year to year and produce enough food throughout the year to meet their dietary needs.

The Zapotec Indians of the village of Santa Tomas in semiarid Mexico farm year-round on four types of land—irrigated, wet, unirrigated flatland, and communal land that is usually dry and hilly. The wet and irrigated lands are the most desirable and most expensive; they can yield two or three crops per year, while dry land can yield only one. The Zapotecs grow early and late varieties of corn, beans, and squash (milpa crops) on the dry and communal lands; beans alone on better unirrigated land; peanuts and chick peas on communal land; and alfalfa, vetch, lima beans, and chick peas on the irrigated or wet lands. Successful farming depends on fallowing (that is, leaving dry plots to return to their natural state before burning the growth to restore soil fertility), supplying water through irrigation, and maintaining soil fertility on the wet and irrigated lands through manuring and chemical fertilizer. By farming for the entire year with some crops always under cultivation, the Zapotecs maintain an adequate supply of food.

The 50,000 or so Aith Waryaghar, Berber people of the Rif Mountains in northern Morocco, must survive in a locale that is dry with poor soil that is subject to erosion from heavy rains. Their solution is a combination of dry and irrigated agriculture, like the Zapotecs, supplemented by animal husbandry. This approach produces small quantities of a great variety of foodstuffs. Cereal crops—barley, wheat, and rye—are grown in dry fields, while fields irrigated with water from mountain streams are used for vegetable gardens (including vetch, corn, beans, tomatoes, garlic, onions, eggplant, and squash) and orchards (figs, olives, grapes, peaches, pears, pomegranates, apricots, plums, almonds, and walnuts). Animals raised include cattle, mules, donkeys, goats, sheep, and chickens.

Unlike the previous cultures, Taiwanese farmers grow food to feed themselves and also to raise cash crops that are sold to external markets. From at least the seventeenth century, some Taiwanese villagers have grown rice, sweet potatoes, and other crops for their own consumption and sugar cane for export. For example, in the village of Ying-Ting, sugar cane was a major crop for several hundred years; under Japanese control beginning about 1900, the activity was expanded. The Japanese imported new varieties of cane from Hawaii and Java, constructed modern refineries to replace local operations, and built an irrigation system. Today, the same crops are grown with newer varieties of seeds, chemical fertilizers, and modern techniques on a mixed crop rotation cycle necessitated by a shortage of water for irrigation. The irrigation system, built in 1930, provides enough water for only one-third of the village land available for cultivation. Each farmer has one or more 150-hectare units of land divided into three zones of 50 hectares each. Ideally, the extent of irrigation and types of crops grown are on the three-year cycle shown in Table A-1 (Chen 1983:56).

As producers of a cash crop, the villagers are linked with other organizations. Most important is the Taiwan Sugar Company that purchases the cane, hires crews to harvest it, and ships the cane to the refineries. In addition, farmers often hire others in the village to help with the rice and jute crops that require more labor than a single farm family can provide during the transplanting and harvesting periods. Other important organizations are the farmers' associations; the extension service; and the moneylending club that provides loans for the purchase of seed, fertilizer, and equipment.

Serbs of the rural regions of the former Yugoslavia, both in the past and to a large extent today, have an economic system based on a combination of agriculture and animal husbandry. This system characterized much of Europe for

TABLE A-1	CROPS GROWN ACCORDING TO THREE-YEAR IRRIGATION ROTATION		
	Zone 1	**Zone 2**	**Zone 3**
Year 1	Irrigated often. Wet rice.	Irrigated periodically. Sugar cane.	Not irrigated. Sweet potatoes and dry crops.
Year 2	Not irrigated. Sweet potatoes.	Irrigated often. Wet rice.	Irrigated periodically. Sugar cane.
Year 3	Irrigated periodically.	Not irrigated. Sweet potato and dry crops.	Irrigated often. Wet rice.

some 5,000 years and has changed markedly only since World War II, with a shift in some locations to agribusiness. The Serbs produce some food for their own use and some for sale. They have the benefit of fertile soil, flat or gently rolling land, and ample supplies of water. The two staple crops are wheat, which is grown to make bread for home use, and corn, which is grown as livestock fodder. Wheat is supplemented by rye, oats, and barley, which along with the wheat is rotated among fields from year to year. Flax, which in the past was grown by women to make clothing, has become unimportant with the availability of manufactured cloth. Each family keeps a vegetable garden near the home where women grow a wide variety of plants including tomatoes, eggplant, peppers, garlic, onions, cabbage, beans, potatoes, and peas. The vegetables are consumed by the family and sold at markets. Many rural homesteads also have a nearby orchard of plum trees; the plums are used at home to make plum brandy and jam and are exported. Other tree crops include apples, pears, peaches, and walnuts. The Serbs keep cows as beasts of burden and for their milk and meat, horses, sheep, poultry, and bees. For the Serbs, as for many other peasant farmers, farming and rural living is a cooperative enterprise that requires cooperation among both community and family members. At the community level, families routinely help each other with plowing; hoeing; harvesting; and building and repairing houses, outbuildings, and farm equipment. At the family level, all family members participate in agricultural tasks as indicated by the following list of some chores performed by the members of one Serbian family over the course of a year (Halpern 1958:72).

Husband (55 years old)—feed and water stock, pick grapes, chop wood, clean stable, mend boots, fence, sow corn, thresh wheat

Wife (56 years old)—feed chickens, prepare lunches and take to the fields, pick grapes, prepare supper, care for grandchildren, milk cows, make dough, bake bread, spin, make cheese, wash clothes

Son (34 years old)—feed pigs, haul water, pick grapes, transport grapes by wagon, chop wood, feed, water stock, shop in town, clean stable, thresh wheat

Daughter-in-law (32 years old)—milk cows, haul water, pick grapes, make supper, feed chickens, weave, make breakfast, make and bring lunch to fields, work in vegetable garden

Grandson (12 years old)—pick grapes, go to school, do homework, whittle, play flute, haul and stack firewood, gather kindling, graze pigs, herd pigs, watch cows

Granddaughter (9 years old)—help haul water, go to school, pick grapes, learn to knit, sing, help clean up kitchen, watch sheep, do homework

Plantation agriculture has produced a sizable percentage of the world's food since the beginning of Western colonialism in the fifteenth century. Tea, coffee, tobacco, sugar cane, bananas, pineapples, and rubber are a few of the products of large-scale plantation agriculture established by colonial powers in the Caribbean, South America, Southeast Asia, and Oceania. Plantation agriculture is based on the exploitation of the local environment and an indigenous or imported labor force, monocropping, intensive use of fossil-fuel energy, and the export of the raw or finished product to European or other external markets. A modern example of plantation agriculture is the commercial growing of pineapples in Hawaii. The Maunaloa pineapple plantation on the Hawaiian island of Molokai is a commercial operation designed to grow pineapples on nearly 10,000 acres of land. As with all types of plantation agriculture, the goal is profits; Maunaloa is structured and functions as a business. The labor force is structured like a pyramid with a small number of managers with European and Japanese ancestry at the top, then a small group of technical specialists such as bookkeepers, mechanics, foremen, and several hundred laborers, 94 percent of whom are Filipinos born in the Philippines and living in the "company town" that borders the plantation. The plantation benefits from the rich volcanic soil on which it is located but suffers from less-than-adequate rainfall that makes it somewhat less productive than are pineapple plantations that have rich soil and adequate rainfall. The plantation ownership and management is a profit maximizer as it seeks to produce as many pineapples as possible with the lowest possible investment in people, equipment, and supplies. In line with this profit maximization strategy, all fields are in use at all times with pineapple plants in different stages of growth and the fruit at different stages of ripeness. Thus, coordination is a major management concern as the right mix of labor, equipment, and supplies must be in the right fields at any given point in time. Management also seeks to use machines rather than human labor whenever possible. About 250 large pieces of equipment such as harvesters, tractors, tankers, trucks, and cranes are used and maintained on the plantation, and pesticides are sprayed by airplane. Soil fertility is maintained by the application of chemical fertilizers and weed killers and by leaving the cut plants to decompose on the ground. The plants themselves are treated with pesticides, fertilizers, and growth stimulants. A plantation agricultural experimentation station functions to genetically refine the plants and to develop more efficient agricultural practices. Pineapple shoots are collected from plants before harvest and planted by hand; the pineapples are picked from the machine-cut plants by hand. All other major operations rely on machines. Harvested pineapples are trucked and then shipped to other islands for canning within 24 hours of picking.

Sustainable Agriculture

Also called alternative agriculture, sustainable agriculture is a type of farming system that is designed to be both economically viable and nondestructive to the environment while at the same time enabling family farms and farm-based communities to be self-sufficient within the context of modern industrial and postindustrial societies that derive their food from energy intensive agriculture. Sustainable agriculture minimizes the use of fossil-fuel energy by restricting or eliminating the use altogether of fossil-fuel-based fertilizers, pesticides, and herbicides and by using agricultural practices and technologies that do not erode the soil, pollute groundwater, or deplete soil fertility. Sustainable agriculture relies on the rotation of crops, intercropping, manuring of fields, mulching with plant matter, using cover crops in winter or terracing to control erosion, composting, rotational cattle grazing, cultivating legumes such as beans to fix fertilizers in the soil, and minimal tilling of the soil. As a social and economic system, sustainable agriculture in the modern context is meant to keep control of land in the hands of farm families and to ensure that farm communities are economically viable without destroying the farmland that is their most important resource. However, since the product of sustainable agriculture is self- or local consumption, sustainable agricultural families often supplement their incomes by engaging in wage labor.

Sustainable systems around the world include irrigated wet rice agriculture in China and Southeast Asia, terraced farming by the Ifugao in the Philippines, traditional methods of Swiss farming in Europe, and Amish farming in the United States. Amish farming incorporates many of the features of sustainable agriculture and also points to the difficulties of maintaining sustainable practices in the context of modern agribusiness. The Amish are a people of German ancestry who first came to the United

States in 1727 and today number about 130,000 in the United States and Canada. The majority live in rural communities in Pennsylvania, Ohio, and Indiana. The Amish subsist mainly by farming; their goal is to maintain family farms, with each newly married couple given enough land to establish their own farm. While seeking isolation from the non-Amish world, the Amish do turn to outsiders for legal, medical, and economic services, and an increasing number of Amish are turning to wage labor outside the community in response to the pressures caused by the rapid increase in the Amish population and the limited availability of low-cost, high-quality farmland.

The Amish believe that humans were placed on the earth to look after the land for God. It is a man's and woman's responsibility to cultivate the land and to keep it attractive and orderly. Both the Amish approach to farming and their specific methods, as well as the Amish lifestyle that stresses moderation in behavior and consumption, fit within the framework of sustainable agriculture. The Amish arrived in the New World with a reputation as excellent farmers and have maintained that reputation for over two centuries. Only recently have neighboring non-Amish farmers using energy intensive methods produced more per acre than the Amish using sustainable methods. Although Amish groups in different states and counties vary in their farming practices, most in the past or today follow the same general pattern. The Amish plant a mix of crops including grains such as corn, oats, rye, barley, and alfalfa and a wide variety of vegetables and fruit trees. They keep an equally wide range of livestock including beef cattle, dairy cattle, horses, hogs, poultry, and sheep. Soil fertility is maintained through crop rotation on three- or four-year cycles, manuring, and the application of chemical fertilizers. In response to land pressure caused by the rapidly growing Amish population and a rise in the cost of land, some

communities in recent years have used herbicides to control pests. Fields have been terraced and tractors have been used in place of human and animal power. Harvested food is stored in large silos and barns and vegetables and fruits stored by traditional methods. Most Amish communities remain completely dependent on non–fossil-fuel energy sources including human and animal power, windmills, and waterwheels. Thus, Amish farming has adjusted to contemporary conditions that have forced some communities to adopt nontraditional methods in order to remain self-sufficient and separate from the non-Amish world.

See also ANNUAL CYCLE; GARDENS AND GARDENING; GREEN REVOLUTION; HORTICULTURE; IRRIGATION; PASTORALISM; TERRACES.

Boserup, Elizabeth. (1965) *The Conditions of Agricultural Growth: The Economics of Agrarian Change under Population Pressure.*

Chen, Chung-min. (1983) *Ying-Ting: A Cultural-Ecological Study of a Chinese Mixed Cropping Village in Taiwan.*

Cohen, Mark N. (1977) *The Food Crisis in Prehistory: Overpopulation and the Origins of Agriculture.*

Granskog, Jane E. (1979) *Efficiency in a Zapotec Indian Village.*

Halpern, Joel M. (1958) *A Serbian Village.*

Hart, David M. (1976) *The Aith Waryaghar of the Moroccan Rif.*

Hostetler, John A. (1980) *Amish Society,* 3d ed.

Netting, Robert McC. (1968) *Hill Farmers of Nigeria.*

Norbeck, Edward. (1959) *Pineapple Town Hawaii.*

Schusky, Ernest L. (1989) *Culture and Agriculture.*

Turner, B. L. II, and Stephen B. Brush, eds. (1987) *Comparative Farming Systems.*

White, Benjamin N. F. (1976) *Production and Reproduction in a Javanese Village.*

ANIMAL DOMESTICATION

Domesticated animals are animal populations that have been selectively bred by humans over many generations to produce individual animals with characteristics that fit human purposes. Domestication always involves changing the genetic structure of the animal population and results in the development of new breeds of the species. A breed is "a group of animals that has been selected by man to possess a uniform appearance that is inheritable and distinguishes it from other groups of animals within the same species" (Clutton-Brock 1981:26). The term "appearance" is used here not to mean just physical appearance but also other genetically determined features of an animal such as quantity and quality of milk produced or the color of the female's eggs. Thus, the development of domesticated animals and different breeds thereof is not the product of biological evolution through natural selection but the product of selection controlled and managed by humans. For some domesticated animals, such as chickens raised by agribusiness methods, and some breeds, such as dogs raised for show, the process has gone so far that these animals cannot survive or reproduce without human support. For all types of domesticated animals, the changes produced by selective breeding will disappear over subsequent generations if the breeding is not managed and maintained by humans.

Considerable confusion accompanies the various words used in reference to animal domestication. Domestication has already been defined above; it differs from taming and herding. A tame animal is one that is incorporated into human society but whose reproduction is not selectively controlled by humans. Taming is quite easy with many animals, some of which can be put in human care before and others after weaning. An example is the falcon used in falconry—it is captured from the wild, raised, and used by humans but not bred selectively. A pigeon used in pigeon racing, however, is a domesticated animal; it is selectively bred to produce traits that enable it to fly long distances rapidly for the benefit of its human owner. Domestication and taming also differ from herding. Herding, like taming, does not involve selective breeding. But unlike taming and more like domestication, herding involves the control of animals so that humans may extract food or other resources from them. Ranching, of course, often relies heavily on domestication to produce breeds that can command the highest market price. Finally, some note should be made of the relation of the term breed, or variety of animal, to the scientific taxonomy used for classifying animals into the categories of genus, species, and subspecies. A breed is roughly the equivalent of a subspecies. The key difference is that a breed is produced through human intervention while a subspecies results from the forces of natural selection operating on a population of animals that is isolated from the general population of the same species.

The first domestic animal was probably the dog, used by hunters perhaps as long as 14,000 years ago to help track and run down game. Animal domestication for food production probably began in the Near East about 9000 B.C. By about 7000 B.C., sheep and goats were herded and domesticated in the Near East; domestication was present in Southeast Asia shortly thereafter. Experts are not sure whether agriculture and animal domestication began at the same time or if one preceded the other. It is clear, however, that in the Old World, agriculture and animal domestication often occurred at the same time in many locales. The joint use of agriculture and animal domestication was, and remains, a major innovation in cultural evolution. This type of farming system—with animals providing meat, milk, manure for fertilizer, and other resources and plants providing food and still other resources—has enabled people in traditional societies to farm the same lands for thousands of years.

Animal domestication was mainly an Old World innovation. Of the 50 or so animals now domesticated, only 5 (turkey, guinea pig, llama, alpaca, and muscovy duck) were domesticated in the New World. Of these 5, only the turkey has spread elsewhere.

The pattern of animal domestication around the world has been the spread of animals from the region of domestication to other regions, and eventually for many animals, to all or most regions of the world. Humans have mainly tried to adapt the same species to new environments rather than use different species in new environments. This practice has produced a very large number of breeds for some species such as cattle, goats, sheep, pigs, chickens, and horses, with each animal bred to best conform to local conditions or needs. For example, a survey of cattle in Great Britain indicates at least 21 breeds.

Aberdeen Angus	Highland
Ayrshire	Jersey
Beef Shorthorn	Lincoln Red
Belted Galloway	Longhorn
British Friesian	Red Dane
Charollais	Red Poll
Dairy Shorthorn	South Devon
Devon	Sussex
Galloway	Welsh Black
Guernsey	White Park
Hereford	

Domesticated Animals

Only about 50 species of animals have been domesticated for human use. However, as domestication of some species continues, new breeds are produced that yield a greater variety of these types of animals. The primary domesticates are as follows:

Major Domesticates

alpaca

bison

buffalo

cage birds (parrots, finches)

camel (one- and two-humped)

carp

cattle

chicken

chinchilla

dog

donkey

duck

elephant

gerbil

goat

goose

guinea fowl

guinea pig

hamster

hinny

honey bee

horse

house cat

llama

mink

mouse

mule

pig

pigeon

rabbit

rat

reindeer

salmon

sheep

silk moth (worm)

silver fox

trout

turkey

yak

Uses of Domestic Animals

Domesticated animals are used in a wide variety of ways by humans across cultures, including as meat for consumption; as a source of food such as milk or eggs; for raw materials such as leather, wool, fibers, glue, manure, and dyes; for transportation and burden carrying; for protection from animal or human predators; for attacking enemies; as a source of energy in farm activities such as threshing grain or turning millstones; as a source of wealth that brings power and status to the owner; as pets for amusement; as objects of religious worship or for sacrifice; for sport and amusement; and as the subject of medical and industrial experiments.

Domesticated animals are an important food resource across cultures. A survey of 186 cultures in the nineteenth and early twentieth centuries indicates that only 4 percent of cultures did not have domesticated animals; most of these were hunter-gatherers such as the San in Africa, Andaman Islanders in South Asia, and the Siriono in South America. Twenty-three percent of cultures kept some domestic animals such as dogs but did not use them for food. Thirty-six percent derived less than 10 percent of their food from domestic animals. Twenty-eight percent derived more than 10 percent mainly in the form of meat, milk, or dairy products but de-

rived food from other sources as well. Eight percent derived a major percentage of their food from domestic animals, mainly cattle, sheep, or goats that they herded. Regarding the types of animals that were kept, 30 percent of cultures kept small animals such as cats, dogs, chickens, or guinea pigs; 26 percent kept cattle, yak, or buffalo; 19 percent kept pigs; 13 percent kept sheep and/or goats; 8 percent had horses and donkeys; and 2 percent each kept reindeer or camels and llama.

In the contemporary world, the most populous domesticates raised primarily for food are chickens (over 10 billion around the world), cattle and sheep (over 1 billion of each), pigs (over half a billion), and goats (about half a billion). Pigs, cattle, and poultry provide the majority of meat consumed around the world, with sheep, goats, horses, and buffalo providing considerably less.

If the practices of hunter-gatherers in modern times are a reliable model of the past, we can assume that the use of animals to manufacture materials predates domestication by thousands of years. In many cultures, animal skin, hair, and fur have been used to make clothing, shelter (for example, a Mongol yurt made from yak hair pounded into felt and Plains Indian tipis made from bison hides), and cordage. Bones have long been used as tools such as shovels and as the raw material for finer implements such as awls and needles. Animal muscle fiber is commonly used for cordage and fat for oil, glue, and other products. Across cultures, the most valuable raw product from domesticated animals such as cattle and pigs is manure that is used as a fertilizer in many farming cultures, as fuel for fires, and as a type of cement in building construction.

The specific animals domesticated or imported to be beasts of burden have varied from region to region. In the South American Andes Mountains, the llama and alpaca served this purpose in the past, but are no longer much used.

Using oxen for plowing in Peru

In the Near and Middle East and Central Asia camels and horses have been widely used. In North America, Plains Indians adopted the horse, which had been brought to the New World by the Spanish (the indigenous variety having become extinct), and switched from being hunter-gatherers or farmers to being horse-borne bison hunters in the eighteenth century. In India and North Africa, the elephant was used for transport and to wage war. Everywhere in the world in the twentieth century animals have been replaced as beasts of burden by fossil-fuel–driven vehicles such as cars, trucks, tractors, and so forth.

Animals—domesticated and wild—have always played a central role in religious belief and practice. Across cultures, people often use animal parts such as feathers or bones as amulets or lucky charms—in American society, for example, the rabbit's foot, a bird feather, or the turkey wishbone. Hunter-gatherers engage in ritual behavior and rituals to ensure a supply of game, a successful hunt, equitable distribution of the meat, and to use magical powers for their benefit. Sacrifice of animals occurs in all types of cultures, with the sacrifice of domesticated animals especially common in pastoral societies. Agricultural peoples are less likely to make bloody animal sacrifices and are more likely to make offerings of grain or other valuable plant foods. Thus, when sacrificed, usually the most valuable animals are killed. Often these animals, like the buffalo among the Toradja of Indonesia, are not normally eaten, except on ritual occasions.

For several thousand years animals have been used in human sports. In some sports, animals are bred and raised by humans to be the competitors—cock fighting, dog racing, falconry, pigeon racing, and bull and bear baiting. In other sports, the animals are bred, raised, and controlled by humans during the competition—dog sled racing, horse racing, horseback riding, jousting, fox hunting, polo, and rodeo. In still other sports, the competition is between humans and animals—kangaroo boxing, alligator wrestling, bullfighting, fishing, and hunting. In addition to sports, humans also breed and raise animals to compete with one another in terms of the animal's appearance and behavior, as in dog and cat shows.

Domestics in Farming Systems

As with agriculture, two major patterns of domestic animal use are found around the world today. The first involves the raising of animals as food as part of the agribusiness system in industrialized societies. In these settings, animals are raised through highly specialized breeding programs to produce animals with characteristics that yield higher profits in the marketplace—for example, sweeter tasting beef with more fat, turkeys with less bone and more meat, chickens with larger breasts and therefore more white meat, chickens that lay eggs of a uniform size, and sheep with nonwrinkled skin that allows the wool to be clipped more easily and cheaply. In the agribusiness setting, physical appearance of the animal is unimportant—most are never seen by humans until they are pack-

Tame parrots perch atop heads of Cuna girls on the San Blas Islands off the coast of Panama.

aged in processed form. Methods used to raise animals for food include those that best control costs and maximize profits, such as the mechanization of feeding, slaughtering, gutting, cleaning, and processing; enriched feeds; antibiotics to control disease and stimulate growth; hormones to stimulate growth; and delivery to distant markets in refrigerated vehicles.

The second use of domesticates in farming systems is in traditional systems, mainly in the nonindustrialized world as part of subsistence or mixed subsistence-cash crop farming systems. These systems take a variety of forms. For example, the Sarakatsani of Greece are primarily herders of sheep and goats, but they also maintain family vegetable gardens in their home villages, keep dogs to drive away wolves from the flocks, use horses for travel, and keep small numbers of pigs and chickens for their meat. Mutton is rarely eaten and sheep are usually killed only as a sacrifice on holy days such as Christmas and Easter, on feast days, and on special occasions such as a wedding or baptism.

More extensive use of domesticated animals is typical of local farming systems throughout rural India. Indian farmers grow a variety of crops including rice or other grains depending on the region and a mix of fruits and vegetables. The typical Indian farmer owns two oxen or buffalo that are used to plow and pull carts, one cow used for its milk and to produce more cattle for use or sale, and chickens. Depending on the region, a farmer might also own a horse, donkey, mule, or camel; goats for their skins; pigs for their meat and bristles for brushes; honey bees; and silkworms or the Indian varieties of the silk moth (*tasar*, *muga*, and *eri*). The cattle are not eaten; instead their manure is used as fertilizer, fuel, and cement in building houses and patios. The skins of cows are processed into leather only when they die.

The Quechua of highland Ecuador also make heavy use of domestic animals in addition to growing corn (the staple crop), vegetables, barley, and beans. The typical family farm has sheep, cattle, goats, pigs, horses, burros, and dogs. The sheep are kept for their wool; pigs for their manure, which is used for fertilizer; hens for their eggs; dogs to watch the homes; horses and burros as pack animals; and cattle, chickens, sheep, and pigs are sold. Llama, which were among the first domesticates in the New World, are no longer commonly used as pack animals. Farmers do not own draft animals; instead, they rent oxen from those who specialize in renting draft animals. In addition, every family raises guinea pigs in its kitchen, which are either sold or eaten. Some families raise *cochineal*, an insect valuable for the purple-red dye extracted from it.

For the Sarakatsani, Quechua, and Indian farmers, animals are valuable because they can be used for a variety of purposes and are sometimes a source of wealth when they are sold. For the Kapauku of the highlands of western New Guinea, pigs are not just a source of wealth—they symbolize wealth itself. The Kapauku subsist through a combination of horticulture (sweet potatoes are the major crop) and pig breeding supplemented by raising chickens, gathering plant foods, fishing, and some hunting. The Kapauku are very concerned with wealth and power; pigs are the primary source of capital that can buy status and power in the village. Pigs are owned, traded, and sold by men, but from the time the piglet is six weeks old it is cared for, often like an infant, by the pig owner's wife. Successful pig raising follows these steps. A young Kapauku man, not yet ready to marry, plants a sweet potato field to provide food for the pig he plans to purchase. With money he has saved from working for other men in their fields, borrowed from kin, or acquired through the payment of a bride-price for his sister by another kin group, the young man purchases a sow. He then raises and breeds the sow and sells all the male pigs, keeping the females so he can breed them when they mature. To keep himself and his growing pig population in food, he must acquire and plant more sweet potato fields and obtain labor from others to manage these larger holdings. He can either hire other men in the village or marry, with his wife helping to care for the pigs and the fields. The cycle then continues with the man planting more fields, buying more pigs, selling pigs, taking additional wives, or hiring more labor and as he becomes richer, eventually gaining political and legal power and influence. This scenario describes the path to wealth and power for Kapauku men. Of course, only some men achieve this goal; the majority have only a few pigs, small fields, one wife, and no hired labor.

As these four examples indicate, no society subsists entirely through animal domestication. In nearly all societies, animal domestication is integrated with farming and sometimes other subsistence activities such as herding, fishing, hunting, and gathering to form a mixed economic system.

Despite the importance of animals as a food source, raw materials, and other resources across cultures, cultures are not consistent in the way animals are treated. In about 48 percent of cultures, at least one species (usually the dog) is regularly treated cruelly. That is, they are poorly fed, left unclean, given inadequate shelter, kicked, hit, teased, stoned, cursed, or whipped. In a smaller number of cultures where animals are used as beasts of burden, horses, camels, and donkeys are regularly mistreated and expected to perform their work despite illness, injury, or malnutrition. In 24 percent of cultures, there is no routine cruelty to animals, although some animals may often be treated cruelly. And in 28 percent of cultures, cruelty to animals is unusual. Included in this group are a number of cultures such as the Blackfoot and Iroquois Indians in North America that prohibit cruelty to animals. Beyond cruelty to animals by individuals, some cultures institutionalize cruelty, often in the form of sport or entertainment such as bullbaiting, bullfighting, and cockfighting and also in the use of animals in religious sacrifice, medical and industrial experimentation, and in agribusiness.

See also AGRICULTURE; FISHING; PASTORALISM; RANCHING; TOTEMISM.

Campbell, J. K. (1964) *Honour, Family, and Patronage: A Study of Institutions and Moral Values in a Greek Mountain Community.*

Casagrande, Joseph B. (1971) "The Indian and Ecuadorian Society" and "Indigenous Society." In *The Condor and the Bull: Tradition and Change in Andean Indian Culture,* edited by Peter T. Furst and Karen B. Reed, 337–489.

Child, Alice B., and Irvin L. Child (1993) *Religion and Magic in the Life of Traditional Peoples.*

Clutton-Brock, Juliet (1981) *Domesticated Animals from Early Times.*

Heiser, Charles B. Jr. (1990) *Seed to Civilization: The Story of Food.*

Kabbadias, Georgios B. (1965) *Mediterranean Pastoral Nomads: The Sarakatsani of Greece.*

Leeds, Anthony, and Andrew P. Vayda, eds. (1965) *Man, Culture, and Animals.*

Murdock, George P., and Diana O. Morrow. (1970) "Subsistence Economy and Supportive Practices." *Ethnology* 9:302–330.

Parsons, Elsie W. C. (1945) *Peguche, Canton of Otavalo, Province of Imbabura, Ecuador: A Study of Andean Indians.*

Pospisil, Leopold. (1964) *The Kapauku Papuans of West New Guinea.*

Shanklin, Eugenia. (1985) "Sustenance and Symbol: Anthropological Studies of Domesticated Animals." *Annual Review of Anthropology* 14:375–403.

Spate, Oscar H. K. (1954) *India and Pakistan.*

ANNUAL CYCLE An annual cycle is the yearly round of subsistence activities that a people regularly engage in from year to year. The survival of peoples who subsist directly from the environment—such as hunter-gatherers, horticulturalists, herders, and farmers—depends on their ability to make effective use of environmental opportunities. That is, they must consider the climate, terrain, length of day, length of the growing season, and so forth in deciding what subsistence activities to engage in at what times during the year. Additionally, they must also often consider other factors such as the payment schedule for the rent on the land they farm or graze, the need to earn money through wage labor, the desire to socialize with others in their culture, and the need to trade with other groups. In most cultures in which people subsist from the environment, the annual cycle is driven by economic considerations. This factor, however, is not true for all cultures. For example, the annual cycle of the Yanomamö, a horticultural society in Brazil and Venezuela, is determined by their warfare practices. In the dry season (September–April), the villages are often empty; the men are off raiding and the women and children are hiding in the forest from raids by other villages, or often all village residents are visiting and feasting in neighboring villages. In the rainy season, the villages are isolated by swollen streams; raiding and visiting is therefore difficult or impossible. Horticultural activities are not on any cycle; instead, gardening is done as food is needed.

The annual subsistence cycle is not the only annual cycle followed in cultures around the world. Equally common is the annual ceremonial cycle of religious holidays and ceremonies. In many cultures, the ceremonial cycle is linked to the subsistence cycle, as the purpose of many rituals is to ask for supernatural help in producing a rich harvest or successful hunt. For ex-

ample, Hopi Indian farmers of Arizona celebrate seven major rites each year, all of which in some way ask for rain, fertility, and a rich harvest. One ceremony held annually in late August is a nine-day rite for rain and for the ripening of the new crop. In some cultures, however, work during the busy periods of the subsistence cycle is so arduous and requires so many hands that rituals are scheduled for slow periods of the year. For example, the Tlingit of the Northwest Coast of the United States are heavily involved in fishing or other activities for much of the year, except for fall and winter when ceremonial activities are scheduled.

For peoples who purchase their food and other materials rather than hunt, grow, or gather them, the annual subsistence cycle is of little importance. As subsistence-level societies and communities become more and more involved in their world economic community, their subsistence cycle changes. As shown in Table A-2, the Tlingit are no longer as likely to move to temporary fishing settlements in the autumn due to the fact that Washington State law mandates compulsory education for their children, making family moves in the fall impossible.

The charts below detail the subsistence cycles of four different cultures who follow different subsistence strategies—Tlingit fishermen, Highland Scot fishermen-farmers, Sherpa herder-farmers, and San hunter-gatherers. A plus symbol (+) indicates that the activity is a major one during that month; a minus sign (-) indicates that the activity is minor. An absence of either sign indicates that the activity is not performed during that month.

As with many peoples whose economy relies heavily on one source of food, many Tlingit subsistence activities take place in the spring when fish migrate into the region. Huge quantities of fish are taken and preserved for use throughout the rest of the year, with additional activities supplementing fishing.

TABLE A-2 ANNUAL CYCLE OF THE TLINGIT

Activity	J	F	M	A	M	J	J	A	S	O	N	D
Deep-sea fishing	-	-	+	+	+	-				-		-
Berry picking						-	-	+	-			
Salmon fishing								+	-	+	-	-
Fur gathering		-	+	-								
Bark gathering				+								
Shellfish gathering	-	-	+	-	-	-				-	-	-
Hunting	-	-		+	-	-				+	-	-
Herb and root gathering					-	-	-	+	-			
Seaweed gathering			+									

TABLE A-3 ANNUAL CYCLE OF THE HIGHLAND SCOTS OF LEWIS

Activity	J	F	M	A	M	J	J	A	S	O	N	D
Fishing	+	+	+		-	+	+	+		-	-	-
Farming	-	-	+	-	+		-	+	+	+	-	
draining	-	-										-
fertilizing			-									
planting and sowing				-	-							
weeding							-					
hay making								-	-	-		
Herding	-	-	-	+	+	+	+	+			-	-
cattle fed indoors	-	-	-									
lambing				-	+							
sheepherding						+	+	+				
lamb weaning								+				
sheep dipping						-	-					
cattle grazing											-	-
Peat cutting and drying				+	+	+	+					
House thatching						-						
Crafts	+										+	+

Table A-3 portrays the annual cycle followed by the Highland Scots of the Isle of Lewis in 1913 and shows a community that was largely self-sufficient through a combination of fishing, herding, and farming. The situation now is much different; the community has been drawn into the regional and world economy since World War I with an end to commercial fishing, the introduction of weaving (Harris tweed garments) as a cottage industry, reliance on food and material goods purchased in stores, and the end of home crafts such as thatching. For the people of Lewis as for many other communities around the world, scheduling income and expenses and balancing the flow of family revenues and expenses has replaced the annual cycle as an organizing principle for the family and local economy.

TABLE A-4 AVAILABILITY OF MAJOR FOOD SOURCES FOR THE SAN

Food	J	F	M	A	M	J	J	A	S	O	N	D
Gemsbok	-	-	-	-		-	-	-				-
Springbok	-	-	-	-	-	-	-					-
Duiker	-	-	-	-		-	-	-	+	+	+	-
Steenbok	-	-	-	-		-	-	-		+	+	
Springhare	+	+	+	+	+	+	+	-	-		-	+
Fox				-		-		-	-	-	-	
Rodents	+	+	+	+	+	+	+	+	+	+	+	+
Birds	+	+	+	+	-	+	-	+	+	+	+	-
Tortoises	+	+	+	+							+	+
Snakes	-	-		-	+	-	-				-	-
Termites	-	-									-	
Fruit—*Bosia albitrunca*			+	+	+							
Melons—*Co. ocynthus citrullus*				+	+	+	+					
Seeds—*Bauhinia esculenta*					+	+	+	+	+			
Leaves—*Aloe zebrina*	-	-	-	-	-	-	-	-			-	-
Leaves—*Talinum arnoti*	-	-	-	-								
Roots—*Coccina rehmanii*	+	+	+	+	+	+	+	+	+	+	+	+
Roots—*Scilla* sp.	+	+	+	+	+	+						
Roots—*Wallera nutans*	-	-	-	-								

TABLE A-5   ANNUAL CYCLE OF THE SHERPA OF NEPAL

Activity	J	F	M	A	M	J	J	A	S	O	N	D
Herding												
Herds near main village, graze nearby										+	+	
Small herds near main village, large herds at low-lying camps; feeding with hay and buckwheat begins											+	+
Feeding with hay and buckwheat	+	+										+
Small herds near main village, large herds taken to high village and fed on hay		+	+									
Small and large herds at high village; all feed on hay			+	+								
All herds taken to medium elevation pastures				+	+							
Large herds to high pastures, some small herds to main village					+	+						
Move all animals to high pastures						+	+					
Grazing in high pastures							+	+				
Move all animals to medium pastures								+	+			
Grazing in medium pastures										-	-	
Farming												
Hoeing and plowing			+									
Repairing stone walls			+									
Manuring			+									
Planting and sowing			-	+	+							
Weeding						-	-					
Harvesting and drying								+	+			
Cutting and threshing buckwheat										+		
Hay making										+		
Threshing barley											-	
Trading				-	-					-	-	

For hunter-gatherers, the annual cycle is seasonal with movements motivated by searching for food. For most groups, from Inuit seal hunters to the San of the Kalahari Desert, these movements involve a pattern of aggregation and dispersal of individuals into larger or smaller camps. For example, in the dry winter months (June and July), the San aggregate in camps composed of a number of families and engage in an active social life of dancing, visiting, feasting, trading, and arranging marriages. In the rainy months (January–March), the camp breaks down into smaller groups (often only a single family) that move off in search of water in small pools, then to larger pools, and finally to permanent sources of water. During the other nonwinter months, movement and group size is based on the search for food rather than water. Table A-4 lists animals and plants hunted and gathered by the San. The table indicates that some plants and animals are available year-round and others only seasonally, and that some are major components of the diet (+) while others are minor (-). San groups hunt for no less than 20 different animals and gather at least 34 different plants. Their annual cycle is geared toward establishing camp in locations where certain foods or water is likely to be available at that time.

For pastoral cultures, the annual cycle involves a balancing of often labor-intensive subsistence activities, movement of part or all of the community and part or all of the herd, and contact with other cultures for trading. Many pastoral societies exist through a mixed economy based in part on the herding of animals for their milk or meat, farming, and trade. These activities need to be scheduled in accord with the climate. Table A-5 outlines the annual activities of the Sherpa of Nepal, who combine the herding of yak with farming (raising potatoes, barley, and buckwheat) and trading. Due to the climatic conditions in the Himalayas, farming and herding activities overlap in time but not always in

Breaking up soil is an important step in the annual farming cycle in agricultural communities such as this one in Nepal.

space as herds might be at high elevations when farming is done near the villages. The Sherpa deal with these competing demands through a division of labor based on sex (men mainly herd, women farm) and combining the activities at the same location whenever possible.

See also CALENDARS; SEASONS; TIME.

Chagnon, Napoleon A. (1968) *Yanomamö: The Fierce People.*

Coleman, Jack D. B. (1976) *Language Shift in a Bilingual Hebridean Crafting Community.*

Frigout, Arlette. (1979) "Hopi Ceremonial Calendar." In *Handbook of North American Indians. Volume 9. Southwest,* edited by Alfonso Ortiz, 564–576.

Fürer-Haimendorf, Christoph von. (1975) *The Sherpas of Nepal: Buddhist Highlanders.*

Irvin, Michael T. T. (1985) *My Grandfathers Build the House: The Tlingit Potlatch as a System of Religious Belief.*

Silberbauer, George B. (1965) *Report to the Government of Bechuanaland on the Bushmen Survey.*

———. (1972) "The G/wi Bushmen." In *Hunters and Gatherers Today*, edited by Mario G. Bicchieri, 271–326.

Tanaka, Jiro. (1980) *The San Hunter-Gatherers of the Kalahari: A Study in Ecological Anthropology.*

ARCHITECTURE

See BUILT ENVIRONMENTS; DWELLINGS; GEOMANCY; SETTLEMENT PATTERNS; SPACE.

ASTRONOMY

See AURORA BOREALIS; CALENDARS; PRECIPITATION; RAINBOW; STARS AND PLANETS; STORMS; SUN AND MOON; THUNDER AND LIGHTNING; UNIVERSE; WEATHER CONTROL; WIND.

AURORA BOREALIS

The aurora borealis is the name given to the two broken rings of light located above the north and south polar regions of the earth. Each ring, or halo, is about 2,400 miles in diameter and ranges from 60 to 600 miles above the earth's surface. Research conducted from space above the halos shows that the halos appear simultaneously and symmetrically. The aurora is produced by particles from the sun that are formed into rings by the earth's magnetic field and colored by gases in the upper atmosphere. When viewed from earth, the aurora comes in many colors—including white, blue, green, and red—and various shapes and sizes, some similar to clouds and others far more spectacular. The aurora borealis is commonly known as the northern lights, although the southern lights are just as common but are seen by far fewer people as the South Pole region has no indigenous population.

The aurora is always present although it cannot always be seen by people on earth. It is visible most often in the Arctic and Antarctic regions; the former is sparsely populated by the native peoples of Alaska, Canada, Greenland, northern Scandinavia, and Siberia and the latter is populated only by visiting scientists. Thus, only a small percentage of the earth's population has regular access to the aurora. In the Arctic region, the aurora can be seen on every clear night from autumn to spring; the lights are not visible in summer because of the bright sunlight and long days. For the rest of the world, visibility waxes and wanes over the years as the rings expand and contract in width. The northern lights are visible further south and the southern lights further north during certain years. This expansion and contraction of the rings has a predictable patterning as the lights tend to expand over a five- to six-year period and become more visible and more spectacular to more people and then contract over the next five or six years. In addition, the lights tend to be more spectacular in color, shape, and movement near the fall and spring equinoxes, are most spectacular around midnight, and tend to be visible for several nights in a row and at 27-day intervals. In general, the closer one lives to the equator, the less likely one will see the lights. If the lights are seen, they will likely not be spectacular in appearance.

The physical limits of the aurora means that it is regularly seen by only a small percentage of people. The northern lights are therefore of interest to only a small number of cultures. Because the aurora does not have the observable effects or associations of other astronomical and meteorological objects or events (such as the sun, moon, stars, or rainbows), in most northern cultures it is not perceived as having the powerful, direct influence on human affairs as do these other objects and events. Additionally, in most northern cultures the lights are not associated with specific supernatural beings such as spirits or souls of specific persons. At the same time, of course, the cosmology of northern peoples does contain beliefs about the origins, nature of, and possible effects of the northern lights. Because of the movement of the lights, a number of cultures, such as some Inuit groups in Canada and the Swedes, Scots, and Finns, associate the lights with dancers and dancing. The Inuit, for example, believe that the lights are the dancing souls of animals important to them as sources of food and raw materials such as the beluga whale, seal, and deer. In some cultures, including the Ottawa and Dogrib in Canada, the lights are seen as a benevolent supernatural force that can be called upon to help in curing diseases. Similarly, the Copper Inuit of Canada see the lights as a manifestation of spirits who will bring good weather. However, the belief that the aurora borealis is a benevolent force is not common to all northern cultures, probably because the lights are not always present or predictable in appearance. Instead, in a number of cultures, the lights are more often associated with death or the dead, although not necessarily seen as harmful. For example, the Chukchee of Siberia conceptualize the lights as several parallel bands across the sky with the upper band inhabited by those who died a "natural" death, the second band by those who were killed by evil spirits, and the third band by those who died by strangulation. In addition, the Chukchee believe that different color spots in the lights have different representations: whitish—the abode of those who died from a contagious disease, red—the abode of those who died by being stabbed with a knife, dark spots—the abode of those who were strangled by spirits of nervous diseases, and spots that change color—the dead playing a ball game with the live head of a walrus. The Samoyed of Siberia also associate the lights with death but also see them as harmful. God sends the lights to cause sickness or harm and the lights may kill reindeer or even humans. Finally, in some cultures, the northern lights are seen as harbingers of the future. The Saami, for example, believe strong northern lights predict snow and storms, lights that straggle across the sky from the southwest predict southwestern winds, and lights that shine on the northern horizon predict a cold spell.

Bernatzik, Hugo A. (1938) *Overland with the Nomad Lapps.*

Bogaras, Waldemar. (1904–1909) *The Chukchee.*

Rae, Edward. (1881) *The White Sea Peninsula: A Journey in Russian Lapland and Karelia.*

Savage, Candace. (1994) *Aurora: The Mysterious Northern Lights.*

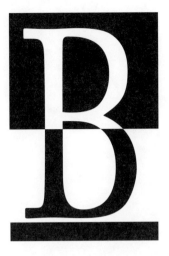

buildings or monuments, and forts or citadels. In 53 percent of traditional cultures, the largest structures are dwellings that are all much alike in size and shape; there are no large or impressive structures. In 13 percent of cultures the most impressive structure is the dwelling of the community leader, the major kinship group, or a wealthy person or family. In 17 percent of cultures the most impressive structure is a building used by the public or some segment of the public such as a meeting hall or a men's house. In 15 percent of cultures the most impressive structure is a church, temple, mosque, or a monument. And in 2 percent of cultures the most impressive structure is a fort or citadel.

From a cultural perspective, the built environment involves not simply the physical forms themselves, but also the organization of space, time, meaning, and communication by the humans who design, construct, use, and experience the built forms. The organization of these four components of the built environment represents an effort by humans to adapt built forms to meet human needs and the changes humans make in their behavior to adjust to the limitations and opportunities created by built forms.

Across cultures, the built environment serves a variety of either instrumental or symbolic functions. Instrumental functions are practical, such as providing shelter from the elements, channeling water to irrigate fields, or fencing in livestock. Symbolic functions are closely related to their role in expressing meanings shared by members of the culture. Three levels of meaning can be communicated by built forms: (1) low-level meanings such as the social situation or cues for behavior; (2) mid-level meanings such as identity, status, and power; and (3) high-level meanings such as worldview and cosmological beliefs.

Built forms provide low-level meanings by creating ambiance that makes it easier to focus on the task at hand, by providing amenities that make it easier to complete the task, and by

BUILT ENVIRONMENTS

The built environment is "any physical alteration of the natural environment, from hearths to cities, through construction by humans" (Lawrence and Low 1990:454). The built environment is sometimes called "fixed feature space" or "architecture," although use of the term *architecture* is often limited to structures purposefully designed and built by specialists. Major categories of built environment forms include buildings; bounded and defined spaces such as courtyards, gardens, fields, pastures, roads, and irrigation ditches; sites such as landmarks, shrines, and monuments; site plans that include clusters of buildings; features of buildings; and the interior plan of buildings. Hearths and dwellings are the only major built environment forms that are found in all cultures. Cultures, otherwise, vary widely in the alterations they make to the natural environment when they build structures or other forms. One indicator of this variability is the cross-cultural distribution of large or impressive structures such as elegant dwellings, public buildings, religious or ceremonial

Building a house in Fiji

fostering interactions through a communications net. In addition, symbolic functions, such as reflecting the social organization of the group and creating a mood through the organization of time and space, create an environment in which appropriate social interaction is possible.

Regarding mid-level meanings, the exclusive use of certain built forms by certain categories of people indicates that those people are different than others. For example, in some cultures menstruating women are confined to special buildings called menstrual huts and are forbidden to interact with men. In many of these cultures, the menstrual huts symbolize the belief that menstruating women are unclean, ritually polluting, and, therefore, dangerous to men. Another example is the use in some societies of men's houses, buildings in which men routinely sleep and socialize with other men while their wives and children live in separate dwellings. This arrangement symbolizes the close ties between men—especially between men who are kin in these cultures—and places relatively less emphasis on the marital relationship. Built forms also commonly symbolize social status for different groups in a society. For example, the requirement in many European nations that Gypsies reside on the edge of a town signifies their low social status and the associated belief that they were dangerous and dishonest. In the United States, the different architectural styles associated with different immigrant groups served as a marker of group identity. And in many developing nations, those who are wealthier or have more political influence live in Western-style housing while others live in traditional-style housing that is smaller, has fewer rooms, and is made of local materials.

High-level meanings reflect cultural beliefs about complex matters such as the nature of relationships between people and the environment, between different cultures, and between people and the supernatural world. The investment of considerable societal resources in the building and maintenance of religious structures such as churches, temples, mosques, or shrines and the restrictions placed on the use of these buildings symbolizes the importance of religion and also the belief that humans can influence the supernatural world through their behavior. The building of monuments to political leaders symbolizes the importance of the values displayed by those leaders. The location of settlements within fortifications indicates a belief that other cultures are likely to be hostile rather than friendly.

One reason why the built environment plays a major symbolic role across cultures is that it is malleable. That is, given certain environmental and climactic constraints, humans have considerable leeway in the plan, design, size, style, form, location, orientation, and decoration of built forms. This leeway is reflected both in the variety of built forms found across cultures as well as the variety within single cultures. While it is not clear what factors influence human decisions about their built environment, it is clear that neither the environment nor the climate is the major determinant and that cultural factors play a major role. One important cultural factor is the level of complexity of the society. Cultures with larger, more densely settled populations and that produce food through agriculture or intensive fishing tend to build larger, rectilinear-shaped buildings, with more rooms per buildings and more monofunctional rooms. They are also more likely to build other types of structures such as irrigation channels, roads, ceremonial structures, public buildings, and fortifications. Other cultural factors of importance are the type of family, as extended families require larger houses divided into rooms for the constituent families, and type of political organization, as cultures with a strong, centralized government tend to organize villages as grids, radiating from a central plaza that is often where the government offices are located and the community leaders live. In cultures with weak centralized leadership, on the other hand, village plans tend to be

A village composed mainly of circular, conical thatched dwellings in Upper Volta. The size and arrangement of the dwellings reflect local kinship organization.

circular, implying an absence of centralized control, or haphazard, implying an egalitarian ethos.

See also DWELLINGS; GARDENS AND GARDENING; GEOMANCY; MOBILITY AND SEDENTISM; PLACE NAMES; SETTLEMENT PATTERNS; SPACE; TIME.

Duncan, James S. (1982) *Housing and Identity: Cross-Cultural Perspectives.*

Gutman, Robert. (1976) "The Social Function of the Built Environment." In *The Mutual Interaction of People and Their Built Environment*, edited by Amos Rapoport, 37–49.

Kent, Susan, ed. (1990) *Domestic Architecture and the Use of Space: An Interdisciplinary and Cross-Cultural Study.*

Lawrence, Denise L., and Setha M. Low. (1990) "The Built Environment and Spatial Form." *Annual Review of Anthropology* 19:453–505.

Murdock, George Peter, and Suzanne F. Wilson. (1972) "Settlement Patterns and Community Organization: Cross-Cultural Codes 3." *Ethnology* 11:254–295.

Rapoport, Amos. (1994) "Spatial Organization and the Built Environment." In *Companion Encyclopedia of Anthropology*, edited by Tim Ingold, 460–500.

although the concept of a day is known in all cultures. Most cultures developed lunar calendars to mark the months and other time periods such as seasons. However, even though the concept of a day as a unit of time is a cultural universal, a day may be measured in different ways. For example, Polynesians traditionally count by nights, not days, and the Jewish ritual calendar marks the day as beginning at sundown.

Calendars are used to structure one's physical and social environment. Although in the contemporary world we think of calendars as a tool for structuring business, social, and religious activities, in many nonstate societies the calendar was more closely linked to the physical environment, especially to changes in climate, plant growth, and animal behavior that impacted subsistence practices. Thus, the monthly calendar told people when to begin planting, when to expect food to be scarce, when to move their livestock, and so forth. It also told them when to hold various religious rites that were often tied to subsistence activities such as planting and harvesting. For the Seminole of Florida, for example, the year began in the month of the Big Ripening Moon (August) and was marked by the Green Corn Dance.

Today, the Gregorian calendar (instituted by Pope Gregory XIII in 1582), with an average over 400 years of 365.2425 days per year and 12 months with an extra day added every fourth year (leap year), is the standard around the world and is used in virtually all nations for government and commercial activities. However, in many cultures, people structure their lives and measure time by using more than one calendar system. In the United States, for example, in addition to the Gregorian calendar used by all, most people also must consider the October–September year used by the federal government; school calendars that run from September through June; fiscal years used by businesses that often run from July though June; and religious calendars followed by Muslims, Hindus, Jews,

CALENDARS

The basic units of time in a full calendar are the day, month, and year. But many calendars also mark other units of time including portions of days such as minutes; portions of minutes such as seconds; seasons; and multiples of a year such as decades, centuries, millennia, and eras. There is considerable variation over human history and across cultures in the types of calendars used and their importance in the society. Full calendars are found only in state-level societies—that is, societies often referred to as civilizations—that have a large and settled population, a system of writing, governance by a centralized political authority, a social structure based on hierarchical distinctions such as those of class or caste, a monotheistic or polytheistic religion, trade, the collection of taxes, and the storing of food surpluses. Thus, calendars were developed by the Egyptians, Babylonians, ancient Hebrews, ancient Muslims, Chinese, Hindus, Greeks, Romans, and others in the Old World and the Maya, Inca, and Aztec in the New World. Nonstate societies generally did not develop full-scale calendars,

Chinese, Native Americans, and others. The same situation occurs in many other cultures. In rural Taiwan, for example, people routinely follow three calendars: the Gregorian calendar for government and business activities such as school, tax collecting, and military service; the traditional lunar calendar for religious purposes such as setting ritual days, visiting the temple, and ancestor worship; and the traditional solar calendar for selecting the earliest and latest possible planting dates. Although it need not be done in practice, the calendars can be aligned so that any event can be marked on each of the calendars. For example, the best time for planting a second crop of rice seedlings is the week preceding or following the Great Heat on the solar calendar, which is July 23 on the Gregorian calendar and the seventh day of the sixth moon on the lunar calendar. The need to use more than one calendar in Taiwan and other cultures around the world today is the result of three major factors. First, because of Western influence, the Gregorian calendar is now the international standard in government and business. Second, because non-Western religious traditions are still vital in many cultures, the traditional religious calendar that was usually lunar must still be used. And third, because the solar calendar best marks seasonal change, it must be followed to best exploit the physical environment.

In accord with their function of structuring the social and physical environment, particular days on calendars often have special meanings. In many cultures, some days are considered unlucky (Friday the Thirteenth, for example) and others lucky (St. Patrick's Day for the Irish, for example). Some days are considered a good time for certain activities; others are not. Similarly, in many cultures certain days are designated as secular or religious holidays and some as days of rest, when normal activities are restricted or prohibited. While Sunday is a day of rest and prayer for Christians around the world, the Shona of East Africa designate four days called Chisi in

each lunar month as days of rest—the day of no moon and the following fifth, fifteenth, and twenty-fifth days. Within the current calendar Chisi always falls on a Friday; all work and ritual sacrifice is forbidden. If a person does not rest as required, the Shona believe that the entire community will be punished by the tribal spirit, who at some later time will cause a drought, flood, famine, or other catastrophe.

In some cultures, the calendar is not just a means of keeping track of time and environmental change but also provides guidance about one's activities. This guidance is often provided in the form of written almanacs that are consulted by individuals on a daily or regular basis. The *Farmer's Almanac* is one such guidebook, as are the numerous almanacs used by families throughout rural China. Traditionally, these booklets were routinely consulted as guides to one's daily activity, although government bans have now restricted their distribution. A sample from one almanac indicates the detailed advice they provide for scheduling one's activities.

March 1st (1936), Sunday; 8th of 2nd month.
　　Birthday of Chang Ta Ti (God of flood).
　　Good for: Offering sacrifice, praying, asking for prosperity, making petitions, visiting relatives, trading, accepting office, arranging marriage, offering marriage gifts, wedding, entering new houses, changing lodging, tailoring, mending buildings, laying foundations, fixing beams, mending storerooms, opening market, making contracts, opening storerooms, planting, breaking soil, burying dead.
　　Bad for: Thatching roof, introducing water to field, hunting.

March 2nd, Monday; 9th of 2nd month.
　　Good for: Visiting relatives and friends, catching animals.
　　Bad for: Making accusations in court, curing diseases, taking medicines.
　　(Plants begin to bud.)

March 16th, Monday; 23rd of 2nd month.
　　Good for nothing.

Bad for nothing.

March 27th, Friday; 5th of 3rd month.

Good for: Taking a bath, fishing, catching animals, clearing houses.

Bad for: Fixing a bed, buying land and other properties.

(Beginning of thunder.)

Of course, individual Chinese differed in the faith they put in the predictions and the extent to which they followed them. These Chinese almanacs actually allow users to reckon the day using any one of three calendars—the Gregorian calendar indicating the name and day of the month and the name of the day, the traditional lunar calendar indicating the day and the se-quence of months, and the agricultural calendar as indicated by environmental features in parentheses.

Calendars in Nonstate Societies

Traditional peoples in nonstate societies generally did not develop lunar-solar calendars. Their calendars instead were mainly lunar and thus had 12 months, even though not all peoples actually recognized that there were 12 months. Because the 12 lunar phases are 11 days shorter than the solar year that influences the seasons and because in many cultures the lunar calendar was used to mark key environmental changes related to subsistence practices, the lunar calendars needed to be adjusted to conform to the solar

Aztec calendar

year. These adjustments usually took the form of adding a month periodically to keep the lunar months in line with the environmental changes associated with the solar year. The Hopi in Arizona and the Belau in Oceania, as in many cultures, add a month every few years. The Belau add an extra month to their 12-month lunar calendar every third year or so. When the Pleiades does not line up correctly with the moon at the start of a new year, the Belau say they have "lost count" of the months and simply add another one. In some cultures—perhaps because the months are indicated more by environmental changes than by the phases of the moon—people are less concerned about keeping the months exactly in line with the solar-determined year. For example, the Kpelle of Liberia reckon the beginnings and ends of their 12 months very loosely, with no clear start or end for each. Instead, predictable environmental changes such as rain or stormy periods and plant growth determine the months; the year begins when the agricultural work cycle begins. For the Kpelle, the key measure of time is not the lunar calendar or annual agricultural cycle but the schedule of four-year Poro initiation schools.

In cultures without full lunar-solar calendars, the past is not marked by reference to the years on the calendar. Instead, events of daily life and one's age are generally calculated by reference to some major event. The Kpelle of Liberia, for example, followed this practice and might locate an event of some weeks past by placing it in "The week I went to Monrovia." In some cultures without writing systems, the passage of time and major events were recorded by notching sticks, by making and keeping symbolic drawings, and on pictographs.

The lunar calendars used in many traditional cultures and the names assigned the months reflect the close tie between the calendars and environmental impact on subsistence activities over the course of a solar year. In some cultures, the names for the months are based on environ-

mental and climate features such as the 12 months of the Iroquois of New York that translate into English as follows:

1. The sun is large again
2. Leaves (fall) down into the water
3. The leaves are much immersed
4. Plants stand up again
5. Fruits are getting ripe
6. Plants growing
7. Plants growing more
8. The harvest is gathered
9. The field is harvested
10. The cold is coming again
11. Again it is cold greatly
12. The sun is returning

In other cultures, the names of the months reflect a consideration of both the physical and social environment as with the names for the 12 annual and 1 intercalary (a month added periodically to bring the lunar months in line with environmental changes of the solar year) Hopi months:

1. Initiates' Moon
2. Dangerous Moon
3. Water Moon
4. Purification Moon
5. Whistling or Cactus Moon
6. Windbreak Moon
7. Waiting Moon
8. Planting Moon
9. Nameless Moon
10. Nameless Moon
11. Nameless Moon
12. Autumn Moon
13. Harvest Moon

Similarly, the names for the 12 lunar months of the Turkana of East Africa reflect social and environmental considerations:

1. Vegetation (when rain falls and plants grow)
2. Mud (when dung looks like mud after a short rain)
3. Luxuriant (when grass is green and high)
4. Flowering
5. Ceremonies
6. Separation (when nomadic pastoralism begins)
7. Nothing to eat
8. To cook (when animal's blood is eaten)
9. Leaf (when trees lose their leaves)
10. To cover (when it is cloudy and rainy)
11. White (when the sun shines brightly)
12. Elapse (the dry season)

Major Non-Gregorian Calendars

Around the world today, a number of non-Gregorian calendars are routinely used by many people. These calendars were developed in different cultural traditions than the Christian world that produced the Gregorian calendar. Depending on where the users of these calendars live, they may guide only religious activity (as for most Jews in North America) or they may still be routinely used in daily life (as among Hindus in India) alongside the Gregorian calendar. Four of these calendars are the Jewish calendar, the Hindu calendar, the Muslim calendar, and the Chinese calendar.

The Jewish era is dated to 3761 B.C., meaning that the year 1995 in the Gregorian calendar aligns with the year 5756 on the Jewish calendar. According to Jewish tradition, the earth was created in the year 3761. The modern Jewish calendar dates to about A.D. 350 with clear influences from earlier Hebrew and Babylonian calendars. It is both lunar and solar with 12 months of 29 or 30 days (some alternate between the two lengths in different years) and 7 leap years of an extra month in each 19-year cycle.

Thus, 19 years in the Jewish calendar contain 6,935 days, equal to the number of days in a solar year. The year begins with the month of Nissan in the spring.

The Muslim era is dated to A.D. 622, the year the prophet Mohammed migrated from Mecca to Medina. It is a lunar calendar of 12 months alternating between 30 and 29 days, with a year of 354 days. Sometimes the last month has an extra day, making a 355-day year. The lunar year is 10 or 11 days shorter than the solar year. Over the course of 32.5 years, the lunar months regress through the seasons. This means that the months change alignment with the seasons from year to year. The year begins with the month of Muharram; the most important month is the ninth month, Ramadan, a month of fasting for all Muslims around the world. Islamic nations in the Middle East vary in the use of the Islamic calendar. Some such as Saudi Arabia and Yemen use the Islamic era, others like Egypt use both Christian and Islamic calendars, while Turkey stresses the Gregorian calendar. Regardless of government policy, Muslims around the world use the Islamic calendar for religious purposes.

The Chinese calendar system is older and more complex than either the Jewish or Muslim. The Chinese solar calendar of 365.25 days and lunar calendar of 29.5 days per month date to the fourteenth century B.C. As early as 770 B.C., the Chinese also recognized the Metonic cycle—periods of 19 years with 7 seasons added at intervals that then equal 19 solar years. The traditional Chinese solar calendar still in use (although replaced since 1912 to some extent by government sanction of the Gregorian calendar) dates to the third century B.C. and is based on a meteorological cycle of 24 points that equal 15 degrees apart on the ecliptic plane. As the plane is 360 degrees, it takes 1 solar year to complete it, making the cycle and the calendar a solar one. The Chinese also employ a lunar calendar of 12 months of 29 or 30 days each, with an extra month added at 7 points in the 19-year cycle. This calendar is used primarily to determine the date of religious holidays. The Chinese also have used a unique 60-year cycle based on a combination of 10 celestial stems and 12 terrestrial branches. The concepts and methods for figuring the units and branches are based on the Chinese philosophical and cosmological systems and are exceedingly complex. The cycle produces a symbolic system in which a particular animal and stem is associated with each individual and is used in fortune-telling. Additionally, 60 years is considered a significant number and those who live beyond 60 years are looked upon kindly by the gods.

Even more complex is the calendar employed in Hindu India. The system results from the complexity of Hindu conceptions of time and the basic calendar, the simultaneous use of the general Hindu calendar and local and caste-based religious calendars (Hinduism has been called the religion of 1 million gods), and the official use of the Gregorian calendar. The Hindu calendrical system uses ages, eras, solar and lunar years, and solar and lunar months. For Hindus, time is divided into two broad periods of Existence (Kalpa) and Dissolution (Pralaya). The Kalpa and Pralaya ages each consist of four ages; Hindus currently believe that humankind is in the Kali or final stage of Dissolution or, more precisely, in the 5,094th year (in 1994) of the 432,000 solar years in this age. In reckoning the beginning of the calendar currently in use, both the Samvat (beginning in 57 B.C.) and Saka (beginning in A.D. 78) are used. Hindus have used a combined lunar-solar calendar since 1181 B.C. The lunar year consists of 12 months with an extra month added about every 2.5 years. The solar calendar is based on 12 solar and 27 lunar divisions based on astrology, with 1 year being the time it takes for the sun to pass through all the divisions—the equivalent of 1 solar year. The names for the lunar moths rather than the solar months are generally used. The lunar days,

which number 30 per month, may begin or end at different times depending on which rites are celebrated that day. The week contains 7 solar days based on the movement of the planets, with the civil day beginning at sunrise and ending at sunrise the following day. Although this system seems extraordinarily complex to non-Hindus, in actual practice Hindus have little trouble marking or telling time with their calendar, as those in contact with one another use the same era, the same month names (usually lunar names), the same astrological system, and celebrate the same religious holidays.

The system outlined above describes the Hindu calendar only in very general terms. In fact, there is considerable variation throughout Hindu India as local communities have developed and use their own calendars with their own eras, sequence of months, and ritual days. Thus, villages, village clusters, and even people of different occupation castes in the same village may follow somewhat different ritual calendars.

See also ANNUAL CYCLE; SEASONS; TIME.

'Ali, 'Abdullah Yusaf. (1937) *The Holy Quran: Arabic Text with an English Translation and Commentary.*

Barnett, William K. (1971) *An Ethnographic Description of Sanlei Ts'un, Taiwan, with Emphasis on Women's Roles, Overcoming Research Problems Caused by the Presence of a Great Tradition.*

Best, Günter. (1983) *Culture and Language of the Turkana, NW Kenya.*

Fei, Hsiao-tung. (1946) *Peasant Life in China: A Field Study of Country Life in the Yangtze Valley.*

Frigout, Arlette. (1979) "Hopi Ceremonial Calendar." In *Handbook of North American Indians. Volume 9. Southwest,* edited by Alfonso Ortiz, 564–576.

Gallin, Bernard. (1966) *Hsin Hsing, Taiwan: A Chinese Village in Change.*

Gelfand, Michael. (1959) *Shona Ritual with Special Reference to the Chaminuka Cult.*

Johannes, Robert. (1981) *Words of the Lagoon: Fishing and Marine Lore in the Palau District of Micronesia.*

Klass, Morton. (1978) *From Field to Factory: Community Structure and Industrialization in West Benegal.*

Trepp, Leo. (1980) *The Complete Book of Jewish Observance.*

Underhill, Muriel M. (1921) *The Hindu Religious Year.*

Waugh, Frederick W. (1916) *Iroquois Foods and Food Preparation.*

Westermann, Diedrich H. (1921) *The Kpelle: A Negro Tribe in Liberia.*

CARRYING CAPACITY

The concept now called carrying capacity was first introduced in 1872 by Robert Malthus, who pointed out that subsistence practices limit the growth of human populations. Malthus further suggested that societies have a marked tendency to expand in size beyond the number of people that can be supported by the subsistence system. He also reasoned that this population growth is controlled either by factors such as famine or disease that increase the mortality rate or factors such as celibacy or infanticide that lower the birth rate. Since this initial formulation, demographers, ecologists, anthropologists, sociologists, economists, and others have been interested in what is now called the carrying capacity of a population. In this respect, the population is a specific community, such as hunter-gatherer societies, horticultural societies,

agricultural societies, entire nations, regions, or the entire human population on earth. Thus, subsistence practices of horticulturalists are analyzed in terms of their carrying capacity; specific nations are categorized as having a high carrying capacity (Japan, Austria, Spain), a low carrying capacity (Burma, Norway, Nigeria), or as not yet approaching their carrying capacity (Laos, India, Jamaica). The world is described as having exceeded its carrying capacity of about 5.5 billion people in 1992.

Numerous definitions of carrying capacity have been suggested and used, with a general one that encompasses all viewpoints being "the maximum population density [and population] that can be supported by that society using its kind of cultural adaptation in its specific environment" (McCoid 1984:32). This definition includes a number of concepts: (1) population density—the number of people in some defined space such as a square mile; (2) population size—the number of members of a culture or society; (3) cultural adaptation—the subsistence system and other cultural practices relevant to resource use such as trade, warfare, and population-limiting customs; and (4) specific environment—the actual resources exploited for food and the potential food resources in the environment inhabited by the group.

The idea of carrying capacity is appealing because it formalizes the commonsense assumption that the availability of resources limits population size and density. When the resources are greater than needed to support the existing population, population growth can be expected. When the resources and population are about equal, growth is limited. And when population growth exceeds resources, a crisis situation exists. While this idea seems quite logical, the actual application of the concept of carrying capacity to real-life situations is open to various interpretations and is marred by technical difficulties. One problem with the concept is that it means different things to different people. For example, ecologists see carrying capacity as a major determinant of population growth rates and population density while economists view the carrying capacity of any society as limitless due to technological innovations and policy interventions. The technical difficulties encountered in using the concept in reference to real cultures include the following: (1) it is impossible to count all potential food resources; (2) not all resources (trees, for example) are used as food resources; (3) not all resources are used at a steady or equal rate; (4) long-term environmental change is hard to identify and measure; (5) the quantity of food taken from the environment changes in response to population growth as population expansion often leads to technological innovations that increase resource use; and (6) cultures that are described as having reached or even exceeded the carrying capacity of their environments continue to experience population growth.

People in non-Western, nonindustrialized societies who subsist by hunting, gathering, horticulture, herding, or subsistence agriculture know that there is a close relationship between the population size and density of their settlements and food resources, even though they do not use the technical term carrying capacity. Across cultures, various mechanisms are used to regulate both population and the availability of food resources in order to maintain a balance between the two. Mechanisms for adjusting the population size and density of a group include fissioning by which one large group divides into two or more smaller groups, either on a seasonal or cyclical basis or in response to unpredictable food stress; flexible group membership that allows individuals or families to move freely to different settlements or other nomadic bands; methods that lower the birth rate such as abortion, infanticide, and a lengthy postpartum taboo on sexual relations; and methods that increase the death rate such as gerontocide or warfare. Mechanisms for increasing the food supply

include raiding other societies for land, crops, or animals; using more land to grow crops and slaves, children, or hired labor to work the land; following an annual cycle that maximizes use of environmental resources; migration to locales with more resources; increasing soil fertility through manuring, growing of nitrogen-fixing crops such as beans, and water control; increasing the crop yield through multicropping and crop rotation; storing food; sharing food; utilizing a mixed subsistence strategy with seasonal adjustments; and trading with other communities or societies.

See also AGRICULTURE; ANNUAL CYCLE; ENVIRONMENTAL UNCERTAINTY AND RISK; GREEN REVOLUTION; MOBILITY AND SEDENTISM.

Chen, Robert S., et al. (1990) *The Hunger Report.*

Dewar, Robert E. (1984) "Environmental Productivity, Population Regulation, and Carrying Capacity." *American Anthropologist* 86:601–614.

McCoid, Catherine H. (1984) *Carrying Capacity of Nation-States.*

COLLECTING

See HUNTING-GATHERING.

COLOR

Color is a physical attribute of objects in the environment and also a matter of considerable variation and subjective meaning for peoples around the world. From a purely physical point of view, different wave lengths of light are perceived by humans as different colors. When white light waves are refracted through a prism, one can see the spectrum of hues. Water droplets in the atmosphere act like prisms, refracting light and producing a rainbow. From a cultural perspective, interest in color has focused on two major topics: first, variation in the use of different words (color terms) across cultures and second, the function and symbolic role of color in different cultures.

In the mid-nineteenth century, British statesman William Gladstone first noted that cultures vary in the number of terms they use for colors. He also pointed out that in Plato's poetry certain colors such as blue and brown were never mentioned. Subsequent research has shown that cultures do indeed vary in the color terminology of their languages. For example, the Aranda, a foraging people of Australia, had only

4 color terms: *tutuka* (red), *churunkura* (white), *urapulla* (black), and *tierga* (yellow, green, blue). The Western Shoshone of North America had 6 terms for white, black, yellow, gray, green, and red. The Blackfoot of the North American plains had 11, the English translations of which suggest the origin of the color terms in the source of the colored material—yellow earth, Buffalo earth, red earth, many times baked paint, red many times baked, white earth, and so forth. In the United States, the 329 color chips in the Munsell system represent the range of hue and brightness in color symbolized by words in English.

Linguists distinguish between Level I and Level II color terms. Level I terms such as black, white, red, yellow, green, and blue are highly inclusive and also the most common colors referred to by terms in most languages. Level II terms such as violet or orange are less inclusive of a range of colors and less often used. They

TABLE C-1 COLOR NAMES FOR THE ELEVEN FOCAL COLOR TERMS IN FIVE LITERARY LANGUAGES

English	Spanish	French	Russian	Japanese
white	blanco	blanc	belyj	shiro
black	negro	noir	chernyj	kuro
red	rojo	rouge	krasnyj	aka
green	verde	vert	zelenyj	midori
yellow	amarillo	jaune	zheltyj	kiiro
blue	azul	bleu	goluboj sinji	ao
brown	moreno pardo	brun	korichnevji	chairo
purple	purpura cardeno	pourpre	purpurnyj	muraski
orange	naranja	orange	oranzhevyi	orenji
pink	rosado sonrosado	rose	rozovyi	mamairo
gray	cano gris	gris	seryj	haiiro

also tend to have appeared in the language later than Level I terms. Eleven colors are focal colors and terms that refer to them are called focal or basic color terms. A focal color term is a word whose meaning is not based on the component parts of the word, is of symbolical importance to the people who use it, is not restricted in application, and does not name a range of colors with a class name used by another term. The 11 focal color terms are black and white (both of which appear in all languages or, at least, all peoples distinguish conceptually between light and dark), red (91 percent of cultures), green and/or yellow (74 percent of cultures), blue (55 percent of cultures), brown, pink, orange, purple, and gray. Table C-1 (see page 41) lists words for the 11 focal colors in five literary languages.

Early theorists attempted to explain the cross-cultural variation in the number of color terms in a language on the basis of evolutionary ideas in which the larger number of terms in Indo-European languages spoken by European colonists were seen as a sign of cultural superiority. This notion has now been discarded and replaced with a different evolutionary explanation based on systematic cross-cultural comparisons that focus on the development of language. The 11 focal terms develop in a predictable sequence in most known languages. Black and white terms appear first, followed by red, then green or yellow, then yellow or green, followed by blue and brown, and then pink, orange, purple, and gray in no particular order. If a language has any term near the end of the list, it will very likely have all terms that precede it. Another possible explanation for the variation of the number of color terms across cultures is that the more common the color is in the culture, the more terms will be used for different hues of that color. This explanation does not explain basic color terms but does help account for situations like that of the Saami noted below where a large number of terms is used to distinguish among related environmental features.

Typically, in many societies with a short list of color terms, a range of related colors that would be identified by Westerners as different colors are lumped as one color and named with a single term. For example, the Seminole in Florida traditionally lumped various colors ranging from violet to green as blue, colors ranging from scarlet to pink as red, and those ranging from dark orange to light yellow as yellow. This practice of using one color term for two or more color categories is known as semantic color identity. The most common form is when one term is used for both blue and green (56 percent of cultures); followed by blue and black (22 percent); green, blue, and black (13 percent); and red and yellow and yellow and green (11 percent each). A marked regional variation exists within these patterns, with the blue-green semantic identity most common among native North and South Americans; blue-black among Africans; green-blue-black among Australian aboriginals and Africans; yellow-red among Australian aboriginals; and red-yellow among native South Americans, Australian aboriginals, and Africans. These patterns suggest a physiological basis for some semantic identity patterns as does biological research suggesting a link between residence closer to the equator and diet to perception of color. People in cultures near the equator are darker pigmented than those further north and south; this factor may influence their perception of the colors blue, red, and yellow and lead to what others classify as "color confusion."

In many cultures, color is of considerable functional importance. One major function is as a criteria for identifying and classifying things in one's social and physical environment. The Trobriand Islanders off the coast of New Guinea, for example, use the color of coconut husks to classify coconuts into five types: *lukumitamata* (green), *lukubwebweria* (red), *lukwaygibu* (brown), *lukulawata* (white or pale), and *lukukwalu* (orange). Similarly, the Saami (Lapps) of Scandinavia use color as the basis for the names assigned to 50 different types of reindeer. Up to seven classes of reindeer are distinguished by their body color—black, brown, gray, yellow-gray, light gray, whitish, and snow white. Each of these general categories is subdivided on the basis of colors of body parts such as the flanks or neck; the colors and shapes of spots or patches are also considered. This use of color enables the Saami to identify different reindeer that appear to be all the same to a non-Saami.

In addition to the physical environment, color is also commonly used around the world to sort people into different categories. The need to sort others in our environment into categories seems to be a human universal and is perhaps related to our somewhat limited ability to recognize and remember others by name and our need to base our pattern of interaction with other people on our perception of their status relative to our own. Thus, appearance is important in classifying people so that we may interact with them in appropriate ways. Skin color, because it is so obvious and immutable, is an important criterion for classification around the world. The much-used, although inaccurate and misleading, classification of the peoples of the world into three "races"—Mongoloid (yellow), Negroid (black), and Caucasoid (white)—is based in large part on skin color. Skin color is also often afforded a powerful symbolic meaning, with skin color linked to various behaviors and the color of one's own group considered superior to that of other groups. For example, the Amhara in Ethiopia see themselves as brown, a color they believe to be superior to black, the color of neighboring peoples who are considered inferior.

Colors beyond those of the skin are also used to classify people. The Hmong in both Laos and the United States identify specific clans (large, extended family groups) with specific colors. In one California community, for example, the Ly clan is identified with white, the Moua with white, and Vang with multicolors. In Laos, these colors are tied to traditional clothing and thus enable others to identify the clan affiliation of an individual on sight. In Highland Ecuador, traditional and assimilated Quechua can be differentiated by their clothing. Traditional Quechua wear light- and bright-colored ponchos, shirts, and shawls; assimilated individuals wear more white-style clothing and "white" colors—that is, dark subdued colors. Colors also signify religious differences in some cultures. The Basques in Spain distinguish among Christians and Turks in their Christmas pageant by Christians wearing blue clothing and never red and Turks the reverse. In Bangladesh, Bengalis who are ascetics devoted to Siva wear red clothes to distinguish themselves from other categories of adherents. Finally, the status of an individual can be indicated by colors. The Aymara in Peru follow customs that dictate the colors to be used at funerals, depending on the age, sex, and marital status of the deceased. For example, the wreath for an older, married man is preferably black, dark blue, and violet while one of black with two light blue colors is not considered appropriate.

In many cultures, color is of considerable symbolic importance; specific colors are considered omens or can be used to protect oneself from harm. In numerous Native American cultures, colors were and continue to be associated with direction and with objects and events in the natural and human worlds. The Hopi of Arizona use the following symbolic system:

Direction	Color	Natural Feature
northwest	yellow	flowers
southwest	blue or green	sky, water, vegetation
southeast	red	blood
northeast	white	purity

In addition, mythical beings and other natural features such as trees and shrubs are associated with each direction and color. The Cherokee of North Carolina believed that "The south wind was white and brought peace; the north wind was blue and meant defeat; the west wind was black and brought death. The wind from the east was red. It brought power, and war." The Pawnee of the Midwest associated colors with the four directions, natural forces, animals, and trees.

Such symbolism is not confined to North America. The Javanese in Indonesia, for example, link red with fire, black with earth, yellow with air, and white with water. In many cultures red is associated with blood or life and black with death or evil. However, among the Zulu of South Africa blackness is associated with the king and symbolizes perfection, completeness as a person, luck, and fertility. To ensure that a king is completely black (beyond his skin color), he must undergo a smoking rite. Because red is associated with life, it is often seen as protective—the Sarakatsani of Greece believe that it protects one from the evil eye. The Andaman Islanders in South Asia daub a sick person with red paint to increase his or her vitality.

Color is also of considerable symbolic and emotional importance in Western culture. Some colors such as soft reds are perceived as warm or cheerful and make people happy. Some people seek color healing or therapy, as with the Andaman Islanders who believe in the healing powers of certain colors. One only has to think about the thought, planning, and expense people go to when decorating their homes to realize just how important color is in Western culture.

See also HOT AND COLD STATES.

Alaiza, Carol Ann Harrington de. (1989) *Santa Grazi Pastorala: A Critical Study of the Basque Pastorale as Contemporary Tradition.*

Berlin, Brent, and Paul Kay. (1969) *Basic Color Terms: Their Universality and Evolution.*

Berry, John W., Ype H. Poortinga, Marshall H. Segall, and Pierre R. Dasen. (1992) *Cross-Cultural Psychology: Research and Applications.*

Bishop, Kent A. (1986) *The Hmong of Central California: An Investigation and Analysis of the Changing Family Structure during Liminality, Acculturation, and Transition.*

Bornstein, Marc H. (1973) "The Psychophysiological Component of Cultural Difference in Color Naming and Illusion Susceptibility." *Behavior Science Research* 8:41–101.

Christensen, Karen. (1989) *Home Ecology: Making Your World a Better Place.*

Cole, John T. (1969) *The Human Soul in the Aymara Culture of Pumasara: An Ethnographic Study in the Light of George Herbert Mead and Martin Buber.*

Collinder, Bjorn. (1949) *The Lapps.*

Ember, Melvin. (1978) "Size of Color Lexicon: Interaction of Cultural and Biological Factors." *American Anthropologist* 80:364–367.

Hays, David G., Enid Margolis, Raoul Naroll, and Dale Revere Perkins. (1972) "Color Term Salience." *American Anthropologist* 74:1107–1121.

Kabbadias, Georgios B. (1965) *Mediterranean Pastoral Nomads: The Sarakatsani of Greece.*

MacCauley, Clay. (1884) *The Seminole Indians of Florida.*

Malinowski, Bronislaw. (1935) *Coral Gardens and their Magic: A Study of the Methods of Tilling the Soil and Agricultural Rites in the Trobriand Islands.*

Östör, Akos. (1980) *The Play of the Gods: Locality, Ideology, Structure, and Time in the Festivals of a Bengali Town.*

Radcliffe-Brown, Alfred R. (1922) *The Andaman Islanders: A Study in Social Anthropology.*

Raum, Otto F. (1973) *The Social Functions of Avoidances and Taboos among the Zulu.*

Reid, John P. (1970) *A Law of Blood: The Primitive Law of the Cherokee Nation.*

Rubio Orbe, Gonzalo. (1956) *Punyaro.*

Spencer, Walter B., and F. J. Gillen. (1927) *The Arunta: A Study of a Stone Age People.*

Weiss, Jerome. (1978) *Folk Psychology of the Javanese of Ponorogo.*

Weltfish, Gene. (1965) *The Lost Universe: With a Closing Chapter on "The Universe Regained."*

Whiting, Alfred F. (1939) *Ethnobotany of the Hopi.*

Wissler, Clark. (1910) *Material Culture of the Blackfoot Indians.*

and "across side" (north). The Taos and Hopi Indians of New Mexico and Arizona, respectively, have five and six cardinal directions. For the Taos these cardinal directions are east, west, north, south, and between east and north—or the place where the sun rises. Rather than running vertical and horizontal on a compass, the Taos directions are skewed slightly to the left. The Hopi's six cardinal directions of northwest, southwest, southeast, northeast, up (above), and down (below) are integrated into their belief system and linked with cultures and features of the environment as discussed below. The inclusion of up and down reflects the Hopi conception of the universe as being divided into upper and lower portions. The Saami of Scandinavia call direction "knowledge of the forest" and have nine directions: north, south, east, west, northwest, northeast, southeast, southwest, and between west and northwest. For the Saami, direction can be difficult to reckon in the harsh winter months or in the forest, thus they look to nature for signs:

Birch bark is darker and thicker on the north side

Birch bark is whiter and broken on the south side

A loose strip of birch bark curls to north

Moss is thicker on the north side of a tree

Tree branches are thicker and longer on the south side

Anthills have sticks and hay on the north side

Stones have more lichen on the north side

The traditional compass of the Chukchee of Siberia marks 22 directions:

West

Sun has come in or gone out of sight

It is still day

DIRECTION

In all cultures, people need a sense of direction to exploit nature and a shared understanding of what is meant by each direction to communicate meaningfully with other members of one's culture. In addition to—or perhaps because of—its practical importance, in many cultures direction is also imbued with considerable ritual and symbolic importance and is used to order the social relations of the living and the deceased in the afterworld.

While no culture recognizes less than four directions, cultures do vary in the number of directions considered important and the meanings associated with each direction. The Mongols have four cardinal directions that correspond to south, west, north, and east: front, right, rear, and left. When killing a sheep, the Mongols believe it is best to have the sheep's head to the west because west is the most honorable direction and is also good for the sheep's departing soul as the sun sets in the west. The Highland Quechua of Peru also have four cardinal directions: "the sun comes out" (east), "the sun goes down" (west), "the other side" (south),

Twilight has come
Twilight has become narrow
Twilight has been extinguished
In the evening
Night recently came

North

Midnight has come
Midnight has passed by
Dawn has approached
Light has burst forth
It has dawned
Darkness has gone
It has well dawned

East

Sun has risen
Sun has ascended
Sun has climbed
To the midday it has gradually approached

South

Midday has come
Midday has passed by
Sun descending has come
Sun has become low

Each of these directions except midday and midnight changes seasonally. Each direction is also linked to a benevolent spirit and those directions are sacrificed to when seeking the assistance of the spirits.

Direction is often considered in the placement of dwellings. For the Quechua, the concern is mainly practical—houses are built facing west to protect the front from the strong southeast winds of the July to September dry season. The Plains Indians in traditional times were less concerned with practical matters than with symbolism when they used the concepts of center, axis, and direction in erecting tipis and orienting each tipi. In general, the camp opening and each tipi entrance faced east as did openings to other structures such as sweat lodges. But in spe-

TABLE D-1 ATTRIBUTES LINKED TO DIRECTION AMONG THE HOPI OF ARIZONA

Direction	north	south	east	west	up	down
Color	yellow	blue	red	white	black	all
Number	one	two	three	four	five	six
Clouds	yellow	blue	red	white	black	all
Corn	yellow	blue	red	white	black	sweet
Winds	cold	summer	dusty	strong	whirl	tornado
Birds	oriole	bluebird	macaw	magpie	blackbird	all sacred
Animals	lion	wolf	coyote	wildcat	eagle	badger
Trees	spruce	fir	willow	aspen	——	——
Beans	French	butter	dwarf	lima	——	——

cial situations, the orientation might be different. The Osage placed the entrance to the west when on an expedition that involved killing. West was the direction of the sunset and the land of the dead.

As with dwellings, direction is often a consideration in the location of graves and the placement of bodies in them. The Quechua prefer that the deceased be buried with their heads to the south; the Shona orient the head to the north, the direction from which the ancestors came. The Aymara orient the entire funeral, including the position of the mourners and the body, to the west. The Senoi require that a man be buried oriented to the direction of the sunrise and a woman to the direction of the sunset.

Perhaps the most elaborate symbolic and ritual use of direction is by the Hopi of Arizona. As noted above, the Hopi reckon six directions and each is linked to specific colors, numbers, plants, animals, and environmental features, some of which are listed in Table D-1.

Direction is also central to the ritual life of the Western Apache of Arizona who associate environmental features with each of their four cardinal directions and use the scheme in all religious activity.

Right and Left

Across cultures direction is commonly expressed as right or left. The concepts of right and left in general and right hand and left hand in specific carry considerable symbolic importance. Across cultures there is a clear pattern of symbolic and behavioral associations with right and left:

Right	Left
male	female
superior	inferior
purity	impurity
good luck	misfortune

Both Muslims and Hindus associate good things with the right side and use the right hand for good acts such as eating, giving alms, and greeting a person, and use the left hand for impure acts. For the Tamil in India, for example, the use of left or right in daily life is governed by beliefs about ritual purity. The left hand is the "hand for dirt" and cannot be used for eating or watering plants; only the right hand can be used for such purposes. The left side is associated with female and the right with male and thus a palm reader will read a man's right hand and a woman's left hand. Men wear ceremonial threads on their right side and women on their left. Similarly, the Aymara prefer that a wife not sit to her husband's right. The burial of men and women in opposite directions by the Senoi points to the association of direction with gender in some cultures. In general, across cultures the right side is associated with good fortune and the left with misfortune. Thus, for example, the Chagga in East Africa do not allow left-handed men to accompany war parties. There are, however, some cultures that associate the left side with good fortune: the Masai of Kenya, for example, throw a stone or branch with their left hand at the new moon to bring luck.

See also GEOMANCY; SPACE.

Bogoras, Waldemar. (1904–1909) *The Chukchee.*

Bullock, Charles. (1950) *The Mashona and the Matabele.*

Cole, John T. (1969) *The Human Soul in the Aymara Culture of Pumasara: An Ethnographic Study in the Light of George Herbert Mead and Martin Buber.*

Dumont, Louis C. J. (1957) *A Subcaste of South India: Social Organization and Religion of the Pramalai Kallar.*

Fraser, Douglas. (1968) *Village Planning in the Primitive World.*

Hieb, Louis A. (1972) *The Hopi Ritual Clown: Life as It Should Not Be.*

Itkonen, Toivo I. (1948) *The Lapps in Finland up to 1945.*

Lattimore, Owen. (1941) *Mongol Journeys.*

Needham, Rodney. (1973) *Right and Left: Essays on Dual Symbolic Classification.*

Parsons, Elsie W. C. (1945) *Peguche, Canton of Otavalo, Province of Imbabura, Ecuador: A Study of Andean Indians.*

Pittman, Anne M. (1972) *Recreation Activities Instrumental to Expressed Life Goals of San Carlos Teen-Age Apaches.*

Reynolds, Holly B. (1978) *To Keep the Tali Strong: Women's Rituals in Tamilnad, India.*

Trager, Felicia H. (1968) *Picuris Pueblo, New Mexico: An "Ethnolinguistic" Salvage Survey.*

Werner, Roland. (1975) *Jah-het of Malaysia: Art and Culture.*

DWELLINGS

Dwellings are a human universal. In all cultures, at least at some times, people need to shelter themselves from the environment. Exactly what constitutes a dwelling varies across cultures and is distinguished between a "dwelling" and a "dwelling area." A dwelling is a roofed structure in which people sleep and perhaps also cook, eat, socialize, engage in ritual activities, and store personal belongings. Of these activities, sleeping is the most important; sleep is the only activity engaged in by people in dwellings in all cultures. In many cultures, roofed structures separate from dwellings are often used for activities other than sleeping such as cookhouses, eating huts, storage sheds, council houses, churches, and men's houses. A dwelling area is the segment of space regularly used for domestic activities and in-

cludes the dwelling proper; other roofed structures such as cookhouses; and unroofed space such as courtyards, porches, and rooftops if these are used for domestic activities. In many Middle Eastern cultures, for example, much socializing takes place not in the house but in the walled courtyard. In the American Southwest, the flat roofs of pueblo houses are used for socializing and observing events in the plaza below.

Based on the use made of the dwelling, cultures can be categorized as either outdoor or indoor cultures. Outdoor cultures, like the San of Botswana, use shelters primarily for protection against the elements—rain in the wet season, sun and heat in the dry season, and cold nights—but otherwise conduct all activities outside the hut in uncovered space, usually in front of the hut. Indoor cultures, on the other hand, such as the rural Irish who reside in two- or three-room stone, thatched houses, use shelters for most domestic purposes such as sleeping, cooking, eating, and socializing. Across cultures, outdoor cultures are more numerous than indoor ones.

This article focuses on primitive or vernacular dwellings. Although the two terms, along with folk dwellings, are often used interchangeably, a distinction can be made. Primitive dwellings are made from indigenous materials, are relatively impermanent in that they may be moved or abandoned frequently or the building materials such as mud or grass are impermanent, and are constructed without the assistance of building specialists. Vernacular dwellings are much the same except they may be influenced by some major architectural tradition, such as dwellings of the wealthy in rural Thailand, and may also be made of some imported material, such as corrugated iron for roofs.

While dwellings are an adaptation to the physical environment and the materials used to construct them are influenced by the environment, dwellings also have enormous social and ritual significance. Owning a dwelling is a significant event in the lives of most people in

A homestead in Karkar, New Guinea

most cultures and building and maintaining a dwelling a major activity throughout one's life. Thus, it is not surprising that in cultures with permanent dwellings, the building and occupation of the dwelling is often marked by public or religious rituals. In the Andes, for example, Quechua Indians hold new house fiestas and invite close friends and relatives to eat, drink, and assist the carpenter in the final construction details. Upon completion, others in the community join in three days of drinking, feasting, and dancing and in the process tamp the loose earth into packed floors suitable for habitation. The Lao Song Dam in Thailand, like many peoples in Asia, believe that supernatural forces will determine the luck or success they have in their new home and, therefore, engage in much ritual activity meant to influence the ancestors and other spirits and to bring good fortune. A

ritual specialist similar to a geomancer in China is employed to select a site and orient the dwelling so that it does not interfere with the movement of spirits in the area. Buddhist monks are asked to bless the first dwelling posts and post holes. The dwelling owner hosts an ancestor ceremony to please his deceased ancestors and a merit-making ceremony to meet his obligations to the Buddhist monks. In addition, rituals are carried out to please less important spirits. At the beginning of the rice season sacrifices are made to the guardian spirits of the villages and houses. In many parts of the world the importance of houses is indicated by signs or symbols placed on them such as a horseshoe or hex sign designed to keep evil spirits away.

A dwelling is a structure is which people carry out various activities, although which activities are carried out and the extent to which they are carried out vary widely across cultures. Thus, the dwelling is a venue for social interaction and its features are shaped in part by beliefs and customs governing social interaction, role relationships, and social status. In cultures where dwellings are grouped in residential compounds, residents of the compound may be kin, as with patrilineal kin who share the same compound among the Yoruba in Nigeria, or they may be relatives by marriage, such as the husband and his wives in societies with polygynous marriage whose dwellings are near each other in the husband's compound. In many cultures, the appearance of one's dwelling is a sign of the owner's prestige or status in the community. Therefore, wealthy or powerful people often have larger houses, houses marked by walls, and houses that are more "modern."

The salient features of a dwelling are its size, shape, style (how it appears on the outside), form (the internal arrangement of rooms), orientation,

site, construction material, permanence, decorative features, and the composition of the household. A key feature, since it is consistently related to other aspects of culture, is the shape of the basic floor plan—whether it is rectilinear or curvilinear. Dwellings with a rectilinear plan tend to have flat, gabled, hipped, or shed roofs; be made of rigid materials such as wood, stone, or adobe bricks; are relatively large, averaging 300 square feet; have more than one room; and are found in cultures with permanent settlements, large communities, social class distinctions, monogamous marriage, and a subsistence system based on agriculture. Curvilinear dwellings, on the other hand, tend to have conical, beehive, or domed roofs; be made of pliable material such as grass, felt, hides, or snow; are relatively small, averaging 100 square feet; have only one room; and are found in cultures with mobile settlements, small communities, a preference for polygynous marriage, and a subsis-

Building the conical roof for a dwelling in Nigeria

Kazakh yurts in Zinjian Province, China

tence system based on hunting-gathering or herding.

Materials

By definition, vernacular dwellings are made from natural materials, most importantly soil; snow; dung; stone; mud; bricks and mortar; plant material such as wood, bark, bamboo, reeds, and grasses; animal skin; and cloth. Soil in its natural state is used as a covering for semi-subterranean earth lodges. Snow is used for snow houses in the Arctic region. Dung is used as wall plaster in India and parts of Africa. Although stone is widely available, it is not used everywhere for dwellings because it is too hard to cut or shape, it cracks easily under pressure, or because it takes too much time and effort to gather and transport. Although often used for dwellings in some regions such as the Middle East, the British Isles, and southern Europe, stone is more often

reserved for the houses of the wealthy; for large, permanent buildings such as ceremonial centers; and for public projects such as forts, village walls, or aqueducts. Mud is commonly used for dwelling siding and interior walls in Africa, Central and South America, India, China, and Southeast Asia. Mud is often used as a plaster over a stick, reed, or grass framework or as sun-dried mud bricks reinforced with plant matter. In all regions, mud siding is susceptible to erosion from heavy rains. Dwellings, therefore, are often designed to control this problem. Solutions include plastering the siding with an outer coat of materials that shed water such as a plant oil or dung, adding runoff spouts to the roof to direct water away from the siding, cutting slits in the wall to channel the water away quickly, and regular re-plastering of mud. The use of bricks and mortar requires a greater technological investment than stone or mud as the bricks must be shaped and fired to the appropriate size. As with stone, the use of brick and fire-backed clay tiles is often associated with wealth in rural communities or, because of their relative permanence, are used mainly for public buildings.

As noted below, more dwellings around the world are made entirely or partly from plant materials than any other type of material. Even when the sides are of stone or mud, the roof is usually of plant material such as grass or reeds. Wood or bamboo is often used as the framework for dwellings and may take the form of unworked poles, split timber, or squared timber. The framework is often lashed together with twine made from plant fibers such as spruce root or coconut husk fibers. The thatch used for roofs and siding is often made from bundles or mats of grass or reeds; in some cultures, tree bark is used alone or with these other roofing and siding materials.

In addition to mud, plant materials, and bark, in some cultures roofs and siding are made from animal hides or cloth woven or pounded from animal hair or plant material such as cotton.

Types of Dwellings

A survey of the primary vernacular dwelling style in 186 cultures around the world indicates four primary types that include ten subtypes and an additional three other types that do not fit into the four primary categories.

I. Circular with Continuous Roof and Siding. The first general category of dwellings includes those with a circular or similar floor plan and with a covering in which the roof and siding are of the same material and are not constructed as distinct features of the dwelling. Such dwellings are found in about 14 percent of cultures and are of three major styles across cultures.

A. Dwellings of beehive shape with a pointed top from which the roofing material slants directly to the ground are rare, being used in only 1 percent of cultures, most of which are in Africa. The Ganda of Uganda have traditional dwellings of a beehive shape hut with a roof and siding of continuous bundles of dried grass placed over a framework of cane poles.

B. Cone-shaped dwellings with a pointed peak and siding flowing directly to the ground are found in about 7 percent of cultures. The best-known example of this style is the tipi of the Plains Indians of Canada and the United States. Although details vary from group to group, the tipi is a cone-shaped structure with a framework of wood poles supported by a framework of poles set in a main frame of either three or four poles and covered with processed bison hides. A smoke hole at the forward top with flaps to adjust ventilation to wind direction is a common feature that distinguishes the tipi from other conical dwellings with a central smoke hole such as the hide-covered lodges of the Chukchee in Siberia or the bark-covered lodges of groups in Alaska and Canada. The tipi is also larger than these other cone-shaped dwellings and contains more sophisticated design features such as the pegging of the covering to the ground and an optional inner wall in the winter. The tipi is no longer the primary dwelling type of Plains Indians but is still used on ceremonial and public occasions and it has been adopted for use as a dwelling by some non-Indians.

C. Dome, or hemispherical-shaped, dwellings without a peak are found in about 6 percent of cultures, with the best-known varieties being the wigwam, igloo (snow house), and hogan in North America. The igloo is constructed entirely of snow (as are the sleeping and sitting surfaces within it) and is used by some Inuit peoples of northern Canada. Contrary to popular belief, not all peoples

Stilt houses like this one in Benin are commonly used in wet regions of the world.

called "Eskimo" used the igloo; some used tents, wooden huts, and earth lodges. Those who did used the igloo only in the harsh winter months, using the other types of dwellings in the warmer months. The wigwam was the most widely used of the various types of dwellings used by the indigenous peoples of North America, with its distribution ranging from the East Coast west to the Mississippi River, north into Ontario, and south to North Carolina. A wigwam is a relatively small dwelling constructed with a framework of bent saplings to which sheets of bark and/or woven grass or reed mats are attached as the roof and siding. The hogan is the traditional dwelling of the Navajo Indians of the Southwest and is usually six- or eight-sided and constructed from logs, stone, and mud. As with the igloo and wigwam, the hogan has one entrance and, like the wigwam, a smoke hole or chimney in the roof. Unlike the wigwam, the hogan is not portable.

II. Rectangular with Merging Roof and Siding.
The second general category of dwellings—found in 6 percent of cultures—includes those that typically have a rectangular floor plan, with the roof and siding merging on at least two sides.

A. In 3 percent of cultures, the primary dwelling is a rectangular building with a two-slope roof supported by a center ridge pole. An example is the *ruka* of the Mapuche of Chile, which had an oval, rectangular, or polygonal floor with a framework of wood or cane poles supporting a thatch roof that extended almost to the ground. The ruka was a basic Mapuche building style; a wealthy family would have a ruka for sleeping and separate ones for eating, storage, and sheltering sheep.

B. Another 3 percent of cultures typically use long, rectangular dwellings with a half-barrel shape. One of the best known of these is the longhouse of the Iroquois and other groups in the eastern United States. Longhouses were usually built inside palisaded villages and on average were 25 feet wide and 80 feet long with a barrel-shaped, vaulted roof. The roofs and sides were covered by slabs of elm bark, supported by a framework of logs and poles. The interior was divided into a central hallway, with apartments on each side for individual families, and storage space above.

III. Circular with Distinct Roof and Siding. The third general category of dwellings includes those with a circular ground plan and clearly distinct roofs and siding. Most of the 12 percent of cultures with this type of dwelling are found in sub-Saharan Africa.

A. All dwellings of this type take the same basic form with cylindrical walls often of mud or sticks reinforced with mud and a dome-, beehive-, or cone-shaped roof of thatch. One type of Lozi dwelling in Zambia, for example, is made with a framework of reeds plastered with mud and a roof of wood or grass.

IV. Rectangular with Distinct Roof and Siding. The fourth general category includes dwellings that usually have a rectangular floor plan with a clear distinction between the roof and siding and accounts for the primary type of dwelling used in 51 percent of cultures. There are four major varieties of this general type.

A. In 6 percent of cultures, the primary dwelling has walls of mud, mud bricks, or stone and a flat roof. In addition, in many cultures these dwellings are built close to-gether, often with walls touching or sharing a common wall, and sometimes in house blocks several stories high or long. The adobe dwellings of the Pueblo Indians of the Southwest—such as the Zuni, Hopi, Acoma, and Taos—are of this type; some of the dwellings are nearly 1,000 years old. The original construction material was coarse adobe; after the Spanish conquest of the region, sun-dried adobe bricks were used. In more recent times, cinder blocks covered with stucco or adobe are used in some communities. Today, entrance is through the front door; in the past, it was through the roof, which was reached by ladders that could be pulled up to protect the dwelling from intruders. In the Punjab region of India and Pakistan, dwellings are of dried clay and are aligned in long rows with outer walls joined along streets. As with pueblo dwellings, entry is through the roof and, because houses abut each other, residents can walk along the roofs to get from one house to another. Similar style dwellings are also found in rural Middle East communities. Across cultures this style—with the close alignment of houses with thick walls, high walls, and multiple stories—serves the dual purpose of keeping the dwelling cool in warm climates and protecting the residents from intruders.

B. A second variety of this general style is the rectangular dwelling raised off the ground on piles with a slanted roof. This type of dwelling is found in 10 percent of cultures, nearly all of which are located in wet, damp, swampy environments that make it difficult to prevent wood from rotting when it is in direct contact with the ground. The Iban in Indonesia build large longhouses with verandas, porches, living areas, and storage space in the rafters raised off the ground on wood pilings and accessed by ladder. The

Warao of Venezuela build their dwellings on log stilts at or above the high tide mark on riverbanks with floors of palm truck wood and roofs covered with palm leaf thatch. A related type of dwelling is the chickee of the Seminole of Florida, which is a raised, open-sided structure with a thatch roof. As with the other dwellings in this category, the pilings protect the dwelling and its residents from the swamp water and the open sides allow cooling breezes to blow through in the humid climate.

C. Rectangular dwellings with slanted roofs and walls of stone, adobe, brick, plaster, or other mineral material are common in 10 percent of cultures. The rural Irish traditionally built long, one-story cottages with three rooms; stone walls; wood beam rafters; and a thatched, two-slope roof. The Santal of India build a square dwelling with two rooms, a veranda, a tile roof sloping on all four sides, and mud plaster walls. The Basques of Spain, as in many cultures in southern Europe, build a three-story stone house with a stable on the ground floor, the living area on the second floor, and a hay loft on the third.

D. The most common type of house across cultures, found in 26 percent of cultures, is the rectangular dwelling with slanted roof and walls made from plant matter such as wood, bamboo, wattle, or woven mats of grass or reeds. This style is especially common in Southeast Asia, Oceania, East Asia, and northern South America. The central Thai build a low-pitched, gable-roofed house supported by a bamboo frame. The roof is thatched with palm leaves or grass with walls made of the same material or of woven bamboo mats. The Saramaka of South America build small houses with walls of wood planks and woven palm fronds with roofs of thatch or corrugated iron. Romonum Islanders in the Caroline Islands build an open-sided,

steeply gabled dwelling suited to the warm, humid climate. The frame is made from breadfruit tree timber cut square on all dimensions, sennit coconut twine for lashing the parts together, and roof thatch from the leaves of the ivory nut palm.

V. Other Dwelling Types. In addition to these four general categories and ten specific types are three other types of dwellings that defy easy categorization.

A. First are semi-subterranean dwellings that share the common feature of being partly underground but otherwise vary in shape, size, and roofing materials. Such dwellings are commonly used, for at least part of the year, by about 4 percent of cultures, and mainly by peoples living in cold, wet environments such as the Nivkh in Siberia, the Aleut off the coast of Alaska, and the Klamath in northern California. Earth lodges in North America and Siberia were generally very large and were built partly underground in a dug hole with the aboveground section covered by earth, logs, sticks, and grass mats. Entry was through a covered hatchway in the roof reached by a ladder laid on the roof or steps cut into the roof. The Saami of Scandinavia build a different type of earth lodge; theirs is built above ground on the slope of a hill with a wooden framework covered by bark sheets and then a heavy layer of soil.

B. Tents, which are used in 5 percent of cultures almost all of whom are nomadic pastoral peoples, come in a wide variety of forms. The black tent made from dyed goat hair has been used for thousands of years by nomadic pastoralists in North Africa, the Middle East, and Central Asia such as the Berbers, Bedouin, Lur, Basseri, and Taureg. The mat-skin tent—covered with bark, animals skins, or woven mats—that resembles

A house constructed of mud and sticks in Nairobi, Kenya.

North American wigwams in framing and shape is also found in the Middle East, although they are less common than the black tent. The yurt, or ger, is a large, circular tent with a domed roof used by the Mongols, Kazakhs, Kirghiz, and other peoples in Central Asia. Because of its size, the intricacy of the construction, and its relative permanence, not all experts classify the yurt as a tent. The framework is of wood poles, with the wall frame made from joined sections of wooden latticework slats hinged together by lashing or screwing. The framework is covered with thick felt mats that may be protected from the elements by an outer layer of woven mats or canvas.

C. The final category of dwellings includes those that are only partly enclosed—caves, windbreaks, and lean-tos—and are used by about 5 percent of cultures. Although caves have been used for shelter by humans for hundreds of thousands of years, cave dwellers today usually alter the basic cave to make larger and more permanent dwellings. Gitano Gypsies in Spain, for example, plaster the interior walls and add doors, while people elsewhere cut rooms into soft tuft rock and add masonry entranceways, doors, and windows. Hunter-gatherer peoples in warm climates such as the Aranda and Ngatajara in Australia, Vedda in Sri Lanka, Semang in Malaysia, and Siriono in Bolivia often use temporary shelters such as lean-tos, semicircular bough shelters, or windbreaks made of poles and leaves during the cold and rainy seasons.

Variation within Cultures

As this survey indicates, it is possible to classify the cultures of the world in terms of the primary dwelling style used in the culture. However, such classification is an oversimplification of the reality that in most, if not all, cultures,

more than one dwelling style is often used. For example, the Lozi in Zambia use three types of dwellings: (1) a double concentric hut with one large room with a cone-shaped roof and an attached, smaller hut with a vaulted roof; (2) a cylindrical hut, which is a smaller, cruder version of the double concentric dwelling; and (3) a gable-roofed, rectangular hut, sometimes divided into two rooms. For another example, in the Highland Quechua town of Ariasucu in Ecuador, of 629 people in 148 households, there are seven house styles—straw roof, tile roof, tile roof with three or more rooms, tile roof with two stories, flattop roof with two stories, earthquake relief house, and dilapidated house.

One major source of variation in dwelling style within a culture is seasonal variation in the climate. For example, some Eskimo groups would use a snow house or an earth lodge in the harsh winter months and portable hide-covered tents in the warmer months. A second major source of variation is the mobility pattern of the group, which is often related to seasonal change and subsistence activities. For example, in some horticultural societies where the farm plots are far from the village, small huts will be built in the plots during the harvest season, while larger, permanent dwellings are used year-round in the village. Similarly, transhumant herders often keep permanent dwellings in a village and smaller, dispersed huts in the fields where shepherds stay with the herds. A third, and perhaps the most important, source of variation is wealth and status distinctions in the community. Across cultures, it is common for those who are wealthy to live in dwellings that are larger, of a different style, and constructed from different materials than the dwellings of commoners. For example, in Ariasucu, Ecuador, wealth is demonstrated by building and owning a large, urban-style home, even though one may never live in it. Perhaps the greatest degree of dwelling style variation is found in the contemporary United States where the existence of the surviving indigenous styles of Native Americans alongside the dozens of styles brought with them by settlers from Europe and new styles developed in the United States have created a diversity unmatched elsewhere in the world.

Finally, it is important to note that dwelling style in a culture changes over time. Throughout the twentieth century across cultures there has been a steady movement away from traditional dwellings and a shift to Western-style dwellings characterized by a rectangular floor plan; walls and roofs of solid materials such as concrete, brick, cinder block, lumber, tin, and corrugated iron; pitched roofs; a floor plan with separate rooms for living, sleeping, and cooking; and doors and windows. The development of dwellings conforming to this general design in much of the world and especially in Africa, the former Soviet Union, and on Indian reservations in the United States is largely the result of colonial domination in which the values of the dominant nation, as reflected in their dwelling style preferences, were forced on the indigenous inhabitants of the nation. In other situations, change in dwelling style is not forced on a population but instead results from a conscious choice made by community members. For example, on Long Bay Cays in the Bahamas, dwelling style has evolved through three distinct stages. Stage one was the nineteenth-century house, first a one-room house, then one with two rooms and a detached kitchen and barn. This was followed in the early twentieth century by the larger Georgian house, first with two bedrooms and pantry and then three bedrooms and more decorative features than the nineteenth-century house. The third stage is the modern house, first with three bedrooms much like the Georgian house and then a later L-shaped style with three bedrooms, in-house kitchen, and dining area. The two forces driving the change in house style and form were prestige—a desire to have "modern" houses—and convenience—having the kitchen inside, more bedrooms, a porch, and so forth.

Households

The group of people who occupy a dwelling is called the household. The ideal type of household in the Western world, a single building occupied by a single family, is also the most common form across cultures, being the primary type in 47 percent of cultures. However, it is not the only type. In 20 percent of cultures, the primary type of household is the family homestead, a single dwelling occupied by one family but with important outbuildings such as barns, stables, granaries, or separate quarters for slaves or servants nearby. Such homesteads are found most often in southern Europe, Asia, and Oceania in cultures that subsist through agriculture and therefore need the additional building to store equipment and harvested crops and house domesticated animals. In about 26 percent of cultures the household is organized as a multi-dwelling compound. Residential compounds, which are found most commonly in sub-Saharan Africa, are of three major forms: (1) a number of related families occupy separate dwellings in a compound or in close proximity to one another (13 percent of cultures); (2) a number of related families live in a compound or near one another with each married man and woman occupying their own dwellings (9 percent of cultures); and (3) a polygynous family lives in a compound or in a cluster of dwellings with each wife and her children occupying a separate dwelling and the husband-father living with the wives in rotation (4 percent of cultures). Other household forms found across cultures are the communal dwelling—a large structure occupied by the entire community (3 percent), apartment houses (2 percent of cultures), and mother-child households in which a mother and her children occupy a dwelling and the husband-father resides elsewhere such as in a men's house that houses all the men of the community (2 percent).

See also DIRECTION; ENVIRONMENTAL DISASTERS; GEOMANCY; SETTLEMENT PATTERNS; SPACE.

Brown, Barton M. (1987) "Population Estimation from Floor Area: A Restudy of 'Naroll's Constant.'" *Behavior Science Research* 21:1–49.

Colloredo-Mansfeld, Rudolf. (1994) "Architectural Conspicuous Consumption and Economic Change in the Andes." *American Anthropologist* 96:845–865.

Faegre, Torvald. (1979) *Tents: Architecture of the Nomads.*

Laubin, Reginald, and Gladys Laubin. (1957) *The Indian Tipi: Its History, Construction, and Use.*

LeBlanc, Steven. (1971) "An Addition to Naroll's Suggested Floor Area and Settlement Population Relationship." *American Antiquity* 36:210–211.

Levinson, David, ed. (1991–1995) *Encyclopedia of World Cultures.*

Levinson, David, and David Sherwood. (1993) *The Tribal Living Book.*

Murdock, George P., and Suzanne F. Wilson. (1972) "Settlement Patterns and Community Organization." *Ethnology* 11:254–295.

Naroll, Raoul. (1962) "Floor Area and Settlement Population." *American Antiquity* 27:587–589.

Oliver, Paul. (1987) *Dwellings: The House across the World.*

Otterbein, Keith F. (1975) *Changing House Types on Long Bay Cays.*

Pedersen, Lise Rishoj. (1982) "The Influence of the Spirit World on the Habitation of the Lao Song Dam, Thailand." In *The House in East and Southeast Asia*, edited by K. G. Izikowitz and P. Sorensen, 115–128.

Rapoport, Amos. (1969) *House Form and Culture.*

Robbins, Michael C. (1966) "House Types and Settlement Patterns." *Minnesota Archaeologist* 28:2–26.

Turner, Victor W. (1952) *The Lozi Peoples of North-Western Rhodesia.*

Upton, Dell, ed. (1986) *America's Architectural Roots: Ethnic Groups That Built America.*

Weissner, Polly. (1974) "A Functional Estimation of Population from Floor Area." *American Antiquity* 39:343–350.

Whiting, John W. M., and Barbara Ayres. (1968) "Inferences from the Shape of Dwellings." In *Settlement Archaeology*, edited by K. C. Chang, 117–133.

Ideas about the earth, land, and soil are found in all cultures. In most cultures, these ideas are imbedded in a broader belief system that seeks to explain the earth, land, and other features of the universe such as the sky or sea as an interrelated system. For example, Trobriand Islanders off the coast of New Guinea conceive of the universe as a system composed of the sky, land, and the sea. The sea brings turbulence to the system, the sky brings mobility, and the land brings stability—it is the resource for gardening and also the place from which the ancestors emerged, bringing with them the traditions followed by the Trobriand Islanders today. For some peoples the earth, or land, may occupy a position of central importance in their belief system. This is the case for many aboriginal peoples of Australia including the Aranda. The Aranda believe in powerful beings who are the ancestors of the contemporary Aranda as well as the shapers of the landscape. Every prominent and not-so-prominent feature of the landscape is associated with the ancestors including trees,

EARTH, LAND, AND SOIL

waterholes, mountain ridges, special rocks, caves, trees, and creeks. The Aranda divide their world into seven regions, with a different ancestor responsible for each. For example, physical features of the first region were made by Intwailiuka, the ancestor of a group of northern Aranda. Long ago, as Intwailiuka walked across the earth, he created the landscape one now sees. He first appeared on earth at Emily Gap in the Macdonnell Ranges. When he put his foot down, he pushed up the earth to create a hill called Unjailgi-i-danuma. He walked a little further and created another hill, Unjailgo-kunia-kurta, and then sat down, creating Heavitree Gap. And so it went as Intwailiuka and other ancestors moved across the earth creating the Aranda environment landscape.

From a cross-cultural perspective, two sets of ideas about the earth, land, and soil are especially noteworthy: first—the ideas agricultural peoples have about the land and soil from which they make their living, and second—Native American beliefs about the earth and land and human relationships to them. These ideas have come to play a central role in efforts to control and prevent environmental degradation around the world.

Land in Agricultural Societies

Of the four major subsistence systems around the world—hunting-gathering, horticulture, pastoralism, and agriculture—people in agricultural societies have the greatest concern about the land; they must subsist on crops grown on the same land year after year. This concern is manifested across agricultural cultures in two general ways: first—in classification systems that differentiate among different types of land and their economic uses, and second—in classification systems that differentiate among different types of soil and their relative fertility. Both of these classification systems enable people to control their environment by identifying available resources, marking their boundaries, and using them over time and space and across members of the community in optimal ways.

The Tamil of southeastern India divide their region into five ecological use zones: (1) mountains used by hunters; (2) forest used by herders; (3) fertile plains used by farmers; (4) the coast on the Indian Ocean used by fishermen, pirates, and divers; and (5) the desert used by warriors. Central Thai rice farmers also distinguish among five types of land on the basis of the elevation of the land and its suitability for wet rice farming: (1) mountains and hills used to gather raw materials such as wood, bamboo, and grasses; (2) forest or bush that is unused; (3) land that is at an elevation too high for agriculture because it will not flood even during heavy rains; (4) land at the correct elevation for rice growing; and (5) land that is too low to control flooding during the rainy season and therefore not suitable for farming. The Central Thai also distinguish among five types of bodies of water or waterways, a central concern because of their use in irrigation: swamps or ponds, lakes, streams, rivers, and canals.

The Ifugao of the Philippines who grow wet rice in irrigated terrace fields differentiate among eight types of land in their mountainous homeland on Luzon Island:

1. Grassland that is little used except for roof thatch
2. Forest used for fuel wood and hunting
3. Cane land used to collect grasses for fencing
4. Woodlots used for firewood and to control flooding in lower-level farm fields
5. Swidden fields used to grow dry field crops such as manioc, corn, millet, and taro
6. House terraces used for settlements and work areas
7. Drained fields used to grow dry crops such as sweet potatoes
8. Pond fields used to grow wet rice and other crops

As noted above, in some agricultural societies, land classification is by soil type rather than land type. Sherpa potato farmers of Nepal classify soil into five categories, based on its suitability for growing potatoes: (1) black, neither sandy nor clay, that is excellent; (2) yellow, not sandy, that is good; (3) sandy that is fair; (4) yellow clay that is poor; and (5) black clay that is also poor. The Amhara of Ethiopia recognize ten types of soil that are important because they enable all extended family members to be allocated some good and some poor land:

1. Male soil that is rich in humus and very fertile
2. Female soil that is sandy and not as fertile
3. Dark soil that is used for luxury crops such as wheat
4. Sandy soil that can be only lightly plowed
5. Mobile soil that is rarely used because it erodes easily
6. Poorly draining soil that becomes muddy and difficult to plow
7. Eroded soil made unusable in the rainy season
8. Alluvial soil created by silt deposited by rivers
9. Infertile soils including pasture land, dry land, and land that had previously proved infertile
10. Hard-to-penetrate soil that makes plowing difficult or impossible because of rocks

Native American View of the Earth and Land
Environmentalists and others concerned about the pollution and degradation of the earth, land, water, and air have often pointed to the traditional Native American view of the earth and land and human relationships to them as an alternative to the Western view that emphasizes the exploitation of the land and other natural resources. Although variations in beliefs about

and the utilization of the earth and land exist among the hundreds of Native American cultures, a number of beliefs are associated with many groups across the continent.

1. The earth was created by a great supernatural force, identified variously as the Maker, God, Mother Earth, the Cosmos, or the Great Spirit, among others, who has given the earth as a gift for humans to live on and use.

2. The earth is an irreplaceable resource that is the source of all life. Unlike living things on earth such as humans, animals, and plants, the earth cannot be destroyed and then replaced. Once it is destroyed it is gone forever.

3. The earth cannot be owned, bought, or sold.

4. In utilizing the resources found on earth, human beings must maintain a balance among all things.

5. Mother Earth is the mother of all human beings because she furnishes all sustenance in the form of animals and plants. Animals and plants allow humans to consume them so that humans can dwell on the earth.

6. To mark Mother Earth's importance and to thank her for providing plants and animals for human use, humans must give thanks through prayer, ritual, and offerings.

Similarly, there are a number of core beliefs about the land that are followed in many Native American groups.

1. Land is a constant of life, the center of the universe, and the focus of man's and woman's existence. At the same time, the land coexists with the system of the broader universe that includes the underworld, the sky, the supernatural world, the weather, and the seasons.

2. Land is an irreplaceable resource that is the source of all life.

3. As a gift from the Maker, land cannot be treated as a commodity that can be won or lost, bought or sold. Only the Maker can take the land away.

4. Land can be given in reciprocity as a gift but not for compensation.

5. Land should be worked carefully with hand tools such as hoes and digging sticks not with plows and other equipment that will injure Mother Earth.

6. Land belongs equally to people living in the present and those who will live in the future. Those living in the present have no authority to sell the land; doing so violates their responsibility as custodians of the land for future generations.

7. Native Americans have been designated as the caretakers of the earth and land because of their special knowledge of animals and plants and the laws of nature.

While ideas such as these are commonly and rightly associated with Native Americans and contrasted with Western and especially Euro-American ideas about the earth and human relationships to it, other peoples in the world also have similar ideas. For example, Mongol pastoralists believe that the world should be in a state of balance between human control of the environment and their dependence on it. Thus, in using the land, humans should balance their needs and the needs of their herds against the needs and rights of the land. In rural Haiti, land is considered by farmers to be their most precious possession and is kept even when not used. Haitian reverence for the land comes from their belief that the gods live in it, the reality that their ancestors are buried in it, and that food and wealth come from land and their acquisition of it through the Haitian Revolution in which the French colonists were defeated.

See also AGRICULTURE; GEOMANCY; HORTICULTURE; IRRIGATION; PLACE NAMES; SPACE; UNIVERSE.

Clemmer, Richard O. (1973) *Directed Resistance to Acculturation: A Comparative Study of the Effects of Non-Indian Jurisdiction on Hopi and Western Shoshone Communities.*

Conklin, Harold C. (1967) "Some Aspects of Ethnogaphic Research in Ifugao." *Transactions of the New York Academy of Sciences.* Series II, 30:99–121.

Jacob-Pandian, Ebenezer T. (1972) *Dravidianization: A Tamil Revitalization Movement.*

Lattimore, Owen. (1941) *Mongol Journeys.*

Leyburn, James G. (1966) *The Haitian People.*

Messing, Simon D. (1957) *The Highland-Plateau Amhara of Ethiopia.*

Reno, Philip. (1963) *Taos Pueblo.*

Riley, James N. (1973) *Family Organization and Population Dynamics in a Central Thai Village.*

Snyderman, George S. (1951) "Concept of Land Ownership among the Iroquois and Their Neighbors." In *Symposium on Local Diversity in Iroquois Culture*, edited by William N. Fenton, 13–34.

Spencer, Walter B., and F. J. Gillen. (1927) *The Arunta: A Study of a Stone Age People.*

Stevens, Stanley F. (1989) *Sherpa Settlement and Subsistence: Cultural Ecology and History in Highland Nepal.*

ENVIRONMENTAL DISASTERS

Environmental disasters are events or a process that cause environmental change that in turn seriously disrupts the lives of a large number of people. Individual victims of a disaster commonly experience the disaster as an event beyond belief and are left feeling out of control over their own lives. The number of people affected and the large amount of damage done distinguishes a disaster from an accident or an emergency.

Environmental disasters can be classified as caused by either nature or humans and as either of quick onset or chronic. Natural disasters are precipitated by environmental events that are not the result of human action and that seriously damage the environment. The damage turns into a disaster through human acts of omission or commission before, during, or following the environmental event that causes large numbers of people to suffer serious disruptions to their lives. Quick onset natural disasters are often referred to as "acts of God," a conceptualization that tends to free humans from responsibility for the damage caused by the disaster. A belief in the supernatural basis of natural disasters is common across cultures. Muslims believe that disasters befall those who act immorally. The Santal of India attempt to end a drought by appealing to the deities and making offerings when the rains come; they respond to disease epidemics in the same way. The Central Thai, who suffered from cholera, smallpox, and other epidemics until the arrival of Western medical treatment in the twentieth century, blamed these outbreaks on the Epidemic Ghost who they believed came from a different ethnic group such as the Lao. The Ghost is still believed to cause animals such as water buffalo to fall ill; farmers will seek a cure by sacrificing a chicken to the Ghost. In the Western world, up to the Lisbon earthquake of 1755, natural disasters were attributed to supernatural causes. Only after 1755 did scientific explanations replace supernatural ones.

The major quick onset natural disasters are earthquakes, tsunamis, volcanoes, floods, hurricanes, fires, insect infestations, and disease epidemics. Less widespread disasters include ice and hail storms, frost, avalanches, and floods caused by the collapse of glacial dams. Not all societies or even all regions within a societal territory are threatened by all natural disasters. For example, the western United States is more prone to dam-

Children collecting roots for food following flooding in Bangladesh in 1991.

age resulting from earthquakes and fires, the Midwest to floods, and the Southeast to hurricanes. However, some societies are subject to the effects of many damage-producing natural events. For example, between 1900 and 1990, the Solomon Islands in the South Pacific experienced 61 earthquakes, 42 volcanic eruptions, 37 hurricanes, 17 tsunamis, 11 floods, 8 storms, 3 droughts, and 3 landslides. The hurricanes and droughts caused the most hardship, resulting in 134 and 106 deaths, respectively. The other six types of events caused only 20 combined deaths.

Hurricanes, as in the Solomon Islands, cause the most deaths of all types of natural disasters. Hurricanes generally strike floodplains that are heavily populated by farmers who prefer to live there because of the rich soil and because the land is often free or inexpensive.

The amount of damage caused by earthquakes is influenced by the soil and rock conditions under buildings and the materials used in building construction. In industrialized nations, buildings in earthquake-prone regions are built with foundations, reinforced supports, and flexible structures that can withstand earthquakes. Earthquakes, therefore, cause relatively limited damage and few deaths. Elsewhere in the world, however, dwellings are often built of mud, sticks, and straw or of stone with no foundations. These dwellings are quickly destroyed by earthquakes. If the dwelling is in use when the earthquake strikes—such as during the night when people are sleeping—loss of life can be extensive.

Tsunamis are giant ocean waves resulting from earthquakes or underwater volcanoes that can cause extensive damage when they hit communities located by the ocean's shore. Like hurricanes, tsunamis can also cause considerable erosion of sand and soil.

Most volcanoes are found in the zone called the "ring of fire" that includes Japan and East Asia, the west coast of North and South America from Alaska to Chile, and the Pacific islands. The most damaging volcanoes occur in tropical regions with fertile soil that attracts large populations. The volcanic eruption of Mount Lamington in northern New Guinea in 1951, for example, killed about 4,000 Orokaiva and caused another 5,000 to be evacuated. Volcanoes can also cause avalanches.

Floods are caused by excessive water and are made worse by various human-induced conditions such as deforestation. Floods cause considerable damage and often many deaths because many people live in river deltas or along rivers where rich soil for farming is found. A special kind of flood is the lake rupture (called *jokulhlaup* in Iceland and *tshoserup* in Nepal) caused by a glacial dam giving way and allowing the water behind it to rush through the valley below. Such lake ruptures cause extensive damage and may also alter the environment by eroding riverbanks or even rerouting rivers.

While insect predation and disease are not usually considered natural disasters because they arise in humans' biological rather than physical environment, they too can cause considerable damage to crops and human life. For example, a mealybug infestation in northern Zambia in 1985–1989 caused shortages of cassava that led to famine and ultimately to a shift to the growing of corn instead.

Human-induced disasters involve human action or failure to act that causes damage to the environment that in turn damages humans and their communities. Quick onset human-induced disasters include those caused by oil spills such as the *Exxon Valdez* spill off the south coast of Alaska; technological accidents such as the gas leak at the Union Carbide plant in Bhopal, India; the leak of buried chemical waste at Love Canal in upstate New York; and nuclear accidents like that at Chernobyl in the former Soviet Union.

Chronic human-induced disasters are now the greatest threat to cultures around the world.

Rather than just threatening one region, these processes have the potential to affect the entire world. At this point, the effects are not fully known and experts disagree about how damaging they may prove. For example, environmentalists claim that global warming will produce food shortages early in the twenty-first century while many economists say that agriculture can be adjusted and no food shortages will occur. Major chronic human-induced disasters include the so-called greenhouse effect, ozone depletion, desertification, deforestation, depletion and pollution of freshwater, depletion of fisheries, salinization of irrigated land, and soil erosion. The greenhouse effect is caused by carbon dioxide pollution that limits the reflection of solar heat back toward the sun. This effect might eventually raise temperatures by about 2–3 degrees Celsius and lead to other unpredictable climatic changes that will affect agriculture. Stratospheric ozone depletion is a thinning of the ozone layer—the atmospheric layer that helps protect the earth from ultraviolet radiation from the sun. Desertification is the transformation of agricultural or grazing land into desert that is no longer useable for food collection or production. Desertification occurs most often in arid or semiarid regions and is caused by overgrazing of herd animals and nonsustainable agricultural practices. Among the results of desertification are droughts, famine, migration, poverty, and ethnic conflict. Deforestation is the harvesting of large tracts of trees in such a manner that the soil is left bare. It results from the cutting of wood for lumber, the clearing of forests for other uses such as farming or herding, pollution, mining, fire, and drought. The effects of deforestation on peoples living in forests mainly in tropical regions include disruption of their traditional ways of life, involvement as low-paid laborers in a wage-base economy, migration, illness, and death. The effects of deforestation on the environment include floods; erosion; and a loss of many species of animals, birds, and other living things in the forest. Overfishing is the taking of more fish than can be replaced naturally. The depletion of fish resources results from the "tragedy of the commons"—the overuse and misuse of the oceans because they are open for use by all and therefore can be overfished by those who derive limited benefits from maintaining the resource but are not inclined to do so. Depletion results mainly from modern, industrialized fishing methods rather than traditional techniques. The depletion of water resources is due to pollution from industry that makes freshwater unsafe for human use. Water-based disasters are also caused by the construction of large dams such as the Aswan Dam in Egypt or the Akosombo Dam in Volta that required the relocation of much of the local population and subsequent changes in their economic, political, and social systems. Salinization results from irrigation without adequate drainage in which salts drawn up through the wet soil leave deposits on the surface, rendering the land useless for agriculture. Erosion, which can result both from natural and human-induced disasters, is the wearing away of soil that leaves the land unsuitable for human exploitation.

Human Factor in Disasters

The human role in disasters becomes clear when one considers the effects of disasters in three different societal situations—traditional societies, economically developing nations, and economically developed nations.

The greatest damage caused by disasters in traditional societies is the loss of their food supply. While this loss may be only temporary, in many situations in the past, months or even years were needed to rebuild the indigenous subsistence system. Until that time, the people would have to either move elsewhere or suffer from famine. For example, heavy frost periodically destroys the sweet potato crop of the Fringe Enga in New Guinea who, before the availa-

bility of government aid, would then migrate to lower elevations and live with the Central Enga for up to six years until Fringe Enga could reestablish productive sweet potato gardens. In northern Zambia, when a mealybug infestation from 1985 to 1989 destroyed the cassava crop, the people lived in famine and eventually adjusted by switching to the growing of corn. In the Mortlock Islands in Oceania, the greatest damage caused by hurricanes is the inundation of inland freshwater taro swamps with seawater. The saltwater causes the crops to die, destroys boundaries between plots, and means the loss of years of work creating the rich swampland plots. In good years with plenty of rain, it takes from 6 to 12 months for the saltwater to be replaced by freshwater before reconstruction can begin. In general, before aid from outside sources such as the national government, the United Nations, or nonprofit organizations was available, people in traditional cultures dealt with disasters by eating less, diversifying their subsistence practices and diet, sharing, reducing community size, raiding other societies for food or land, and by moving elsewhere and living with kin.

In the twentieth century, disaster relief is provided more frequently by nonindigenous organizations and recovery efforts are directed and supported by government agencies. The underlying philosophy of many of these efforts and programs is that the indigenous subsistence economy is not capable of sustaining the society after disasters and that it must be modernized. Thus, natural disasters in traditional societies now speed along the modernization process and leave the communities dependent on outside sources of assistance, capital, and political support. Major changes include drawing the culture into a market economy; the replacement of kinship ties with ties based on employer-employee or seller-buyer relations; women working outside the home; men migrating to cities or towns for wage labor; changes in agricultural practices such as multicropping, food storage, and the planting of disaster resistant crops; and changes in local leadership in which younger men with experience outside the community replace the traditional elders. Some experts see these changes as damaging to the traditional ways of life of these cultures while others argue that in the modern world no traditional culture can be self-sufficient.

Disasters such as earthquakes in Peru and Central America, hurricanes in Bangladesh, and drought in the Sahel of Africa often cause large-scale damage in developing (Third World) nations. These nations often experience enormous loss of life beyond what is found in traditional societies (because they have small populations to begin with) and developed nations (because they have effective warning, evacuation systems, and safer buildings) and massive destruction of dwellings. These two results of disasters are linked, because in many developing nations, large populations aggregate in specific locations where land is free or cheap and the soil suitable for farming. Also in many developing nations, dense settlements called squatter settlements are built on the outskirts of cities often on unstable hillsides by poor migrants from rural sectors. Thus, the combination of a large, dense population living in poorly constructed housing in areas prone to natural disasters such as hurricanes or earthquakes makes wholesale damage inevitable. For example, on 29 April 1991, a hurricane (called a cyclone in South Asia) struck the delta region of southern Bangladesh killing 67,000 people, mostly poor farmers and their children. So many people died for a number of reasons, all having to do with human behavior rather than the storm itself. First, 97 percent of the houses were built of straw and mud and could not withstand the high winds. Second, the high population density of nearly 9,000 persons per square hectare placed many people at risk. Third, the storm shelters provided by the government were too few and inadequate. Fourth, the people did not

fully understand the warning signal system. In the system, eight, nine, or ten signals all meant the same thing—great danger. But many people believed that fewer signals meant less danger so that when the first warning was with ten signals and the second was nine, many thought the danger had decreased. Fifth, the people did not take the warnings seriously because of false alarms in the past. Sixth, some people refused to leave their homes because they feared looting in their absence. Seventh, people did not believe a severe storm would hit in April. And eighth, some groups such as women and children at home were placed at especially high risk and suffered the greatest loss of life.

Disaster relief efforts in developing nations tend to be highly politicized. Often, the government attempts to downplay the extent of the disaster to prevent scaring off tourists or investors. Also, governments may not ask for help from international organizations in an attempt to conceal government incompetence or corruption. Postdisaster recovery efforts are also highly politicized: those in power direct a disproportionate amount of aid to their constituents, developers and investors seek access to lucrative replacement projects, poor farmers are displaced from their land, and out-of power political parties use the handling or mishandling of the situation by the party in power as an issue to attract the support of voters.

In both traditional and developing nations, disaster relief efforts may make the disaster worse by stressing short-term solutions that create long-term vulnerability to disasters. For example, government intervention and support programs weaken indigenous support systems such as kin ties and trade patterns and also make the local communities dependent on the bureaucratic services provided by the government. As indicated above, the provision of these services is often influenced by political considerations. For example, a hurricane struck the Mortlock Islands in 1976 and caused varying amounts of damage to different communities ranging from nearly complete destruction to little damage. However, the communities with the least damage received the most relief for two reasons: first—communities with power in the central government were sent more aid, and second—local officials who distributed relief supplies sent more to the districts where they had relatives.

Developed nations are effected least by natural disasters. Property damage is the major result with relatively few deaths and no food shortages. Recovery is managed by the government (local, state, and national), private organizations, and insurance companies. The major problem in providing assistance is coordinating the actions of the numerous agencies and companies involved in the effort. Developed nations, unlike traditional cultures and developing nations, experience no long-term societal changes.

See also ENVIRONMENTAL UNCERTAINTY AND RISK; FAMINE; STORMS.

Abbink, Jon. (1993) "Famine, Gold, and Guns: The Suri of Southwestern Ethiopia, 1985–1991." *Disasters* 17:218–225.

Aptekar, Lewis. (1994) *Environmental Disasters in Global Perspective.*

Belshaw, Cyril S. (1951) "Social Consequences of the Mount Lamington Eruption." *Oceania* 21:241–252.

Blong, R. J., and D. A. Radford. (1993) "Deaths in Natural Hazards in the Solomon Islands." *Disasters* 17:1–11.

Brower, Barbara A. (1987) *Livestock and Landscape: The Sherpa Pastoral System in Sagarmatha (Mount Everest) National Park, Nepal.*

Button, John. (1988) *A Dictionary of Green Ideas.*

Hansen, Art. (1994) "The Illusion of Local Sustainability and Self-Sufficiency: Famine in a Border Area of Northwestern Zambia." *Human Organization* 53:11–20.

Homer-Dixon, Thomas F. (1994) "Environmental Scarcities and Violent Conflict: Evidence from Cases." *International Security* 19:5–40.

Marshall, Mac. (1979) "Natural and Unnatural Disaster in the Mortlock Islands of Micronesia." *Human Organization* 38:265–272.

Mukherjea, Charulal. (1962) *The Santals.*

Mushtaque, A., et al. (1993) "The Bangladesh Cyclone of 1991: Why So Many People Died." *Disasters* 17:291–304.

Stern, Gerald M. (1976) *The Buffalo Creek Disaster: The Story of the Survivors' Unprecedented Lawsuit.*

Textor, Robert B. (1973) *Roster of the Gods: An Ethnography of the Supernatural in a Thai Village.*

Torry, William I. (1978) "Bureaucracy, Community, and Natural Disasters." *Human Organization* 37:302–308.

———. (1978) "Natural Disasters, Social Structure, and Change in Traditional Societies." *Journal of Asian and African Studies* 13:167–183.

———. (1979) "Anthropology and Disaster Research." *Disasters* 3:43–52.

ENVIRONMENTAL ETHICS

Ethics are beliefs that guide human action. Environmental ethics are beliefs that guide human relationships with the physical environment and thus guide human behavior that effects the natural environment. The environmental ethic of any culture exists within the broader context of each culture's cosmology and worldview that together define the natural world, denote the place and role of human beings within the natural world, and define the relationship between humans and other creatures and features of the natural world. Cultures differ markedly in their environmental ethics. The environmental ethics associated with the major world religions range widely from those where the environment is considered unimportant to those that are subject to various interpretations to those that clearly view humans as having a role in protecting the environment.

Confucianism provides little guidance for its adherents regarding their relationship to the environment. Confucianism is concerned mainly with the order in the social and political spheres of human existence.

The Judeo-Christian environmental ethic is traced from the sections of the Book of Genesis about the creation of the earth and human responsibility for other creatures and natural features of the earth. These sections have been interpreted in three different ways, making it unclear what the Judeo-Christian environmental ethic actually is. In the Despotic Interpretation, humans are seen as being made in God's image and are the rulers of the earth, including all other living things on it. Thus, in this view it is the human right, both individually and collectively, to exploit the environment for one's own gain with no concern for the short- or long-term effects of that exploitation on the environment. The second interpretation is the Stewardship Interpretation in which humans are viewed as having an obligation to wisely rule the earth with destruction of the earth being a violation of the trust God has placed in humans as the custodians of the earth. In the third interpretation, the Citizenship Interpretation, all creatures are seen as equal and humans behave sinfully when they view the human form as superior to other creatures.

Native Americans in Montana holding ceremony for the "underwater people"

As with the Judeo-Christian tradition, religious texts central to Hinduism also provide an unclear message as to basic Hindu environmental ethics. On one hand, Hinduism strongly emphasizes the soul and its existence apart from the material world, suggesting that the physical environment should be of little concern. But on the other hand, Hinduism includes a belief in the transmigration of souls with the human soul becoming the soul of an animal in another life and also an array of lesser gods who manifest themselves in natural forms such as trees, plants, or animals. These beliefs suggest a unity between humans and other living creatures and plants.

Buddhism and Taoism are much clearer about environmental ethics. In Theravada Buddhism, humans are seen as a part of nature with the human-natural world relationship defined as one based on respect, care, and compassion. Zen Buddhism is less concerned with ethics than with aesthetics and provides a prescription for an open and free human-environment relationship. Taoism provides the clearest environmental ethic—one in which humans are expected to develop a close relationship with nature, limit population size and the use of material goods, and derive their own sense of personal harmony from their relationship with the natural world.

The actual influence these ethical beliefs have on the behavior of adherents is unknown; some, such as those associated with Zen Buddhism and Taoism, are often used by non-adherents as a model for ethical environmental behavior. Another environmental ethic commonly used as a model for behavior is that associated with Native Americans. In fact, since Native Americans are not a single culture but rather several hundred cultures, there is no single Native American environmental ethic. However, a number of environmental beliefs are common to many Native American cultures, which are different than the Judeo-Christian Despotic Interpretation. These beliefs include the following:

1. Humans are a part of the universe.
2. All elements of the universe coexist in harmony.
3. There is no clear distinction between the natural world and the supernatural world.
4. The basic relationship between humans and nature is human dependency on nature.
5. Humans have moral obligations to other living things and features of the universe that include not destroying the environment and exploiting the environment to ensure that all species of plants and animals will survive.

In many Native American cultures this ethic is manifested in how people behave in relation to the environment and also in religious beliefs and rituals that reflect those beliefs. For example, the Tlingit acknowledge their moral obligations to plants and animals by speaking to them. Similarly, the Zuni refer to an object as a "living person" although humans are considered "cooked" and other things "raw." And the Klamath, like many groups, express their sense of oneness with other creatures through rituals performed before and following hunting, fishing, and gathering activities. The Native American environmental ethic described above is typical of many Native American cultures as well as many nonindustrialized cultures elsewhere in the world such as the Aranda in Australia, the Maori in New Zealand, and the Amhara in Ethiopia.

See also TOTEMISM; UNIVERSE.

Bunzel, Ruth L. (1929–1930) "Introduction to Zuni Ceremonials." *U.S. Bureau of American Ethnology, Annual Report* 47.

Callicott, J. Baird. (1994) *Earth's Insights.*

Firth, Raymond W. (1959) *Economics of the New Zealand Maori.*

Laguna, Frederica de. (1972) *Under Mount Saint Elias: The History and Culture of the Yakutat Tlingit.*

Spencer, Baldwin, and F. J. Gillen. (1927) *The Arunta: A Study of a Stone Age People.*

Stern, Theodore. (1965) *The Klamath Tribe: A People and Their Reservation.*

Young, Allan L. (1970) *Medical Beliefs and Practices of the Begemder Amhara.*

ENVIRONMENTAL UNCERTAINTY AND RISK

All people in the world continually face uncertainty in their lives. Uncertainty refers to an individual's lack of knowledge about the world. Uncertainty is a human universal because no features of the environment are constant. Rather, environmental features are all variable and humans have only a limited capacity to predict the timing, intensity, and duration of their variation. Uncertainty usually brings with it risk—for an individual acting without the benefit of full information there is always a probability that his or her actions will produce a result that is harmful. Behavior is more risky when the probability is high that the outcome of the behavior will not be the desired one. Risk-taking behavior involves assessment of what is at risk for the individual (for example, loss of money, physical injury, crop destruction), an evaluation of the degree of risk involved in different possible courses of action, and taking action.

Human beings face uncertainty from the three major environments in which humans live: the physical environment, the biological environment composed of nonhuman organisms, and the social environment composed of members of one's own and different cultures. Uncertainty arising from the physical environment includes variation in the climate, weather, and natural disasters. Uncertainty arising from the biological environment includes variation in predation by insects, disease, and the behavior of nonhuman organisms. Uncertainty arising from the social environment includes variation in conflicts within one's own group and competition between different groups.

Of these three sources of uncertainty, physical environment uncertainty has drawn the most attention for scientists interested in human behavioral responses to uncertainty. However, despite less research, it is also clear that biological uncertainty is a major cause of uncertainty, especially in cultures that subsist at least partially on the food resources they collect or produce. In these cultures, parasitic diseases, introduced diseases to which the people have no natural immunity, diseases affecting their livestock, and changes in the annual migration patterns of animals and fish the people hunt and collect are all major sources of uncertainty and therefore major causes of various actions taken to reduce uncertainty or to control its effects. Thus, as discussed in this article, environmental uncertainty refers to physical and biological uncertainty, with the emphasis on the former.

Variability of Food Resources

The primary manifestation of environmental uncertainty for human beings is variability in food resources. Variability of food resources refers to two related phenomena: first, the actual variation in food resources used by an individual or group, and, second, the effect of factors such as climate and human risk-taking behavior that affect the availability of specific food resources. The major ways in which food resources vary are

1. Time—how often it occurs, how long it lasts

2. Geographical spread—size of area affected and whether entire area or only parts are affected

3. Intensity—severity of the shortages

4. Predictability—relative predictability or unpredictability such as seasonal, annual, or cyclical weather changes that are predictable to some extent versus pest infestations, shifts in animal migration routes, long-term climatic cycles, or environmental disasters that are not predictable

One element of environmental uncertainty that is both predictable and unpredictable across cultures is seasonality. All cultures—even those in tropical regions with only two seasons per year—are affected by seasonal changes in the climate and the effect of those changes on the availability of food resources. Thus, in all cultures, seasonal change and usually the general nature of the change (hot to cold, rainy to dry, and so forth) and its effect on food resources (food shortages in certain seasons) are known and are therefore certain. However, in many cultures, along with the certainty of seasonal changes comes uncertainty about the actual time and duration of the food shortages, the extent of their geographical spread, and their intensity.

While the focus of this article is on non-Western cultures that to various degrees live on the food that they collect or produce, it should be noted that modern, industrialized societies are also affected by environmental uncertainty. For example, the ongoing debate about the effects of global warming on crop production does little to reduce uncertainty about this long-term environmental change or to help people act in ways that will reduce the possible effects of global warming. One group of scientists argues that global warming will markedly reduce crop yields and will lead to famine. Others argue that the effects of global warming will be considerably less severe and can be controlled by changes in farming techniques and crops. Similarly, the appearance of the HIV–III virus and AIDS and the failure to reach a cure, the appearance of antibiotic-resistant tuberculosis, and the long-term effects of childhood polio were not predicted and point to the continuing high level of biological uncertainty faced by all humans.

The effects of food shortages resulting from environmental uncertainty are predictable across cultures. They include, in the order of appearance and severity, hunger, starvation, famine, and death. Biologically, an individual's food shortage produces hunger, malnourishment, weight loss, increased susceptibility to illness, lower fertility, and eventually death. For cultural groups, food shortages can lead to increased competition and less cooperation, conflict, violence, the breakup of families, a reduction in community size and population density, population relocation, and the dissolution of communities. As discussed below, these effects are the result of a combination of factors including features of the community or culture itself, the nature of the food variability, and the mechanisms used to cope with or to control the food shortages.

At some time in all cultures, communities and some individuals experience food resource variability and food shortages. In one cross-cultural survey of from 114 to 145 cultures around the world mainly in the nineteenth and twentieth centuries, 26 percent of cultures faced famine once or more often every 25 years, 45 percent of cultures faced weather or pest threats to food once or more often every 25 years, and 14 percent of cultures had chronic resource problems in not having enough to eat.

As these statistics suggest, considerable variation exists across cultures in resource variability and food shortages. This variation comes from different sources. First, in some cultures people can seemingly tolerate greater levels of food shortages than can people in other cultures. For example, in traditional East African cultures many people were somewhat malnourished even in "good" years. However, even in these groups, at some point individuals will suffer weight loss, illness, deaths, lower fertility, and so forth. Second, some regions have higher environmental uncertainty and greater resource variability than other regions. For example, the Sahel region of Africa has long periods of drought and parts of eastern, central, and southern Africa experience drought every four or five years. At the other extreme are environments where cultures usually have abundant food resources such as those in the Northwest Coast of North America before European settlement. But even in these regions, food or certain foods are sometimes scarce and accommodations must be made. Third, the basic subsistence system of a culture is related to the amount of uncertainty it faces. Cultures with mixed subsistence systems—such as pastoralists who herd sheep, farm, and trade with villages or hunter-gatherers who also fish and trade—face less uncertainty because they draw on a wider subsistence base than do cultures reliant on only one type of subsistence. This factor is probably the main reason that most hunter-gatherer, horticultural, pastoral, and fishing cultures that have survived into modern times have mixed subsistence systems. Those cultures in the past that relied on one type of system could not compete and eventually disappeared or were absorbed by other groups. The one exception to this pattern are agricultural societies who often subsist by one strategy and sometimes mainly on one crop such as rice or wheat and experience less food resource variability than other societies. However, in agricultural societies, it is not the subsistence system alone that reduces uncertainty but also the size and density of the population, the ability to store and transport large quantities of food, trade with other societies, and the ability to expand their territory or take food from other peoples through warfare and conquest.

Responses to Variability

Cultures attempt to deal with food resource variability in a number of ways. These mechanisms as a group are called "coping strategies," "coping devices," and "buffering mechanisms" and include appeals to the supernatural, storage,

mobility, diversification, exchange, and territorial expansion. The effectiveness of these mechanisms rests on the match between each mechanism's capacity and scale with those features of the variability whose effects the mechanism is expected to manage. While each of these six mechanisms is discussed separately below, it is key to remember that all cultures use a combination of these mechanisms most of the time. The case studies at the end of the article indicate how these different mechanisms are used in conjunction with one another.

Appeals to the supernatural are common across cultures. In many cultures, no distinction is made between the supernatural and natural worlds. Therefore, features of the physical and biological environments such as the weather or animal behavior are believed by peoples in many cultures to be under the control of supernatural forces. These supernatural forces may be the essence of the natural feature itself, or resident in it, or may control it from outside. Thus, in these cultures, people routinely deal with uncertainty both as individuals and as a culture through prayers, offerings, and rituals designed to influence the supernatural and ensure good environmental conditions and adequate food resources. In some cultures, such as the Hopi of Arizona who are concerned about adequate rainfall, such appeals to the supernatural are part of all ceremonies. In other cultures, such as the Zulu of South Africa, ritual specialists are charged with the supernatural management of different aspects of the environment. Zulu rain, hail, and lightning "doctors" are charged, respectively, with seeing that an adequate amount of rain is produced, that hail and lightning storms are prevented, their damage controlled, or the victims helped to recover. In many other cultures, the supernatural is communicated with directly by individuals involved in subsistence activities. For example, Eskimos in northern Alaska believe that animal behavior is controlled by spirit-beings resident in the animals. Thus, hunting success depends on the inclinations of these beings that are the spirit of the species (*inua*), the breath spirits (*ilitkusiq*), and the spirit doubles (*taktok*). To ensure that the species spirit will not warn the animals away from the hunters, rituals are performed before the hunt. For example, to prevent contamination of sea life with land life, all weapons used in hunting caribou are cleaned before hunting for whales. Failure to clean the weapons would cause the whale spirit to direct the whales away from the hunters. After the hunt, the breath spirit and spirit double need to be satisfied with ritual. The Eskimos believe that animals allow themselves to be killed because they want something from humans. To ensure that the breath spirit tells others of its good treatment by humans, the head of the animal is cut from the body to free the breath spirit and special wishes of the spirit are granted. These special wishes often relate to the needs of the animal's spirit double, which is the spirit of another species in the opposing environmental resource zone. For example, the spirit doubles of sea animals are land animals and vice versa. Giving the spirit of a whale freshwater or that of a caribou whale blubber or some other similar activity satisfies the requirement to attend to the needs of the spirit double.

Whether religion provides an effective coping mechanism is an unsettled question. Believers themselves, of course, place great faith in the supernatural while scientists tend to regard religion as having no direct effect on environmental uncertainty. Whether religious belief and action affects the environment, it clearly does have a psychological function in giving people a sense of control over their environment, providing an explanation for naturally occurring events, and freeing people from personal responsibility for food shortages. As non-Western cultures have been drawn into the world economy, many of the foods that they formerly collected or produced for only their consumption have become commodities that are traded or sold. This shift to commodification has been accompanied by a decline in the importance of religious ritual in collecting and producing food. Religion has thus become less important as a resource variability control mechanism in the contemporary world. While the use of religion to influence the environment might be dismissed as something outside the realm of "rational" decision making in the modern world, it should be noted that such practices are still quite common even in the modern world, such as the blessing of the fishing fleet in many seaports each year.

Physical storage means that people store surplus food at one time for use later when the food item is scarce or as a replacement for scarce foods. Food storage varies across cultures in its importance, in the methods of storage, in the types of food stored, the quantity of food stored, the length of time food is stored, and in who controls the stored food. A survey of 186 non-Western cultures mainly in the nineteenth and early twentieth centuries indicates that 30 percent of cultures do not store food. These include mainly hunter-gatherers who are nomadic, cultures that rely on fish that are available all year, and pastoral societies whose storage is in the form of the milk or meat of their herd animals. Another 4 percent of cultures store food to meet occasional food shortages. The largest group of cultures (35 percent) store food in preparation for predictable shortages during lean seasons. For example, some San in Botswana store water in ostrich eggs in the sand for use during the dry season. Or on a much larger scale, the Tlingit and other peoples of the Northwest Coast of North America traditionally preserved large quantities of salmon and other fish taken during spawning runs for use during the remainder of the year. Some 6 percent of cultures store food to protect against food shortages in "bad" years rather than during off seasons. And in a few cultures (1 percent) storage takes the form of large-scale storage facilities, bureaucratic distribution, and trade. In societies that store food,

A store of yams in the Trobriands

the food is often processed in some way before storage by drying, smoking, salting, or converting into another form such as drying root crops (such as cassava) and then processing them into flour. Food is stored in four general ways across cultures: (1) in households, in outbuildings, or in private caches; (2) in warehouses controlled by the community; (3) in warehouses controlled by a centralized political authority; and (4) in warehouses controlled by a centralized political authority, with the acquisition of food for storage and its distribution under the bureaucratic or market control of middlemen. To some extent, food storage is incompatible with some other mechanisms of variability control. For example, cultures that are highly mobile cannot store much food and in cultures where people routinely share food with others, there might be little surplus to store for future use. Finally, in the contemporary world, surplus food storage is sometimes managed by other societies and delivered to drought regions or regions hit by natural disasters through international relief agencies or the United Nations.

Mobility means that one moves away from an area of scarcity to an area where there is more food. For mobility to be a viable mechanism it requires open territory and free access to resources—a disappearing condition in the modern world. Traditionally, mobility was most common in hunter-gatherer and pastoral societies, both of which have been often and incorrectly characterized as being always nomadic. Nomadic hunter-gatherers use open territory and flexible group membership while pastoralists are often transhumant, moving to different areas in different seasons. For example, the Bedouin of Libya say that "When we have a bad year, we take our animals to the grasses of our relatives. When they have a bad year, they come here." To be successful, mobility requires that people have accurate information on environmental conditions elsewhere. This information might come from previous experience or may be provided by others in the culture.

Sometimes, and especially in the contemporary world, planned temporary moves can become permanent relocations. For example, the Libyan Bedouin herder when faced with more than one bad year of drought may not be able to live with relatives. Instead, he may have to sell his herd, find work as a wage laborer, and move permanently into town with his family. While not always leading to massive population relocation, extended food shortages caused by drought such as that in the Sahel can lead to some relocations, the movement of women and children to towns, and a pattern of men periodically moving back and forth from cities to the rural communities in search of work.

Diversification is the broadening of the subsistence base and is universal across cultures. The reliance on a mixed subsistence base is the best protection against the effects of uncertainty. When used as a mechanism to deal specifically with resource variability, diversification takes a variety of forms. For hunter-gatherers, diversification may involve exploiting a wider territory that provides a greater variety of foods or using a greater variety of foods in the same territory. For example, the Mescalero of the Southwest preferred mescal but would also collect sotol in "bad" times. The Mohave of southern California preferred to farm but in drought years would expand their territory and do more hunting, gathering, and fishing. In some cultures, a specific subsistence activity itself might be diversified to deal with resource variability. For example, the Aka of central Africa increase the number of hunting trips, hunt more often in groups, and change their hunting strategy to hunt alone at certain times of day and in groups at other times. In addition, they share any meat taken and preserve meat to trade with neighboring agricultural peoples. Horticulturalists and agriculturalists rely on a variety of diversification methods such as using dispersed fields, mixing different crops in the same fields, planting at different times, and rotating fields. The Sherpa of Nepal, for example, plant potatoes at different elevations so that if rain or frost ruins one crop it will not damage others. Similarly, many horticulturalists plant different crops in the same garden so that if plant diseases, predators, or insects destroy some plants, others will go unharmed. Pastoralists diversify by keeping mixed herds, by keeping herds in different locations, or by keeping some animals for one purpose such as milking and others for other purposes such as sale or transportation.

Exchange, in the form of sharing or reciprocity, is a cultural universal and a common mechanism for dealing with resource variability. Exchange takes a variety of forms including giving aid to others (people more often give aid to kin than to nonkin), trade, barter, sale, and reciprocal relations among friends and fictive kin such as blood brothers or godparents and godchildren. Exchange, like storage, is especially effective in controlling the variability of time in resource variability. The examples of the Bedouin moving to the land of relatives or Aka communal hunting mentioned above are two types of exchange as is the assistance high island Trukese in Oceania provide to low islanders when the latter's coconut, breadfruit trees, and taro crops are destroyed by hurricanes. The high islanders ship in food by the boatload, take in relatives, and even give them temporary rights to land that the low islanders may use until they can resume economic activities on their home islands.

A sixth and final possible response to variability and uncertainty is raiding and warfare, or negative reciprocity. Raiding, which is common across cultures, is usually conducted to obtain some item such as women to enslave, horses, cattle, or camels and less often for food. Thus, raiding provides cultures with a hedge against uncertainty by providing capital that can be invested in subsistence activities. Women taken in raids are commonly used in domestic labor (freeing native women for more productive work) or as field hands. Camels can be traded. Horses taken by Plains Indians in the nineteenth century were used in bison hunting and also in future raiding. Raiding can also be used to alleviate food shortages in times of stress, by one group raiding another for food.

Warfare can reduce uncertainty by both enabling a culture to expand its territory and therefore the diversity and size of its subsistence base as well as reducing its own population through battle deaths, thereby placing less pressure on resources. In the past, non-Western cultures were more likely to go to war to acquire environmental resources as a hedge against environmental disasters that periodically destroyed their resources. In the contemporary world, environmental uncertainty and resource shortages play a role in conflict between nations and between groups within nations. In the twentieth century, at least 12 wars between nations have been fought over access to resources, mainly oil and mineral wealth. The migration of people from a region of scarcity to one with more resources is a major cause of violent conflict, especially between the host and the newly arrived ethnic groups. And environmental degradation can disrupt the equal distribution of goods and services in a society leading to inequalities and strife.

Not all of these six mechanisms and their variants are used in all cultures (although all cultures use more than one) and not all are used equally across cultures. A number of factors influence which mechanisms are used. For example, a culture with a large population that is usually dependent on only a few foods is less likely to diversify or move and its members are less likely to share food, but it is more likely to raid or make war on weaker neighbors. Transportation technology is also important—an efficient road or railway system will allow for rapid mobility and food exchange as well as increasing the distance over which resources can be shared. Finally, the physical environment itself influences cultures in ways that make them more or less amenable to different mechanisms. For example, population density tends to be lower in dry climates with variable rainfall. Mobility is more common in cultures in climates that are cold and have droughts.

Case Studies

The following summaries of attempts to manage resource variability by the Efe of Zaire, the Tonga of Zambia, and the Enga of New Guinea point to two basic characteristics of how people customarily employ resource variability control mechanisms. First, in every culture a number of different mechanisms are used. Second, in all cultures these mechanisms are often sequenced, with new mechanisms or more extreme forms used as the food shortage worsens.

The Efe of central Africa are usually classified as tropical rainforest hunter-gatherers, although they actually get the majority of calories in their diet from crop foods obtained from the neighboring Walese. The Efe work in Walese gardens and are paid in foods such as cassava, peanuts, and rice that they are allowed to harvest for themselves. The Efe also consume wild plant foods, meat, honey, and other foodstuffs they hunt and gather in the forest. They also trade these items for food and material goods. The Walese, and therefore the Efe, often experience food shortages in April, May, and early June when the previous crop is depleted and the new crop is not yet ready for harvest. While these annual shortages are predictable, the Efe face uncertainty over when the shortage will start and end, how severe the shortage will be, what other foods can be obtained in place of the garden crops, and how plentiful these other foods will be. The Efe deal with the food shortage and accompanying uncertainty by first increasing their hunting and gathering activities in the forest. They do not move into the forest, preferring instead to remain near Walese villages. Women

build dams, collect fish, and increase their time spent searching for edible wild yams and nuts. Efe men hunt more often and over a wider territory. In addition, this increased hunting and gathering might be supplemented by searching abandoned Walese gardens for cassava in the ground, stealing food from gardens not yet completely harvested, and asking for food in the villages. If conditions worsen, some Efe will use marriage or kinship ties established by intermarriage over several generations and move into Walese households; others will move to other villages where food is available.

The Tonga do not face annual, predictable food shortages like the Efe. But they do experience "bad" years due to drought in which there is not enough to eat. The Tonga employ a number of mechanisms to deal with the shortage and the uncertainty that remains until the following year (or in more recent times, until government aid arrives): diversify economic activities, store food, store and share information about famine foods, convert surplus food into trade items, and use existing social relationships to gain access to resources elsewhere. The Tonga utilize these devices in a rough sequence, adding mechanisms as conditions continue to worsen. At first they stop eating preferred foods that they can trade or sell for other foods. They then begin preparing and consuming food far more conservatively than in good years—for example, husks are ground in with the grain and the grain is ground thoroughly. If conditions fail to improve, each woman moves her grain processing equipment indoors, reduces how much the family eats, reduces the number of daily meals, and changes family eating habits so that all members of the household eat together and men eat with women. If conditions continue to worsen, these food conservation measures are not enough and the Tonga begin to make basic economic changes. Food that has been stored because of its trade value is now sold to other villages for cheaper, less desirable foods. Meat obtained through hunting is also sold, and production and sale of trade items such as baskets, pottery, and mats is increased. If conditions worsen even more, the Tonga begin engaging in high-risk behaviors that endanger individuals and even the survival of the group. People may begin stealing from one another, families move from the village to their field houses from which they search for plant foods, older people and children might be sent to live with relatives in other villages, and some men will migrate elsewhere for wage labor. Finally, whole families will leave the village and settle elsewhere. In the past before colonization, they may have also sold children into slavery to reduce the population or made war against neighboring groups to take food or expand their territory into regions with food or more rain. Today, many latter-stage mechanisms need not be used as government aid often arrives in time.

For the Enga of the New Guinea highlands, the major threat to their food supply is frost. For Enga living at the highest elevations (above 7,000 feet), minor frosts occur every year and heavy, killing frosts every 10 to 30 years. These frosts kill sweet potatoes that, until recently, were the dietary staple and also provided food for domesticated pigs. The Enga attempt to control the uncertainty caused by the threat of or actual heavy frost in two ways. First, they garden in ways that increase the chances of some plants surviving a frost. All crops are grown in large mulch mounds that raise the temperature around the plants about 3 degrees Celsius over the temperature of nonmulched earth. And they diversify their gardening by planting gardens in different locations—some in the valleys, some on the slopes, some near the village, and some in other locations several miles away. Dispersed gardens increase the chances that some will survive a heavy frost. Second, when the plants do die and food shortages result, the Enga adjust their eating habits, primarily by slaughtering pigs, which both reduces the demand for sweet

potatoes as food for the pigs and also provides more food for the Enga. However, this step is usually not enough and the Enga then relocate en masse to villages at lower elevations where they are hosted by kin or by those who have been trading partners. The Enga may remain in the lower villages from three to six years, gardening there while returning to the higher elevations to reestablish their gardens to which most eventually return. In recent years, the Enga response to uncertainty has been modified by their involvement in the regional economy and development efforts by the government. New, frost tolerant food plants such as Kikuyu grass for pig feed, potatoes, peas, and other vegetables mean that a frost no longer destroys all food crops and makes migration to lower elevations largely unnecessary.

See also ANNUAL CYCLE; ENVIRONMENTAL DISASTERS; FAMINE; HORTICULTURE; HUNTING-GATHERING; IRRIGATION; MOBILITY AND SEDENTISM; PASTORALISM; SEASONS; SUBSISTENCE SYSTEMS; WEATHER CONTROL.

Bahuchet, S. (1988) "Food Supply Uncertainty among the Aka Pygmies (Lobaye, Central African Republic)." In *Coping with Uncertainty in Food Supply,* edited by I. de Garine and G. A. Harrison, 118–149.

Bailey, R. C., and N. R. Peacock. (1988) "Efe Pygmies of Northeast Zaire: Strategies in the Ituri Forest." In *Coping with Uncertainty in Food Supply,* edited by edited by I. de Garine and G. A. Harrison, 88–117.

Baksh, Michael, and Allen Johnson. (1990) "Insurance Policies among the Machiguenga: An Ethnographic Analysis of Risk Management in a Non-Western Society." In *Risk and Uncertainty in Tribal and Peasant Economies,* edited by Elizabeth Cashdan, 193–228.

Basehart, Harry W. (1974) "Mescalero Apache Subsistence Patterns and Socio-Political Organization." In *Apache Indians XII*.

Cashdan, Elizabeth, ed. (1990) *Risk and Uncertainty in Tribal and Peasant Economies*.

Colson, Elizabeth. (1979) "In Good Years and in Bad: Food Strategies of Self-Reliant Societies." *Journal of Anthropological Research* 35:18–29.

Garine, I. de and G. A. Harrison, eds. (1988) *Coping with Uncertainty in Food Supply*.

Ember, Carol R., and Melvin Ember. (1992) "Resource Unpredictability, Mistrust, and War." *Journal of Conflict Resolution* 36: 242–262.

———. (1992) "Warfare, Aggression and Resource Problems: Cross-Cultural Codes." *Behavior Science Research* 26:169–226.

Findley, Sally E. (1994) "Does Drought Increase Migration? A Study of Migration from Rural Mali during the 1983–1985 Drought." *International Migration Review* 28:539–553.

Fürer-Haimendorf, Christoph von. (1975) *Himalayan Traders: Life in Highland Nepal*.

Gladwin, Thomas, and Seymour B. Sarason. (1953) *Truk: Man in Paradise*.

Halstead, Paul, and John O'Shea, eds. (1989) *Bad Year Economics: Cultural Responses to Risk and Uncertainty*.

Homer-Dixon, Thomas F. (1994) "Environmental Scarcities and Violent Conflict: Evidence from Cases." *International Security* 19:5–40.

Levinson, David. (1994) *Aggression and Conflict*.

Low, Bobbi S. (1990) "Human Responses to Environmental Extremeness and Uncertainty: A Cross-Cultural Perspective." In *Risk and Uncertainty in Tribal and Peasant Economies*, edited by Elizabeth Cashdan, 229–256.

Minc, L., and K. Smith. (1989) "The Spirit of Survival: Cultural Responses to Resource Variability in Alaska." In *Bad Year Economics: Cultural Responses to Risk and Uncertainty*, edited by Paul Halstead and John O'Shea, 8–39.

Moshen, Safia K. (1971) *The Quest for Order among Awlad Ali of the Western Desert of Egypt*.

Murdock, George P., and Diana O. Morrow. (1970) "Subsistence Economy and Supportive Practices." *Ethnology* 9:302–330.

Obermeyer, Gerald J. (1969) *Structure and Authority in a Bedouin Tribe: The 'Aishaibat of the Western Desert of Egypt*.

Stewart, Kenneth M. (1983) "Mohave." In *Handbook of North American Indians. Volume 10. Southwest*, edited by Alfonso Ortiz, 55–70.

Vayda, Andrew P. (1976) *War in Ecological Perspective*.

Waddell, Eric. (1975) "How the Enga Cope with Frost: Responses to Climatic Perturbations in the Central Highlands of New Guinea." *Human Ecology* 3:249–273.

shortages of particular types of food, changes in consumption practices such as eating less or eating foods not otherwise eaten, and worry about not having enough to eat. The survey indicates that seasonal starvation occurred in 34 percent of cultures around the world. Famine is a form of starvation that is indicated by a high death rate and the disruption of customary activities. Famine is reported as having occurred in 68 percent of cultures.

Famine can be described in terms of its severity, persistence, and recurrence. Severity means the extent of disruption to community life. Famine of limited severity takes the form of people having to eat less-preferred foods, preparing foods in different ways such as mixing grain husks with the grain when it is ground, restrictions on sharing food, people moving elsewhere in search of food or aid, and the acceptance of food from relief agencies or other communities. More severe famine takes the form of entire families—or even the entire culture—moving to a locale with food or employment opportunities, riots, stealing, and epidemics of starvation-related or -caused diseases. At least on some occasions, famine has been limited or severe in 48 percent of cultures. Persistent famine is famine that occurs more than once in the recent past in a society and occurred in 26 percent of cultures. Finally, famine that recurs more than once in a 100-year period is described as recurrent and occurred in 5 percent of cultures.

Throughout human history, famine has been associated with rural populations such as those covered in the survey noted above and peasants in nation-states. The victims of the largest famines have been peasant farmers such as the 3.25 million who died in India in the famine of 1899–1901, the 16 to 30 million who died in the China famine beginning in 1931, the 1.8 million who died in the Bangladesh famine of 1973–1975, and the millions who have died in the famine effecting the Sahel region of Africa since the early 1970s. This pattern through human history

FAMINE

Famine is ". . . a reduction in a normally available food supply such that individuals, families, and eventually whole communities are forced to take up abnormal social and economic activities in order to ensure food" (D'Souza 1988:7). Famine is the extreme form of starvation. Starvation is the physical condition that results when an individual consumes food that does not provide adequate calories. Endemic starvation is the situation where some members of a community or society suffer undernourishment in times when the food supply is considered to be at normal levels. A survey of food conditions, primarily in the nineteenth and early twentieth centuries in 186 nonindustrialized cultures, indicates that in about 13 percent of cultures some people suffered from endemic starvation. Epidemic starvation is episodic and effects a larger percentage of the community population. Short-term starvation epidemics last only a few days to several weeks and were reported as occurring in 7 percent of the cultures in the world survey. Seasonal starvation occurs at specific times each year and takes the form of

of people who produce their own food being most impacted by famine suggested to some experts in the past that famine was the result of environmental changes that led to food shortages. However, it is now clear that famine is rarely caused by changes in environmental conditions or by natural disasters that produce food shortages. Instead, famine is caused by economic, political, and social factors that lead to unequal distribution of food, with some groups having less access to food than other groups. Thus, famine can and does occur in a world, a region, or nation where there is adequate food; the problem is that not all people have equal access to the food.

The interaction of three sets of interrelated factors lead to famine: (1) the physical environment, (2) the sociopolitical system, and (3) the economic system. The physical environment provides the context in which famine occurs, with change in the environment that produces food shortages one possible factor in causing a famine to occur. Rainfall variability is a major factor as either too little rainfall causing drought or too much causing flooding can lead to a food shortage that may eventually become a famine. Other environmental factors include insect predation that destroys crops, animal diseases that kill herd animals, erosion and lowering of soil fertility caused by overcropping and overgrazing, and deforestation caused by logging and conversion of forest into agricultural land. The article in this volume "Environmental Uncertainty and Risk" details the sources of environmental uncertainty that may produce food shortages and the mechanisms used across cultures to mitigate food resource variability such as exchange, mobility, storage, prayer, war, and diversification.

Given that the environment provides the context for famine and that certain environmental events may set the process in motion, the basic cause of famine is the rules of property ownership and exchange in a society that may under

certain conditions prevent the flow of food to certain segments of the society. Thus, famine is not caused by an individual's ability to produce food but rather by restrictions on an individual's ability to acquire food through purchase or trade. Sociopolitical factors that can restrict access to food include ethnic discrimination by the government against certain groups, warfare in which one society destroys or blocks the food supply of another nation, government famine relief policies and practices that fail to get the food to those most in need, and cultural beliefs and practices about sharing.

At the economic level, whether famine occurs and how severe it becomes is influenced by the food production system, rural nonfood production system, urban nonfood production system, and the food delivery system. These four economic subsystems interact with one another in the context of the physical environment and under government control (through laws, policies, and taxation) to create an economic system that either functions in a way that prevents famine or allows famine to occur for a segment of the population. The food production system includes agricultural practices and technology, the size of the crop, the timing of the crop, labor, and land ownership—all of which can impact the ability of food producers to produce a harvest of the correct size for the market at the right time. The rural nonfood production system includes secondary economic activities, such as fishing, that are susceptible to environmental uncertainty and therefore may not always be available as secondary sources of income. The rural nonfood production system also includes people who live in the rural region such as blacksmiths or shopkeepers who purchase rather than produce their own food. These people may be the victims of famine when their rural customers experience bad years. The urban nonfood production system controls the flow of money to the rural sector through food purchases, loans, and land ownership and also provides a haven for those fleeing famine. The food delivery system includes traders who act as middlemen between the rural food-producers and merchants; the merchants; and the actual railways, shipping, and highways transportation infrastructures themselves.

Across cultures in the modern world, under optimal conditions, food produced in the rural sector flows through the food delivery system to the mainly urban markets; money flows from the urban markets back to the rural sector, with a balance between supply and demand so that those in the rural sector earn enough to purchase food. However, if environmental variability such as too much or too little rainfall, warfare, ethnic discrimination, low demand for a food, oversupply that drives down prices, or some other factor disrupts the adequate flow of food to the urban sector or money to the rural sector, famine may result.

The famine of 1943 in the Bengal region of India near the city of Calcutta is an example of the interplay of the forces that create the conditions for a famine, how famine is dealt with, and the consequences of famine across cultures. In 1942, the Japanese controlled most of nearby Burma and the British, who then controlled India, were preoccupied with the threat of Japanese expansion into India. Of the 60 million Bengal residents, 44 million were farmers whose staple food was rice. However, crop yields had been poor since 1934 and only in 1937 were imports of rice not needed to feed the Bengal population. At the same time, the British stored masses of rice for use in the war effort. In 1942, the winter crop was poor in most locales and destroyed in other areas by a hurricane and floods. As a hedge against anticipated shortages, the farmers kept a third more rice for themselves, thus sending that same third less to be sold. Finally in April 1943, the government pulled some 25,000 boats out the water in response to the Japanese threat. These actions meant that rice farming in delta areas ceased. All of these events

and actions served to drive up the price of rice and by May 1943, the price had risen 600 percent in Bengal markets. The farmers began to suffer and sought alternative sources of money and food and also to lower their demand for food. They sold family and personal ornaments and the doors and iron roofs from their homes. They began collecting foods such as wild grasses and snails that would not be eaten in better times. Widows were asked to leave the homes of their deceased husband's brothers, families split up, and children were abandoned—some were left at the gates of homes of the wealthy. The effects of the famine spilled on the streets of Calcutta as people fled there in search of food, shelter, and employment. They lived on the sidewalks and in railyards and were given food by private and government relief organizations. But they also acted in ways otherwise unheard of such as eating dogs, foraging in garbage dumps, selling their children, and Hindus and Muslims exchanged food with one another. By July 1943, at least 100,000 people had moved to Calcutta. Despite reports that hundreds of people were dying in the village every week, in November and December 1943 and January 1944, the police following a new law sent more than 43,000 people back to the rural areas. In January 1944, nearly 23,000 people died. It was not until October 1943, after months of public denial, that the government admitted that "Bengal is in the grip of an unprecedented famine." Finally, by the end of 1943, the combination of famine, cold weather, and a shortage of clothes and shelter added malaria and cholera to the disaster. In early 1944, a good crop was harvested and all returned to prefamine conditions, with the governor of Bengal noting that "I am convinced that there is plenty of rice in Bengal for all the people of Bengal. The difficulty is that it is unevenly spread. Our task is to spread the butter evenly on the bread." While the famine may have ended, villagers were still commonly finding skeletons in their rice fields 25 years later.

A food line during relief effort in Ethiopia in 1984

In the contemporary world, the short-term effects of famine, such as malnourishment and disease, are mainly dealt with through the intervention of international organizations who import food and distribute it to those living in famine conditions or through the migration of those suffering from famine to other regions where food is available. However, the success of such efforts is often determined by local, regional, national, and international politics than by the needs of the famine victims, the availability of food, or the condition of transportation systems. In Ethiopia and Somali in the 1980s and 1990s, the problem in obtaining relief was not a shortage of food but a combination of indifference outside the region and local political conflicts that channeled food to some groups but not to others. However, since all cultures and communities are effected by external political, economic, and social factors as well as resource variability, it seems unlikely that most communities in developing nations can be en-

tirely self-sufficient and can survive in times of famine without outside help. One group who did manage to survive on their own are the Suri of Ethiopia. After several years of difficult circumstances, they suffered a severe drought and famine beginning in late 1984 and lasting into 1991. The drought destroyed their sorghum and corn crops, decimated their cattle herds, and forced many Suri to migrate to Sudan. By late 1991, the Suri had recovered, without any outside aid, and their traditional economy was restored with fields of sorghum and corn, cattle herds back to pre-1986 size, and many people returned from the Sudan. For the Suri, however, the key to their success was the mining of gold in their territory that could be sold to purchase food, seeds, fertilizer, cattle, and automatic rifles to keep neighboring groups away. Thus, by exploiting a new resource, the Suri restored their traditional economy and built a defense system to protect themselves from human predators. Across cultures, however, few cultures have such new resources available to deal with famine.

See also ENVIRONMENTAL DISASTERS; ENVIRONMENTAL UNCERTAINTY AND RISK.

Abbink, Jon. (1993) "Famine, Gold, and Guns: The Suri of Southwestern Ethiopia, 1985–1991." *Disasters* 17:218–225.

Desai, Meghnad. (1988) "The Economics of Famine." In *Famine,* edited by G. Ainsworth Harrison, 107–138.

Dirks, Robert. (1993) "Starvation and Famine: Cross-Cultural Codes and Some Hypothesis Tests." *Cross-Cultural Research* 27:28–69.

D'Souza, Frances. (1988) "Famine: Social Security, and an Analysis of Vulnerability." In *Famine,* edited by G. Ainsworth Harrison, 1–56.

Hansen, Art. (1994) "The Illusion of Local Sustainability and Self-Sufficiency: Famine in a Border Area of Northwestern Zaire." *Human Organization* 53:11–20.

Harrison, G. Ainsworth, ed. (1988) *Famine.*

Keen, David. (1994) "In Africa, Planned Suffering." *New York Times,* 15 August 1994: A15.

Morehouse, Goeffrey. (1972) *Calcutta.*

Seavoy, Ronald E. (1986) *Famine in Peasant Societies.*

Sen, Amartya. (1981) *Poverty and Famines: An Essay on Entitlement and Deprivation.*

FIRE

Fire is the major means by which humans convert nature to human use. Every known society uses fire and every society except for one—the Andaman Islanders of the Indian Ocean—discovered or invented a way to make fire. Even the Andaman Islanders probably knew how to make fire in the past but lost that knowledge as part of the general cultural disintegration they experienced prior to contact with Europeans in the nineteenth century. The heat produced by fire is an agent of transformation. While the transformations of most interest in Western societies are the physical transformation of the fuel to produce heat or illumination and the transformation of objects into forms suitable for human use, in some other cultures the transformational power of fire is conceived of in broader terms. For example, the Senoi of Malaysia see heat as transforming raw food into cooked food that they can eat, jungle into fields that they can cultivate, and humans into supernatural beings or other species such as tigers. The Senoi further believe that the essence of the fire itself is transformation—the flames turning into smoke, the heat of the flames into the coolness of the smoke, and the red of the flames turning into the white of the smoke. Thus, as discussed below, in many cultures fire is not simply about physical transformation but is also imbued with mythical meanings and is therefore commonly used for symbolic and ritual purposes. In addition to having a broader view of the transformational nature of fire, in some cultures fire in not conceived of as something under human control. For example, the Warao of Venezuela like many groups in South America believe that fire has always existed—at first, according to their myth, in the body of the Toad Women, and then in the bodies of various trees. Thus, making a fire to the Warao actually means "extracting" it from the wood where it exists so it can burn on the hearth rather than in the tree.

When human ancestors first began to use, make, and control fire is not absolutely known. Hearths dating to 1.5 million years ago have been found in East Africa and suggest protohuman use of fire but do not clearly establish protohuman fire-making ability. Fires associated with protohuman occupation of caves in southern Europe date to about 1 million years ago, but again it is not clear if the occupants made the fires or if the fires resulted from natural events such as lightning or volcanic eruptions. Hearths in China dating to about 400,000 to 500,000 years ago are likely associated with human use of fire. It is certain that by about 200,000 years ago humans were producing fire through the use of fire drills and fire saws based on friction. The major problem in dating the first control of fire by humans is that preindustrial tools used to make fire—the fire drill and fire saw—are made of wood themselves and do not survive for future analysis.

Fuel and Fuel Procurement

Across cultures, the preferred fuel is wood; the procurement of wood for fires is a major activity around the world. It is estimated that 50 percent of the worldwide consumption of wood is for fuel. And in developing nations, about 90 percent of wood that is collected is used to produce heat. In sub-Saharan Africa, wood is used in cultures with an adequate supply at the rate of about 1 cubic meter per person per year.

Wood is not always readily available in all cultures; about 1 billion people commonly experience firewood shortages requiring the use of other fuels in place of wood. Firewood is becoming scarce in many parts of the world because of the growth of the indigenous populations, a reduction in the amount of wood available because of the conversion of forests to agricultural or ranch land or their use for industry or towns, and the mass harvesting of wood by the lumber industry for export to the industrialized world. Another cause of firewood shortages, especially in regions where firewood is limited to begin with, is tourism. In Nepal, for example, tourism in the form of trekking parties, hotels, and tea houses has created a great demand for scarce firewood. Tourists, suppliers of service to them, and the indigenous Sherpa who rely on collected firewood for fuel have been forced to cut live trees when the Sherpa in the past subsisted on dead wood alone. Tourists and tourist facilities use far more wood per person than do the Sherpa, further contributing to the shortage. The Nepal government has attempted to deal with the problem by encouraging the use of kerosene, establishing tree farms, restricting collecting by the Sherpa to certain tracts, and establishing national parks where cutting of trees is prohibited. These measures have failed to control the problem, forcing the Sherpa to search further and further away for wood and creating a situation that might lead to long-term environmental damage including soil erosion, destruction of the forests, loss of wildlife, and a decrease in soil fertility. Such problems already exist in other parts of the world such as in the Andes that have been deforested in part by the procurement of ever greater amounts of firewood. In addition to environmental problems, firewood shortages also effect the people who rely on the wood. Because of supply-and-demand forces, firewood or desirable woods can become a product to be sold rather than used. This switch from use to sale leads to injuries because people travel to dangerous places to obtain wood, carry loads that are too heavy, and use undesirable woods at home where the smoke causes discomfort and disease and is less useful for some purposes such as smoking meat or the performance of rituals such as the Sherpa Buddhist ritual of burning juniper branches each morning to ritually purify themselves.

In addition to these social, political, and economic factors that effect firewood procurement, two environmental factors are especially important in influencing the amount and types of wood that are available for human use. First is temperature, which determines how much wood people need to use to produce heat and also influences the growth of vegetation and thereby determines what kinds of wood and how much is available. In the extreme north, for example, firewood is generally unavailable and Inuit cultures have had to rely on other fuels, mainly seal blubber and also polar bear fat, with vegetation such as heather or seeds from cotton grass used as wicks in oil lamps made of stone. The second environmental factor is rain, which, like temperature, also influences the amount and types of firewood available and also the types of food available that vary in their cooking requirements. For example, in desert regions, the availability of firewood along with rainwater and plant and animal foods are all considered when a group such as the San in Botswana makes a decision about moving camp.

Across cultures, there are four primary ways of obtaining firewood: (1) gather fallen wood, (2) cut or burn down trees and gather the wood, (3) cut down trees on a large-scale basis such as for commercial sale of the cut wood as firewood or during a specific time of year, and (4) plant and cultivate woodlots for use as firewood. The gathering of fallen wood, which is the most common means across cultures, is mainly women's work. In 70 percent of cultures, gathering firewood is done mainly by women, often with help from their children; in 7 percent by women or men; and in 22 percent mainly or exclusively by men. Firewood gathering is mainly women's work because, like other tasks usually done by women in nonindustrialized societies, it is often done near the home and is therefore compatible with childrearing and is also associated with related tasks done by women such as hauling water, washing laundry, preparing food, and cooking.

In all cultures, there is a clear preference for some types of wood as fuel for fires. For example, the Cherokee prefer hard woods such as oak and hickory that burn very hot and avoid soft woods such as pine that smokes heavily and woods such as chestnut and hemlock that send out too many sparks. Similarly, the Blackfoot of the American–Canadian Plains preferred cottonwood to pine for fires in their tipis, as pine gave off too much smoke and cinders that floated about and burned clothes and other objects in the tipi.

Cottonwood was preferred because it produced a cleaner, hotter flame; left glowing embers that were used in rituals; and also worked well for burning incense.

In cultures where fire is commonly transported from place to place rather than started new each time or where people leave the camp for days on end, the preference is for wood or other fuel that will smolder for long periods without igniting. The Andamanese prefer such wood and cover a smoldering log with wet leaves so they can relight the fire when they return. The Blackfoot transported fire in a fire horn and glowing coal was carried in a bison horn lined with damp, rotten wood and plugged with a piece of wood. For cultures in which people travel by boat or fish from boats on trips that keep them away from home overnight, a special platform of mud or stones is constructed in the center of the boat to serve as a hearth. The Tonga of Polynesia, for example, used a shallow wooden box filled with stones and earth as the hearth on their outrigger canoes.

Alternatives to firewood include fossil fuels, dung, and crop residues. Charcoal, which is preferred in some cultures, is not an alternative fuel as it is made from wood. Of the alternatives, dung is the most common, with cultures in the Andes using llama dung, in India cattle dung, in the Himalayas yak dung, and in the Middle East camel dung. While dried dung is often readily available and makes an adequate fuel, its use can cause economic problems. For example, the Burusho of India prefer to use dung as a fertilizer and thus place their crops at risk when they must use it as fuel instead of a fertilizer.

Fire Production

As noted above, all 2,000 or so cultures that have survived into modern times have had the knowledge that enables them to make fire. Fire is produced across cultures by three major methods: friction, percussion, and compression. Fire produced by friction is either by rotation as in drilling or by reciprocating motion as in the use of fire saws and plows. A fire drill is the most often used fire-making tool around the world. The Yao of Mozambique use a drill consisting of a flat platform (a log with one side cut flat) with a depression drilled in the center and a groove down one side. Tinder is put at the bottom of the groove and when a drill stick is rotated rapidly in sand in the depression, the sawdust that results starts to smolder and then falls on and ignites the tinder. Fire saws and plows, like drills, also require two pieces of wood. With the saw, one piece such as a sturdy vine is used to cut into the other with the friction causing the sawdust to smolder and ignite the tinder. With the plow, a piece of hardwood is sawed across a piece of softwood, again dropping smoldering sawdust into the tinder. Percussion involves striking materials such as flint, pyrite, quartz, or sulfur together or against other materials to produce a spark that will ignite tinder placed underneath. Percussion is especially important in the Arctic where wood for plows, saws, or drills may not always be available or always be dry. The use of compressed gas to produce fire is less widespread than the other methods and is used mainly in Asia. The tool for producing fire by compression is the fire piston, consisting of a wood cylinder, a wood piston, and tinder. Heat is generated by driving the piston into the cylinder, which in turn ignites tinder tied to the bottom of the piston. These methods have now largely disappeared around the world, as nonindustrialized peoples were quick to begin using other fire-making means such as matches, flints, lighters, and such as soon as they were introduced by outsiders. In some cultures, however, such as the Warao in Venezuela, there is a preference for using traditional methods for lighting fires for important rituals.

Fires are usually made and contained in hearths, which vary widely in size, shape, and construction material across and even within cultures. The common characteristic of a hearth is that it must be made of or lined with noncombustible material, usually stone (although the stones must be ones that will not explode or shatter from the heat) or earth. Hearths are generally differentiated less by their appearance than by where they are located and their use, which is tied to location. For example, the Warao use eight types of hearth: in the kitchen or cooking area of the dwelling, in the sleeping area of the dwelling, in the village church, in the priest's house, in the "new kitchen" of the annual festival, in the forest, in menstrual huts, and on boats.

Uses of Fire

Uses of fire by humans fall into two categories: habitat fires that are used to alter the physical environment and domestic fires that are used to meet human needs in and around the household. Both uses have an impact on the physical environment, with habitat fires generally having the greater impact. The exploitation of forests for firewood can have long-term environmental effects in many regions, particularly in the late twentieth century as populations dependent on firewood have increased and the forests have shrunk due to logging, use for agriculture, and human settlement.

Across cultures, the most common use of habitat fires is to prepare garden plots for planting in horticultural societies. In slash-and-burn horticulture, which is still practiced by hundreds of cultures in tropical and subtropical regions of the world, plots are cleared by cutting down the growth and fertilized by burning the slash and sometimes wood and brush brought in for this purpose from adjacent forests. These fires are carefully controlled, often by firebreaks cut around the site or fire rings in which the fire is directed inward. In traditional horticulture in which these plots are used only for two or three years and then left to fallow for a dozen or more years and only a small semipermanent population is supported, the fires and clearing do little long-term damage to the environment. The practice may, in fact, actually help the environment by allowing bushes and other secondary growth to thrive on the fallow plots. However, in the contemporary world, with horticultural societies now more populous due largely to the control of disease through the use of Western medicine and with less land to use, much destruction does result from slash and burning as plots are not left to fallow for adequate periods, too many plots are used at one time, and the natural fertilizers are supplemented by chemical ones. Other uses of fires to alter the habitat include the use of fires by hunter-gatherers to drive animals to places where they can be easily killed, such as over cliffs or into narrow valleys; to attract game; to destroy grasses or other plants that are not used; to cut paths through heavy vegetation; to clear campsites; and to drive off undesirable wildlife.

The Cherokee of the southeastern United States, like other indigenous cultures in the New World, used fire as a primary forest management strategy for at least 2,000 years. The Cherokee made fires to remove worthless vegetation such as white pine, hemlock, maple trees, and grass to allow more useful vegetation such as the acorn-bearing oaks to grow. They also burned off brush to allow blueberry and other fruit-bearing plants to flourish and to create favorable foraging conditions for game animals such as turkeys and deer. In addition, they routinely cleared woods near the villages to prevent fires from spreading to their dwellings. Cherokee forest management by fire helped them in a variety of ways including reducing the number of wild fires, improving travel conditions, making it more difficult for enemies to launch a surprise attack, driving out unwanted animals such as reptiles, attracting game animals, and improving visibility in the forest. This use of fire in forest management and other practices by North and South American cultures before European settlement, such as horticulture and heavy exploitation of certain game animals, casts doubt on the validity of the "Pristine Myth" in which the New World environment is described as being pure and unaltered prior to European settlement. In fact, the environment was used and altered by the native peoples; during the period beginning with European settlement up to the westward expansion in North America in the nineteenth century, the land probably returned to a more natural state.

Domestic fire use can be subdivided into a number of categories—practical, ritual, social, and curative. Regarding the practical use of fire, people across cultures commonly use fires for warmth, illumination, to drive off insects, to keep predators away, to cook food, to preserve meat, to produce ashes for soap and to flavor food, to lure animals or insects, for sale for money, to fell trees, to size logs to length, to hollow out canoes and other objects, to shape tools, to summon warriors or warn of the enemy, to heat water for washing, and for metal smithing. A survey of fire use in 41 African cultures indicated the following percentages of cultures using fire in 12 practical ways:

Use	% of Cultures
Cooking	100%
Metal working	51%
Pottery making	51%
Cottage industries	39%
Warmth	37%
Illumination	34%
Preserving food	24%
Producing smoke	17%
Heating bath water	12%
Laundry	7%
Ironing	7%
Kindling nonwood fires	5%

These percentages indicate that in many cultures the use of fire for practical purposes involves not just use in the home for the needs of family members but also the use of the fire to provide energy for economic activities conducted in the home. In addition to the practical uses of fire in these cultures, over half also use fire for ritual purposes and nearly half use fire in the treatment of disease.

The social uses of fire cover a wide range of customs and beliefs. The Andaman Islanders, like many peoples who rely on wood fires for warmth, cooking, and illumination, view the fire as the center of their social universe, as indicated by the household families who gather around the hearth in the evening and the returning hunters who gather around the communal cooking fire to swap stories after returning from the hunt. For the Cherokee of North Carolina and the Iroquois of the eastern United States, fire in the form of the council fire symbolized unity among the tribes and clans that formed the political community while lighting and smoking the peace pipe symbolized peace.

Across cultures, fire is often used to mark the status of individuals or groups within the community. For the Blackfoot, fire is a key component of the all-important Sun Dance and helps mark warriors as especially brave. A fire pit is dug along the east side of the lodge, and as victorious warriors enter the lodge to participate in the ceremony they recount their brave deeds and place a stick on the fire in the pit after each recitation. Those warriors whose sticks make the fire blaze are admired for their success and bravery as warriors. For the Tonga of Polynesia, fires mark the status of a departed high chief. When a chief is dying, fires are kept burning around his household during his last night. After death, torches are set at night in sand-filled hearths around the house, with each torch guarded by three men or women, with one holding it in a horizontal position facing in the direction of the chief's body lying in state in the house. The torch fires are kept alive throughout the night, with new torches lit from the flames of dying ones. And for the Bemba in Africa, fire is the key part of the initiation ceremony for girls that marks a change in their status from girls to adults.

As with the social uses of fire, symbolic and ritual uses are very common and varied across cultures as well. The Aranda of Australia are totemistic in that they link both individual human beings and groups to features of the natural environment, including fire. The Aranda believe that fire began with a spark of fire that rose into the sky at the Place of Fire in the north and was then blown by the north wind to a spot on what is now known as Mount Hay. The spark fell to earth and caused a great fire and from its ashes arose the Inaputua creatures, the ancestors of people today of the fire totem.

The Andaman Islanders are typical of a number of cultures who believe that fire or the light given off by it can drive off evil spirits including the feared sea and forest spirits. To protect themselves at night when it is dark, a state they consider unnatural and evil and the result of two ancestors fighting in the distant past, they hurl burning logs into the forest around the camp and always take a torch with them in the forest at night.

Fire plays a role in many religious rituals in most religions and involves the use of special fuels, special containers for the fire, certain times for lighting and extinguishing the fire, and offerings and prayers. The Gond of India, for example, when about to conduct a ritual sacrifice always kindle the fire with fire taken from the Hearth of the Departed in the house.

In many cultures fire is also used to predict the future. Aymara seers in Peru, for example, predict the future by watching the color, density, and direction of smoke rising from a fire, while old Bororo men in Brazil carefully watch the fire as it goes out and the remaining ash to "learn the future."

A common symbolic and ritual use of fire across cultures is the "first fire" that marks some important first event, usually in the annual cycle. The use of fire in the form of the Olympic Torch and Flame to mark the opening and closing of the Olympic Games is an example of a "first fire." There are numerous other examples of culturally defined "first events." For example, Basque priests in Spain traditionally marked the opening of the sheepherding season by having all village residents extinguish their homes' fires and then relight them with fire carried from a fire built by the priest on the church stairs. For the participants, the resulting fire and heat in their homes was "like the love that God has for us." Similar to the Basque ritual, though completely separate in origin, is the Cherokee Festival of Purification held each fall when all fires in the villages are extinguished and then rekindled with fire taken from a central fire. The cleaning out of the fireplaces and the use of new fire is a form of ritual and actual cleaning that is accompanied by personal cleansing in the form of drinking special teas during the Black Drink Ceremony.

See also HORTICULTURE; HOT AND COLD STATES; SUN AND MOON; TECHNOLOGY; THUNDER AND LIGHTNING.

Bouroncle Carreón, Alfonso. (1964) "Contribution to the Study of the Aymara." *América Indígena* 24:129–169, 233–269.

Brower, Barbara A. (1987) *Livestock and Landscape: The Sherpa Pastoral System in Sagarmatha (Mount Everest) National Park, Nepal.*

Cipriani, Lidio. (1966) *The Andaman Islanders*, edited and translated by D. Taylor Cox.

Colbacchini, Antonio, and Cesar Albisetti. (1942) *The Eastern Bororo Orarimogodogue of the Eastern Plateau of Mato Grosso.*

Collocott, Ernest E. V. (1922) *Tongan Astronomy and Calendar.*

Ewers, John C. (1971) *The Blackfoot: Raiders of the Northwestern Plains.*

Fisher, James F. (1990) *Sherpas: Reflections on Change on Himalayan Nepal.*

Goodwin, Gary C. (1977) *Cherokees in Transition: A Study of Changing Culture and Environment Prior to 1775.*

Grigson, Wilfrid V. (1949) *The Maria Gond of Bastar.*

Grinell, George B. (1962) *Blackfoot Lodge Tales: The Story of a Prairie People.*

Hamel, Paul B., and Mary U. Chiltoskey. (1975) *Cherokee Plants and Their Uses—A 400 Year History.*

Howell, Signe. (1984) *Society and Cosmos: Chewong of Peninsular Malaya.*

Hungry Wolf, Adolf. (1977) *The Blood People, a Division of the Blackfoot Confederacy: An Illustrated Interpretation of Old Ways.*

Jenness, Diamond. (1922) *The Life of the Copper Eskimo.*

Kilpatrick, Jack F., and Anna G. Kilpatrick. (1967) *Run toward the Nightland: Magic of the Oklahoma Cherokee.*

Lewis, Henry. (1994) "Fire." In *The Encyclopedia of the Environment*, edited by Ruth A. Eblen and William R. Eblen, 248–250.

Lorimer, Emily O. (1938) "The Burusho of Hunza." *Antiquity* 12:5–15.

Man, Edward H. (1932) *On the Aboriginal Inhabitants of the Andaman Islands.*

Ott, Sandra. (1981) *The Circle of Mountains: A Basque Shepherding Community.*

Radcliffe-Brown, Arthur R. (1922) *The Andaman Islanders: A Study in Social Anthropology.*

Spencer, Walter B., and F. J. Gillen. (1927) *The Arunta: A Study of a Stone Age People.*

Tobe, John H. (1960) *Hunza: Adventure in a Land of Paradise.*

Wilbert, Johannes. (1967) "Secular and Sacred Functions of the Fire among the Warao." *Anthropologica* 19:3–23.

Williams, Paula J. (1983) *The Social Organization of Firewood Procurement and Use in Africa: A Study of the Division of Labor by Sex.*

In the most general sense, fishing refers to the taking of fin fish, shellfish, and sea mammals from the water for human use. In terms of the technologies and strategies used, a distinction can be made among fishing for fin fish, hunting for sea mammals, and the gathering of shellfish. However, this distinction is not always perfect as small fish are gathered by hand in tide pools, sea mammals such as dolphins are caught in nets, fish are sometimes taken by spearing or shooting with arrows, and deep-sea lobstering relies on trawling with nets.

With the exception of the gathering of small fish and shellfish near shore, fishing in ocean waters is the most uncertain of all major subsistence activities. For that reason, there are few societies in the world that rely primarily on fishing for their food and none that rely on fishing for all of their food. A survey of 186 societies indicates that in only 8 percent does fishing provide more food than all other subsistence activities; in another 6 percent fishing provides the most food, but less than 50 percent of all food; in 34 percent more than 10 percent of food, but at least one other activity produces more food; and in 50 percent less than 10 percent of the food supply. Most non-Western cultures that traditionally relied heavily on fishing were found in the Northwest Coast region of North America from Washington north to southern Alaska. Although traditional methods of fishing for migratory salmon and other species of fin fish have now largely disappeared, many of these groups are active participants in the commercial fishing industry. Fishing also contributes much to the diet of peoples in Oceania, although on most islands the primary subsistence activity is horticulture. Similarly, numerous fishing villages can be found on the coasts of all nations with coastlines on oceans or seas such as Canada, Mexico, Brazil, Japan, Indonesia, Korea, Great Britain, and Spain. While in the past, much of the fishing conducted from these villages was for subsistence or local consumption, in the last few decades most of these communities have been drawn into the regional, national, or international fishing system and traditional methods have given way to modern, mechanized fishing for the commercial market. In the developing world, most fishing communities are now fishing-farming communities with fishermen either both farming and fishing or a division in the community between those who farm and those who fish. This pattern is consistent with the nature of fishing communities throughout human history as rarely being entirely self-sufficient by fishing alone.

As noted above, the level of uncertainty is much greater with fishing than with hunting-gathering, horticulture, pastoralism, and agriculture. This uncertainty comes from a number of sources. The primary source is that human beings are not biologically fit to function and survive in the water. A second source of uncertainty is the physical heterogeneity of the fishing environment. Fishing environments vary from place to place—swamps, bays, sounds, seas, oceans, rivers, streams, lakes, ponds, and so forth. And within one location the size, depth, ecology, temperature, and wave action of a body of water can change on an hourly, daily, weekly, monthly, or seasonal basis in response to weather and climate changes. The fish being sought also form a heterogeneous population that varies in any location in the number of species, the size of schools, fish size, specific location both in distance from shore and depth, and spawning patterns. Another source of uncertainty is the time, effort, and money that must be given to making and repairing fishing equipment; it is never certain that the investment will pay off in a good catch. In addition to these sources of uncertainty that arise from the physical environment, in most societies fishermen in the past and today occupy a marginal economic position and thus the amount of income they can derive from fishing is dependent not just on their skill but also on the amount of competition from other fishermen, market conditions that drive up or down the price of fish, and outsiders who buy their fish and finance their operations.

Traditional fishing societies adapt to this uncertainty in two general ways: first—by discovering and inventing diversified and specialized technologies and implementing strategies to use those technologies in the most productive ways, and second—through specialized forms of sociocultural organization and relationships that allow human time and energy to be used in such a way as to maximize the exploitation of marine resources. In addition, in many fishing societies the emotional issues created by the danger and uncertainty of fishing are dealt with through religious ritual and folklore.

Technology and Strategy

It is probably impossible to fully catalog all the equipment, methods, and strategies used around the world to catch fish. All fishermen use more than one method and in all cultures different methods are used for different types of fish, in different seasons, and under different water and climate conditions. For example, Belau fishermen in Oceania consider the month of the year, the winds and weather, currents, and the wave action in deciding what methods to use and what species to fish for. For the Belau, juvenile reef fish are especially abundant in late February and March when the winds are easterly and light, the current is weak, and the waves are low. Similarly, fishermen off the coast of Kalanatan and Trengganmu in Southeast Asia handle the variable and changing conditions by using 26 different methods with five types of hook and lines, seven types of gill nets, six types of lift nets, five types of seines, and three types of traps. The availability of fish varies seasonally, and thus all fishermen must schedule activities and methods in response to unpredictable fish behavior. In most fishing societies, different fish are taken at different times of the year. In Okayama Prefecture of Japan, for example, coastal fishermen follow the following schedule and methods for commercial and subsistence fishing:

Month	Method	Fish
Aug.–Sept.	drifting gill net	butterfish
May	drifting gill net	mackerel
	trap	goby
Apr.–Nov.	floating gill net	herring
Jul.–Oct.	trap	octopus
Oct.–Dec.	floating gill net	sea bass, herring
Sep.–Oct.	stationary gill net	crabs
Apr.–Dec.	stationary gill net	small fish,
	trap net	squid, mullet, black porgy
All Year	digging	clams

Methods used across cultures can be classified as either yielding single fish at a time or yielding fish en masse. The two categories are not mutually exclusive in time or place and sometimes the two are combined, as among Northwest Coast Native Americans who would block migrating salmon with fences and then spear them from shore or canoes. The major categories of traditional fishing methods found across cultures are the following.

Manual collection is employed most often for shellfish such as muscles, clams, cockles, and crabs but is also used for collecting fish in shallow water or tide pools. Fish are sometimes taken by hand, but more often a basket is used for fin fish and hooks and rakes for shellfish.

Spearing with lances, spears, and harpoons or shooting fish with arrows is commonly used in shallow or clear water. An able spear or arrow fisherman knows how to correct for the distortion created by the light hitting the water. Across cultures there are numerous varieties of spearing weapons including single- and double-barbed spears, tridents, harpoons with detachable and permanent heads, and long-shafted arrows.

Hooking fish with gaffs is commonly used to land fish already hooked. Large hooks and other implements may also be thrown into schools or dragged along the bottom to hook fish through their bodies.

Angling involves fishing with a line and a hook and takes a wide variety of forms including the hand line, the floated line, and the rod and line. Equipment used in angling varies not just from culture to culture but from fisherman to fisherman. Fishermen in all cultures expend considerable time in acquiring, making, maintaining, and repairing angling equipment—lures, hooks, line, sinkers, and floats. Three types of hooks are widely used—barbed, nonbarbed, and gorges, which are sticks sharpened at both ends that when picked up by a fish can be jerked to lodge sideways in the mouth.

Fishing with pots and nets in Nigeria

Noose fishing is used in Malaysia and some Oceanic islands to catch specific species of fish such as shark or gar whose sharp teeth easily tear fishing line. The noose can be attached to line so that it slips around the head when the fish takes the bait or attached to a line or pole with a bait fish suspended inside the loop and the noose tightened when the fish takes the bait.

Torch fishing is done at night with a light source (torch or fire in the past, electric or gas lights in modern times) used to cast light on the water to attract fish, which can then be taken by spearing, netting, angling, or other methods.

Suspended angling refers to techniques that allow the angler to place the bait and hook further out over the water than can be done from shore. Kite fishing is used in the Pacific to catch fish far offshore without a boat. A baited hook is strung to a long line hanging from a kite that is flown out over the water. In South America, lines are hung from trees over rivers.

Log fishing takes advantage of the fact that fish often seek shelter from the sunlight under objects. A log is floated in the water and then fish are taken when they collect near or under the log.

Trolling is towing a hook and line behind a moving boat at the correct depth and speed to incite fish to bite. Trolling is done with a motor or sailboat.

Fencing is the erection of barriers to stop the movement of fish or direct them in a certain direction. The purpose is to create large pools of fish that can be taken en masse. A simple form or fence used in ocean fishing is a weir, an enclosure erected on the beach that prevents fish that came into shore during high tide from moving back out as the tide falls. At low tide, the fish can then be collected by hand. The simplest form is simply a barrier of rocks, low enough to be submerged during high tide but high enough to block fish as the tide goes out. More complex barriers include nets stretched across the beach and fences built across rivers.

Trapping is done with portable traps or pots usually of mesh to allow water to flow through. Most have a funnel-shaped opening that allows fish to enter but not escape and a door opened by the fisherman to empty the trap. A wide variety made for specific species and water conditions are used in many fishing communities. In Singapore, for example, fishermen use coral fish, shallow water and deep water traps, and a fish pot with wings (a trap with netting extending from each side) to direct the fish into the trap. A more complicated version is the palisade trap also used in Singapore that traps fish at the bottom of a river and then directs them through funnel-like openings into chambers near the surface from where they can be harvested.

Directing involves altering features of the land or sea so to direct fish to the fisherman or to a spot from where they can be taken. For example, Indians on the Northwest Coast cut paths through seaweed beds and then floated above the path in their canoes to spear migrating salmon.

Netting is used both to collect fish directly and to assist in other fishing methods. Among the wide variety of nets are lift, drop, hoop, bag, and scoop nets.

Entangling is a form of netting in which fish become entangled in the net and cannot escape. Gill nets trap single fish in the mesh. Tangle nets are used mainly for shellfish. Reef nets are set near shore, in areas of large schools.

Engulfing involves dragging nets through the water to trap any fish encountered. Drag

Fishing from stilt bars in the Indian Ocean off of Sri Lanka

seines can be pulled by hand or by boats. Trawls are large and are pulled by power boats.

Sweeping and raking are primitive forms of seining with long brooms or rakes moved through the water to herd fish so they can be collected.

Poisoning usually involves dumping a substance that either stuns or kills fish in the water or less often, placing the poison in bait. Fish are then stunned by the bait and float to the surface. A major problem with poisons and the reason they are used only rarely and are banned by most locales is that they can kill or harm more fish than can be used, kill other forms of plant or animal life, and may destroy the environment as when poisons used in coral reefs kill the coral.

Exploding is rarely used today but was used in some locations after World War II when surplus ammunition was left behind. The idea is to stun the fish so they float to the surface to be collected. As with poisoning, exploding easily results in overharvesting and damage to the environment.

The Problem of Common Property

On of the major problems facing people such as fishermen who exploit an area that is an open resource available for all to use is that the resource will be overused and undermaintained and therefore depleted. When a resource is free and open, people are likely to take as much from it as possible and invest nothing in its maintenance, as that investment is more likely to benefit others who use it. This situation is called the "tragedy of the commons" and is a major reason that many bodies of water around the world are now badly overfished and polluted.

Traditional fishing cultures have generally dealt with this problem by controlling access to fishing waters in a variety of ways. In Micronesia, for example, four different sea tenure systems are used: (1) a reef or lagoon is owned by all villagers or all residents of the island, (2) kin groups such as clans or lineages own all the lagoons or reefs, (3) kin groups such as clans or lineages own specific areas of lagoons and reefs, and (4) families own the reefs or lagoons. Each of these ownership systems ensures that access will be restricted to a certain number of people and that outsiders will be denied use, although use rights may be requested and are sometimes granted. A common way of assigning fishing rights across cultures is for individual fishermen to identify and keep secret specific fishing spots that they believe yield an especially rich supply of fish or highly desirable fish. Off the coast of Brazil, for example, all fishermen share knowledge about the fishing grounds, but individual fishermen discover and keep secret fishing spots that they exploit. Similarly, fishermen in the Brazilian Amazon have favorite spots on rivers. In both these situations, as elsewhere, this information is passed on from fishermen to their sons. The Tlingit of the Northwest Coast also traditionally established fishing rights, by driving off rival groups, to spots on rivers where salmon runs were heavy. Control of the spot was then maintained by the community leader who determined when fishing should stop so as not to overfish the river. While these sea tenure customs do not ensure a successful catch, they do reduce the amount of competition a fisherman faces from other fishermen and give each sea-owning group a stake in seeing that the resource is maintained. Even a passive maintenance practice such as not fishing a territory for a time to allow fish to spawn or to return can have long-term benefits. Sea tenure systems do not operate in isolation from other sociocultural and economic features of a society and often, in fact, are extensions of land tenure customs and the organization of social relationships in the community.

The traditional system of the Belau of Micronesia provides an example of the workings of a sea tenure system. Village clusters own the rights to fishing grounds. Village chiefs control the rights for their villages. If a poacher is caught, he will first be warned and then his chief will be fined by the Belau high chief. The fined chief loses face and fines the kin group of the poacher to compensate himself. In the past, a poacher might simply be killed if caught. The village chief also has the right to share or rent fishing grounds. In the past, the Belau also conserved by keeping only the fish they planned to eat and releasing the remainder of the catch and also by storing any extra fish by smoking or making fish stews that were preserved by reheating each day. The Belau also protected the coral reefs by not using poison near the coral and took certain species of fish only at certain times, such as when storms interfered with the availability of preferred species.

Sociocultural Aspects

Traditional fishing communities differ in important ways from communities that subsist by other means. One major difference is that in many fishing communities both the people themselves and outsiders view the fishing community and its members as in some ways different than other people and communities in the society. In some societies this difference is ethnic, as fishermen are often from one specific ethnic group (although not all members of the ethnic group are fishermen). For example, in Gloucester, Massachusetts, fishermen are mainly of Italian ancestry while fishermen in New Bedford, Massachusetts, are mainly of Portuguese ancestry. In the Puget Sound area of Washington, fishermen were often Norwegian or Croatian in ancestry. Similarly, some fishing villages in Japan are the home of people referred to as *eta*, formerly considered outcasts in the Japanese social order even though they are ethnic Japanese. When members of the fishing community cannot be distinguished by ethnic background from the general population, they are still perceived as being different. This perception is largely due to the nature of fishing as a technological activity and especially the danger and high level of uncertainty involved, the fact that it is largely a male activity, and the need to respond to the conditions created by the environment rather than control the environment. For example, men must often fish or travel at night, arriving home early in the morning with their "workday" ending at about the time that of nonfishermen begins. Bars filled with fishermen at 10:00 A.M. might suggest to the outsider accustomed to drinking in the evening that fishermen are drunks. Instead, it simply means that fishermen operate on a different schedule than others.

Just as fishing communities see themselves and are seen by outsiders as different, so too are individual fishermen. Compared to people who engage in other occupations, fishermen are more careful planners, more independent, more fearless, and more able to defer gratification. These personality characteristics all serve well one who is engaged in a dangerous and uncertain activity such as fishing.

In traditional fishing communities and to a large extent in fishing communities now involved in the fishing industry, various social arrangements were used to reduce some of the uncertainty. These arrangements include paying the crew in fish rather than in money to ensure that all have a stake in the success of the venture; an egalitarian ethos among members of the crew with the work of all considered valuable; selecting crews on the basis of kinship, friendship, or shared ethnicity; and maintaining long-term relationships with middlemen who serve as the conduit through which fish flow from the sea to urban markets. In many communities, middlemen also played a major role in the early days of conversion from traditional to modern fishing methods as suppliers of the capital for the purchase of equipment. However, in some situations, these relationships were exploitive, with the fishermen locked into an endless cycle of using profits to pay off debts.

Across cultures, the work involved in preparing to fish, fishing, and processing the fish is allocated usually on the basis of gender. In a sample of 186 cultures, in all cultures that hunt for large aquatic animals such as whales and seals the hunting is performed only by men. In 143 cultures that derive some food from fishing, men do all or most of the fishing in 90 percent of the cultures, men and women both fish in 6 percent, and women mainly fish in only 4 percent. The gathering of small sea creatures such as shellfish falls mainly to women in 71 percent of cultures, is done by both men and women in 2 percent, and mainly by men in 27 percent of cultures. Men also perform most technical tasks related to fishing such as boat building (in 96 percent of cultures) and net making (in 68 percent of cultures) while women more often process and preserve the fish (65 percent of cultures). A survey of fishing by women in Oceania supports this general worldwide pattern. With the exception of the interior of major islands such as New Guinea, the majority of animal protein in the diet of Oceanic cultures comes from fish, with a considerable percentage, although generally less than half, provided by women who collect shellfish and small aquatic animals such as octopus on the island reefs. However, in 50 percent of the 36 societies surveyed, women also fish on the reefs with nets, hooks and lines, and traps; in 8 percent they engage in all types of fishing except for the largest fish such as tuna and bonito; and in 1 society, the Marianas, they engage in all types of fishing. Both the Oceanic and worldwide pattern of men doing most of the fishing and especially fishing by boat away from home while women fish or collect near the home conforms to the general pattern of the division of labor by sex in technological activities found around the world. Because women are the primary caretakers for children in nearly all cultures, women tend to perform tasks that are compatible with child care—tasks that can be done near the home, that are relatively safe, and in which children can participate. Men perform tasks that require travel away from the home and are less safe such as deep-sea fishing. This division of labor is also reflected in some cultures by customs that prohibit women from being near fishing spots. The Tlingit, for example, prohibited menstruating women from going near fishing places on the streams, fearing that their presence would contaminate the river and cause the fish to disappear. With the shift from traditional to commercial fishing, women's roles can change. For example, women may participate in all types of fishing when demand for fish is high and there are not enough men to fish,

they are employed in canneries as among Northwest Coast Native Americans, and the collection of shellfish may decline in importance as the community becomes involved in trade relationships and purchases food rather than collects it.

Because fishing takes place in a hostile environment, fishing is a dangerous activity and fishermen are often hurt and not infrequently killed. This danger effects not only the fishermen but also their families, who when the men leave for sea can never be sure that they will return. No other subsistence activity is as risky as deep water ocean fishing. In many fishing communities the dangers are often not discussed openly and many fishermen ignore basic safety measures. At the same time, however, because of both the uncertainty and danger, fishing is

Carib Indian in Brazil fishing with bow and arrow

Fishing with throw nets is a common technique in lakes and rivers such as this one in Guyana.

accompanied by much religious ritual that serves to alleviate some of the emotional stress associated with fishing. For example, in Singapore, the Malays believe that each boat has a soul, called the *mayor prahu*. Fishing success depends on the strength of the boat's mayor. And after a long run of poor luck, a fishermen will hire a ritual specialist who summons the boat's mayor, while a sweetened rice mixed with saltwater is placed as an offering on each rib of the boat. A feast is then held with fowl, sheep, or goat meat offered to the mayor. Offerings are always made on Friday, because spirits have the most power on that day. Among the Native Americans of the Northwest Coast, fishing—especially salmon fishing—was accompanied by considerable ritual and ceremony. Although varying from group to group, these rituals included the First Salmon Ceremony that opened the fishing season, prayers to the first fish encountered, cleaning fish in the correct manner such as with the head pointing upriver, and eating the fish and disposing of its bones in a manner that showed respect and allowed the soul of the fish to escape and then reappear in the future in the body of another fish. Fishing is also associated with an extensive body of magical beliefs, beliefs based on experience, folktales, songs, and rhymes, all of which, like religious ritual, help alleviate the stress that is associated with fishing. Some beliefs from the Texas Gulf Coast are as follows:

Whistling on a boat is bad luck.

Bad luck on the first day out means bad luck the rest of the time.

It is good luck when a porpoise meets you coming in.

Waving a red cloth will scare away evil spirits.

A circle around the moon means bad weather.

When there is no moon the fishing is best.

Transition to Modern Fishing

Modern fishing is an industry with fish a commodity sold in the international marketplace. A combination of overfishing and pollution has depleted the fish and sea mammal population in many onshore and offshore fishing locations and has also rendered many fish unsuitable for human consumption. Modern fishing based on large trawlers, on-ship processing plants, and a distribution network designed to move fish from the coast to urban markets has either destroyed or markedly altered traditional fishing communities around the world. In many nations, governments initiated programs that encouraged the formation of fishing cooperatives to enable fishermen to be more efficient, to increase cooperation, and to decrease the importance of middlemen. So far, it is not clear that cooperatives have generally had these effects, with both local and national politics often making cooperation difficult.

Around the world, all traditional fishing communities have been changed by modern fishing, although the change began at different times in different places. In Korea, for example, the traditional fishing system began to change after the arrival of the Japanese in 1910 with the earliest changes being the introduction of sailboats and line fishing for rays, eels, and croaker; the use of nets; and the involvement of fishing communities in the national economy in the form of the trade of fish through middlemen to canneries and urban fish markets. This commodification of fish conflicted with the traditional role of fish as a medium of exchange that was used in gift-giving to fulfill obligations or gain favors, as a present, or traded for agricultural foods. By the 1960s, the coastal fish population off the Korean coast was so depleted that fishermen were forced to move further out to sea. This change required large, in-board fishing boats and more expensive equipment as well as new skills at navigation and fish-finding. To finance their deep-sea fishing, fishermen were forced to borrow money from fish dealers and they would pay on the principal and interest with fish. However, because the initial financial investment is high, boats and equipment need continual maintenance. The fish haul is uncertain and fishermen quickly became caught in a cycle of low profits and high expenses with the process managed by the middleman traders, some of whom exploited the fishermen.

Even when small-scale fishing continues, fishermen use modern, purchased equipment in place of traditional handmade equipment. For example, in Belau, motorboats replaced dugout canoes, nylon nets replaced locally made nets, and spear fishermen used underwater spear guns and goggles and cut the glare of the sun with polarized sunglasses. Despite the use of modern equipment in traditional fishing, fishing declined and is no longer a subsistence practice of any importance in Belau, as most food is purchased and several hundred thousand tons of fish are imported every year, usually in cans. No fish is exported.

In the Northwest Coast of North America, which was the home of the largest concentration of fishing societies around the world, most cultures were drawn into the commercial fishing industry in the late nineteenth century, with men working as fishermen and women in the canneries. When the canneries closed in the early to mid-twentieth century, women sought other employment outside the home while men continued to work as fishermen.

Thus, for many fishermen around the world, the traditional uncertainties associated with fishing such as danger and the exploitation of a hostile environment remain, now supplemented by uncertainty created by fluctuating demand for fish in the world marketplace, depletion of resources, pollution, and control of the industry by large fishing corporations.

See also ENVIRONMENTAL UNCERTAINTY AND RISK; TRAGEDY OF THE COMMONS.

Acheson, James M. (1980) "Anthropology of Fishing." *Annual Review of Anthropology* 10:275–316.

Annandale, Nelson, and Herbert C. Robinson. (1903) *Fasciculi Malayenses.*

Boxberger, Daniel L. (1994) "Ethnicity and Labor in the Puget Sound Fishing Industry, 1880–1935." *Ethnology* 33:179–191.

Burdon, T. W., and M. L. Parry, eds. (1954) *Papers on Malay Fishing Methods.*

Chapman, Margaret D. (1987) "Women's Fishing in Oceania." *Human Ecology* 15:267–288.

Firth, Raymond W. (1946) *Malay Fishermen: Their Peasant Economy.*

Forman, Shepard. (1980) "Cognition and Catch: The Location of Fishing Spots in a Brazilian Coastal Village." In *Maritime Adaptations: Essays on Contemporary Fishing Communities*, edited by Alexander Spoehr, 15–24.

Hardin, G. (1968) "The Tragedy of the Commons." *Science* 162:1243–1248.

Jackson, Jean E. (1983) *The Fish People.*

Johannes, Robert. (1981) *Words of the Lagoon: Fishing and Marine Lore in the Palau District of Micronesia.*

Laguna, Frederica de. (1972) *Under Mount Saint Elias: The History and Culture of the Yakutat Tlingit.*

Mullen, Patrick B. (1988) *I Heard the Old Fisherman Say: Folklore of the Texas Gulf Coast.*

Murdock, George P., and Diana O. Morrow. (1970) "Subsistence Economy and Supportive Practices: Cross-Cultural Codes 1." *Ethnology* 9:302–330.

Murdock, George P., and Caterina Provost. (1973) "Factors in the Division of Labor by Sex." *Ethnology* 12:203–225.

Norbeck, Edward. (1954) *Takashima: A Japanese Fishing Community.*

Oliver, Douglas L. (1989) *Oceania: The Native Cultures of Australia and the Pacific Islands.*

Poggie, John J., Jr., ed. (1980) *Maritime Anthropology.* Special Issue of *Anthropological Quarterly* 53.

Ruddle, Kenneth, and Tommoya Akimichi, eds. (1984) *Maritime Institutions in the Western Pacific.* Senri Ethnological Studies, no. 17.

Sahrhage, Dietrich, and Johannes Lundbeck. (1992) *A History of Fishing.*

Sinclair, Peter R., ed. (1988) *A Question of Survival: The Fisheries and Newfoundland Society.*

Stewart, Hilary. (1977) *Indian Fishing: Early Methods on the Northwest Coast.*

FORAGING

See HUNTING-GATHERING.

might have an appreciation of naturally growing flowers and use them for personal adornment or in religious rituals.

Land used for gardens is of four types: (1) adjacent or near homes or other buildings such as churches, (2) between buildings, (3) alongside open-use areas such as rivers or roadways, and (4) large open areas such as parks. In altering the environment to create gardens, designers combine aesthetic and physical components through the use of design principles. Aesthetic components include the use of elements such as space, mass, line, color, light, shade, texture, and scent. Physical components include natural ones such as soil, rocks, water, and plants and human-made ones such as paths and terraces, walls and fences, buildings, fountains, and furniture. These components are united to form a garden by the use of design principles such as unity, variety of elements, balance, contrast, accent, size, and proportion. How these elements are combined and which design principles are used are largely determined by the beliefs, values, and aesthetic sense in the culture. Thus, garden design varies both across cultures and over time in a single culture. In addition, there has been much borrowing between cultures (such as from China to Japan, across Europe, and from Europe to North America) in garden design so gardens in many cultures are shaped by both internal and external influences.

Across cultures and over the course of human history, gardening has been found almost exclusively in state-level societies—that is, societies with large, dense populations; cities; occupational specialization beyond that based on sex or age; social stratification; and centralized government. Gardens are not found in most hunter-gatherer, horticultural, or mainly pastoral societies. Thus, the beginning of gardening and the most elaborate gardens are associated with the agricultural civilizations of the ancient Near East (such as Egyptian, Assyrian, and Babylonian) and those of Bali; China; Japan;

GARDENS AND GARDENING

The term *gardening* is used here to mean the growing of plants for aesthetic rather than for utilitarian purposes. A garden is a feature of the built environment and is a natural area whose features are purposefully altered in some way to conform to a human-imposed design. In the real world, of course, gardens can serve both aesthetic and practical purposes. For example, sunflowers are often grown in gardens because of the enjoyment people get from viewing their size, shape, color, and the bees they attract. But at the end of the growing season, the large heads are often harvested and dried and the seeds removed and eaten. Similarly, rural Serbs grow sweet basil in their household gardens because they like its appearance and also because of its ritual importance in Serbian Orthodox ceremonies. However, in all cultures with gardens, a distinction is made between land used to grow plants for food or other reasons and land used to grow plants for their beauty. Gardens are not a cultural universal and in many non-Western cultures people do not make gardens, although they

A formal English garden on the grounds of the restored Tryon Palace in New Bern, North Carolina, features elaborate low hedges enclosing mass plantings of tulips.

India; the Aztecs in Mexico; the Inca in Peru; Greece; Rome; and later the colonial nations of Europe such as England, France, and Belgium.

In many of these societies, two types of gardens can be distinguished. The first type is the royal garden, built and owned by the rulers with wealth collected by taxing citizens or conquering other societies and with the labor of commoners or slaves. These gardens, which are now open to the public in many nations, were typically very large, enclosed, and elaborate and, as with the ruler him- or herself, were meant to symbolize the society's relationship with other features of the universe. These gardens also symbolized the power of the rulers and the social hierarchy of the society through the eviction of peasants in order to use the land for royal gardens, the enclosure of the gardens, restricted access to them, and the exploitation of peasant or slave labor. The second type of garden is the private or household garden, including those owned by the elite which were often small-scale imitations of the royal gardens and the gardens of commoners that are found in nearly all societies with gardening. Flower gardens, for example, are a common feature of homesteads in rural, urban, and suburban America. In Serbia, most rural homes have carefully tended flower gardens bordered by white stones with sweet basil, irises, lilacs, tulips, carnations, hyacinths, roses, peonies, and geraniums grown in pots placed on doorsteps or windowsills. In rural Taiwan, many homes also have gardens with flowers raised for their beauty and herbs grown for their medicinal uses in the home. Buddhist temples in central Thailand have flower gardens tended by the priests and novices. Traditionally flowers were grown by the farmers both for their own use and less importantly for sale to vendors who sold them in towns and cities. On the island of Tonga in Polynesia, most homes have carefully tended courtyard gardens with shrubs and flowering trees.

Across cultures the actual work involved in gardening—designing, clearing the land, preparing the soil, planting, weeding, fertilizing, trimming, and harvesting—is marked by a rigid division of labor. In many cultures the division of labor is based on sex. In royal gardens, the gardens were usually planned by men and the actual gardening done by men. While some women might be involved in planning their own royal-style household gardens, such work was usually also done by men. In agricultural and horticultural societies around the world, regardless of the purpose of the garden (aesthetic or practical), men more often clear the land (93 percent of cultures) and prepare the soil (69 percent) while women more often plant the seeds or plants (56 percent), harvest (67 percent), and tend the crops (66 percent). In general, across cultures men care for the larger, food-producing plots while women tend the smaller flower, vegetable, and herb gardens nearer the home. This same pattern holds in the private gardens of modern societies. Men tend the vegetable gardens, mow grass, and trim shrubs; women weed and tend the flower and herb gardens, even in cities. The Serbs are typical of many cultures when they say that "It is possible to tell if there is a young girl in the household by the condition of the [flower] garden." In some cultures a specific category of people is associated with gardening. In California, for example, Japanese-Americans and more recently people of Mexican ancestry often work as gardeners, and in a number of locales such as northern California and New York, Italian immigrants often grew flowers for sale in urban markets. Such groups often gain a reputation among their clientele as having special skills at gardening. In northern India the Malis, an occupational caste of several

million, grow and sell flowers, basil leaves, and wood apples to Hindu worshippers.

Symbolism of Gardens

Although a feature of the built environment with no or only limited practical purpose, gardens do, nonetheless, have important functions in all gardening cultures. One major function is to provide people with a pleasurable experience, whether that pleasure is gained from working in the garden, viewing the flowers or design of the garden, or smelling the plants. Gardens also play an important symbolic role. In this sense, gardens and gardening are a form of expressive culture as they symbolize the relationships between different categories of people, the relationships between humans and nature, and the relationships between humans and the supernatural world.

As noted above, royal gardens in Europe as elsewhere symbolized royalty's exalted status and their power over the rest of the population, but these gardens have other symbolic meanings as well. As represented by the Garden of Eden, gardens in Europe and the Western world in general symbolize purity and paradise and glorify the serene, close-to-nature rural way of life in comparison to the corrupt, loud city life. In the past, royal gardens symbolized humans' control of nature. Construction of these gardens required massive alteration of the landscape on which a large, enclosed garden was built. The elements in the garden included flowering plants, shrubs, trees, lined walkways, pools of water, fountains, statues, benches, and other built features. All were usually aligned symmetrically and at sharp angles to one another, and the garden was often divided into rectilinear interior sections. The garden has little relationship to the surrounding environment and demonstrates the human capacity to alter the environment to meet human wishes. In the twentieth century in Europe there has been a movement away from such formal gardens toward more natural gardens that conform to natural features of the environment. The traditional and modern European views of gardens as control of versus living in accord with nature are set forth in the lines of poet W. S. Merwin in the "Gardens of Versailles":

At what moment can it be said to occur
the grand stillness of this symmetry
whose horizons become the horizon
and whose designer's name seems to be Ours
even when the designer has long since
vanished and the king his master whom
they call The Sun in his day is nobody again
here are the avenues of light reflected
and magnified and here the form's vast claim
to have been true forever as the law
of a universe in which nothing appears
to change and there was nothing before this
except defects of Nature a waste of marshes
a lake a chaos of birds and wild things
a river making its undirected
way it was always the water that was
motion even while thirty six thousand men
and six thousand horses for more than three
decades diverted it into a thousand
fountains and when all those men and horses
had gone the water flowed on and the sound
of water falling echoes in the dream
the dream of water in which the avenues
all of them are the river on its own way

Quite the opposite are traditional Chinese gardens that symbolize harmony with nature through the use of winding waterways, trees, rocky hills, lakes and islands, and a conformity to the surrounding landscape. Chinese gardens reflect Taoist beliefs about harmony and balance and opposition among elements of the universe and attempt to re-create those principles in small-scale form with the viewer given the opportunity through the careful placement of benches and pavilions to view the different scenes.

Islamic gardens in the Middle East are also large and grand but feature the use of water—a scarce resource in this arid region—in fountains, channels, ponds, and waterfalls. Thus, Islamic gardens symbolically recognize the importance of a scare but vital resource, represent in small-

scale the waterworks constructed by people to control the resource, and express people's concern about the certainty of that resource.

Finally, in south India and Sri Lanka, Buddhist gardens are filled with quiet pools, baths, and flower beds to encourage the private contemplation of the universe while Hindu gardens contain many trees that have been venerated for centuries by Hindus.

Anderson, William. (1967) "A Journal of a Voyage Made in His Majesty's Sloop *Resolution* May 16th, 1776." In *The Journals of Captain James Cook on His Voyage of Discovery*, edited by J. C. Beaglehole, 721–986.

Bhattacharya, Jogendra N. (1896) *Hindu Castes and Sects.*

Gannon, Martin J., and Associates. (1994) *Understanding Global Cultures: Metaphorical Journeys through 17 Countries.*

Goody, Jack. (1993) *The Culture of Flowers.*

Gould-Martin, Katherine. (1977) *Women Asking Women: An Ethnography of Health Care in Rural Taiwan.*

Halpern, Joel M. (1958) *A Serbian Village.*

Hoyles, Martin. (1991) *The Story of Gardening.*

Ingersoll, Jasper C. (1964) *The Priest and the Path: An Analysis of the Priest Role in a Central Thai Village.*

Jellicoe, Sir Geoffrey, et al. (1986) *The Oxford Companion to Gardens.*

Mijatovich, Chedo. (1914) *Servia of the Servians.*

GEOMANCY Geomancy is the art and/or science of site selection. Geomancy is now a generic term, referring to a number of related practices and beliefs, all having to do with using knowledge of features of the natural environment to select sites for human use—communities, buildings, and graves. The emphasis is not on observable physical features of the environment in and of themselves, but rather on unseen forces in the earth and universe that must be utilized to achieve harmony with nature. In the past, the term was used interchangeably with *feng shui (fung shui, feng-shui)*, the traditional Chinese method of site selection. Feng shui is still used in modern China, although it and other religious and cosmological beliefs and practices have been restricted in the Communist era, and also in Korea, Hong Kong, and Singapore. It is also practiced by non-Han peoples in China such as the Miao, Hakka, and Zhuang, to whom it diffused from the Han. Earlier in the twentieth century the Miao were described as more serious adherents than the neighboring Han in southern China. In the twentieth century, geomancy has been adopted by some in the environmental design movement as a technique for guiding site selection. While tracing its roots to Chinese feng shui, modern geomancy also considers knowledge derived from Western science such as the effect of electromagnetic fields that were unknown to but still may have played a role in the success of traditional geomancy. Modern geomancy is also selective in the beliefs and practices borrowed from the traditional Chinese system and has evolved more into a system concerned mainly with maintaining a balance between human beings and the universe as an end in and of itself rather than as a system, as in China, for using that balance to materially benefit human beings. Also different in the Western version is the use of geomancy to select sites for housing rather than for graves and tombs, the major use in China.

The origins of feng shui are unclear. Some experts claim that it originated in simplified form among the Mongols and other nomadic peoples north of China in their belief in a "code of the laws of nature and the harmony of man with

nature." The Mongols, for example, required that nobles and lamas make camp upstream or uphill from commoners to avoid the latter ritually or materially polluting the former. Feng shui then diffused to China during the period of frequent and often violent contact between the nomads and the Han dynasty beginning about 206 B.C. and lasting to A.D. 8. During this period, the more elaborate form of feng shui developed and was called by a number of names including *khan yu* (heaven and earth) and *ti li* (influences of the earth). Feng shui means "wind and water," the symbolism of which is discussed below. The underlying principle of feng shui is found in ancient Chinese writings, perhaps the oldest of which states (de Groot 1912:287)

> By looking up, in order to contemplate the constellations, and by looking down to examine the influences or laws of the Earth, Man may understand the explanations of mysterious and intelligible matters.

The origin of the name *feng shui* is unclear, but in one version it is attributed to the spring and summer winds that bring the monsoon rains needed for raising crops. In another view, "wind and water" is seen as referring to all features of the environment that influence the currents of the winds and the flow of waters. In this sense, "features of the environment" refers not just to physical features observable by the five human senses but also unobservable forces in the earth and universe.

In Korea, feng shui is called *pangsu* or *chigwon* and flourished during the Koryo period (935–1392). As in China, a geomancer is a man (almost all are men) of considerable reputation and influence who is consulted by those who can afford his services in all matters requiring the selection of building and burial sites and the best time to build or bury the dead. Some geomancers may also be involved in selecting the best day for a wedding.

The practice of feng shui is a product of the traditional Chinese cosmology and the multiplicity of religious systems that required specialists to interpret the cosmology and apply it to daily life for the commoners as well as the wealthy and powerful. Geomancers, along with fortune tellers and other diviners, who used scapulimancy (divining the future by observing the cracking of a mammal's scapula) and milfoil (divining with the yarrow plant), were one category of such specialists. Feng shui is one component of traditional Chinese folk religion, which of course differed over time and across regions but is considered a system of religious belief and practice distinct from the major traditions of Confucianism, Taoism, and Buddhism. Among the key beliefs that feng shui draws upon or is integrated with are a belief that the earth is a living organism, a belief in the duality and opposition of elements in the universe (especially the forces of yin and yang), ancestor worship, and the elaborate associated funerary customs. Most important is the belief in the earth as a living organism with internal channels whose locations and points of convergence are beneficial for human beings and that these channels can be blocked, thereby disrupting the harmony of the universe. The geomancer's special gift is the ability to identify these channels and to use that knowledge to determine the best location for a building site or grave. In his work, the geomancer is guided by printed instructions, intuition, knowledge of the landscape, the hidden meanings of visible natural features, and the ability to use a complicated compass to divine a suitable site where the characteristics of the inhabitant (often reflected in his or her date of birth), the nature of the site, and the heavenly bodies are in harmony in space and over time. Thus, feng shui is used to select a site for a house and other buildings and the grave or tomb site for a deceased relative. Such matters are of considerable importance as the use of a suitable site will bring prosperity to the individual or his family while the wrong site can bring disaster. In fact, poverty or disasters are often blamed on the location of an ancestor's grave or tomb in a site that ignores the forces of feng shui.

Alterations to the adjacent environment, however, can reduce or destroy a site's suitability, meaning that the geomancer's work does not end with the selection of a site. He may also be employed to correct a feng shui that has gone awry because a neighbor has dug a grave nearby, a stone has been moved, or a nearby hill has been cleared of trees or mined. Thus, any change in the physical landscape at or near the site—and this is especially true for tombs and graves of ancestors—can cause a suitable site to be viewed by its owners as no longer suitable. The worst offense is the digging of another grave near the first one. Such a grave will cut off the underground channels and cause harm to the ancestor's soul, thereby interfering with the ancestor's ability to provide assistance to his living descendants. Geomancers are called upon to help restore the suitability of the site or to negotiate a settlement when the disruption is caused by the acts of other persons. However, since both parties to the dispute may have made their site choices on the basis of feng shui, both are reluctant to change their sites, resulting in threats, violence, court battles, and sometimes vandalism of the graves. In addition to disputes over graves, such conflicts also concern villages and conflicts between neighbors over building sites and especially additions to existing buildings that alter the physical landscape. In feng shui, any alteration to the physical landscape alters the flow of unobservable forces and may disrupt the harmony of the elements that make for a suitable feng shui—thus, the frequent and often intractable conflicts.

Although geomancy is basically about human-environment interaction and human attempts to utilize the structure and forces of the environment, geomancy does not exist apart from social, political, and economic considerations in Chinese and other societies. First, it is important to note that not all Han Chinese, Koreans, Miao, and others believe in feng shui. Even in a single small community only some believe, others are uncertain, and still others do not believe at all. And even among believers, feng shui may be but one of a number of factors mentioned as an explanation for a family's economic success, with other factors such as individual ability, fate, and moral qualities given equal or even greater weight.

From the perspective of social stratification in rural communities, feng shui can be interpreted as a belief system that tends to reinforce the status quo—that is, the wealth of some families can be attributed to the beneficial effects of feng shui while the poverty of other families can be similarly explained as a consequence of their less than suitable feng shui. In this regard, the feng shui of ancestors' graves and tombs is especially important, thus the frequent disputes noted above. Such a belief system both frees humans from bearing directly responsibility for their own status and places the responsibility on forces beyond their complete understanding and direct control. Since wealth can buy the services of the best geomancers and the poor often cannot afford their services at all, the belief system is self-perpetuating over the generations. But because in this context feng shui is a cause of one's status, it can be the source of conflict in communities—different families desire the best sites for their ancestor's graves and tombs. As noted above, even the slightest alteration to a site or adjacent land may disrupt the feng shui, lead to conflict, and require the services of a geomancer to rectify the situation. Some experts suggest that geomancers are expert at exploiting such situations for their own financial gain. While this may or may not be true, it is clear that feng shui is a source of conflict in many communities and that geomancers play a major role in conflict management and resolution. Thus, feng shui may serve as the vehicle through which conflicts over land rights and wealth can be voiced and resolved indirectly, thereby mitigating the more prolonged conflict that might result if the actual issues were faced openly.

See also DIRECTION; SETTLEMENT PATTERNS.

Building with Nature. (1992) September–October.

Friedrich, Paul, and Norma Diamond, eds. (1994) *Encyclopedia of World Cultures. Volume 6. Russia and Eurasia/China.*

Groot, Jan Jacob Maria de. (1912) *Religion in China: Universism. A Key to the Study of Taoism and Confucianism.*

Harrell, Clyde Stevan. (1983) *Belief and Unbelief in a Taiwan Village.*

Knez, Eugene I. (1970) *Sam Jong Dong: A South Korean Village.*

Lattimore, Owen. (1941) *Mongol Journeys.*

Wang, Hsing-ju. (1948) *The Miao People of Hainan Island.*

GREEN REVOLUTION

Green Revolution refers to the partially successful effort by Western nations to dramatically increase the agricultural productivity of less developed countries through the development and introduction of new varieties of basic food or commercial crops. The revolution began in Mexico in 1944 with United States–backed research to produce hybrid varieties of corn and wheat more suitable to climatic and soil conditions in Mexico. Subsequently, especially in the 1960s and 1970s, hybrid development has focused on wheat, corn, rice, and cotton; new varieties have been introduced on a broad scale in many nations including Mexico, the Philippines, India, Pakistan, Brazil, Kenya, Indonesia, Iraq,

Women in India plant rice seedlings on a Japanese-designed experimental farm.

Iran, and Turkey. The goal of the Green Revolution—supported by the United Nations, the World Bank, and other international organizations—was to make less developed nations self-sufficient in food production. In all areas where Green Revolution plants and farming methods have been introduced, the existing system was based on sustainable methods such as crop rotation, intercropping, and green and animal manuring that generally produced enough food for local consumption but little for sale.

The Green Revolution rests on the genetic engineering of food plants; heavy use of chemical fertilizers, pesticides, and herbicides; irrigation; and mechanized farming based on tractors, combines, and water pumping systems. The goal of the genetic engineering has been to produce new varieties of seed that produce higher yields.

Thus, hybrid plants have been produced that are disease resistant, that mature earlier and thus can produce more than one crop per year, that produce more food as a percentage of plant size, that are highly responsive to fertilizers and sunlight, and that can withstand harsh climatic conditions such as high winds. Such plants are labeled High-Yielding Varieties (HYV) and require large quantities of fertilizer and water to produce at maximum levels. Thus, the Green Revolution is fossil-fuel dependent and uses large quantities of energy to produce fertilizer, run the farming equipment, and operate the irrigation pumping systems. This fact has led critics of the Green Revolution to label the plants Energy-Intensive Varieties (EIV).

Since the beginning, and especially since the oil crisis of the early 1970s, which dramatically raised the cost of fuel, the Green Revolution has been controversial. Proponents claim that it benefits farmers by enabling them to produce more on less land, which means that some crops can be grown exclusively or mainly for sale and that the cost for basic foods will be lower. Critics argue that the fuel and financial requirements of the Green Revolution are beyond the reach of most small-scale farmers who do not have enough land to farm nor adequate irrigation systems nor money to invest in equipment and fertilizer. Thus, the real beneficiaries of the Green Revolution have been those who already owned much land and who can now sell their produce in urban or overseas markets—practices that do little to make the local communities self-sufficient in food production. Critics further claim that the heavy reliance on fertilizers, fossil fuel, and water is environmentally unsound and has led to the depletion of nonrenewable resources, land degradation, and air and water pollution.

It is now clear that the Green Revolution has not led to self-sufficiency in all local communities in less developed countries around the world. Although in many nations, such as India, food production is now much higher than before the Green Revolution, results at the local level are mixed, with some communities thriving as a result of the Green Revolution, others little changed, and others transformed to agribusiness operations under the control of wealthy investors. In addition to change in the farming system, communities involved in the Green Revolution also undergo major social and political transformation; the focus of their economic activities shifts from the family and community to the region and nation. Thus, farms become larger, wage labor common, food is purchased rather than grown, political leadership is achieved by those able to deal with outsiders such as government officials and traders, and villages are drawn into the world economy. In general, where the Green Revolution has been successful—in the sense of increasing yields without major disruption to the local community—it has been because of five reasons: (1) a suitable irrigation system already existed or was developed by the government; (2) fertilizer is relatively cheap; (3) the government supports the farmers through low-interest loans, agricultural extension services, and the establishment of farming cooperatives; (4) electricity is already available or is provided at low cost; and (5) traditional farming methods such as the use of animal fertilizers or nitrogen-fixing crops or trees have been used with Green Revolution methods.

See also AGRICULTURE; IRRIGATION.

Leaf, Murray J. (1984) *Song of Hope: The Green Revolution in a Punjab Village.*

Schusky, Ernest L. (1989) *Culture and Agriculture: An Ecological Introduction to Traditional and Modern Farming Systems.*

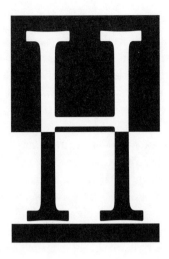

See PRECIPITATION.

HORTICULTURE

Horticulture is a food production subsistence strategy based on the "growing of crops of *all* kinds with relatively simple tools and methods, in the absence of permanently cultivated fields" (Ember and Ember 1990:93). There are two major forms of horticulture. The first type of horticulture is the growing of a variety of plant species in a garden plot for a few years until the soil is no longer fertile and then shifting to a new plot for several years and so on. Although there are variations from culture to culture, shifting cultivation is usually characterized by the following features:

1. Extensive rather than intensive use of land with a shifting to and creation of new garden sites every few years and the abandon-

ment of old sites so that they can return to their natural vegetative state

2. Use of solar energy stored in vegetation as the basic source for minerals to increase the fertility of the soil

3. The use of natural fertilizer in the form of ash from the vegetation cleared from and burned on the garden site to fertilize the soil

4. The use of relatively simple technology such as axes, machetes, hoes, digging sticks, and fire to clear the land and plant the crops

5. Cultivation of a variety of crops mixed together in a single plot or over several plots

6. Cultivation of plants over the course of an entire year through sequential planting of the same or different crops

7. Horticulture serves as a food storage mechanism through multicropping and the long growing season

A worldwide survey of 563 cultures mainly in the nineteenth and early twentieth centuries indicates that 36 percent were reliant on shifting cultivation for a substantial portion of their food, with most of these cultures located in the tropical regions of Central and South America, Melanesia, and Southeast Asia. No culture known to human history, however, has been wholly reliant on shifting cultivation as a source of food. Instead, all horticultural societies only partially rely on horticulture; food is also obtained through hunting, gathering, fishing, animal husbandry, and exchange.

The second, and less common, form of horticulture is the harvesting of edible plant matter such as fruits, nuts, and the pulp of long-growing trees or bushes. Harvesting of such foodstuffs is often done in cultures that also practice shifting cultivation or other forms of food production, but in about 10 percent of cultures, mainly on islands in Oceania, gathering from long-growing trees is an especially important means of obtaining food. On many

Oceanic islands such as Samoa, Belau, and the Trobriands, people traditionally harvested coconuts, breadfruit, bananas, the starchy pulp of the sago palm, and the pineapple-like fruit of the pandanus, or "screw pine." This harvesting was accompanied by other food collecting and producing activities such as shifting or permanent cultivation of root and other crops, gathering of wild plant foods, raising animals such as chickens and pigs, and fishing in the lagoons or on the reefs around the islands. In addition, after Western contact, people in many Oceanic cultures also harvested, sundried, and processed coconut meat into copra for sale for processing into coconut oil.

Shifting Cultivation

Shifting cultivation first appeared about 10,000 B.C. in the Middle East and subsequently appeared elsewhere either through independent invention or diffusion from one culture to another. It first appeared in Europe about 5000 B.C. and was the primary subsistence strategy used to clear the forests following the Ice Age and to convert much of the European landscape into farmland. In most of Europe, shifting cultivation was replaced hundreds of years ago by mixed farming with crop rather than field rotation and lasted only into the twentieth century in northern Europe. Prior to the spread of Western-style intensive agriculture based on irrigation, artificial fertilization, mechanized farming, and monocropping in the nineteenth and twentieth centuries, horticulture was a worldwide subsistence strategy. Of the 46 percent of the world's cultures that relied in part on horticulture for food in the eighteenth through the early twentieth centuries, 29 percent were located in sub-Saharan Africa, 28 percent on the islands of Southeast Asia and Oceania, 24 percent in South and Central America, 10 percent in North America, 7 percent in East Asia, and only 2 percent in the Middle East and Europe.

Shifting cultivation is known by a variety of other names. Social scientists, agronomists, and government officials often use forest fallow rotation, slash-and-burn agriculture, fire agriculture, and swidden farming for what here is called shifting cultivation. Names used regionally or by horticultural peoples themselves include in Africa: *masole, chitemene,* and *tavy*; in Central and South America: *milpa, coamile, ichali,* and *conuco*; and in Asia: *chena, bewar, kaingin,* and *tagal*. The term *swidden* refers to the plot of land—the garden—cleared by slashing and burning and comes from an old English word for "burned clearing." The term *fallow* is used both in reference to the garden plot that is left to return to its natural vegetative state and to the period of time it is in the fallow state before it is slashed and burned into a swidden.

The two key features of horticulture as a subsistence activity are clearing the swidden and fertilizing it through the slash-and-burn strategy and field rotation—from fallow to swidden and back to fallow. While the details of the slash-and-burn technique vary from culture to culture, the overall process is largely the same. First, a site must be selected and often permission to use it obtained from the village headman or kin group leader. The trees on the site are then felled, girdled, or stripped of some or all of their branches and the underbrush cut away and spread across the site. Sometimes, additional brush will be brought in from the nearby forest or from a firebreak cut around the site. The slash on the site is allowed to dry and is then set on fire and reduced to a layer of ash covering the entire swidden. Then, before the rains begin, the plants, seeds, roots, cuttings, and so forth are planted in the soil. After one to rarely more than three years, the swidden soil gives out; the swidden is abandoned; and a new site selected, slashed, burned, and planted. Usually, each horticulturalist has a number of swiddens planted and a number in fallow at any point in time.

Although horticulture involves far less permanent alteration of the environment than does agriculture, horticulture does require some alteration including the following:

1. Altering the terrain ranges from no alteration at all—especially where the land is flat, to the building of fences to keep out animals, to the building of terraces or ditches to manage the flow of water.

2. Clearing the land includes simply cutting off tree branches to allow sunlight to reach the ground, leaving all or some of the trees standing but clearing all other plants, clearing all vegetation from the swidden, and clearing all vegetation and also all roots.

3. Preparing the garden soil generally includes fertilization by slashing and burning, leaving the fertilized soil unworked and simply planting seeds or roots in it, more careful distribution of the ash on top of and also beneath the surface, mounding the soil, and the building of large mounds and hills separated by ditches.

4. Placing the crops in the swidden includes random planting, planned intercropping, and segregation of crops in separate sections or even in separate gardens.

While horticulture, when compared to other major subsistence strategies, requires less use of technology and less investment of time, it does require considerable knowledge by the horticulturalists. Most important is knowledge of the environment that must be used in selecting the garden site such as the condition of the soil, the location of the site in relation to a water source or neighboring villages, and knowledge of the uses and growth patterns of plants. The use of different types of terrain, different garden plans, and different plant placement strategies is a key element of successful horticulture and is typical of most horticultural societies. For example, the Dyaks of Borneo grow some 92 species of plants through the strategic use of a mix of four types of gardens: home, farm, swidden, and the fallow area. Home gardens are located near the households or communal longhouses or near the village and are used for growing nonstaples such as vegetables, spices, and ornamental and medicinal plants. The swidden is the primary garden and is cleared by slashing and burning and cultivated for 1 to 3 years and then left to fallow for 5 to 25 years. The main swidden crop is rice with the intercropping of corn, cassava, and sweet potatoes. Sugar palms, candlenuts, sago palms, and banana trees are left standing in the swiddens and their products are harvested as well. Farm gardens are much like the home gardens but are located within the large swiddens, but unlike the home gardens are abandoned when the swidden is left to fallow. The fallow area is used to gather wild plant food such as watermelons and ginger as well as serving as a source of bamboo and as a place to hunt game.

Horticultural Societies

Studies of traditional horticultural societies prior to massive change from Western contact suggested that they can be divided into two groups—small-scale and complex. Small-scale horticultural societies that in the twentieth century are found only in the Amazon basin in South America, the highlands of New Guinea, and parts of Southeast Asia accounted for about 22 percent of horticultural societies in modern times. They are characterized by relatively small populations of several thousand individuals who live in semipermanent villages with populations of about 100 people on average per village. In some groups, however, the villages may contain only a few dozen people and in others several hundred. The villages are autonomous political units usually governed by a headman or council of headmen whose authority is based on their kinship ties and their skills and powers of persuasion. Ties among villages are based on kinship (often through intermarriage), trade, reciprocal religious obligations, and alliances in warfare waged by villages against each other or against another society. An example of a modern small-scale horticultural society is the Yanomamö of the rainforest of southern Venezuela and northern Brazil. Estimates place the number of Yanomamö at about 20,000 living in some 360 villages. Villages consist of one large circular palm-thatch dwelling house with each family occupying a section of it. Settlements are abandoned periodically, primarily during periods of warfare with other villages and, more recently, in response to incursions by non-Indians. Each village operates as an independent unit although alliances between villages are common and important. Villages affairs, both internal and external, are managed by the headman who comes from the largest patrilineal kinship group in the village. Some Yanomamö are known for the almost continual state of violence that characterizes relations among men in the village and different villages. Others, however, are more peaceful. Yanomamö subsistence centers on horticulture that provides some 85 percent of food, although occupies less time than do hunting, fishing, and gathering that provide most of the additional 15 percent of food. Yanomamö swiddens—ideally made in lightly vegetated areas of the forest near a water source—are cleared, planted, and prepared with axes and digging sticks, and the slashed underbrush burned to form a layer of ash. The most laborious task is the transport of the heavy plantain cuttings to new swiddens. The primary garden crops are bananas and plantains that are supplemented by plantings of sweet and bitter manioc, taro, sweet potatoes, maize, tobacco, cotton, and the harvesting of tree fruits and nuts. Gardens are moved periodically when the soil gives out or, in villages engaged in warfare, when they are forced to flee to a safer location.

Complex horticultural societies in modern times are found in sub-Saharan Africa and Southeast Asia and account for about 78 percent of horticultural societies around the world. They are characterized by the indigenous manufacture and use of iron tools and much larger populations and settlements than small-scale horticultural societies. Complex horticultural societies may range in size from several thousand to several million, with villages averaging 280 inhabitants across cultures. In the past, some horticultural societies such as the Maya and Yoruba supported urban centers with large populations. These cultures are labeled advanced because their economic, social, and political systems are more multilayered and complex than in small-scale societies. This complexity includes multiple layers of political organization often with a king at the top, social stratification based on wealth, slavery, occupational specialists who subsist by selling their products and services, and large, permanent villages. As with small-scale horticulturalists, kinship ties remain important but are now but one of many sets of relationships that structure relations in the society. An example of a modern horticultural society are the Yoruba of West Africa, who number about 20 million and live mainly in southern Nigeria and also neighboring Benin and Togo. Over the centuries at any point in time, Yoruba settlements have ranged from small camps to cities of up to 60,000 inhabitants. The traditional political system centered on rulers of specific kingdoms and a council of chiefs who represented the religious, kinship, military, economic, and other segments of Yoruba society. Villages followed the same basic structure with representatives of the king maintaining ties to the villages. An individual's and family's social status was and continues to be based on sex (men have higher status than women in general), kin group affiliation, and wealth. Craft specializations include weavers, wood carvers, carpenters, tailors, and shoemakers, in the past organized into craft guilds. Other important occupations are traders, government officials, and priest and priestess. The traditional economy, which in the past 50 years has given way to agriculture and industry to some extent, was based on subsistence and cash horticulture and trade supplemented by hunting, fishing, and the selling of manufactured goods. The main subsistence crops, whose value varies across Yoruba regions, are beans, yams, cassava, and maize. The swiddens are cleared with hand tools and burned and then the crops are both intercropped and planted in sequence to ensure a supply of food for the entire year. The fallow period varies from region to region and can range from two to ten years. The major cash crops are cocoa and kola in the forest regions and cotton and tobacco in the savanna regions.

Horticultural Societies Today

Today, horticultural societies are found almost exclusively in tropical and savanna regions north and south of the equator in Central and South America, Africa, and insular Southeast Asia. Traditionally and today, horticulture requires a relatively small population, low population density, and a considerable amount of open land to regularly yield enough food over the years to support semipermanent villages. In tropical regions, horticulture traditionally was a successful subsistence strategy because it controlled many of the problems that resulted from the heavy, seasonal rains and poor soil typical of the tropics. These problems include erosion of the soil and the leeching out of nitrogen and phosphorus, two elements necessary for plant growth. Slash-and-burn horticulture controls these problems by directly returning phosphorus to the soil though the ash, indirectly returning nitrogen through bacterial action stimulated by the plant matter added to the soil, and by preventing erosion during swidden years by means of the dense plant coverage and during the fallow period when the swidden is overgrown with plants. Additionally, a proper mix of techniques enables horti-

culturalists to grow a variety of staple crops and secondary crops and to continually exploit the swidden even after it is left to fallow. Horticulture also produces a high return in food calories in relation to the calories invested in it, although it also produces a relatively low yield in relation to the amount of land used.

The conditions that made horticulture a viable subsistence strategy—small population, low population density, much land—are now changing around the world and horticulture is rapidly disappearing. Although some 300 million people still derive much of their food from horticulture, their numbers and the number of horticultural societies are decreasing. One major factor in the demise of horticulture is a shortage of land caused in part by private interests and governments in the Third World that acquire or take land previously controlled by horticultural peoples and use it for farming, ranching, mining, industrial complexes, roads, airstrips, and towns. Additionally, the size and density of horticultural societies have been increasing over the twentieth century, largely due to better medical prevention and treatment programs. The combination of more people and less land has initiated a sequence of events in many horticultural societies in which more land is used for gardening, fallow periods are shortened, and eventually there is no longer enough land to support the larger population. Horticulture is no longer a sustainable activity. This pattern not only damages the horticultural economy but also often the environment—much land is left uncovered by plant growth leading to often extensive erosion, especially in mountainous regions. As a consequence, many horticulturalists have been drawn into national or regional industrializing economies in which wage labor replaces subsistence horticulture. Efforts to sustain horticulture through the use of chemical fertilizers, the mixing of cash crops with subsistence crops, and the use of imported plant species with shorter growing seasons or which are drought or disease resistant have generally not been successful.

Bascom, William. (1969) *The Yoruba of South-western Nigeria.*

Chagnon, Napoleon A. (1968) *Yanoamo: The Fierce People.*

Christensen, Hanne, and Ole Mertz. (1993) "The Risk Avoidance Strategy of Traditional Shifting Cultivation in Borneo." *The Sarawak Museum Journal* 44:1–18.

Ember, Carol R., and Melvin Ember. (1990) *Cultural Anthropology.* 6th ed.

Lenski, Gerhard, and Jean Lenski. (1974) *Human Societies: An Introduction to Macrosociology.*

Murdock, George P. (1981) *Atlas of World Cultures.*

Oliver, Douglas L. (1989) *Oceania: The Native Cultures of Australia and the Pacific Islands.*

Russell, W. M. S. (1977) "The Slash-and-Burn Technique." In *Man's Many Ways: The Natural History Reader in Anthropology*, edited by Richard A. Gould and *Natural History Magazine*, 71–76.

Schusky, Ernest L. (1989) *Culture and Agriculture: An Ecological Introduction to Traditional and Modern Farming Systems.*

HOT AND COLD STATES

In physical terms, hot and cold refer to the relative temperature of an object. Temperature is often judged in everyday life relative to the temperature of the human body, in accord with personal preference, or is measured on the Fahrenheit or Celsius scales—while scientists use the Kelvin scale. While temperature can be measured objectively, in many cultures hot and cold take on symbolic meanings that go well beyond temperature as a measurable form of energy. The emotional and symbolic content of hot and cold is suggested by just a few definitions in the *Concise Oxford Dictionary*:

> *cold*—lacking ardour, friendliness or affection; depressing, dispiriting, uninteresting (cold facts); at one's mercy (he had me cold), sexually frigid; without preparation or rehearsal

> *hot*—ardent, passionate, excited; eager, keen; fresh, recent; very skillful; strongly rhythmical or emotional; stolen goods

These definitions and others of hot and cold are reflected in numerous words and word combinations in English such as coldhearted, cold-blooded, cold shoulder, hot potato, hot stuff, and hot tempered. In other cultures, the meanings associated with hot and cold also go beyond the measurable temperature of an object. The Shona of Kenya equate cool with calm and are much concerned about keeping the spirit of a deceased person cool to discourage the spirit from entering the deceased's village and causing harm to others. Through rituals and strict adherence to burial customs, the spirits are kept cool. Special attention is given to the spirits of chiefs and adults with children as their spirits are believed to be more capable of causing serious harm. In Inner Mongolia, a person's eyes are considered cold and therefore will be weakened by hot objects and must be treated with cold medicines. One man reported than his eyes were damaged from using binoculars because such instruments are hot, as proved by the ability of a lens to cause fire.

In some cultures, entire categories of people are classified as either hot or cold. In Europe, for example, people from Mediterranean nations such as Spain and Italy are considered hot—lively, loud, fun-loving, sexual—while those from northern nations such as England or Sweden are considered cold—reserved, quiet, serious, modest. These beliefs may derive from climatic differences between the north and south. Among the Tzeltal in Mexico, the reverse is believed to be true: lands of the northern communities are considered hot and more fertile and those of the cold south. In other cultures, specific categories of people are considered to be either hot or cold. Among the Tamil in southern India, menstruation and pregnancy are considered hot states and therefore the bodies of women in these conditions are considered hot. Considerable concern is shown over girls experiencing their first menses and efforts such as altering their diet are made to control their hot state. Since the hot state is thought to be of a sexual nature, marriage and frequent sexual intercourse are sometimes recommended as a permanent cure. Pregnant women are not allowed to eat foods such as garlic or chicken as these are hot foods that will make them even hotter and cause boils or other skin problems. After birth, the mother's body is considered to be cool and she is then fed these foods to make her hotter. Control of diet including fasting (which increases heat) is used by the Tamil because they believe that heat is stored in the belly where it can concentrate and increase. Eating and baths are used to dissipate the stored heat.

The Chewong of Malaysia use the concepts of hot and cool in a more general sense than in most cultures to help them order their world and make distinctions between the natural world, the world of humans, and the supernatural world. Just as culture and nature and culture and the supernatural are seen as opposites, so too are the states of hot and cold. Everything classified as either hot or cold is considered harmful and is linked with disease. Coolness, on the other hand, is associated with health, immortality, and fertility. Human beings and the world they live in and create are hot while the world of the supernatural and supernatural beings are cool. The aspects of nature that are not used by humans, such as the forest, are also considered cool. To communicate with the supernatural and to use supernatural forces to cure

illness, the Chewong communicate through powerful healers who are believed to have exchanged their hot blood with the cool blood of supernatural figures. Other healers take cold baths or cool their faces and bodies with special smoke to become cool. In curing the sick, the healer's goal is to make the sick person cool through spells, application of dew, blowing of smoke, or sleeping on the ground in the forest. As certain foods are considered hot, the diet is altered to eliminate meat—a primary source of heat, salt, oil, lemongrass, and other hot foods. The Chewong employ the concepts of hot and cool in these symbolic and ritual ways to help maintain the balance between nature and culture and their day-to-day world and the world of the supernatural.

Bourdillon, Michael F. C. (1976) *The Shona Peoples: An Ethnography of the Contemporary Shona with Special Reference to their Religion.*

Howell, Signe. (1984) *Society and Cosmos: Chewong of Peninsular Malaya.*

Lattimore, Owen. (1941) *Mongol Journeys.*

Redfield, Robert, and Alfonso Villa Rojas. (1939) "Notes on the Ethnography of Tzeltal Communities of Chiapas." *Contributions to American Anthropology and History* 5:105–119.

Reynolds, Holly B. (1978) *To Keep the Tali Strong: Women's Rituals in Tamilnad, India.*

HUNTING-GATHERING

Hunter-gather cultures are food collectors. They derive all or most of their subsistence from wild plants, animals, fish, shellfish, reptiles, insects, and other natural food sources in their environment. The hunter-gatherer subsistence system (also called foraging or collecting) in its various forms around the world differs from other major subsistence systems—horticulture, agriculture, and pastoralism—in that the other systems are based on food production rather than collecting. While hunting-gathering is usually discussed as a single type of subsistence system, there are in fact four different subtypes of hunter-gatherers as described below: the classic nomadic hunter-gatherers, affluent hunter-gatherers, hunter-gatherers of the tropical rainforests, and horseback hunters.

Hunting-gathering was the only subsistence strategy used by human beings for several million years up to the appearance of horticulture, agriculture, and pastoralism beginning about 10,000 years ago. Thus, for over 99 percent of human existence, humans have been hunter-gatherers; the long-ago ancestors of all modern humans were hunter-gatherers. Since the beginning of continual Western colonial expansion and domination, the percentage of hunter-gatherers in the world has been rapidly decreasing as a percent of the entire world population. These decreases in the percentage of hunter-gatherers and the actual number of hunter-gatherer cultures and of hunter-gatherers is due to a number of factors: (1) the dramatic growth in the number of people living in other types of cultures, especially agricultural ones and (2) the disappearance of hunter-gather cultures and hunter-gatherers through genocide; epidemics of introduced diseases; displacement from indigenous territories; forced settlement on reservations; and involvement in local, regional, and international economic systems. In the contemporary world, pure hunter-gatherers—those who live exclusively or almost exclusively on wild foods—are extinct. At the end of this article is a list of some hunter-gatherer peoples known to have survived into the nineteenth or twentieth century and whose traditional way of life has been described by ethnographers.

Hunter-gatherers have always fascinated people living in industrialized societies. At various times hunter-gatherers have been stereotyped in idealized and romanticized terms as "uncivilized savages," "helpless children," and most recently as "noble savages" who live in harmony with nature. The most recent demonstration of fascination with hunter-gatherers was the so-called "discovery" in 1971 of the 26 Tasaday of the Philippines who lived in caves and ate only wild foods such as frogs, bananas, and berries they collected but lived an easy life in which they collected food only two to three hours per day. The Tasaday were the subject of numerous newspaper and magazine articles and films around the world. Subsequent research showed that the Tasaday were a people who had previously been farmers but in the 1880s split off and moved into the forest where they lived much like other Philippine hunter-gatherers—by hunting, gathering, growing rice and root crops, and trading with villages two-and-a-half miles away.

None of these stereotypes, like that of the Tasaday, are accurate for two reasons. First, all are based on perceptions of outsiders whose knowledge of hunter-gatherer life is often minimal. Second, the hunter-gatherer subsistence systems vary across cultures with a number of different subtypes. Thus, it is inaccurate to think of all hunter-gatherers as being the same except for their reliance on food collecting as opposed to food production.

Modern hunter-gatherers are of interest also because their way of life might tell us something about the way of life of hunter-gatherers of the past; that is, the way of life of the ancestors of all modern peoples. For this to be the case, modern hunter-gatherers would need to be survivals from the past whose way of life has gone unchanged for tens of thousands of years. Unfortunately, while the study of modern hunter-gatherers can be helpful in reconstructing hunter-gather life in human prehistory, their

A Cherokee in North Carolina demonstrates hunting technique with a blowgun.

value in this regard is limited by four realities. First, modern hunter-gather groups live in marginal environments—deserts, the arctic, and tropical rainforests—while earlier hunter-gatherers lived in all ecological regions. Thus, the adaptation patterns of modern groups in limited environments may not tell us much about the adaptation of earlier peoples in richer environments. Second, modern hunter-gatherers are not survivals from the past, but each group has an evolutionary history just like all cultures. Some have evolved from peoples who were hunter-gatherers long ago, but others such as the Tasaday have devolved from other forms of subsistence. Third, many hunter-gatherers, like the Tasaday, the San-speaking peoples in southern Africa, and aboriginal peoples in northern Australia, have been in contact with non–hunter-gatherer cultures for hundreds or even thousands of years. In fact, it is likely that all hunter-gatherers in tropical rainforest environments in Africa, South and Southeast Asia, Australia, and Central and South America in both the past and present have had trade relations with other non–hunter-gatherer groups. They traded forest products for cereals, fish, meat, and other foods as well as for material goods. In South America, many hunter-gatherers also engaged in some farming themselves. This contact often involved trade that supplied food necessary for survival and introduced new cultural elements that altered hunter-gatherer settlement and food-getting practices. Fourth, the lifeways of many hunter-gatherers have changed since the beginning of European colonization in the 1400s. The use of the hunter-gatherers' traditional territories for mining, lumbering, farming, and ranching; the closing of traditional territories by national borders; involvement in the fur trade; the replacement of traditional technology with manufactured goods; settlement on reservations; and other factors have changed most if not all hunter-gatherer cultures. (See Table H-1 for a list of long-standing hunter-gather cultures

that survived into the nineteenth or twentieth century.)

The changes undergone over the past several hundred years by hunter-gatherers and the current situation of some hunter-gatherers are indicated by the San-speaking peoples of southern Africa. San is the general name used for over ten different groups in Botswana, Namibia, and Angola who in the past or now are described as living a hunting-gathering way of life. Estimates place the number of San at about 50,000 in these three nations with the majority in Botswana. Commonalities in geophysical features across this large region include a hot season from October to May, heavy rains during that season, hot summers, and cold winter nights. The San live in extended family homesteads with a settlement containing up to 300 persons. Houses are mainly single-room of wattle-and-daub construction with thatched roofs. Grass huts are used in temporary camps; some nomadic San use simple windbreaks. Most San live in the permanent villages and travel to temporary camps near water sources to hunt and collect plant foods. Although well known as hunter-gatherers in a seemingly harsh environment, today—and probably for some time—only about 5 percent of the San subsist mainly by hunting and gathering. For about 500 years, most have subsisted through a combination of hunting, gathering, herding, farming, and trade with neighboring non-San peoples. Hunting and gathering has been most common in times when these other subsistence practices were difficult because of drought or interference by national governments. Land rights are held by sets of related families and others must ask permission to use the land. Leadership traditionally rested with a "chief," whose role is now much reduced.

As noted above, there are different types of hunter-gatherers with distinctions made among food storers and nonstorers, nomadic and sedentary, sharers and hoarders, poor and affluent, and on the basis of the basic subsistence

TABLE H-1 SOME CLASSIC AND TROPICAL FOREST HUNTER-GATHER CULTURES THAT SURVIVED INTO THE NINETEENTH OR TWENTIETH CENTURY

Africa
Aka
Dorobo
Efe
Hadza
Koroca
Mbuti
San

Asia
Agta
Andamanese
Aru Islanders
Ata
Batak
Batek
Birhor
Boyas
Chenchu
Irula
Jalaris
Ket
Korwa
Kubu
Kuki
Kurumba
Malapantaram
Mamanwa
Nyaka
Paliyan
Penan
Punun
Raji
Ruc
Saoch
Semang
Semaq Beri
Sulung
Tac-Cui
Toala
Vedda
Yanadi

Yerkulas
Yumbri

Australia and Oceania
Aranda
Asmat
Dieri
Kamilaroi
Karadjeri
Kariera
Mardudjara
Ngatatjara
Pintubi
Tiwi
Warlpiri
Wik Mungkan
Wongaibon
Yir Yoront
Yolngu
Yukaghir
Yungar

North America
Achomawi
Baffinland Inuit
Cahuilla
Central Yup'ik Eskimo
Chimariko
Chipewyan
Chugach
Coast Yuki
Copper Inuit
Cowichan
Cree
Digueno
Dogrib
East Greenland Inuit
Flathead
Hare
Ingalik
Ingulik Inuit
Inughuit
Kaibab

Karok
Kaska
Kutchin
Labrador Inuit
Lake Yokuts
MacKenzie Inuit
Modoc
Montagnais
Netsilik Inuit
North Alaskan Eskimos
Nunamiut
Panamint
Pomo
Seri
Tubatulabal
Tututni
Washo
West Greenland Inuit
Wintu
Yavapai

South America
Ache
Akuriyo
Aweikoma
Bororo
Botocudo
Chamacoco
Choroti
Guato
Heta
Maku
Mataco
Mocovi
Nambicuara
Ona
Paraujano
Shiriana
Siriono
Warrau
Yahgan
Yuqui

technology—hunting, gathering, or fishing. In addition, there are specialized types including affluent hunter-gatherers and horseback hunters.

Hunting-Gathering-Fishing

All hunter-gatherers traditionally lived by either hunting, gathering, fishing, or some combination of the three. One survey of 180 hunter-gatherer cultures in the seventeenth through the twentieth centuries indicates that 30 percent subsist mainly by gathering, 25 percent by hunting, and 38 percent by fishing.

Hunting involves the use of weapons (bows and arrows, lances, spears, blowguns with darts, harpoons, stones, and so forth); nets; traps; and snares to capture and kill land animals, sea mammals, birds, waterfowl, and large reptiles. Hunting is a male activity and can be done by individuals or more commonly, for large game, by groups of hunters. Depending on the environment, hunter-gatherers collected a wide variety of foods including wild animal products such as eggs and honey, insects, small reptiles, herbs, leaves, blossoms, edible tree pith, seeds, fruits, vegetables, berries, nuts, shellfish, and also dug roots and tubers. Gathering was usually women's work and in many cultures contributed a substantial amount of protein to the diet. In addition to food, fuel, raw materials such as reeds and grasses, and clay were gathered to make vessels; materials for dwelling construction were also gathered. The collection of water was the most important collection activity. Fishing took the form of catching true fish with hooks, nets, traps, baskets, dams, and by poisoning. In some cultures, both hunting and gathering techniques are used in fishing—such as the spearing of fish or shooting them with arrows or the damming of rivers and then the collection of the trapped masses of fish in baskets or with hooks.

In many cultures, traditional hunting and fishing (and sometimes gathering) were group or communal activities. Cooperative hunting involving a number of men was common when large animals such as seals, whales, buffalo, or kangaroo were hunted. These activities were conducted communally when a large quantity of animals, fish, or insects could be taken at one time. Communal foraging took the form of either surrounding an animal so it could not escape and then killing it or driving a single animal or a herd into a trap or over a cliff where they were killed and butchered. For example, Shoshone Indians in Utah traditionally drove grasshoppers into large pits where they were killed; Caribou Inuit women and children acted as beaters, driving caribou herds into ravines or water or over cliffs; Australian aboriginals would surround a kangaroo or emu at a waterhole or prevent these animals from escaping by building a fire around them.

Hunter-gatherers utilize five types of sites: residential base camps, foraging locations, field camps, caches to store food, and stations. In utilizing these sites, they use two different mobility strategies. One type of hunter-gatherer culture, called foragers, uses a residential pattern of movement with moves made on the basis of the availability of different plant or animal foods in their foraging territory. Another type of hunter-gatherer culture, called collectors, uses a logistical strategy in which they base their activities at a residential camp and use the other sites as needed. Some hunter-gatherers mainly use the residential pattern, others the logistical pattern, and still others combine elements of both. For example, the Kawich Mountain Shoshone use the residential strategy; their neighbors, the Owens Valley Paiute, use the logistical strategy; and another neighboring group, the Reese River Shoshone, use both, transporting food to residential camps in the winter and moving to food location sites during the summer.

Within the hunting-gathering-fishing framework are many hunter-gatherer cultures who fit the model of the "classic" hunter-gatherer. Additional cultural features associated with this type of hunter-gatherer culture are small communities; low population density—each community collects food over a very large territory; free access to land; frequent movements in search of food or water; an egalitarian social order with leadership based on knowledge or skills; and a division of labor based on sex in which women gather, perform domestic chores, and care for the children while men hunt or fish. The following descriptions of the Ache of the forest in Paraguay and the Copper Inuit of northern Canada point to the basic features of the "classic" hunter-gatherer culture as well as differences among hunter-gatherers and to their fate in the modern world.

The Ache live in the forest of the mountains and foothills of eastern Paraguay and have been there since at least the 1600s, although continual contact with Westerners began only in the early 1960s. The five related Ache groups number about 600 and since 1976 have all lived on reservations or in communities associated with missionaries. Before placement on reservations, the Ache lived in nomadic bands ranging in size from 3 to 160 persons who moved about once a week. Campsites were selected because of access to food—either palm trees for their fiber and heart or wild game. Water was widely available and was not a factor in selecting campsites. Ache sleep on the ground on leaves or leaf mats and build only small palm-covered huts to protect themselves from heavy rains. Today, the Ache subsist through a combination of growing manioc and corn, wage labor, and traditional hunting and gathering in the forest. Men hunt either alone or in groups with bows and arrows for peccaries, monkeys, rodents, deer, and other animals and collect honey. Women gather plant foods and fruits, transport the family's goods, and care for the children. Food is shared among members of the band. The Ache continue to make most of their material objects themselves including bows and arrows, clubs, palm-leaf baskets, clay pots, stone axes, and bamboo flutes. Membership in bands was fluid although rela-

tives tended to join the same band. The nuclear family was the basic unit of production and consumption. All Ache were free to use the forest as they pleased; they had no concept of land ownership or territorial control. Today, the Ache are confined to four small reservations with use of the forest limited to hunting and gathering trips. Traditionally, there were no leaders although a few older men in each band made the major decisions for the group. Today, a clear leadership role has emerged and such positions are often held by younger men who are used to dealing with non-Ache.

Copper Inuit (formerly Eskimo) is a term used by outsiders for a number of related Inuit communities who occupy Victoria Island and the adjacent mainland in the Canadian Arctic. This region is one of extreme cold, snow, and ice with snow on the ground from September until June and the temperature below 50 degrees Fahrenheit year-round. Continual Western contact began in 1910, although the Copper Inuit had both peaceful and violent relations with the neighboring Netsilik, Caribou, and Mackenzie Inuit before then. The Copper Inuit were settled in government-sponsored communities in the 1950s and 1960s that, along with involvement in the fur trade earlier in the century, markedly altered the traditional hunting and fishing economy. Other than brush used occasionally for lighting lamps, the Copper Inuit used no plant matter. Their subsistence was based on an annual cycle of winter seal hunting, fishing on inland lakes, caribou hunting, and fishing on rivers. Food was stored for use in the fall before the seal hunting season began again in December. In the winter months, they resided in temporary houses made of snow (igloos) in communities of about 100 residents, many of whom were related to one another by marriage. These camps relocated about once a month when seal hunting declined. In the spring, they lived in dwellings with snow walls and skin roofs; in the summer, the camps broke up into smaller units

Cofan hunter applying curare to dart point

that moved almost every day, living in skin tents. Men hunted while women and men fished and built the dwellings; women alone sewed the clothing and tents, handled domestic chores, and supervised the children. Today, in the permanent villages, men hunt fox for their furs and engage in wage labor. Included in the basic Copper Inuit tool kit were harpoons, lances, bows and arrows, and sleds. Dogs assisted in hunting but became useful as pack animals only after Western contact and involvement in the fur trade. Groups were identified with a particular territory but there was no sense of land ownership. Leadership was situational, with the advice of those who had proved knowledgeable about the task or situation in the past followed by the community.

These two cultures along with the San described above indicate some of the common features of hunter-gatherer life around the world, despite differences in environment: migration in order to optimize use of natural resources; seasonal shifts in subsistence activities; a division of labor based mainly on sex; weak leadership; and a decline in hunting and gathering as these peoples are settled and drawn into regional, national, and the world economies.

Affluent Foragers

Affluent foragers are the same as classic foragers; they derive all or most of their food by collecting it. They differ in that they have much larger populations, live in permanent or semipermanent communities, have a higher level of technological sophistication used to exploit natural resources, preserve and store large quantities of food for future use, have considerable material wealth beyond food and technological equipment, and are organized internally into distinct social classes. Thus, except for their food collecting subsistence strategy, affluent foragers more closely resemble agricultural societies. Cultures that traditionally fit the affluent forager model are the Ainu of northern Japan, the Gilyak and Itelman of Siberia, and dozens of Native American cultures along the Northwest Coast of North America and in central California. Groups in Japan, Siberia, and the Northwest Coast subsisted mainly by collecting large quantities of fish (of which salmon was the most important) during seasonal spawning runs and then preserving and storing them for use during the remainder of the year. Fishing was usually supplemented by other activities such as gathering plant foods, hunting land animals, and trade with other groups. Affluent foragers in California utilized acorns and processed acorn flour as their year-round staple and also relied on supplemental gathering, hunting, and fishing. For affluent foragers, the season when their basic staple was not available—the season of scarcity—was a time for social and ritual activities and for the making and maintenance of equipment used during the fishing and gathering season.

Affluent foragers, in contrast to classic hunter-gatherers, were able to live a settled life because of the large quantities of food they collected and stored. Storing the food year-round meant that they had no need to move regularly in search of food and also made it difficult to move. The steady food supply and living a settled life meant that women had more time free from subsistence activities and therefore could care for more children at one time. This led to a higher birth rate and more frequent births than is typical of classic hunter-gatherers and larger communities. These communities were also densely settled in villages, as the large food store could adequately support them throughout the year. Finally, the accumulation of wealth in the form of food and equipment such as canoes to obtain the food meant that excess food or personal skills such as canoe making could be exchanged for goods such as blankets or copperplates that carried with them value and status for the owner. This unequal distribution of material wealth within the communities then led to social inequality that on the Northwest Coast manifested itself in most groups having three social classes—high, commoner, and low—as well as craft specialists such as canoe makers, totem pole carvers, coppersmiths, and slaves who were captured or purchased from other cultures in the region. The following two cultures—the Tlingit of southern Alaska and the Yokut of central California—point to the essential features of affluent foraging as it existed during the 1880s.

In the past and today, the Tlingit occupy villages and own land along the southern coast of Alaska. Tlingit villages are located in protected coves along the Pacific Coast where they have access to drinking water and shellfish, beaches on which to store their canoes, and access to salmon migration routes. The Tlingit took huge quantities of salmon with hooks and nets and dried and smoked them for consumption in the winter months. They also hunted bear, deer, and goats, among others; fished for several species

An Efe man in central Africa making a honey basket.

of fish; and collected shellfish and wild berries and fruit. In addition to subsistence activities, some members of the communities also specialized as carvers, basket makers, weavers, and metalsmiths. The Tlingit traded some of what they collected, hunted, and produced with the other groups in the region and later with non-Indians for manufactured goods. Men hunted, fished, and carved; women cleaned the fish, gathered plant foods, and handled domestic chores. Tlingit society was organized into kinship groups and three social classes—high class, commoners, and the low class. Kinship clans owned the rights to fishing streams and hunting grounds. The Tlingit suffered serious depopulation and economic and political hardships following the acquisition of Alaska by the United States. Following some 50 years of struggle for their rights and aboriginal land, the Tlingit are now organized into nine village corporations with substantial landholdings. Some Tlingit men work as commercial fishermen while women work in canneries and make craft items.

Yokut is the name applied to some 40 different groups who, prior to European settlement, lived in south-central California primarily in and around the San Joaquin Valley. The Northern Yokuts subsisted on salmon collected with nets and spears in the fall and acorns collected in the spring, summer, and fall supplemented by the hunting of geese and ducks. The abundance of these resources enabled the Yokut to live in permanent settlements, with occasional use of hunting or fishing camps. The Yokuts also collected tule used for making baskets, roofing, rafts, cradles, and numerous other items. Men hunted, fished, and made tools; women gathered and wove items from tule and handled domestic and child-care responsibilities. Each Yokut group was lead by a hereditary headman and each group owned its own territory with each member hav-

ing rights to use it. Yokuts today live on reservations and earn their living by leasing land to non-Indians or working as wage or migrant laborers.

Horseback Hunters

The Native Americans of the Great Plains who hunted buffalo from horseback in the eighteenth and nineteenth centuries are an economically specialized type of cultural system. In some ways they were hunter-gatherers, as the hunting of buffalo was their major economic activity and the buffalo provided meat for food and raw material for clothing, tipi covers, furniture, containers, and various tools. However, unlike other hunter-gatherers, they did not rely solely or mainly on their own energy to collect food, but instead relied heavily on horses that had been first brought to the New World by the Spanish and had migrated northward. The Plains Indians also seemed like pastoralists in that they kept

Mbuti trading with Bantu-speaking neighbors in central Africa, a common practice among tropical forest hunter-gatherers

herds of horses on the open plain and an individual could amass personal wealth and prestige through horse ownership. Prior to the arrival of the horse, peoples who became horseback hunters were hunter-gatherers, farmers, or some mix of the two. The arrival of the horse changed their subsistence system and their way of life for a short period of about 100 years or less until the buffalo gave out and the Indians were defeated and placed on reservations by the United States. The Cheyenne were one such culture.

Originally, the Cheyenne lived on the grass-covered plains from what is now Montana south to Colorado and Kansas. Prior to their adoption of the horse by 1770, the Cheyenne had been mainly settled farmers and middlemen traders in the fur trade. With the adoption of the horse, the Cheyenne became nomadic bison hunters who traveled much of the year in ten separate bands, camping near rivers and coming together as a group in the summer for ceremonies. Hunting bison from horseback was the primary activity supplemented by the gathering of wild plant foods. The bison produced meat and raw materials for their own use as well as for trade with non-Indians. Men hunted, fought with other groups and the Americans, conducted ceremonies, and made all items for their own use. Women handled all domestic chores, gathering, and child care as well as moving and making camp. All Cheyenne could use resources in Cheyenne territory; each band used a particular region. Cheyenne society was organized by kinship and various social groups such as the ten bands, societies for men and women, and military societies with overall leadership in the hands of a council of 44 leaders representing the ten bands. Relations with the in-moving non-Indians became hostile after 1840, and by 1879 all the Cheyenne were defeated and placed on reservations in Oklahoma, Montana, and South Dakota where they continue to live and work as loggers, ranchers, and farmers.

Bailey, Robert C., et al. (1989) "Hunting and Gathering in Tropical Rain Forests: Is It Possible?" *American Anthropologist* 91:59–82.

Barnard, Alan. (1991) *Hunters and Herders: A Comparative Ethnography of Khoisan Peoples.*

Bicchieri, M., ed. (1972) *Hunters and Gatherers Today.*

Binford, Lewis R. (1980) "Willow Smoke and Dogs' Tails: Hunter-Gatherer Settlement Systems and Archaeological Site Formation." *American Antiquity* 45:4–20.

Damas, David. (1984) "Copper Eskimo." In *Handbook of North American Indians. Volume 5. Arctic*, edited by David Damas, 397–414.

Ember, Carol R. (1978) "Myths about Hunter-Gatherers." *Ethnology* 17:439–448.

Forbis, Richard G. (1978) "Some Facets of Communal Hunting." *Plains Anthropologist* 23–82:3–8.

Headland, Thomas N., ed. (1992) *The Tasaday Controversy: Assessing the Evidence.*

Hill, Kim, and M. Hurtado. (1989) "Hunter-Gatherers of the New World." *American Scientist* 77:436–443.

Jenness, Diamond. (1922) *The Life of the Copper Eskimos.*

Koyama, Shuzo, and David H. Thomas, eds. (1981) *Affluent Foragers.* Senri Ethnological Studies, no. 9.

Lee, Richard B., and Irven DeVore, eds. (1968) *Man the Hunter.*

Levinson, David, ed. (1991–1995) *Encyclopedia of World Cultures.*

Lustig-Arecco, Vera. (1975) *Technology: Strategies for Survival.*

Moore, John H. (1987) *The Cheyenne Nation: A Social and Demographic History.*

Murdock, George P., and Diana O. Morrow. (1970) "Subsistence Economy and Supportive Practices: Cross-Cultural Codes 1." *Ethnology* 9:302–330.

Parry, William. (1992) *An Ethnographic Bibliography for South and Southeast Asian Hunters and Gatherers.*

Tindale, Norman B. (1974) *Aboriginal Tribes of Australia: Their Terrain, Environmental Controls, Distribution, Limits, and Proper Names.*

Tollefson, Kenneth. (1976) *The Cultural Foundations of Political Revitalization among the Tlingit.*

Wallace, William. (1978) "Northern Valley Yokuts." In *Handbook of North American Indians. Volume 8. California*, edited by Robert F. Heizer, 462–470.

Wilmsen, Edwin. (1989) *Land Filled with Flies: A Political Economy of the Kalahari.*

Winterhalder, Bruce, and Eric A. Smith, eds. (1981) *Hunter-Gatherer Foraging Strategies: Ethnographic and Archeological Analyses.*

ICE

See PRECIPITATION.

IRRIGATION

Irrigation is the deliberate supply of freshwater to soil to promote the growth of crop plants. Irrigation involves human-made alterations to the natural environment, the use of technology to make those changes, and specific social and political arrangements to manage the system. Irrigation is a productive form of water control; it involves human intervention meant to exploit more fully water resources as opposed to protective forms of water control such as dams or drainage and flood control systems designed to prevent or control the potentially harmful effects of water to human settlements. While irrigation systems across cultures vary widely in scale, technology, and the administrative arrangements to manage them, all systems require a source of water, a means of delivering the water from its source to the fields to be irrigated, and a method of distributing the water in the fields.

The archaeological record shows that irrigation dates to several thousand years B.C. and is associated—although on varying scales—with the emergence of major state-level societies (civilizations) in Egypt, Mesopotamia, China, South Asia, South America, and Middle America. Prior to Western expansion that spread irrigation further and intensified its use where it already existed, irrigation was practiced by indigenous peoples in the highlands of western South America and Middle America, in East and South Asia, the Middle East, North Africa, southern Europe, southwestern North America, and on some islands in Polynesia and Micronesia. Irrigation is used mainly by farmers in rural areas and most often in valleys that are fed by rivers and streams or by springs from the surrounding hills and mountains. Today, all nations in tropical and temperate climates rely heavily upon irrigation to grow crops; some 320 million acres around the world are under irrigation. The trend around the world is for systems that were based on low-level technology to be replaced by larger, centralized systems based on gas or electric pumping systems.

Irrigation systems can be differentiated from one another in three ways: (1) by the primary irrigation technique, (2) by the technology used to acquire the water, and (3) by the form of sociopolitical organization used to manage the system. The major irrigation techniques used around the world are surface irrigation in which fields or furrows are flooded by water flowing onto them, sprinkler irrigation in which water is sprayed from above down onto the soil surface, and subirrigation in which pipes bring water to the plant roots.

The primary technologies used in irrigation systems are either gravity or pumps. Gravity systems rely on water sources flowing on the

An irrigated rice paddy in Thailand

surface such as rivers, streams, and springs. Water is brought to the fields in open ditches, lined channels, or pipes and then allowed to spread across the field or along furrows by opening or closing a series of dams or sluice gates. To be effective, such systems must have a steady supply of water (or a means of storing water such as in a reservoir for future use) and the water must flow in the desired direction and at the right speed. Pump systems use pumps powered by humans, animals, gas, electricity, or wind to bring underground water to the surface and then move it along channels or through pipes to the fields. Pump systems based on gas or electric pumps take water from deeper in the earth and can spread it more widely and more precisely than gravity systems. For most of human history, gravity systems have been the norm, although they have been rapidly replaced by pump systems around the world during the twentieth century.

Not all gravity systems are reliable. Over the course of human history various tools have been developed to raise water that flows below the level of the fields. Prior to the introduction of gas-powered pumps, Egyptian farmers used a variety of water-raising methods, all of which were also used at some point in other cultures as well. The simplest and least effective method was for humans to haul water from rivers or wells in containers or for men to stand in the river and pitch water up onto the field with large, flat pans. More effective methods that lessened the reliance on human power were the shadoof, waterwheel, and Archimedes' screw. The Archimedes' screw, or water-lifting auger, is a barrel-shaped device with a large wooden screw auger inside. The barrel is placed at an angle with the lower end in water and the screw turned with a crank at the top, bringing the water up to the top where it is allowed to spill into a ditch for conveyance to the field. A waterwheel contains wheels aligned with one another so that when the large wheel, set parallel to the ground, is turned counterclockwise, the vertical wheel, with pots attached to it, moves through the water filling the pots and dumping their contents in a ditch as they reach the riverbank. The waterwheel was generally powered by a blindfolded animal such as an ox or buffalo driven by a boy around and around in a circle. A shadoof is an invention of Egypt designed to make the transfer of irrigation water from the riverbed to higher land easy and efficient. A shadoof consists of a pivoted beam attached to a post or two posts sunk into the ground, with a water container at one end and a weight of rock or mud at the other. The beam is lowered into the water to fill the container, and then a gentle push by the operator effectively utilizes the counterweight to raise the container and then dump the water into an irrigation ditch. To raise water from an especially low riverbed, two or three shadoofs set one above the other can be used. While the shadoof was a major improvement over hauling water by hand, using it was long and difficult work nonetheless, as made clear by the following song of shadoof operators:

> Hast thou resolved upon strangling me, O God?
>
> Loosen the noose!
>
> No mother weeps [for me],
>
> No aunt,
>
> No sister!

Irrigation systems can also be classified on the basis of who owns or manages the system. In centralized systems, the system is managed and water rights are generally controlled by some central authority such as the national, state, or local government. Traditional systems, on the other hand, are managed by the farmers themselves either alone, in neighborhood or family groups, or in more formal local associations. These two categories of ownership are not mutually exclusive; in many cultures, both exist simultaneously.

In a general sense, irrigation is used to help produce a richer harvest of crops. Across cultures, farmers use irrigation to achieve this general goal in a variety of ways: (1) to control water shortages, (2) to supplement inadequate rain in the rainy season, (3) to replace evaporated rainwater, (4) to allow for cultivation in the dry season, (5) to extend the length of the growing season by planting a second crop, (6) to protect winter crops, (7) to have an earlier crop, (8) to plant on land not otherwise suitable for agriculture, and (9) to plant a greater variety of crops.

While irrigated fields are usually seen by outsiders as mainly or exclusively for growing crops, it is important to note that in some cultures in which irrigated fields are a part of everyday life, the fields can serve many other purposes. For example, the Ifugao of the Philippines who farm wet rice and other crops on spectacular irrigated terraces use the top layer of soil in their terrace pond fields for at least ten purposes other than growing crops. These include as a coating for dams, as a soaking pool to soften fiber used for rope, as a tank for catching small fish and snails for eating, as a playground for children, and as a breeding ground for edible insects. Irrigated land is also valuable property in cultures reliant on irrigation agriculture. Ownership of such land can be a source of prestige, status, and economic and political power. Because of its value in and of itself and apart from the value of the crops raised on it, the disposition of such land in many cultures is controlled by various written and unwritten laws that stipulate how much land may be sold or leased, to whom (kin, nonkin, outsiders, and so forth), for what purpose (profit, marriage transaction, inheritance), and for how much.

Although seen in most cultures as a highly effective means for exploiting the environment and relatively free of environmental problems, irrigation can have negative consequences. First, irrigation alters the ecosystem often by expanding the habitat of many animals who then compete with humans for food. For example, the rat population may expand rapidly and they may destroy some of the additional crop grown on irrigated land. Irrigation systems, especially those in tropical regions that utilize reservoirs of standing water, also can serve as breeding grounds for insects such as mosquitoes that spread diseases like malaria. Second, and most importantly, irrigation, especially large-scale pump irrigation, can cause environmental degradation. This degradation occurs through salinization—a process that occurs when irrigation causes the water table to rise and underground water to seep up to the surface through capillary action. As the water evaporates, it leaves behind salts that inhibit plant growth and may eventually make the soil unsuitable for some crops or ruin the field entirely. Such degradation through salinization has occurred in the Indus Valley in South Asia, near the Aswan Dam in Egypt, and on a smaller scale elsewhere. Lowering the water table with a drainage system can prevent salinization, although most irrigation systems are not built with accompanying drainage systems. Third, large-scale irrigation systems can also have the reverse effect and lower the water table, thereby causing water shortages and the disappearance of natural water resources as with the Aral Sea in the former Soviet Union and desiccation caused by decreased soil moisture. A final problem associated with irrigation is an escalation of conflict in communities that rely on irrigation. In all communities, irrigation is accompanied by disputes over water rights, ownership of water resources, responsibility for building and maintaining the system, and theft of water. Various attempts to control conflict are discussed below under Social and Political Aspects. Additionally, the introduction of irrigation or its transformation from a traditional to a centralized or

a gravity to a pump form may have a deep and permanent effect on social, political, and economic relations in the community. Common effects across cultures include absentee landowners, the intensification of wage labor, the replacement of subsistence crops with commercial crops, and involvement in the regional or national legal system. For example, in Sri Lanka in 1935, the government attempted to institute laws to control the sale or transfer of small irrigated holdings to prevent the division of farms into units too small for productive use.

Varieties of Irrigation Systems

The examples that follow summarize the nature and use of irrigation systems in different cultures. Three relatively simple systems are used by villagers in southern Spain, the Amhara in Ethiopia, and the Marquesas Islanders in Oceania. Traditionally, the countryside of southern Spain and other parts of Mediterranean Europe were dotted with small family farms, called *huertas* in Spain. These farmlands were irrigated by spring water flowing from the hills that were assigned by tradition to certain lands, with the amount of water available for irrigation determining the size of the farms. Farmers also used pumps in the field to bring ground water to the surface. The irrigation water was traditionally available to the farmers only during certain months (for example, 24 June–29 September in one community) and only on certain days (for example, Tuesdays and Saturdays) and to individual farmers for only a few hours on those days. At all other times, the flowing water was used in the mills. Disputes over water rights were a major source of conflict in these rural communities.

The Amhara of Ethiopia irrigate with river water to produce an early crop of barley that can be harvested before the rains in June. The irrigation system consists of sod- or stone-lined ditches running off the rivers and then channels into the fields that fall apart during the rainy season and must be rebuilt each year. The irrigation is highly effective when river water is plentiful. The green, irrigated fields stand out among the brown, unirrigated ones during the dry season.

The Marquesas Islanders use stream water to irrigate terraces on which they grow taro. Stone-lined ditches carry water to the terraces that are built in rows running parallel to the stream.

For several thousand years, communities in India have relied on irrigation to produce a succession of crops, a greater variety of crops, and to keep more land under cultivation than would be possible relying on rainwater alone. More recently, India has also converted irrigation water to other uses, such as to produce hydroelectric power. In general, irrigation has made life more secure for Indian farmers who would otherwise be reliant on the monsoon rains, but it has also led to many of the problems associated with large-scale irrigation such as salinization and the spread of insect-borne diseases. Across India, the general irrigation technologies used are canal, tank, well, and a variety of small-scale techniques. Canals that run parallel to rivers are used for inundation of fields but their value can be limited since they may run dry during the dry season. More reliable is perennial canal irrigation based on the control of river water flowing through pumping stations. Tanks (the name used in South Asia for what elsewhere are called reservoirs) have long been associated with irrigation in South Asia and continue to be used in India. They are mainly used in irrigation to supply water for wet rice cultivation on terraces and are not an especially efficient method; much of the water is lost to evaporation, many tanks run dry, and others fill with silt. Well irrigation is used by farmers in small fields. In the past these farmers used buckets, shadoofs, waterwheels, and other mechanical devices to bring the water to the surface. Today, gas or electric pumps are commonly used. The other forms of irrigation

A waterwheel on the White Nile in Sudan being used to irrigate a field

that are used include temporary dams and channels, the partial damming of rivers to create moist fields above the dam, water taken from waterholes or directly from rivers, and shafts driven into the ground to bring water from high water tables to the surface.

In the Oaxaca Valley of Mexico farmers irrigate in different seasons for different purposes. In the summer they irrigate to compensate for irregular rainfall and evaporation, in fall to plant a second crop or to keep the soil moist for the spring planting, and in winter to protect the alfalfa crop and to plant a second crop of corn. The farmers exploit rainwater, stream water, and groundwater, using each in different ways. They use rainwater in the summer when heavy rainfalls produce heavy flows of water in gullies down the hillsides. In a heavy rain, farmers rush to their hillside fields and dam the gullies with brush, channeling the water over their adjacent fields. When their fields are adequately irrigated, they release the flow and the next farmer down the hillside then takes his share of water. Stream-fed irrigation relies on a series of dams, canals, and subcanals, aqueducts across gullies, and gates to bring the water from hillside steams to the fields on the valley floor. In the past, the system was constructed of stone, brush, logs, and soil; more recently, canals have been lined with cement, reservoirs have been constructed, and underground channels that date back 2,300 years have also been lined with cement. Some farmers are also able to utilize water from high water tables by digging shallow wells in their fields and dumping water hauled up in buckets directly on nearby vegetable and flower plants.

Taiwan—like the United States, China, republics of the former Soviet Union, India, and Mexico—is heavily reliant on irrigation. The problem in Taiwan is that rain falls mostly only in May, June, and July and this water must be stored and distributed to agricultural land at other times during the year. Most communities rely on both the public irrigation system managed by the government and private systems managed by local cooperatives. The public system uses water flowing in rivers from the mountainous interior toward the coasts. On the plains the water is diverted by dams into canals and then into ditches running out to the rice fields. Water is then allowed to enter the field either through holes in ditch walls or is pumped up to the field by human-powered waterwheels or motor-driven pumps. The fields are allotted water on a rotating schedule, with those nearest the main canals and dams taking water first and those farthest away receiving it last. The area near the water source is called the water head and has an earlier growing season than the water tail area that is farthest from the water source. The water tail is also more likely to suffer during periods of water shortage. The private pumping associations develop and manage pumping

operations to irrigate land that is not covered by the public system. These systems can range in size from those owned by a few farmers and managed informally to large ones with a formal structure. Farmers become shareholders in the cooperative, entitling them to a share of water or, if a local association allows, a farmer may purchase water without becoming an owner. This privately irrigated land often gets water earlier and more reliably than tail areas irrigated by the public system and thus has become economically important land.

These examples of irrigation indicate that irrigation is used for different purposes, relies on different technologies, and is of considerably different scales in different societies around the world. However, regardless of differences in purpose, technology, and scale, the development and use of irrigation often has profound implications for the social and political organization of the culture and community.

Social and Political Aspects

For irrigation to be beneficial to the community, rules of behavior and an administrative structure must be developed and maintained. These rules and the administrative structure must deal with the construction and maintenance of the system and the allocation of the water. Construction requires the acquisition of building materials, equipment, labor, and sometimes special knowledge and skills. Maintenance requires surveillance, cleaning, and repair. Allocation requires the development and administration of rules and procedures for assigning water rights, collecting fees, accounting for use, and resolving the inevitable conflicts. Variation across cultures in the social and political arrangements relating to the management of irrigation systems is due to a mix of factors including the size of the system, whether it is a traditional or centralized system, whether the resource is used by one community or shared by a number of communities, the nature of the water source, and the type of technology used to exploit it.

One basic issue is who controls the water—a concern in all societies with irrigation except for those with very informal systems used by only one person or family. In modern, centralized systems such as the public system in Taiwan, water is controlled by a centralized political authority such as the nation or state and managed by an administrative bureaucracy under centralized control, often with local representatives involved at some level. In other societies, control may rest with the chief—as in traditional Hawaii where chiefs employed local leaders to manage the systems, with village councils, the kin group, or irrigation associations. Different systems in one society may be controlled by different groups, as in Taiwan.

Another issue is how to recruit labor to maintain the system, a dirty and onerous task in cultures with systems constructed of dirt, brush, and stones. In some cultures, cooperation is encouraged by turning the work into a village festival or by placing the burden on neighborhood, village, or kinship groups who cooperate in other tasks. In other cultures, coercion is more often employed such as hiring village leaders to supervise work teams or denying water to families who do not do their share.

A third issue revolves around controlling and settling conflicts that inevitably arise over water rights, access to water, and theft of water. Theft of water occurs with both gravity and pump systems. With gravity systems, it can take the form of diverting water to which another is entitled, irrigating one's fields for a longer time period than is allowed, or placing a field closer to a water source than existing fields. Theft of pump water often occurs at night when water is diverted from one field to another or when pumps are turned on or gates opened illegally. One method of controlling conflict is to establish laws governing water rights. The Ifugao of the Philippines, for example, required that

The law as to new fields. If all land below a spring or small stream located on ownerless land, be common land—that is, land without an owner—he who makes the first rice field below the source of the water supply is entitled to all the water needed for his rice field.

The law as to water. Water which has been flowing to an area of irrigated land may under no circumstances be diverted to irrigate a different area, even though that area may be nearer the source of water.

The law as to irrigation ditches. Constructors of an irrigation ditch may sell interest in the ditch. The ditch thus shared with others becomes an equal burden as to upkeep on all the owners.

The Ifugao enforced these laws by punishing multiple offenders. Diversion of water might result in a fine or even death; diversion from a ditch might result in all water being drained from the offender's field or a beating. In other cultures, the village or community leaders are often responsible for enforcing the rules and punishing offenders. In some locales, however, the theft of water becomes routine and while people don't like it, offenders are rarely caught or punished.

Irrigation and the Rise of Civilization

Irrigation of cropland is associated with the appearance of state-level political organizations around the world. Archaeologists have unearthed evidence of irrigation accompanying the development of civilization in China, the Indus Valley in South Asia, along the Nile River in Egypt, in highland Peru, Mesoamerica, and the fertile crescent in the Middle East. Some experts argue that use of irrigation and other water control technologies caused the rise of states by creating a need for a ruling elite to control the water resources, the technology, and the people who managed the system. Others see irrigation as a contributing, but not the only, factor. In one scenario, irrigation is seen as producing an agricultural surplus that, in turn, causes increased land and labor productivity that then results in many of the traits of civilization such as a large population, cities, social classes, and writing. However, the fact that not all cultures with irrigation developed into state-level societies suggests that irrigation alone will not always lead to civilization. Another view is that canal irrigation is the form of irrigation most often associated with ancient civilizations and that the use of canals allowed these states to grow and expand and in the process conquer and displace or subjugate neighboring peoples. Although it is not yet clear exactly how irrigation contributed to the rise of civilization, it is clear that irrigation played a major role and continues to play a major role in economic development around the world today.

See also ENVIRONMENTAL DISASTERS; PRECIPITATION; TERRACES; WATER.

Ammar, Hammed. (1954) *Growing Up in an Egyptian Village: Silwa, Province of Aswan.*

Ayrout, Henry H. (1945) *The Fellaheen*, translated by Hilary Wayment.

Barton, Roy F. (1919) *Ifugao Law.*

Blackman, Winifred S. (1927) *The Fellahin of Upper Egypt, Their Religious, Social, and Industrial Life Today with Special Reference to Survivals from Ancient Times.*

Buxton, D. R. (1949) "The Shoan Plateau and Its People: An Essay in Local Geography." *Geographical Record* 114:157–172.

Cohen, Ronald, and Elman R. Service, eds. (1978) *Origins of the State: The Anthropology of Political Evolution.*

Conklin, Harold C. (1967) "Some Aspects of Ethnogaphic Research in Ifugao." *Transactions of the New York Academy of Sciences.* Series II, 30:99–121.

Gallin, Bernard. (1966) *Hsin Hsing, Taiwan: A Chinese Village in Change.*

Handy, Edward S. C. (1923) *The Native Culture of the Marquesas.*

Leach, E. R. (1968) *Pul Eliya: A Village in Ceylon.*

Lees, Susan H. (1970) *Socio-Political Aspects of Canal Irrigation in the Valley of Oaxaca, Mexico.*

O'Malley, Lewis S., ed. (1941) *Modern India and the West: A Study of the Interaction of Their Civilizations.*

Pitt-Rivers, J. A. (1961) *The People of the Sierra.*

Spate, Oscar B. K. (1954) *India and Pakistan.*

Wittfogel, Karl. (1957) *Oriental Despotism: A Comparative Study of Total Power.*

or cattle have complex measurement systems. Thus, measures and measurement are cognitive tools used by humans to place economic and sometimes social and ritual value on elements of their environment.

All measurement systems require a means to discriminate the object or phenomena to be measured, a means of measuring its attributes, and a known quantity of the same object or of an analogous one to compare it with. The four basic measurements are mass or weight, area, length or distance, and volume or capacity. In the modern world, temperature, luminosity, pressure, electric current, and velocity are also routinely measured.

In the modern world, the four major measurement systems are the English, the U.S. Customary, the Metric, and the International System of Units. However, none of these systems is exclusive and more than one may be and often are used in the same nation or society, sometimes alongside indigenous measurement units. For example, the Highland Quechua of Ecuador operate in an economic environment that requires the use of metric measures such as meter and kilogram, Spanish colonial measures such as the *cuadra* (a measure of area equal to 84 meters on each side), English measures such as the pound, and local measures such as the mule-load.

Measurement Systems

Probably the first quantity to be measured by humans was distance, and the earliest measures were probably based on the length of body parts. One of the earliest known measures, dating to about 3000 B.C., was the Egyptian cubit—the distance from the elbow to the end of the fingertips on an extended arm and hand. This measure was standardized as the royal cubit, with a distance equivalent to 20.62 inches. The ancient Babylonians and Chinese, who also developed measurement systems, also used body-part length to measure distance. In non-Western

MEASURES AND MEASUREMENT

Measurement is the process of assigning numerical value to a physical quantity or phenomena. The term *measure* has a number of meanings, including, when used as a noun, the quantity found through measurement, an instrument such as a vessel or ruler used in measurement, or a unit of measure such as a bushel measure, and, when used as a verb, the actual act of measuring. Measurements made using the human senses alone are actually estimates; measures rely on the use of instruments and thus are more precise and reliable than estimates. Measurement is a cultural universal, although cultures vary widely in the types of measures used, the objects routinely measured, and the complexity of their measurement systems. The degree to which measurement is used and the complexity of the measurement system in a society is largely a function of the extent to which the culture controls and exploits its environment. Cultures that heavily exploit the environment and place economic value on the products of that exploitation such as land, harvested grains, trees,

societies, measures based on body-part length were commonly used in the manufacture of tools, implements, and clothing until these items were replaced by the purchase of mass-produced items in the nineteenth and twentieth centuries. The Blackfoot Indians of the Plains of Canada and the United States, for example, used measures based on the fingerwidth, handwidth, span, and "squaw yard." Stirrup straps were one finger wide, hackamores and bridles were made from bison-hide strips two fingers wide, a woman's belt was three fingers wide, and arrow shafts were made five handwidths and two fingers long. The Blackfoot span was the distance from the tip of the middle finger of a man's extended arm and hand to the center of his chest and was used to measure the length of a man's bow. The Blackfoot "squaw yard" was the distance from a woman's nose to the tip of her fingers on an outstretched hand and arm and was used to measure cloth purchased from traders. The Tonga of Polynesia also used body-part length to measure cloth, with the basic measure being the *haga fesi*, a span measure in which the cloth is spanned and then the hand turned over onto the knuckles to add the length of the first two finger joints to the measure. A piece of cloth is then measured to a size of 2 spans long and 14 or 16 spans wide. The Amhara of Ethiopia use a measure called "throwing the rope" based on the elbow to fingertip distance to measure farm plots. One rope equals about 40 elbow lengths and land might be measured a number of times, such as before and following plowing in order to get an accurate measure.

A particularly comprehensive body-part measurement system is used by the Tzeltal of Mexico:

> *nab*—the distance between the end of the thumb and the extended middle finger

> *chutub*—the distance between the end of the thumb and the extended little finger

shucubil—the distance from the elbow to the end of the extended middle finger

jaub—the distance between both extended arms

yankabal—the distance from the armpit to the extended middle finger of the opposite hand

legua—the distance a man can walk in one hour

In some cultures, the area of farmland is measured by the amount of crops that can be grown on it or the amount or resources needed to cultivate it. The Sinhalese of Sri Lanka measure farm plots by the amount of seed planted on it, with one unit called a *paelo*, and four paelo equaling an *amuno*, which is the equivalent of two acres. The Tzeltal employ the same measure, considering a *milpa* (about 1.5 hectares) to be about 60 ears of corn, the number of ears needed to seed one milpa. The Central Thai measure a farm plot by the amount of land a man and a water buffalo or pair of oxen can plow in a day, a plot of land being a *rai,* which equals about two-fifths of an acre.

It is common across cultures for long distances to be measured by the amount a time it takes to travel the distance. For example, the Toba in Argentina measure distance by a day's travel, and the Tzeltal of Mexico consider the legua (about five kilometers) to be the distance a man walks in one hour. In traditional China, distances in rural regions were measured in units called *li*, with 45 li equaling a typical day's travel. The Khasi of India measured distance by the number of betel nuts chewed on the journey.

Across cultures, the sale of farm produce requires a measurement system so that a market price can be set for the produce. Central Thai farmers sell their rice to rice mills in *tang* baskets that hold about 20 liters, or 10 kilograms. Shonto Navajo farmers in Arizona measure their farm produce such as corn and squash in "pickup truck loads," as that is how they transport crops from the fields to storage bins. However, if crops are sold, they must be weighed to establish a retail price. The Javanese of Indonesia use four measures in their rural markets: (1) piles or bunches of loose produce such as corn or cassava, (2) baskets that hold processed produce such as corn kernels or rice, (3) tins holding about one kilogram, and (4) cups or bowls. The piles and bunches and baskets especially, and the other two measures to a lesser extent, vary from individual to individual. The contents are standardized by adding or subtracting some produce to adjust for their size or moisture content and also by the trader who uses his or her own set of measures.

Across cultures, a finer gradient of measures is used for items important to the culture. For example, the Kpelle of Liberia use an intricate system of measures for their staple crop, rice:

molon kpalan—rice farm, the amount of land needed to grow rice for one family during the year

molon fiyen—rice bundles that are of a size that can be held by a woman between her thumb and fingers

molon kôon—two or three *molon fiyen* tied together

kôpi—one "cup" of rice ready for cooking, sale, or purchase. When purchased, the kôpi is flat bottomed, when sold it is round bottomed, thereby providing the seller a profit.

bôke—a bucket or about 24 *kôpi* of rice

tin—44 cups of rice

boro—a bag of rice, about 100 cups

Symbolism of Measures

While the primary use of measures is practical, in some cultures they are believed to have special ritual or symbolic meanings as well. For example, the Sinhalese believe that some measurements bring good fortune while others cause misfortune. The meanings associated with certain distances are carefully considered when building a house. Astrologers are consulted by some to advise on the measurements to be used when constructing a house; various religious texts provide rules about measurements in building a house (MacDougall 1971:867–868, 876, 880, 885, 901):

42. You should be familiar with the *waDu riyene*, "carpenter's cubit," by which you measure the auspicious post which has been felled properly. It is one *riyene*, "cubit," one *viyete*, "span," and four inches from the right hand. You should understand the *waDu riyene* measure. [A cubit is about 18 inches, a carpenter's cubit about 36 inches.]

43. Using the carpenter's cubit, take, without doubt, a length of five cubits and a breadth of three. If the length of the house is to be six and a half cubits, make the breadth exactly three and a half cubits.

44. For a house which is to be seven cubits long, measure off carefully a breadth of four. For a house which is to be nine cubits long, take a breadth of five cubits. If you take the measurements in this way, fortune will come to the house.

45. For a house with a length of ten and a half cubits, take a breadth of six and a half. For a length of eleven cubits, take a breadth of seven and a half.

46. If the length increases, the wife of the house will die. If the breadth increases, death will come to the husband. If the house has suitable measurements, its inhabitants will be prosperous and happy. Therefore, neither increase nor decrease the measurements.

90. Divide the carpenter's cubit into four equal parts. One of them is called a *paadeye*, "foot." Take eight feet for the length of the door and for the breadth take four and a half.

110. For the inside of the fenced enclosure which surrounds the house, take a length and breadth of sixty cubits. Harmonize these measurements with the four directions.

111. From east to west measure off sixty cubits with a string. From north to south do the same.

112. Fix a third string running from southeast to northwest, and a fourth string running from southwest to northeast.

142. According to the teachings of the sages, it is good to dig a well in the northeast, four cubits away from the house. If you do so, the earth will yield game of various varieties. If the well is dug in the same direction at a distance of twelve cubits, the wealth in cattle of the house will be destroyed.

215. There are five kinds of *titis*, "lunar days," namely, *nanda*, "pleasureful," *bhaddra*, "prosperous," *jayaa*, "victorious," *rikta*, "empty," and *purna*, "full."

216. When you divide each of these *titis* into three *paade*, "feet," you have a total number of fifteen feet. Similarly, when you divide land in this manner, you have a total number of fifteen feet or sections.

217. According to the teachings of the Vedas, the first, sixth, and eleventh feet come under the *nanda titi*. The same Vedas tell us that the second, seventh, and twelfth feet belong to the *bhaddra titi*.

218. The sages say that the third, eighth, and thirteenth feet are called *jayaa titi*. The fourth, ninth, and fourteenth feet are called *rikta titi*.

219. The three feet which belong to the *purna titi* are the fifth, tenth, and the fifteenth. So, first you divide the land into five equal parts, and then you divide it again so that each of the five have three equal parts. This is how you divide the land into *titis*.

220. If the house site falls into the division called *nanda titi*, the owner will not be free from mental grief. The owner of a house on *bhaddra titi* will be happy and prosperous. He will have no worries whatsoever.

221. The owner of a house on *jayaa titi* will be able to avoid quarreling with others, and will prosper like Bandula. He will be happy and proud of his children. Thieves and enemies will enter the house which falls into the *rikta titi*.

Among the Malays, measurement plays a major role in determining whether a sword or other weapons will bring the user good or bad luck. There are various ritual applications of measurement that a warrior can use: requiring measurement of the sword blade with a length of palm leaf, folding the leaf, cutting the leaf to fit the width of the blade at various measurement points, reciting various ritual words, and aligning measurement points with specific words to determine the luck of the sword and its owner. The luck can range from bad (the sword will stick in its sheath, it will break when used), to fair (it will not bring luck when worn on trading expeditions), to good (the user will be successful in all ventures).

Finally, because the Chinese believe that rice is the staff of life, they believe that rice measures are the measure of life and thus the square, wooden measures symbolize justice, mercy, and virtue.

See also GEOMANCY; MOBILITY AND SEDENTISM.

Bromley, Ray. (1981) "Market Center and Market Place in Highland Ecuador: A Study of Organization, Regulation, and Ethnic Discrimination." In *Cultural Transformations and Ethnicity in Modern Ecuador*, edited by Norman E. Whitten, Jr., 233–259.

Buxton, Leonard H. D. (1929) *China: The Land and the People: A Human Geography.*

Collocott, Ernest E. V. (1925) "Supplementary Tongan Vocabulary." *Polynesian Society Journal* 34:146–169, 193–213.

Dewey, Alice G. (1962) *Peasant Marketing in Java.*

Evans, I. H. N. (1927) *Papers on the Ethnology and Archaeology of the Malay Peninsula.*

Ewers, John C. (1970) "Bodily Proportions as Guides to Lineal Measurements among the Blackfoot Indians." *American Anthropologist* 72:561–562.

Gay, John, and Michael Cole. (1967) *The New Mathematics and an Old Culture: A Study of Learning among the Kpelle of Nigeria.*

Gurdon, Philip R. T. (1907) *The Khasis.*

Ingersoll, Jasper C. (1964) *The Priest and the Path: An Analysis of the Priest Role in a Central Thai Village.*

Kerr, John G. (1950) *A Naturalist in the Gran Chaco.*

MacDougall, Robert D. (1971) *Domestic Architecture among the Kandyan Sinhalese.*

Messing, Simon D. (1957) *The Highland-Plateau Amhara of Ethiopia.*

Russell, Scott C. (1983) *Factors Affecting Agricultural Production in a Western Navajo Community.*

Villa Rojas, Alfonso. (1969) "The Tzeltal." In *Handbook of Middle American Indians, Volume 7*, edited by Robert Wauchope, 195–225.

MINING

The mining and quarrying of minerals and the extraction of fossil fuels are two of the major ways humans exploit the physical environment around the world today. The mining industry removes about 28 billion tons of material from the earth each year and uses 5–10 percent of the world's energy each year to extract and process minerals. The importance of mining in the human experience—over time and across cultures—is indicated by the use of the labels Stone, Bronze, and Iron to indicate major ages in the cultural evolution of humans. Large-scale mining as it exists today, however, is a product of the Industrial Revolution with industry creating an insatiable and continually growing demand for minerals and fossil fuels and, in turn, providing the technology needed to locate, extract, and process these minerals.

Of all human exploitive activities, mining has the largest impact on the physical environment in two major ways. First, mining involves the exploitation of resources that are neither renewable nor sustainable. Once a mineral deposit is removed from the earth, it will not be replaced nor can mining at its current rate be sustained indefinitely. At this time, however, there is no immediate threat that mineral resources will run out, as all major resources have reserves that will last at least from several decades to several hundred years. In addition, known mineral resources not yet ready for exploitation far exceed the reserves. The second way mining impacts the environment is as a major agent of pollution. Because of the scale of current mining and processing operations and the nature of the minerals mined, environmental damage is almost always a consequence of mining. Environmental damage resulting from mining and processing includes the physical destruction of human and natural habitats, water pollution, air pollution, deforestation, and the creation of dead zones that can no longer support life. Because the mining process also requires the heavy use of energy, mining contributes to global warming. The extent of damage in any given locale is the result of the interplay of factors such as the nature of the site, the quantity mined, the chemical composition of the mineral mined and the covering or surrounding minerals, and the process needed to convert the minerals into products for consumption. In addition to the environmental costs, mining also has large human costs in the form of peoples displaced from the land located above rich mineral resources, the exploitation of mining labor, disease and injuries, and the social and economic destruction of mining communities when the mine is no longer economically viable.

Minerals

The minerals acquired through mining can be characterized in a variety of ways, including based on their ultimate use—metals, industrial minerals, construction materials, and energy materials—or by their chemical characteristics—metals, nonmetals, fossil fuels—as shown in the list below. The major metals mined around the world are iron, aluminum, copper, manganese, and zinc; the major nonmetals are stone, sand, gravel, clays, and salt.

Metals
Aluminum
Bismuth
Chromium
Copper
Gold
Iron
Lead
Manganese
Mercury
Molybdenum
Nickel
Platinum
Silver
Tin
Titanium
Tungsten
Zinc

Dolomite
Fluorite
Gravel
Gypsum
Lime
Magnesite
Marble
Phosphate Rock
Potash
Potassium Salts
Pyrite
Salt
Saltpeter
Sand
Soda Ash
Steatite
Stone
Sulfur
Talc

Nonmetals
Asbestos
Barite
Bauxite
Cement
Clays
Diamonds

Fuels
Crude Oil
Coal
Lignite
Natural Gas

Mining Process

Around the world today, most mining takes place in less developed nations in Latin America, Africa, and Asia or on land owned or formerly owned by indigenous peoples in the United States, Canada, and Australia. Minerals mined in these nations are mostly exported to industrialized nations, with those from Latin America

flowing to the United States, those from Africa to western Europe, and those from Asia to Japan. In the United States, a substantial percentage of minerals and fossil fuels come from Native American reservations that hold over 50 percent of uranium deposits in the nation, 20 percent of gas and oil reserves, and 33 percent of low-grade sulfur coal in the West. For example, the Wind River Reservation in Utah is a source of coal, oil, natural gas, uranium, phosphate, gypsum, and potash; the Navajo Reservation in Arizona a source of uranium, oil, gas, coal, sand, and gravel; and the White Mountain Apache Reservation in Arizona a source of coal, copper, asbestos, and gold.

The three major processes involved in mining are exploration, development, and extraction. Exploration, which involves locating mineral reserves, measuring their size, and evaluating whether they can be profitably mined at current market prices is a very important step as the value of a mineral deposit is mainly determined at the time of discovery and exploration. Development of the mine centers on creating the plan for extracting the mineral deposit and transporting it for processing or sale. The plan must consider the size and location of the reserve, the nature of surrounding minerals, the most efficient extraction and processing technology, and the location of shafts and support facilities.

Extraction involves the actual removal of the mineral from the ground. In colonized nations in the past and less developed nations today, extraction is labor-intensive, with minerals removed by picks and blasting and hand-loaded onto cars for removal from the mines. Men are coerced into working as miners through taxation systems, indebtedness to labor contractors, or through the purchase of estates that include control of the peasants living there who volunteer for the work because of the relatively high pay or to meet seasonal subsistence shortages. In developed nations, extraction is mainly mechanized, with virtually all tasks previously done by men such as cutting, drilling, blasting, and loading now done by machines, and in continuous mining operations by a single machine. Most mining today is surface rather than underground mining that uses tunnels and shafts. Surface or strip mining is more economically efficient but also produces more waste and potentially more damage to the environment. Strip mining takes a variety of forms, depending on the location of the mineral to be mined, including prairie stripping in which the overburden of soil and rock covering a large area is stripped off, contour in which shelves are cut into hillsides, and auger in which augers are drilled through overburden that is too deep to strip off.

Social and Political Factors

Mining by non-Western peoples prior to or apart from colonization differs markedly from modern, commercial mining. Because of the relatively small communities, the use of minerals by individuals rather than by industry and the reliance on manual labor was small in scale and its impact on the environment. For example, the Hopi of Arizona mine and gather salt, coal, clays, minerals for pigments, and stone. Salt is now gathered from several miles away, as the Hopi believe that the mine was once near the village but was moved away by spirits because of the people's greed. Coal is used to fire pottery and also in the winter when firewood is difficult to obtain. Clay is used in making pottery and minerals are gathered to make paint—yellow from geothite or limonite, red from hematite, purple from manganese dioxide or red iron oxide, blue from copper carbonite, green from malachite, and white from silicious matter or kaolin. Sandstone is carefully quarried by men to produce stones for ovens that will not crack. The rough stones are carefully worked by women to smooth and blacken them. The Cherokee of North Carolina gathered flint, chert, hematite, steatite, clay, and salt and later began mining gold, silver, copper, and lead after the arrival of Europeans.

Perhaps the grandest mining operation was that managed by the Inca of Peru prior to the Spanish conquest in the sixteenth century. The Inca mined gold, silver, copper, platinum, tin, hematite, lead, limestone, diorite, porphyry, and black andesite. The mines were operated for four months each year, from noon to sunset each day. Miners were taken from neighboring provinces in groups of from 20 to 50 men, in the *mita* system of labor recruitment that later became common under the Spanish. All the gold and silver was taken by the emperor who kept it for the royal family and gave some to what he considered to be deserving nobles. Copper was used by all people and was alloyed with tin to make bronze. Metals were processed by smelting, alloying, casting, hammering, repoussé, incrustation, inlay, soldering, riveting, and cloisonné. The Inca considered the hills with mineral reserves and the mines themselves to be shrines and prayed to them and held festivals in their honor so the mines would be generous with their metals.

As noted above, much of the mineral reserves in nations such as the United States, Canada, and Australia are located under land on reservations that are owned or controlled by indigenous peoples. However, the minerals and rights to exploit them are often controlled by private companies who pay lease fees for the land, pay royalties on extracted minerals to the Native owners, and often promise to provide jobs for Natives. For example, 33 U.S. corporations hold interests in uranium and coal mines and power plants on land that was formerly or is currently under Indian control in Montana, North and South Dakota, and Wyoming. In a few situations the Native inhabitants mine minerals themselves. This mining is often only for local use, and the mining operations are based heavily on traditional labor-intensive methods that cannot compete in the national or international market with multinational firms. In general, use of Indian land and exploitation of minerals with

Gold mine and adjacent "town" in Brazil

Indian labor have been less than helpful to the Indian groups. The experience of the Laguna Indians of New Mexico is typical. The Laguna leased 7,000 acres of reservation land to the Anaconda Corporation who strip-mined uranium from 1952 until 1981 and paid the Laguna lease fees and royalties and trained and hired a sizable number of Laguna men as miners, thereby reducing the reservation employment rate to about one-half of other reservations and making the miners "rich" by local standards. In 1981, when the mine was played-out, Anaconda ended its relationship with the Laguna, leaving behind a large crater, piles of radioactive waste, a hundred or so unemployed men with skills not useful in other work, and a reservation dependent on the now-absent mining industry.

Not all indigenous peoples have suffered due to the mining of their land. Nauru Island, in the Pacific Ocean, contains one of the richest phosphate deposits in the world. This deposit will be largely gone by the year 2000. Mining began in 1906 and was under British control from 1919 to 1968 when Nauru achieved independence. The British paid the Nauru residents a royalty of a half penny per ton. Since 1968, the Nuaruese have controlled the mining and have sold the phosphate on the open market, reaping sizable returns that have been distributed among the population on the basis of land ownership and also invested by individuals and the government for the future when the phosphate is gone. Although the center of the island is now uninhabitable—nothing is left but coral outcroppings—the Nauru have used the only resource they have to secure their economic future.

Mines are often located in desolate, isolated areas and, therefore, the mining communities that develop near them are often self-contained communities whose residents include the miners, their families, and persons providing supporting services such as shopkeepers, doctors, and ministers. In Africa, mining communities often took the form of mining camps located at the mine, some of which developed into cities such as Obusai, which was a gold camp, and Kibi, which was a quartz camp. In North America, mining communities in the Appalachia region (a major source of coal, gypsum, manganese, zinc, lead, copper, pyrite, and other minerals) take the form of company towns where all residents are directly or indirectly economically dependent on mining and where most contacts are with others within the small community. As with Indian communities, these company towns also suffer when mining operations cease. For example, the town of Hellier, Kentucky, developed in the 1920s as a supply center for nearby mining camps. Many of its shoppers came from the nearby mining town of Allegheny, built by two mining companies about ten years earlier. In the 1940s, the company sold its mine to another company that mechanized production; in the 1960s, the mine was sold again to another company that moved its coal operation to the other side of the mountain. Within a few years the Hellier city hall was abandoned, stores closed, and the remaining unemployed miners and their families were living on union and welfare payments. Auger strip mining left the hills bare, and rains brought mud and rocks down onto the town. In the words of one observer (Caudill 1963:348):

> Stranded Hellier, forlorn and hopeless, symbolizes the coalfield—indifferent and callous economic masters, helpless and despairing people, a narrow, twisting valley dependent entirely upon a single industry which has withdrawn its benefits from the families so long dependent on it.

Because of these conditions—the social solidarity that develops in isolated mining communities and the leverage that miners have as the sole source of labor—mining operations were often the target of worker unrest. Compared to other industries, mining is far more likely to suffer losses from workers stealing ore (the Inca stationed guards at mine entrances to check miners for gold), vandalism of equipment, strikes, and labor union organization campaigns. In Appalachia, the United Mine Workers was a powerful influence for several decades until mechanization replaced labor-intensive mining. And in its Basque region, Spain experienced its first industrial strike in 1890 when Spanish workers struck against the Basque mine owners and then struck 35 more times in the following 20 years. Complaints focused on long work hours, company control of living accommodations and supply stores, and a blacklist shared by owners that made it difficult for miners to find different employment. Faced with no alternative labor force, the owners quickly gave in to most miner demands.

See also TECHNOLOGY.

Adams, William Y. (1963) *Shonto: A Study of the Role of the Trader in a Modern Navaho Community.*

Caudill, Harry M. (1963) *Night Comes to the Cumberlands: A Biography of a Depressed Area.*

Churchill, Ward, and Winona LaDuke. (1992) "Native North America: The Political Economy of Radioactive Colonialism." In *The State of Native America: Genocide, Colonization, and Resistance*, edited by M. Annette Jaimes, 241–266.

Colton, Harold S. (1974) "Hopi History and Ethnobotany." In *Hopi Indians*, 279–386.

Ellis, Florence H. (1974) "The Hopi: Their History and Use of Lands." In *Hopi Indians*, 25–277.

Ford, Thomas R. (1962) *The Southern Appalachian Region: A Survey.*

Godoy, Ricardo. (1985) "Mining: Anthropological Perspective." *Annual Review of Anthropology* 14:199–217.

Goodwin, Gary C. (1977) *Cherokees in Transition: A Study of Changing Culture and Environment Prior to 1775.*

Heiberg, Marianne. (1989) *The Making of the Basque Nation.*

Jorgensen, Joseph G. (1974) *The Sun Dance Religion: Power for the Powerless.*

Reagan, Albert B. (1930) *Notes of the Indians of the Fort Apache Region.*

Rowe, John H. (1946) "Inca Culture at the Time of the Spanish Conquest." In *Handbook of South American Indians, Volume 2*, edited by Julian H. Steward, 183–330.

Viviani, Nancy. (1970) *Nauru: Phosphate and Political Progress.*

Young, John E. (1992) "Mining the Earth." In *State of the World*, 100–118.

Zirakzadeh, Cyrus E. (1989) *Popular Politics in the Basque Region of Spain: A Study in Political Anthropology.*

MOBILITY AND SEDENTISM

Mobility refers to the frequency with which people in a culture customarily move their settlements. Sedentism refers to the process through which an increasing percentage of people in a culture settle in permanent rather than mobile communities. While it is individuals who are mobile or sedentary, entire cultures can be classified as such on the basis of the relative mobility-sedentism of their members. One classification scheme lists six types of mobility-sedentism: (1) migratory or nomadic bands, (2) seminomadic communities, (3) rotating settlements, (4) semisedentary settlements, (5) impermanent settlements, and (6) permanent settlements. Frequent mobility is associated across cultures with three types of subsistence systems. First, many hunter-gatherers, although not all, were traditionally nomadic, moving frequently throughout the year in search of water to drink, plant foods to gather, and animals to hunt. Second, many pastoral peoples moved nomadically, seminomadically, or occupied rotating or semipermanent settlements throughout the year. Their movements were mainly reactions to seasonal changes in the climate and were motivated primarily by the need to provide water and grazing land for their herds and also for other reasons such as to avoid conflicts or domination by a centralized national government. Third, peoples labeled Gypsies and Travellers were traditionally peripatetic, moving camp periodically in order to locate themselves near populations who demanded their specialized economic services such as horse trading, entertainment, or metal working. Gypsies and Travellers, however, moved in reaction to changes in the sociopolitical and economic environments, not to changes in the physical environment. For the most part, cultures existing by these three subsistence strategies or some modified forms of them in the past are now mainly sedentary due to disruption of their traditional economies by colonial rule and their incorporation into modern nation-states. For example, traditionally nomadic hunter-gatherers in North America, South America, and Australia are now mainly confined to living in permanent communities on reservations or reserves. With access to grazing lands blocked by fencing and laws, many pastoralists the world over have been settled on ranches. Thus, the information that follows describes the world situation as it existed in the late nineteenth century and early twentieth century, not the situation today in which the overwhelming majority of the world's people live in sedentary communities—although as in the United States, a significant portion of individuals in the society may move numerous times during their lifetimes.

Settlement mobility is important because it is predictably related to other features of culture and is a reliable indicator of the overall complexity of a culture. Thus, if we know the mobility pattern typical of a culture, we can predict other customs of that culture. For example, nomadic cultures such as the Mbuti of central Africa, the San of Botswana, and the Vedda of Sri Lanka tend to have small settlements, impermanent buildings, no system of writing, weak or no political leadership, a division of labor based only on sex and age, land transportation by humans or sometimes pack animals, and no social classes. On the other hand, cultures with permanent settlements such as the Ashanti in Ghana or the Chinese are virtually the opposite with social classes; large, densely populated settlements; strong political leaders; and so forth. Knowing a community's settlement-mobility pattern is especially important to archaeologists who often can find features in the ground about mobility and sedentism but less information about other features of culture. Thus, their knowledge of mobility patterns enables them to predict other features of cultures of the past such as those noted above.

The first type of settlement mobility, nomadic bands, are found mainly in hunting-gathering societies where people (usually small family groups) establish temporary camps at different locales as they move throughout the year. While most cultures with a nomadic mobility pattern are hunter-gatherers, not all hunter-gatherers are nomadic. Some, such as those of the Northwest Coast of North America who subsist on rich food supplies such as fish that provide a surplus for year-round consumption, live in large settled villages. A survey of 186 cultures indicates that 14.5 percent are nomadic. The Semang of Malaysia were, and some still remain, nomadic hunter-gatherers. They live in temporary camps of 2 to 20 palm-thatch lean-tos, each housing one family for a total camp population of about 60 persons. These camps are oc-cupied from one day to as long as six weeks depending on the availability of food in the vicinity. Most Semang are now settled in permanent villages under Malaysian government control.

In the 11 percent of cultures with semi-nomadic communities, people occupy nomadic-type camps for much of the year but join together to live in a single, larger settlement for usually one season. This pattern of mobility is typical of traditional hunting peoples in the sub-Arctic region of North America and Siberia as well as peoples such as the Vedda and Andamanese in South Asia. The Montagnais of Canada typify this pattern. In the summer months, several groups numbering about 50 members each would join together and camp along the shores of lakes and rivers. When fall approached, the camp would break up into the smaller groups who then moved about the forest during the remainder of the year, hunting, fishing, and camping in birch-bark wigwams. The larger camps in the summer were made possible by the milder climate and more abundant resources during this season that supported a larger sedentary population. Another form of seminomadism is practiced by the people known as the Sea Nomads of Asia who live on and around the islands running from the Indian Ocean to the southern Philippines. Some Sea Nomads live most of the year on dugout boats with a hearth for cooking and platform living area. They subsist primarily by fishing for consumption and trade for other foods and material goods. Each boat houses one family and from 5 to 10 boats travel together. Once a year, during the monsoon season, as many as 40 boats dock together in bays to ride out the storms.

In the 3 percent of cultures with a rotating settlement pattern, people have two permanent settlements that they occupy in different seasons during the year. This pattern is found most often among some pastoral peoples who move their herds to grazing areas in the spring and then to a more sheltered location in the winter months.

Tuareg women in North Africa erect dry season tent.

For example, the Toda of India, who traditionally herded water buffalo, lived in villages in the more lush highlands with their herds from December and March and in other villages in the lowlands during the rest of the year.

The fourth mobility pattern—semisedentary settlements—is found in 7.5 percent of cultures, most of which are either hunter-gatherers or pastoralists. In this pattern, the entire group lives in a permanent settlement with some segment of the population living elsewhere for part of the year, usually to hunt or graze livestock. The Sarakatsani of Greece, for example, live in settled villages near the coast, but during the warm seasons the shepherds and others take the sheep flocks up into the mountains to graze while some members of the community remain behind in the villages. Similarly, the Aleut of North America and Russia traditionally lived in permanent villages along the coast where they fished, collected sea life, and hunted sea mammals. Village sites were selected for their access to the sea and resources and protection from enemies. Smaller camps for use by hunters were built away from the village for seasonal exploitation of resources near them.

The fifth pattern, impermanent settlements, is found in 8 percent of cultures, mainly horticulturalists in tropical rainforests such as the Yanomamö in Brazil and Venezuela who occupy permanent villages for a period of years and then move and build a new village when the soil is no longer able to produce enough food.

The sixth and final pattern is permanent settlements occupied continuously and for indefinite periods of time. They are the most common form across cultures, used by 59 percent of cultures in the late nineteenth and early twentieth centuries and by an even greater percentage of cultures today. Peoples who live in permanent settlements that are usually larger and more densely populated than settlements in other types of societies typically subsist by agriculture or intensive horticulture.

In addition to these six types of mobility-sedentism, mobility in hunting-gathering cultures can be classified as residential, logistical, or territorial, or may take the form of permanent migration from one territory to another. Residential mobility means that the entire group moves together and continues to reside together, although some families may now and then break off and join other bands. Logistical mobility means that the people live in one location, but hunters or foragers go off from the central camp. Territorial mobility means that over a course of years the people search for food in different territories but always return to territory used previously. This pattern is typical of some hunting peoples and some horticulturalists, the latter leaving previously used land to remain fallow while they plant their gardens elsewhere. Finally, certainly in the past when land was an open resource, some people would migrate into a new territory in search of a more reliable source of food.

For all peoples who are mobile, the two most important considerations in deciding to move are the availability of food and the cost of obtaining that food in their current locale as compared to some other locale. Other considerations are forming larger communities to hold religious rites, to obtain marriage partners, to form political alliances, or to avoid warfare. Additionally, in some cultures with a long history of mobility, some people may simply prefer to move frequently and live with different people than simply stay in one place with the same people for an extended period of time.

See also HUNTING-GATHERING; PASTORALISM; SETTLEMENT PATTERNS.

Binford, Lewis R. (1990) "Mobility, Housing, and Environment: A Comparative Study." *Journal of Anthropological Research* 46:119–152.

Evans, I. H. N. (1937) *The Negritos of Malaya.*

Kelly, Robert L. (1992) "Mobility-Sedentism: Concepts, Archaeological Measures, and Effects." *Annual Review of Anthropology* 21:43–66.

Laughlin, William S. (1980) *Aleuts: Survivors of the Bering Land Bridge.*

Murdock, George P., and Suzanne F. Wilson. (1980) "Settlement Patterns and Community Organization: Cross-Cultural Codes III." In *Cross-Cultural Samples and Codes*, edited by Herbert Barry III and Alice Schlegel, 76–116.

Sopher, David E. (1977) *The Sea Nomads: A Study of the Maritime Boat People of Southeast Asia.*

Walker, Anthony R. (1986) *The Toda of South India: A New Look.*

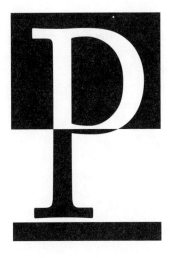

P

Pastoralism is "the raising of livestock on 'natural' pasture unimproved by human intervention" (Salzman 1995). Pastoralism differs from other subsistence strategies that also utilize animals—such as the keeping of domesticated animals, dairy farming, and ranching—in that the environmental resources that are used in pastoralism occur naturally. This definition of pastoralism reflects the ideal situation; in many pastoral societies humans do intervene to alter the environment to maximize its usefulness for grazing. For example, in recent years, the importation of water by truck has been used by pastoralists in the Middle East, reducing the need to move in search of waterholes and vegetation. As a form of environmental adaptation, pastoralism requires the balancing of location and timing to ensure that adequate water and vegetation are available for the herds in a safe location.

Pastoralism is a relatively rare type of subsistence economy. In a survey of 563 cultures, only 12 percent were primarily pastoral, making pastoralism the least frequent subsistence type compared to agriculture, horticulture, foraging, hunting, and fishing. However, despite their few numbers, some of the best-known and most independent societies in human history have been pastoral—the Mongols and Kazakhs in Central Asia, the Saami (Lapps) in Scandinavia, the Bedouin in the Middle East and North Africa, and the Masai of Kenya to name a few. Because of their large territory, the absence of a strong, centralized political system, and their frequent movements, pastoral societies have until the late twentieth century proved themselves to be especially resistant to interference and control by others. Experts at one time believed that pastoralism developed as a highly specialized and environmentally restricted subsistence strategy in environments that were not suitable for horticulture or agriculture. The force behind the appearance of pastoralism in a region was thought to be population growth and the resulting spread of agricultural people into areas not suitable for agriculture. These people then shifted to pastoralism that existed alongside the agriculture of their neighbors. Experts now believe that while pastoralism is a specialized response to specific environmental conditions, it often developed alongside agriculture, not as an offshoot to it. In the Middle East, pastoralism existed at least 5,000 years ago. In other areas, such as East Africa, it developed in a number of societies such as the Jie, Turkana, and Masai independent of agriculture, even though exchange relations were sometimes maintained with neighboring hunter-gatherer societies and no group relied entirely on pastoralism for subsistence. In other regions, pastoralism is a more recent development. For example, among the Saami of Scandinavia, reindeer herding evolved out of reindeer hunting only in the past 200 years, and a segment of the Navajo community in the U.S. Southwest adopted sheepherding only in historic times.

Pastoralism is an Old World economic form, with most pastoral societies throughout human

157

history found in the Circum-Mediterranean region, Central Asia, Siberia, southeast Africa, and mountainous regions of Europe. Depending on the definition of pastoralism, there are relatively few or no pastoralists in the New World. While llama and alpaca herders of the Andes during the Inca period and later were pastoral, they also relied heavily on agriculture and trade with other groups. Some experts classify the horseback riding bison hunters of the North American Plains—such as the Blackfoot, Comanche, and Crow of the 1800s—as pastoralists. Others, however, see these groups as hunters who kept and used horses to acquire food and other material goods. This practice differs from other pastoral societies who obtain food and other items directly from their herds. The major pastoral society in the New World today is the Navajo in the southwestern United States who rely heavily on sheepherding. Navajo pastoralism, however, is not an indigenous practice; it was introduced by the Spanish.

There are three major types of pastoralism—settled, nomadic, and agro-pastoralism. Settled pastoralism is characterized by residence in permanent villages with some of the residents tending the herds or flocks in natural pastures. For example, sheepherders in Sardinia, Italy, tend the flocks while most pastoral Sardinians reside in villages. In contrast, nomadic pastoralists move frequently in search of water and vegetation for their herds. The nomadic sections of the Masai composed of extended families, for example, would migrate at virtually any time with little notice, abandoning their huts and villages for others to occupy. A particular form of nomadic pastoralism is transhumance that involves regular seasonal movements to better pasturage. The Basseri in Iran and some Bedouin groups in the Middle East were transhumant. A third form of pastoralism is agro-pastoralism in which some members of the community grow crops while others tend the herds. The Nuer of the Sudan, for example, subsisted traditionally on a combi-nation of millet farming, fishing, and the herding of cattle, with different communities responsible for the different economic activities. Similarly, nomadic Bedouin (not all are nomadic) often plant grain along their routes for harvesting upon their return. Thus, pastoralism involves a wide mix of strategies for exploiting a limited environment, with considerable variation both across and within pastoral societies. The long list of different species and the varieties of each herded by different pastoral cultures—camels, horses, sheep, goats, alpaca, llama, yaks, reindeer, buffalo—point to the highly specialized environmental adaptations of different pastoral cultures.

Pastoral societies in the past and today are found in climatic regions that did not traditionally support agriculture—deserts, grasslands, savannas, and mountains. Thus, pastoral societies are found mainly in East Africa, North Africa, the Middle East, Central Asia, Siberia, and southern Europe. As noted above, a variety of species are herded by pastoralists with cattle especially common in East Africa; camels and sheep in North Africa and the Middle East; reindeer in Scandinavia and Siberia; sheep in Europe; and mixed herds of cattle, sheep, goats, and horses in Central Asia. Yak are herded by groups such as the Sherpa in the Himalayas and llama and alpaca in the Peruvian Andes.

The world over, the most important product of pastoralism is milk. The herds are often used for other purposes as well such as transportation and as beasts of burden as by the Saami (reindeer), Kazakhs (horses), or Bedouin (camel); for meat for consumption; for blood for consumption as among the Masai and other groups in East Africa; and for raw materials such as hides. The herds also serve social and political functions in many societies. The size of one's herd is a mark of a herder's wealth, and stock is used for marriage payments and also provides nonsubsistence economic benefits when sold or traded. Because of the reliance on milk, many pastoral societies have developed cuisines that emphasize milk-based foods. For example, the Buriat Mongols of Central Asia make and eat butter, several types of cheese, yogurt, vodka from milk, fermented mare's milk (*kumys*), and various dishes based on flour and milk mixtures. Where herd animals are slaughtered for consumption, meat is often an important part of the diet. However, meat is not consumed frequently by all groups. Especially in times of environmental stress, consumption can adversely effect herd size and the herd's capacity to reproduce itself. Some nomadic pastoral peoples are also associated with distinctive forms of dwellings—the Central Asian groups with the yurt and the Bedouin with the multiroom black tent.

Pastoralism as an Environmental Adaptation

As a specialized form of adaptation to the environment, pastoralism is characterized by considerable uncertainty. Pastoralists, however, have more control over their environment than do hunter-gatherers as pastoralists can move their herds to more advantageous locations. And compared to agriculturalists, pastoralists enjoy the advantage of having a mobile and expandable resource—their herds—while agriculturalists cannot simply move their fields in times of drought or flood or easily acquire additional land. In general, however, agriculture is a more efficient exploitation of the environment and can support a larger population, larger settled communities, and a greater degree of occupational specialization.

From the viewpoint of technology, pastoralism requires a number of specialized activities such as regulating the herd size, moving the herd, training herds, protecting herds, and harvesting food and other products. Pastoralism also requires special tools, equipment, knowledge, and skills. The yak and sheepherders of Tibet, for example, make and use knives, ropes, spears, milking hooks and pails, hobbles, cattle pens,

sheepfold, stalls, fetters, tethers, and various receptacles not needed in nonpastoral societies.

As an environmental adaptation, pastoralists often must cope with arid land and capricious rainfall, wide changes in the climate across the seasons, and environmental disasters such as drought and excessive rainfall with flooding. The inability to control rainfall and ensure adequate growth of vegetation has traditionally made pastoralism risky. In addition, herds can be threatened by predators; disease from other animals; and various problems related to herd size, age, sex ratio, the mix of species herded, and the animals' requirements. Thus, pastoralists must adapt to an environment that in the broad sense supports their principal source of capital and material well-being—their herds—but also provides a continual threat to the security of that source of capital. Pastoralists devote considerable resources to securing their herds, making sure they can reproduce, and ensuring the future production of milk. Pastoralists also selectively breed their herds to produce animals best suited for the environment and the pastoralists' food, material, and transportation needs. The "discovery" in 1994 of a new breed of horse in the Himalayas points out the enduring role of pastoralists in diversifying the species they herd.

Pastoralists often adapt to their environments through a combination of mobility (nomadism or transhumance); internal economic differentiation with some communities engaging in other subsistence activities; securing other income or goods through trade or raiding; forms of social organization that make the most efficient use of human power in managing the herds and extracting and processing milk, hides, and other products; and through herding practices that maximize environmental opportunities.

The principal herding practices used by pastoralists are herd mobility, species diversification, herd dispersion, and herd maximization, each of which has advantages and disadvantages that must be weighed by pastoralists in making decisions about environmental exploitation. Mobility is the most obvious practice and, in the most general sense, involves either continual or seasonal movement, although other strategies are often used such as keeping a portion of the herd near the homestead, moving only in certain years, or even not moving at all if the environment permits. Herd diversification means keeping a herd composed of different species such as by the Kazakhs who traditionally kept camels, horses, cattle, and sheep. This strategy extends the period of time milk is available, ensures that the entire herd will not be lost to disease at one time, and maximizes natural resources when some of the herd, such as cattle, graze on grasses and others, such as goats, browse on bushes and trees. Additionally, several smaller herds tend to return more quickly to maximum size after a drought than does a single large herd. Herd dispersion involves dividing the herd into several smaller herds and keeping these in separate locations to reduce the effects of disease, predators, or theft. This practice is sometimes done by dividing the herd in two or at other times through social arrangements in which a household divides in two or a herder loans part of his herd to others. It is also possible that the frequent raiding of other herds by the Bedouin was a way of dividing one's herd. Since the raiding and theft was continual and reciprocal, a herder was generally assured of getting additional stock in the future. Thus, stock stolen and kept by others was really only "on loan." Finally, pastoralists try to maximize their herd by keeping as many female animals as possible and by keeping a herd larger than is required just for subsistence as a hedge against food shortages.

Social and Political Aspects of Pastoralism

There are few, if any, pastoral societies that are entirely self-sufficient. That is, all pastoral societies either maintain some type of exchange relations with other societies or are internally differentiated (as in agro-pastoralism) so that some communities are primarily agricultural or trading and others pastoral. For example, the Sarakatsani, numbering about 80,000, are sheep- and goatherders of the Pindus and Rhodope Mountains of northwestern Greece. They live a transhumant lifestyle, tending their flocks in the mountains from May to November and then wintering on the coastal plains. The Sarakatsani do not own either the winter or summer pastures but lease them from neighboring non-pastoral Greeks. The lease is obtained by the head of the Sarakatsani kinship group composed of a father, his sons, and other close kin who cooperate in economic matters. Sarakatsani life centers around the care of the flocks: milking, shearing, building pens, lambing, cheese making, and related activities. Products produced from the flocks are supplemented by household gardens, the gathering of wild plants, and various crafts such as spinning wool and dyeing cloth. Many Sarakatsani own their summer homes in the mountains but continue to live in the communal groups in their winter villages, at least in part to maintain distance from their Greek neighbors. The Bedouin traditionally sold and traded camels, a major source of income, and maintained relationships with nonpastoral groups. In East Africa, herd size is a sign of wealth, and the distribution of cattle often in marriage transactions is used to cement family ties and to establish a herder's status.

Pastoralism is labor-intensive and requires a large labor pool that in many traditional pastoral societies was composed of a man, his sons, sons-in-law, younger brothers, and nephews. Pastoral societies are described as male-centered in that men perform the primary economic activity—herding and owning the stock—and kinship ties are generally traced through the male line. Additionally, in many pastoral societies, a woman would move to the community or dwelling of her husband's family following marriage. In traditional pastoral societies, there was often a clear division of labor based on gender, with men and boys caring for the flocks while women and girls handled domestic chores, child rearing, and other subsistence activities such as gathering or domestic gardening. Men generally were responsible for slaughtering animals; women processed raw materials into food and material goods. The economic relations between husbands and wives were often complementary with each responsible and in charge of their domains.

In many pastoral societies, ownership of the grazing lands was communal. Members of the society have the right to use the lands, although each extended family might typically use a particular section each year. Who owns the stock, including newborns, is often not a clear issue; the rights to sell, milk, move, dispose of, and slaughter animals might be shared among different members of the family. Efforts by national or state governments to institute private ownership of herds and grazing land conflict with this traditional orientation.

Many pastoral societies have or had a tribal form of political organization with the overarching tribe whose members shared a common language and religion and smaller sections, subsections, lineages, and families. In addition, there are often other structural features such as age-grades among the Nuer, villages, and friendships that create links between individuals. In pastoral societies, people and groups are tied to one another by an ethos that emphasizes the reciprocal obligation to protect and assist one another.

Pastoralism in the Contemporary World

Around the world, pastoralism is in decline, and within pastoral societies, the number of people who live by pastoralism is decreasing. In the regions of the former Russian Empire and Soviet Union, pastoral societies such as the Kazakhs and the reindeer herders of Siberia have been under government pressure for several centuries. In the Middle East, the end of colonialism, the establishment of independent nations with cen-

tralized governments, and economic development have reduced the number of Bedouin camel- and sheepherders and rendered sedentary many of those who remain. Camel herders moving from oasis to oasis are now largely an image from the past. In sub-Saharan Africa and especially in East Africa, pastoralism has been a victim of postcolonial centralized government, economic development, and environmental concerns since the 1960s. And in southern Europe, mountain pastoralists are being rapidly drawn into their national economies. As this world situation suggests, there are five major, interrelated processes pushing pastoralists in the Third and Fourth Worlds (where most pastoralists are found) into decline: population growth and expansion, efforts by national governments to control pastoralists, economic development, concern about the environment, and the introduction of new technology.

Pastoralists pose a problem for centralized national governments that find it difficult to exert political control over pastoral groups with their loose tribal organization, use of large tracts of land, and frequent movements. Thus, many governments in the twentieth century have taken direct and indirect action to bring pastoralists under national control. These actions include settling pastoralists in villages, collectivizing their herding activities, establishing ranches in place of open range, marketing livestock, converting pastures to farmland, settling farmers on former pastures, making land private property, collecting taxes, establishing towns, and building roads across pasturage. These government actions are not always motivated by a desire to control pastoralists but instead reflect population growth and expansion in many nations and efforts to stimulate economic development. In general, whatever the motivation, government actions such as these usually result in a decrease in the number of pastoralists, a reduction in pasturage, and the incorporation of pastoralists into the national and even international economic

Pathan sheepherders in Pakistan

systems. Such government actions also often have a negative impact on the pastoral way of life. Iran in the 1920s, for example, attempted to settle the sheepherding Basseri in villages, a program that led to 70–80 percent of the sheep dying and the resulting shortage of wool, meat, and draft animals throughout Iran. In Kenya, government programs have converted Masai range into ranches, and the government has controlled the number of cattle owned and sold by the Masai. The result has been overgrazing of the inadequate ranchland and degradation of the environment. Recent programs designed to convert some Masai pastureland to national parkland and involve the Masai in the process as well as sharing revenues with them seem more promising.

Pastoralists in East Africa have been criticized by environmentalists who claim that tra-

ditional pastoral stock management practices degrade the environment. Environmentalists charge that common pastures, large herds, and free mobility lead to overgrazing that in turn causes desertification, a claim not clearly supported by research in the region.

Economic development programs and the introduction of nonhuman and nonanimal forms of energy also impact pastoralism. Among the Skolt Saami, for example, the introduction of snowmobiles has had broad effects including making the Saami dependent on fossil fuels and other products that must be purchased from outside sources, a reduction in the number of herders, and the involvement of the Saami in Finnish society to a far greater extent than earlier.

Many of the changes experienced by many pastoral groups and the forces behind those changes in the twentieth century are exemplified by the situation of the Bedouin sheepherders of Syria. In 1952, the Bedouin were 8.1 percent of the Syrian population but by 1978 had declined to only 3.2 percent, largely because of population increases among non-Bedouin Syrians. Traditionally, the Bedouin were transhumant sheepherders who used camels for transport, were governed as a loose confederation by a tribal chief, and who maintained trade relations with merchants in towns. In 1960, the Syrian government replaced the Bedouin system of tribal law with the national civil code and began placing grazing land under mechanized cultivation, thereby reducing Bedouin grazing space and encouraging some Bedouin to become farmers. In 1966, the erection of the Euphrates Dam converted more land to agricultural use and more Bedouin became settled farmers; others began to seek temporary labor as migrant workers in Saudi Arabia. About this time, herding became mechanized with flocks moved by truck, water tanked in, and cars and trucks used in place of camels. Those who had turned to farming settled in villages. Herders built permanent winter homes but continued to use tents during the summer months. And they became less self-reliant, preferring instead to purchase foods and tools. In the future, pastoralism is likely to continue to decline in the face of worldwide population growth and economic development.

See also DWELLINGS; RANCHING.

Cohen, Yehudi. (1968) *Man in Adaptation: The Cultural Present.*

Dyson-Hudson, Rada, and Neville Dyson-Hudson. (1980) "Nomadic Pastoralism." *Annual Review of Anthropology* 9:15–61.

Evans-Pritchard, Edward E. (1940) *The Nuer.*

Forde, C. Daryll. (1963) *Habitat, Economy, and Society.*

Friedrich, Paul, and Norma Diamond, eds. (1994) *Encyclopedia of World Cultures. Volume 6, Russia and Eurasia/China.*

Galaty, John G., Dan Aronson, Philip C. Salzman, and Amy Chouinard, eds. (1980) *The Future of Pastoral Peoples.* Proceedings of a Conference Held in Nairobi, Kenya, August 4–8.

Homewood, K. M. (1988) "Pastoralism and Conservation." In *Tribal Peoples and Development Issues: A Global Overview,* edited by John H. Bodley, 310–320.

Ingold, Tim. (1980) *Hunters, Pastoralists, and Ranchers: Reindeer Economies and Their Transformations.*

Kabbadias, Georgios B. (1965) *Nomadic Shepherds of the Mediterranean.*

Lustig-Arecco, Vera. (1975) *Technology: Strategies for Survival.*

Murdock, George P. (1981) *Atlas of World Cultures.*

Pelto, Pertti J. (1973) *The Snowmobile Revolution: Technology and Social Change in the Arctic.*

Salzman, Philip C. (1995) "Pastoralism." In *Encyclopedia of Cultural Anthropology,* edited by David Levinson and Melvin Ember.

Weissleder, Wolfgang. (1978) *The Nomadic Alternative: Modes and Models of Interaction in the African-Asian Deserts and Steppes.*

PLACE NAMES

The following description of the role of place names in Faeroese culture applies with equal validity to all cultures around the world as place names are a cultural universal. In addition, while the actual places named and the names used vary from culture to culture, the criteria used in selecting places to name, the criteria used in assigning names, and the role of place names in a culture follow the same general pattern across cultures.

> Faeroese place names and person's geographic names tie culture to nature as well as mediate between nature and culture. They instantly refer to and describe parts of the land harnessed by humans—houses, hayfields, pastures, etc.—as well as to inaccessible cliffs and chasms. Contrasting with the fluidity and uncertainty of nature, weather, fishing luck and life in general, place names ad knowable dimensions to the landscape. They provide a grid and groundplan for "placing" culture onto nature (Gaffin 1993:66).

The number of place names known in a cultural group ranges from a few hundred to several thousand. One survey of 12 cultures indicates a low of about 118 place names known to the Quileute of Washington to a high of 4,776 used for some 8,200 places known to the Tonga of Oceania. However, it is rare for an individual to know and use all the place names known in his or her culture. Instead, individuals know and use names only for places important to them; on average across cultures people use about 500 place names with a range from about 200 to 800 names. One of the major factors influencing how many place names a person uses is the human memory, which seems to have a limit of about 500 place names for the average person.

Across cultures, 11 criteria are commonly used to assign place names, although not all criteria are used in all cultures. In most cultures, only 2 or 3 criteria are used for assigning most place names. For example, in the United States, the majority of place names are taken from the names of people, especially the names of towns that are often named after the surname of the first settler, founder of the town, or the first postmaster. In Tonga the names are mainly descriptive or based on incidents with a few also of foreign origin. The 11 criteria used to assign place names are as follows:

1. Descriptive names are ones that identify a place by some distinguishing feature such as its size, shape, color, or other feature. While descriptive names and association ones as well seem straightforward, it is important to note that sometimes they are not completely accurate nor is their use always restricted to one place. For example, Tewa-speaking Indians of New Mexico call the Rio Grande River the "Big River" although the Chama River is just as wide but is never called "Big River." Similarly, each pueblo community traditionally had a "High Hill" nearby on which ceremonies were conducted, but the "High Hill" was not necessarily the highest one near the village. And arroyos from the same water source may all have the same name while streams running in different directions from the same source may also have the same name. Thus, while descriptive terms emphasize physical features of the place being named, the actual process of applying the name is influenced by the beliefs and needs of those doing the naming.

2. Association names are related to descriptive names and are ones that identify a place by some distinguishing feature linked to the generic name for some other place such as Mill River or Flaking Stone Mountain.

3. Possessive names identify a place by a name that links it to a current or previous owner.

4. Incident names are ones that identify a place by an event that took place there. Incidents used as place names range widely and include events such as a flood, the death of a human, the sighting of an animal, and supernatural happenings. In cultures that gather their food rather than produce it, incident names often relate to animal behavior such as the nesting of birds or the trail of migrating animals and thus mark places that are likely to be good locales for hunting in the future.

5. Commemorative names are ones that identify a place by the name of a person, whose memory the people wish to preserve or honor.

6. Commendatory names are ones that identify a place by assigning it a name that creates an image of the place as a desirable place to live.

7. Manufactured names are ones that identify a place by constructing names by combining one or more letters, syllables, or words.

8. Transfer names are ones used to identify a place by naming it after a place in another location and are common in the New World where European settlers named the villages after towns, cities, or counties in their homeland. These names are often combined terms, with the names of the place preceded by New, as in New World itself.

9. False names are those used to identify a place by, in essence, assigning it a new name, which is a new spelling or pronunciation based on an existing name.

10. Number names are ones used to identify a place by using a unique number for it, usually in a consecutive set of numbers followed by a place name. Numbering systems are found most often in modern nations to number buildings or plots of land in sequence such as 127 West Avenue. However, they are sometimes used in other ways as well, such as by the Hopi in Arizona who refer to Tewa pueblos in New Mexico as number one (San Ildefonso), number two (Santa Clara), and number three (San Juan).

11. Mistake names are ones used to identify a place but which have no known or obvious origin, usually because they have been incorrectly translated from another language and their original meaning has been completely lost. The original meanings of place names often are forgotten over time, and in cultures such as the Rural Irish where place names have important symbolic meanings, discussions often take place about the origin and, therefore, the "true meaning" of place names.

The use of a number of different criteria in naming places in a single culture is indicated in the following names, as translated into English, used by the Copper Inuit of Canada for the region north of Bathurst Inlet as shown on the map in Figure 1 on page 166. The 34 Inuit place names listed on the map are of three types—descriptive, incident, and commemorative.

In every culture place names serve a variety of functions including economic, political, social, religious, and those that help define the human-environment relationship. In terms of the human-environment relationship, place names help humans maintain some degree of stability in the face of environmental uncertainty. Place names tell hunters where to hunt and fishermen where to fish, mark trails through the forest, serve as boundary markers for fields, and generally indicate what places are of importance and which are less important. In most cultures, most names that people know and use are for places in their local environment that have economic importance, as with the 34 place names used by the Copper Inuit. Place names also give people a sense of stability when the culture is mobile; the names of places remain the same. In terms of the environment, a key function of place names is to mark dangerous places, as with this tale from Rural Ireland:

> There's somebody lost, I was told, off every bit of the cliffs. In the old days men used to go down often [for wood and salvage]. They used to go down on their own ropes. . . . There was a fellow over in Liscannor who would go down at any time of day or night. He used to go down for lost sheep or lambs. One day a child fell off Aillenasearrach and he went down for the body . . . but when he came up he said he'd never go down again because every rock down

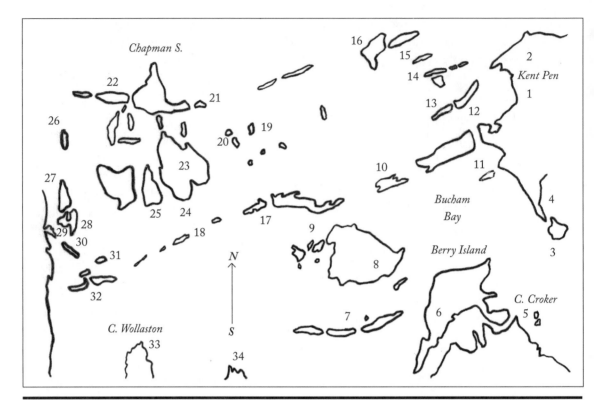

FIGURE 1   THE REGION NORTH OF BATHURST INLET; FROM KENT PENINSULA TO THE
WEST. LOOKING ALMOST FROM SOUTH TO NORTH. FROM A DRAWING BY NETSIT.

1. That which seems to form a conclusion
2. The maggot abounding
3. The little flat one
4. The forefinger
5. The testicles
6. The dear little pissing place
7. The narrow ones
8. The Big Island
9. The after-birth like one
10. Those rich in steep coasts
11. That like a toolbox
12. The big sound
13. Those like a hood
14. Those abounding in hares
15. The one lying across
16. The place where one ties one's kamik-laces
17. Unknown
18. Nakanhunnartuarjok—the name of two
    dangerous spirits
19. An island
20. The two who lie nudging together
21. The place where one can ladle something
22. Those who have laid themselves across
    something
23. The copper
24. Its whip
25. The place where there are bundles (of dried
    meat)
26. The little flat one
27. The place where one waves with skins (to scare
    caribou)
28. That which resembles brains
29. The place where one waits for something to
    end (a hunt, taboo, or life)
30. Where gulls abound
31. The heart-shaped one
32. Those that are good to have as an underlayer
    for protecting the edge of the platform
33. The little ness
34. The place with the big house

below was covered with people sitting on it. People out of the sea they were. . . . Two little girls were lost looking for flowers the fairies put there to grow. The flowers aren't there at all, but are put there just to draw people over the cliff. (Arensberg 1937:203)

Place names also play a real and symbolic role in individuating people in their community and in creating a sense of identity in multicultural settings. For example, the name of the place where one lives often tells others in the community something about the person. In the Faeroe Islands, for example, a person called Leif Post Office would indicate that he is the postman, a position treated with some disdain in Faeroe culture. Similarly, a woman called Woman of the Valley would be seen as sexually promiscuous. In a more general sense, place names are also used as a symbolic shorthand for defining whole groups of people, such as the people Under the Bluff or of the Mound. Finally, place names serve to distinguish among insiders and outsiders and multiethnic communities. For example, in England in 1940, when the English feared a German invasion, signs with town names on them were taken down. The British government reasoned that the missing signs would slow the advance of the Germans as well as identifying as a possible spy an individual who asked for directions from town and town. Place names also distinguish among locals and outsiders when local people use a different name for a place. For example, in the Berkshire region of Massachusetts, the main north-south road is Route 7, and visitors to the region will follow this road. Local people, however, refer to the stretch of road through the town of Great Barrington as Main Street or Up-Street and the six-mile stretch from Great Barrington to Stockbridge as the Stockbridge Road. Similarly, locals refer to the town not as Great Barrington but as Barrington.

Place names are, of course, subject to change, and old names disappear from use and new ones appear with considerable regularity. In general, names fall from use when the place they name becomes unimportant to the users of the name or another name serves the purpose better. For example, in Sheffield, Massachusetts, in 1992, the town residents decided to replace some street names and alter others to eliminate duplicate or similar names and to shorten names so that the local rescue service could respond to calls with less confusion. However, not all names are discarded, even if the place is no longer used. For example, in the Faeroe Islands, the names "Sitting Room Rock" and "Milkmaid's Gate" refer to a house site and path used in the past but now abandoned and unused. And pueblos in the Southwest, such as San Juan, often retained their names when moved to a new location.

Arensberg, Conrad M. (1937) *The Irish Countryman.*

Gaffin, Dennis. (1993) "Landscape, Personhood, and Culture: Names of Places and People in the Faeroe Islands." *Ethnos* 58:53–72.

Gifford, Edward W. (1923) *Tongan Place Names.*

Harrington, John P. (1907–1908) *The Ethnogeography of the Tewa Indians.*

Hunn, Eugene. (1994) "Place-Names, Population Density, and the Magic Number 500." *Current Anthropology* 35:81–85.

Rasmussen, Knud J. V. (1932) *Intellectual Culture of the Copper Eskimos.*

Stewart, George R. (1970) *American Place Names.*

Tooker, Elizabeth, and Harold C. Conklin, eds. (1984) *Naming Systems.*

PRECIPITATION

Precipitation is all the water that falls to earth as rain, snow, sleet, and hail. The water that falls to earth comes from the oceans, lakes, and rivers. While some precipitation in most areas comes from local evaporated water, most is brought from distant oceans by winds. Water in the oceans is evaporated by the heat of the sun and rises as vapor into the atmosphere where it eventually condenses and forms clouds and then falls to earth as rain, snow, or hail. Condensation on the ground or on plants is called dew while condensation occurring near the ground is called fog or mist. Rain occurs when the temperature is above freezing and snow when the temperature is below freezing. In addition to snow, the other major forms of frozen precipitation are hail, sleet, and graupel (soft hail or snow pellets).

Across cultures, people commonly classify different forms of rain, snow, and ice into different categories, with these classification systems varying widely in detail across cultures. One of the most complex systems is that used traditionally by the reindeer-herding Saami of Scandinavia who have separate words for each of the types of precipitation listed below:

1. Rain—cold, drizzle, downpour, strong

2. Fog—thin, dense and dry, frost, winter, low-floating, rising from the ground

3. Haze

4. Dew

5. Hoarfrost—on trees, on the ground

6. Ice—on stones, bushes, and trees; thin layer on snow

7. Frost—hard, cloudy frost weather, on the ground, at the bottom of shallow bodies of water

8. Snow—wet, on the trees, hail snow, dirty looking, pressed down, melted next to the ground, next to the ground, soft snowdrift, hard snowdrift, snowdrift unmelted in the summer, steep snowdrift, snowdrift on a mountain, gently sloping new snow on a mountain, steep snowdrift on a lake, natural snow or ice bridge, thick snow, thick snow in the fall, hard and slippery sheet of snow, bare spot where wind has swept snow away, especially bare spot where wind has swept the snow away, spot where the snow has melted away, ground free of snow or ice

9. Ice—under the snow on lichen, even surface, thin, new and shiny, gray, clear, covered by a thin layer of snow, coarse ice in the spring, single surface of ice, surface of ice with another layer under it, melting, crack in the ice, slush near the shore, firm, black ice, dripping ice

10. Glacier

11. Avalanche

The Saami use a number of principles in assigning their native language terms to these different types of precipitation. These principles include the effect of the precipitation on Saami subsistence resources such as the term for "ice under the snow on lichen" meaning that reindeer will starve because they cannot eat the lichen, the physical appearance of the precipitation itself such as hard or soft snow, the nature of the distribution of the precipitation on the ground or on objects, the season in which the precipitation occurs, and the effect of the precipitation on Saami activity such as "thick snow" meaning that it is hard to ski on. Thus, this long list of terms not only classifies different forms of precipitation for the Saami but also enables them to evaluate these forms in terms of their effect on their life and especially on subsistence activities related to reindeer herding. In this regard, the list actually gets longer—the Saami have several dozen words that describe the condition of snow and ice on the ground or trails and indicate the suitability of these surfaces for human and reindeer use.

Rain

In all cultures, people need water to survive. And in all cultures, both immediate and long-term water needs are met by rain. In most cultures, people differentiate between water and rain. Water such as standing pools of rainwater, rivers, lakes, oceans, lagoons, and so forth are usually considered part of the natural world on earth, while rain, which is beyond human control and prediction, is more often associated with the supernatural world or with both the nature and the supernatural. The Andaman Islanders in the Indian Ocean, for example, look to both nature and the supernatural for an understanding of where rains comes from. They have a number of explanations for rain, including that it is caused by a stone in the sky turning cold and turning the mist into rain, a large pool in the sky overflowing, or by a female rain deity. The Toba of Argentina take a more strictly supernatural view and believe that rain is a one-eyed man, a servant of the spirits, who lives in the northwest sky. When clouds moving across the sky from the south reach this place, they ask his permission to let rain fall and the Master of Rain opens a door and rain falls to earth. The Horia of South America also take a supernatural view and believe that rain is a spirit riding a horse across the sky.

People need a sufficient amount of rain at the right times to grow and harvest crops; water and feed their livestock; have wild plant foods and animals available for gathering and hunting; and slashing, burning, and planting their gardens. People also need rainwater on a daily basis for drinking, bathing, preparing foods, and so forth. Additionally, in tropical climates, rain defines the two seasons of the year—dry and rainy—and thus determines the annual subsistence cycle as well as the scheduling of religious and social activities. The Yanomamö of Brazil and Venezuela, for example, are largely confined to their villages in the rainy season when trails are flooded making the raiding of other villages or peaceful visiting between villages during this time virtually impossible. Similarly, in the hot, dry season it is too hot after early morning for the San of Botswana to do much of anything, so they mainly sit in their huts and talk.

From the perspective of subsistence activities the issue is not simply how much rain but how, when, and local variations of how much

and when. A deluge can rapidly destroy crops causing starvation just as can too little drain cause a drought and also cause starvation. Most peoples are like the Amhara of Ethiopia for whom "rain is important in season." The Amhara say that "In (the month of) Hamle, beating down rain; In (the month of) Sänya, fine drizzle." As Sänye is the beginning of the rainy season, Amhara farmers prefer a fine rain that moistens the soil enough to break it up with a plow. During Hamle, they prefer more rain to water the sprouting grain. Similarly, the Serbs, like most agricultural peoples, hope that a strong rain comes only after the crop is harvested and stored. In most cultures around the world people do worry about rain, when it will come, if there will be too much or too little, if it will come at the right time, and if it will rain too hard or too softly. These concerns are indicated by peoples' recognition of different types of rain. The Saami of Scandinavia, as noted above, recognize rain, drizzle, cold rain, a downpour, and a strong rain. The San of Botswana recognize two types—a hard rain that "speaks loudly" as it often falls during thunderstorms and the preferred "this is good rain, which speaks softly and is gentle." They also distinguish between two types of clouds—"rain-skins" and "rain feathers." In addition to general concerns about rain such as how much and when, some cultures have very specific concerns. The Senoi of Malaysia are troubled by three features of rain that seem unnatural—hot rain, *nyamp*, and rainbows. Hot rain occurs when it rains while the sun is shining, an occurrence the Senoi believe will cause fever and jaundice and which they try to avoid by wearing protective amulets. *Nyamp* is the Senoi term for the condition of the air following a downpour that ends at sunset. The air is heavy and damp and the sunlight colors everything red or light yellow, frightening the Senoi who bring their children inside and temporarily suspend all public activities. Finally, the rainbow, which generally accompanies both hot rain and *nyamp*, also seems unusual to the Senoi and they believe it causes illness.

As with many other aspects of the weather, rain for many peoples across cultures is associated with the supernatural rather than the natural world. That is, rain is believed to be caused by supernatural forces and is thus controllable by appeal to those forces. For the Hopi who grow their crops in the desert conditions of Arizona, rain is a major concern and in a broad sense all Hopi ceremonies conducted during the year are for rain, fertility, and abundant crops. The concern about rain is most evident in the nine-day August ceremony when conditions are dry and rain is needed for a rich harvest. At that time prayers are enacted to bring rain. Unlike the Hopi, the Central Thai get most concerned about rain only when they are threatened by a drought; then they carry out various rites to bring rain. Three ceremonies are used commonly. The first, called *song grabaan*, is a combination of traditional animistic practices and Buddhist rites. Villagers offer the spirits food and clay figures of people and draft animals while priests conduct public merit ceremonies in which they bless merit makers to please the spirits and induce the spirits to let it rain. In a second ceremony, called *suad kaw fon*, Buddhist priests chant in a field to call on the deity, Pra Piruun, who is associated with rainfall. At the same time, some villagers symbolically engage in sexual intercourse with clay figures, with the male figure (symbolizing heaven) asked to drop his semen (symbolizing water) on the female figure (symbolizing earth). The third rite is a traditional ceremony now falling into disuse. In times of drought, a cat is carried from house to house in a cage while people sing songs expressing their wish for rain. The lyrics from one song are:

A widow has many children,
And miserable is she:
There is no rain this year.
The father-in-law and the son-in-law,
They pout their arms on the forehead. . . .
The widow has many children,

And miserable is she: There is no rain this year. . . .
Let the rain fall down, fall down. . . .

At each house the people are greeted and water is thrown on the cat. When the procession is completed, a village feast is held at the temple. A cat is used because it is an animal that does not like water and dousing it with water is a magical act to bring rain.

Among the Shona of East Africa, rain is associated not just with the acts of supernatural beings but also with the actions of humans, and too much or too little rain is blamed on misdeeds by people in the effected communities. In the case of particularly devastating drought and famine, the religious leader will lead the entire community in a ceremony to confess their sins, propitiate the ancestors with beer, and appeal to the Creator for rain. The Shona also look to a medium, designated as the person responsible for rain, to conduct ceremonies when drought threatens.

The San of Botswana, for whom rain is a vital concern, deal with the supernatural somewhat differently than in these other cultures. The San do not ask for rain directly but instead try not to offend their god, N!adima, who is responsible for the rain, and through their sayings and prayers make it clear that they appreciate and are grateful for the rain given to them. In an interesting twist, the San sought to end a flood period that led to an outbreak of malaria by killing a chameleon in order to anger N!adima so that he would stop the rain. The innovation worked but led to a new worry about whether rain would occur the next year.

Frozen Precipitation

Snow is water that freezes in the atmosphere and falls to earth in crystallized form. Hail is a ball of ice that forms when rain droplets are carried up into the colder layers of the atmosphere by strong winds and are coated with layers of ice before eventually falling to earth. Sleet is small ice pellets formed in the same way as hail, except that the original droplets freeze rather than become coated with layers of ice. Sleet is a mixture of rain and snow. Ice is water in its solid state and generally occurs when water or water vapor freezes at 32 degrees Fahrenheit or 0 degrees Celsius.

Snow covers 23 percent of the earth's surface for all or part of the year. The amount of snow on the ground and its distribution across the landscape are determined by a number of facts including the amount of snow that has fallen, the ground conditions it has fallen upon, the air temperature, the wind, and the weight of the snow.

While people in most cultures value rain and, as described above, act in ways designed to bring adequate amounts of rain at the appropriate times of the year, few cultures have a generally favorable view of frozen precipitation. Snow, for example, reflects nearly 90 percent of the sunlight hitting it and therefore can cause snow blindness for people living in Arctic and sub-Arctic regions or at high elevations that are snow-covered for much of the year. People in Greenland, northern Canada, Alaska, Siberia, and Tibet protect themselves from the glare of the sun off the snow with snow goggles made from wood, animal hides, bone, tree bark, and metal. These goggles have narrow slits that block most of the sun but still enable the wearer to see. Similarly, hail, which often falls during heavy thunderstorms, is generally troublesome. The Aymara of Peru describe hail, wind, and ice as three lazy sons who bring misery and ruin to their parents. Frost in the mountains is a concern for the Sherpa of Nepal who can easily lose one-third of their buckwheat and potato crops in the spring to a late frost and, like farmers everywhere, worry about crop-destroying hail in the planting and harvest seasons. Since hail often falls during thunderstorms, protective measures usually involving prayer and the performance of rituals can be placed in the context of efforts to control thunder and lightning and the heavy rains that accompany them. In some cultures, however, special measures may be taken for hail. The Sherpa, for example, might pay a particular family with wheat to perform rituals to prevent hail from falling. The Zulu of South Africa have a special Hail Doctor, in addition to Lightning and Rain doctors, who through their knowledge, lifestyle, and ability to interact with the supernatural are expected to control hail and ritually purify those harmed by it.

See also Environmental Disasters; Famine; Rainbow; Seasons; Storms; Water.

Attagara, Kingkeo. (1968) *The Folk Religion of Ban Nai, a Hamlet in Central Thailand.*

Dentan, Robert K. (1978) *The Semai: A Nonviolent People of Malaya.*

Ingersoll, Jasper C. (1964) *The Priest and the Path: An Analysis of the Priest Role in a Central Thai Village.*

Itkonen, Toivo I. (1948) *The Lapps in Finland Up to 1945.*

Kileff, Peggy, and Clive Kileff, eds. (1970) *Shona Customs: Essays by African Writers.*

Levinson, David, and David Sherwood. (1993) *The Tribal Living Book.* 2d ed.

Messing, Simon D. (1957) *The Highland-Plateau Amhara of Ethiopia.*

Metraux, Alfred. (1946) *Myths of the Toba and Pilaga Indians of the Gran Chaco.*

Pavlovic, Jeremija M. (1973) *Folk Life and Customs in the Kragujevac Region of the Jasenica in Sumadija.*

Radcliffe-Brown, Alfred R. (1922) *The Andaman Islanders: A Study in Social Anthropology.*

Silberbauer, George B. (1981) *Hunter and Habitat in the Central Kalahari Desert.*

Stevens, Stanley F. (1990) *Sherpa Settlement and Subsistence: Cultural Ecology and History in Highland Nepal.*

Tschopik, Harry, Jr. (1951) *The Aymara of Chucuito, Peru: 1. Magic.*

RAIN

See PRECIPITATION.

RAINBOW

A rainbow is a multicolored arc composed of a series of colored concentric arcs. A rainbow is formed and can be seen when light falls on water drops. Rainbows occur most commonly in nature when sunlight falls on the water drops from the rain of a distant rainshower. Rainbows also occur naturally in the same way with the water drops in sprays such as from a waterfall, a fountain, or in fog. The colors result from the refraction and internal reflection of the light through the raindrops.

Rainbows are often visible toward the end of a rainstorm when the sun breaks through clouds and casts light on the raindrops. This pattern is noted by the Hausa of Nigeria who believe that Gajimari, the rainbow serpent, resides in the form of a snake in a well or ant mound and at the end of rainstorm rises up to the sky and causes the rain to stop. Such a serpent is called Masaruwa, meaning "drinker of water." Once the rain ceases, Masaruwa stretches himself across the sky as the red arc in the rainbow alongside the thunder spirit, Ra, who forms the blue arc. Rainbow deities in the form of serpents are common throughout cultures. In West Africa, the Yoruba call theirs Osumare, the Dahomeans call theirs Aido Hwedo, and the Jukun refer to their rainbow serpent as Akuwo. The association of rainbows with serpents is found elsewhere as well. In Malaysia, the Senoi link rainbows with a large subterranean dragon. In the New World, Haitians of West African ancestry believe that Damballa, the rainbow, often lives as a snake and is the source of spring water. The following song, sung at rites aimed at influencing Damballa, points to the fact that Damballa cannot be drowned:

> Papa Damballa you are a snake, oh!
> Why don't you drown?
> Why don't you drown?
> Damballa, why don't you drown in the water?

The symbolic link between the rainbow and serpents is also common in southern South America—among numerous cultures in Argentina, Brazil, Peru, Bolivia, and Chile. The Vilela account for the variety of coloration among birds with their myth in which the rainbow serpent crawled about consuming animals and humans until the birds killed him. The birds then took pieces of his multicolored skin, hence the variety of different colored birds in the Vilela world.

In some Oceanic cultures, the rainbow, while characterized as a special phenomenon, does not carry the influence and symbolism found in West Africa and South America. For example, the Mangaia traditionally believed that the rainbow was the girdle of their god Tangaroa, which he let hang down to earth when he wished to descend.

Because of its association with rain and storms, the rainbow is taken in many cultures as a harbinger of the future. And in others, such as the Hausa where it is attributed supernatural power, the rainbow can be either a malevolent or benevolent force. Copper Inuit hunters in northern Canada, for example, throw a piece of deer skin at a rainbow to bring them good luck. Native Americans of the Pacific Northwest believed that pointing at a rainbow would cause one's finger to wither. The Western Shoshone believed that the rainbow was a good omen. The Andaman Islanders in the Indian Ocean believe the opposite; they believe that the rainbow will cause someone to fall ill, a view shared by the Mbuti of central Africa who link the appearance of a rainbow to sorcery and death. The Senoi of Malaysia believe in different types of rainbows with different spirits associated with each one. In general, they see rainbows as mainly harmful. Walking under one might cause the person to become ill. Rainbows are attributed to a tiger killing a large animal or human and flinging the victim's blood into the sky to form the rainbow. Of the various rainbow spirits, two of whom are a married man and woman, the woman lives at the source of streams and cares for the fish in the stream while than man lives in the ocean and causes storms.

Courlander, Harold. (1960) *The Drum and the Hoe: Life and Lore of the Haitian People.*

Greenberg, Joseph H. (1946) *The Influence of Islam on a Sudanese Religion.*

Jenness, Diamond. (1922) *The Life of the Copper Eskimos.*

Metraux, Alfred. (1946) *Myths of the Toba and Pilaga Indians of the Gran Chaco.*

Mooney, James. (1982) *Myths of the Cherokee and Sacred Formulas of the Cherokees.*

Radcliffe-Brown, Alfred R. (1922) *The Andaman Islanders: A Study in Social Anthropology.*

Steward, Julian H. (1941) *Culture Element Distributions: XIII. Nevada Shoshoni.*

Turnbull, Colin M. (1965) *The Mbuti Pygmies: An Ethnographic Survey.*

Werner, Roland. (1984) *Jah-het of Malaysia, Art and Culture.*

RANCHING

"Ranching is that pattern of land use which is based upon the grazing of livestock, chiefly rudiments, for sale in a money market. This pattern of land use is characterized by control over large units of land, extensive use of that land, and extensive use of labor on the land" (Strickon 1965:230). Cattle ranching is found on the greatest scale on the Great Plains of the United States and Canada, the Huasteca region of Mexico, northern Brazil, and northern Argentina; sheep ranching in Australia; and reindeer ranching in Scandinavia and Siberia. Generally, ranching is found in regions where the land is too poor to support agriculture or where the land has yet to be exploited for agriculture. For example, in North America, open-range ranching flourished on the Plains frontier until ranches began to diminish in size following the arrival of farmers in the region. In the twentieth century, ranching in North America has grown on some Indian reservations such as those of the Western Apache in Arizona and on the Wind River Reservation in Wyoming, in part because of a shortage of quality farmland. However, as with ranching in most of the world today, to be economically viable, these ranches are generally small, with enclosed graze lands, smaller herds, selective breeding, and water supplied through irrigation when necessary.

Types of Ranching

Three different types of ranching are found around the world: proto- or frontier-ranching, collectivized ranching, and Euro-American ranching. As a subsistence strategy, proto-ranching combines elements of hunting, pastoralism, and ranching. It tends to be found in frontier regions that have much graze land but few human inhabitants such as in the Skolt Saami region of Scandinavia and northern Brazil. In proto-ranching, large herds are grazed on large open ranges primarily for subsistence rather than sale, as the ranchers live off the livestock. The herders who assist the herd owners are like kin as they may live with the family and are often given livestock with which to start their own herds. Proto-ranching has often been a transitional subsistence phase utilized by peoples whose economy is changing from pastoral to ranching or to a diversified economy. Among the Saami, for example, free-range grazing became subsistence ranching and then ranching based on roundups organized by reindeer men's associations and the selection and sale of reindeer for slaughter.

Collectivized ranching developed in the former Soviet Union when nomadic pastoral groups such as the Koryak and Chukchee in Siberia were forced to settle in Russian-designed communities and graze their formerly free-roaming reindeer herds on confined ranches. Additionally, the pastoral economies were transformed into diversified economies combining ranching, farming, and wage labor.

The Euro-American ranching complex is what most people mean when they discuss ranching. It is found in three major regions—North America, Argentina, and Australia—with the first two ranching mainly cattle and the last sheep. Longhorn cattle were introduced to the New World in Mexico by the Spanish colonists in the sixteenth century. From there both the cattle and the ranching complex diffused north first into Texas and then through the Great Plains of the United States into southern Canada, where it became firmly established by the 1860s. Euro-American ranching is essentially a product of the industrial and commercial revolutions as it requires a large urban market to serve as a market for the meat, a processing industry to turn the cattle into meat or the sheep's wool into clothing, and a transportation system to bring the cattle to the processing centers and the meat or clothing to the marketplace.

Euro-American Ranching

The key elements of Euro-American ranching are land, livestock, labor, and the market. Thus, Euro-American ranching is both an ecological adaptation and a commercial enterprise whose structure and success depend on the rancher's ability to cope with uncertainties of both the physical environment and external markets for meat.

Ranching requires large amounts of land for, in general, the more cattle raised the more income the rancher can earn by selling them. Thus, the purchase of grazing land is the major capital investment made by ranchers, followed by their investment in cattle, buildings, machinery, and fencing. In the early days of ranching in North America and Australia, ranchland was open country with herds kept separate from one another by the size of the ranch's grazing lands and the distance between ranch homes. In more recent times, pressure from neighboring farms and settlements, the use of barbed wire fences to contain herds, selective breeding, and the introduction of different breeds suited for different environments has meant that ranches have become smaller and the herds confined to smaller ranges. This shift has also led to a change in the rancher's strategy from an emphasis on maintaining large herds to a consideration of both quantity and quality—a limited amount of land can be used more profitably to raise a smaller number of cattle such as Angus or Herefords that will command a higher price on the market. Still, ranches often cover much territory, homes tend to be located far from one another (3 miles apart in parts of Canada to 100 miles apart in central Australia), and ranchers continue to value their relative isolation and self-sufficiency. The telephone, pickup trucks, and in some places helicopters have, of course, made communication and travel much easier today than when ranchers were reliant on horses and horse-drawn wagons and coaches.

Livestock is the second major capital investment for the rancher, and the successful rancher is one who keeps a herd large enough so that he can derive maximum profits in years when demand is high and keep his stock off the market in years when demand is low. In order to maintain stock, the rancher needs land suitable for grazing, a reliable source of water, and laborers to manage the herd. The rancher can also maximize his profit by ranching the stock best suited to the local environment or that which commands the highest price on the market.

Ranching is labor-extensive; that is, the cost of labor per head of cattle declines as the number of cattle in the herd increases. The major labor cost is the wages paid the foreman and the cowboys whose two major responsibilities are to round up the calves for branding and selecting and driving to market those animals to be sold. In addition to the cowboys, other labor costs include the wages paid specialists such as blacksmiths, cowboys who break and train wild broncos, and cooks.

The final element of Euro-American ranching is the market, composed primarily of large urban populations who do not grow their own food. Euro-American ranching emerged in the 1860s in the United States, Australia, and Argentina in direct response to urban market demands. In the United States, the demand came from cities in the East, in Argentina from Europe to which meat could be shipped on refrigerated ships, and in Australia the demand was from England for wool. In addition to a market, ranching needs a regional infrastructure of roads or railways that can be used to ship cattle to the processing houses (St. Louis, Kansas City, and Chicago in the United States during the nineteenth and early twentieth centuries) and then to the markets.

In summary, to be successful, ranching, in either its open or large range form, needs to be based on a balance among the carrying capacity of the range land, the size and breed of the cattle or sheep, the cost of labor, and the level of market demand that can drive the price up or down.

Ranching and Pastoralism

On the surface, ranching and pastoralism appear to be quite similar as both are based on the grazing of herds on open pasturage. However, the two strategies are actually quite different in a number of ways. First, and most important, pastoralism traditionally, and still in some parts of the world, is a subsistence strategy, as those cultures labeled pastoral derive most of their food and other materials from their stock. Ranching is not a subsistence strategy, for while ranchers do get their supply of meat from their stock, the animals are raised mainly to be sold for profit that can, in turn, be used to purchase items in the marketplace. For example, while herders of Central Asia such as the Mongols subsisted primarily on meat and milk from their herds, Native American ranchers on the Wind River Reservation raise their cattle for sale, although they do take meat, hides, and fats—but not milk—for their own use. Second, in pastoral societies, contact between the herders and their herds is continuous throughout the year; the stock must be watched, protected, milked, and periodically moved to fresh grazing land. Ranchers, on the other hand, are in contact with their herds only discontinuously, primarily when they need to be rounded up for branding and rounded up and driven to market for sale. Third, pastoralists deal with predators—human or animal—by being defensive. That is, they will move to avoid conflict with other groups and use dogs or sentinels to guard against incursions on the herd by animal predators. Ranchers, too, are offensive in dealing with predators. In North America, South America, South Africa, and Australia, the native peoples who got in the way of ranching were simply exterminated or pushed off their land. Similarly, possible predators such as wolves or coyotes are killed to the point of extinction. Fourth, ranchers routinely dispose of most of their own herds by selling them for sale while pastoralists, because herding is their main subsistence activity, seek to maintain their herds at maximum size. And fifth, pastoralism is a subsistence strategy that emerged several thousand years ago and has persisted into modern times while ranching is only several hundred years old and has diminished in the twentieth century. However, ranching and pastoralism are similar; their demise or reduction has been due in part to their land being taken over by farmers, a development initially resisted by both ranchers and pastoralists around the world.

The Cowboy Complex

Associated with Euro-American ranching across cultures is a sociocultural pattern known in North America as the cowboy complex. The complex centers on the image of the cowboy (called *vaquero* in Mexico and *gaucho* in Argentina), his values, and his lifestyle. The cowboy complex emerged as part of ranching in colonial Mexico and then spread north along with ranching into the United States and Canada. Although ranching developed somewhat independently in South America and Australia, the cowboy complex emerged in those locales as well. Although romanticized in literature, film, and song as a hero or an outlaw, the cowboy is actually a wage laborer who herds, brands, rounds up, and drives cattle to the market for the ranch owner. A cowboy must be an expert at riding a horse and at roping, herding, and riding cattle. He must be self-sufficient, independent, and brave to be able to deal with threats from hostile predators, storms, and stampeding cattle, and willing and able to settle disputes with his fists or six-shooter.

These skills and personality traits are not just demonstrated day-to-day on the ranch but are also dramatized in rodeos (in the United States) and stampedes (in Canada) in which cowboys compete in calf roping, bull riding, steer wrestling, and saddle bronco and bareback riding—the basic skills of a cowboy. In Australia, dramatization of the stockman's role takes the form of three-day cross-country horse races designed to test the endurance of the ranch hands and the horses. The cowboy's most important possession is his horse and his most important pieces of equipment are his rope—or lariat, saddle, hat, and pistol. Cowboy dress in North America is also closely associated with boots and chaps, equipment not used by cowboys everywhere such as in Brazil. Another actor in the cowboy complex is the gunslinger (*pistolero* in Mexico) who in film and literature usually sides with the farmers or ranchers but in fact equally often sided with the local power structure. The rustling of cattle, the robbing of stagecoaches and trains, bar brawls, and gun battles in the street over women, land, and insults to one's honor and independent, hardworking women living on the rugged frontier round out the popular image of the cowboy complex.

Ranchers and Farmers

In the United States and to a lesser extent in Canada, Australia, and Mexico, relations between ranchers and farmers have traditionally been characterized by conflict. The range wars of the late 1800s in the United States were the culmination of this hostility. The conflicts were mainly about land—the rancher's desire to maintain large, open ranges and the farmer's desire to convert rangeland into farmland—and also about lifestyle and values—the rancher's nomadic independence versus the farmer's settled lifestyle. These conflicts also pitted the ranchers who "tamed" the frontiers against the national governments who passed laws favoring small family farms in the United States and Argentina.

Ranchers referred to farmers in derogatory terms as "land grabbers," "sod busters," and "mossbacks." Their resentment of the farmer ultimately can be traced to the farmer's perceived role in destroying the open range, a sentiment expressed clearly in the will of one rancher from western Canada (Bennett 1969:176):

> This is a codicil to my last will and testament, bearing date the 29th day of September, 1919, and which I direct to be taken as part thereof. I give, devise, and bequeath to George Wincer my Navajo saddle Blanket; to William Vincent Smith my rope; to Pete Lapland my rifle; in recognition of the fact that they are respectively the best rider, the best foot-roper, and the best shot in the Hills. Finally I leave to each and every Mossback my perpetual curse, as some reward to them for their labors in destroying the Open Range by means of that most pernicious of all implements, the plow. As witness my hand this 9th day of May 1922.

In fact, the establishment of farmers and towns with services for the farmers and their families usually meant the end of open range, smaller ranches, and if the region were especially suitable for farming, the end of ranching entirely. In actuality, the development of both ranching and farming on what had been the frontier in the United States, Canada, Argentina, and Australia was the product of the same forces—a large urban population in need of food, free or cheap land on the frontier, and an infrastructure of roads or rails to move cattle or produce to the urban markets.

See also PASTORALISM.

Bennett, John W. (1969) *Northern Plainsmen: Adaptive Strategy and Agrarian Life.*

Getty, Harry T. (1963) *The San Carlos Indian Cattle Industry.*

Ingold, Tim. (1980) *Hunters, Pastoralists, and Ranchers: Reindeer Economies and Their Transformations.*

Osgood, Ernest S. (1929) *The Day of the Cattleman.*

Rivière, Peter. (1972) *The Forgotten Frontier: Ranchers of Northern Brazil.*

Roland, Betty. (1973) "Farmers of the Australian Outback." In *Peoples of the Earth. Volume 1. Australia and Melanesia*, edited by Anthony Forge, 28–33.

Schryer, Frans J. (1980) *The Rancheros of Pisaflores.*

Strickon, Arnold. (1965) "The Euro-American Ranching Complex." In *Man, Culture, and Animals: The Role of Animals in Human Ecological Adjustments*, edited by Anthony Leeds and Andrew P. Vayda, 229–258.

Wilson, Paul B. (1972) *Farming and Ranching on the Wind River Indian Reservation, Wyoming.*

season the Hiwi spend more time working, use more energy, and the fertility rate for women is higher than in the dry season.

The effect of seasonal changes on human behavior has been given official recognition by the American Psychiatric Association who recognizes Seasonal Affective Disorder (SAD) as an emotional disorder experienced by millions of Americans each year during the winter months. SAD is characterized by excessive sleeping, lack of energy, feeling down, weight gain, and a craving for carbohydrates. Even those not afflicted with SAD often feel down in the winter and suffer with cabin fever when the weather is harsh. SAD and cabin fever disappear with the arrival of spring. Like people in temperate climates, the San of Botswana also suffer—but during their hot, not cold season—when food is scarce and the band breaks apart into separate families who must forage on their own for food; this arrangement deprives adults of companions and children of playmates. As with SAD in temperate climates, the San experience boredom, listlessness, and lonesomeness, and their spirits lift with the anticipated arrival of the wet season. Both SAD in temperate zones and the seasonal depression experienced by the San are caused by a combination of environmental factors and the limits these factors place on the opportunity for social interaction. It is also likely that the harsh weather conditions create anxiety about food sources and travel that also contribute to depression in harsh seasons. The Amhara of Ethiopia also view the seasons as influencing one's health, but in a different way. They believe that medical treatment that requires the intervention of the spirits cannot be effective in the rainy season, as the spirits stay inside their grottos just as people stay in their houses. When the rains end, the spirits become active and can then be called on to assist in curing illness.

Cultures in the temperate regions usually experience and mark four distinct seasons such

Seasons

Changes in the weather, animal behavior, and plant growth associated with seasonality are a major influence on human cultures and human behavior. In agricultural and pastoral societies, the ability to grow and harvest sufficient quantities of food or to maintain adequate herds is effected by the seasons. The effect of seasonal changes on subsistence also influences other aspects of culture such as settlement patterns, community size, household composition, political leadership, relations with other cultures, ceremonial practices, and other features of culture. For example, seasonality effects the diet, work effort, nutrition, fertility, and sexual division of labor of the Hiwi hunter-gatherers of Venezuela. Meat is available to the Hiwi all year, but plant foods are more readily available only in the wet season. Thus, in the wet season, both men (who hunt and gather fruit) and women (who gather fruit and roots) get food, but in the dry season most food comes from what the men hunt. This makes women and their children dependent on their husbands and their husband's male relatives. In the wet

as summer, fall, winter, and spring of Euro-American cultures. However, even within the four-season scheme there are variations, reflecting local climatic conditions. The Taos Indians of northern New Mexico, for example, have four seasons—summer (good time), fall (ripe time), winter (still time), and spring (beginning time). However, their winter lasts four months, summer and autumn three months each, and spring only two months, reflecting the climatic conditions at 9,000 feet in the mountains. The San of Botswana have five seasons—*!hosa* (the hot time when the trees flower, *Naosa* (the rain time when the grass is green and the antelope breed), *Badasa* (when the tsama melons are plentiful), *G!wabasa* (when the plants begin to die), and *Saosa* (the cold time).

Cultures in the tropics generally experience only two clear seasons each year. What these seasons mean in different cultures is determined by the specific environments in which these cultures are found. The Tonga in Oceania experience two seasons that are marked in a general sense by differences in day and night temperature during the year. Smaller seasonal changes are noted by the growth of plants and behavior of wildlife. Times when certain plant flowers set buds or fruit and the appearance of particular species of fish in the Pacific Ocean near Tonga mark subseasonal periods within the two major seasons. For the Belau who live in Oceania near the equator there is little seasonal variation, but they still recognize two seasons. As they subsist by fishing, fishing conditions along with changes in plant life indicate the seasons. The *ongos* months from October to April are when the waters are calm due to the easterly winds, the time when fish spawn, and the best fishing season. The *ngeband* months from May to September are when the winds blow onshore, turning the water rough and making for poor fishing. The Turkana of East Africa who subsist by cattle herding recognize a dry season from September to March when there is not sufficient rain to

support vegetation for their herds to graze and a wet season from April to August when there is sufficient rain. As with many pastoral peoples, rain is a major marker of the seasons, as they must move to areas where rain is sufficient to support vegetation to feed their herds. Both the nomadic and transhumant movement of pastoral peoples are mostly due to seasonal changes.

The Aymara of the Peruvian highlands have two seasons that are identified by amount of rainfall and food. The rainy season from October to April is called "green time" or "fat time" meaning that food is abundant. The dry season is called "ice time" or "lean time" indicating that food is scarce. Even though the wet season is one when food is more readily available, it too can be harsh and unpredictable for the Aymara—steady downpours erode the soil and wash away seeds, thunderstorms kill people and sheep, hailstorms destroy crops and damage roofs, and droughts diminish the harvest. Thus, while in most cultures one season or certain seasons are more desirable than others, even the best of seasons are not without their environmental uncertainty. The Hopi of Arizona also have two seasons—summer and winter—which fit with their belief in the duality of the universe. The Hopi look to the behavior of birds to predict the summer season and reduce some of the uncertainty:

> Return of the birds means that summer is near.
>
> When a yellow bird arrives when the peach trees are in blossom it will be a good summer.
>
> When a red-headed bird returns early there will be good pasturage.
>
> When the black bird with a red breast returns it is time to plant the corn.
>
> If the doves return early it will be a good summer.
>
> If the birds return late it will be a bad summer and an early frost.
>
> If the wild ducks head south at the time of peach harvest there will be an early frost.

As with the Hopi, in many cultures a new season—especially the growing season—is accompanied by ceremonies to mark its arrival and to appeal to the supernatural for assistance in producing a good crop. The Sherpa of Nepal, for example, associate a supernatural queen with each season (summer, winter, autumn, and spring) and mark the arrival of each season with a one- to six-day ceremony during which work ceases and all members of the community are expected to attend. The Zulu of South America restrict their behavior in various ways to make seasonal weather more predictable. In summer certain grasses are not cut to prevent storms, certain musical instruments are not played to prevent thunderstorms, and trees that are lightening conductors are not cut down. Such restrictions do not pertain in the winter when the effect of the weather on crops is not important.

See also ANNUAL CYCLE; CALENDARS; TIME.

Beaglehole, Ernest. (1937) *Notes on Hopi Economic Life.*

Collocott, Ernest, E. V. (1922) *Tongan Astronomy and Calendar.*

Fantin, Mario. (1974) *Sherpa Himalaya Nepal.*

Gulliver, Philip H. (1955) *The Family Herds: A Study of Two Pastoral Tribes in East Africa, the Jie and Turkana.*

Hurtado, A. Magdalena, and Kim R. Hill. (1990) "Seasonality in a Foraging Society: Variation in Diet, Work Effort, Fertility, and Sexual Division of Labor among the Hiwi of Venezuela." *Journal of Anthropological Research* 46:293–346.

Johannes, Robert. (1981) *Words of the Lagoon: Fishing and Marine Lore in the Palau District of Micronesia.*

La Barre, Weston. (1950) "Aymara Folktales." *Journal of American Linguistics* 16:40–45.

Messing, Simon D. (1957) *The Highland-Plateau Amhara of Ethiopia.*

Miller, Merton L. (1898) *A Preliminary Study of the Pueblo of Taos, New Mexico.*

Raum, Otto F. (1973) *The Social Functions of Avoidances and Taboos among the Zulu.*

Silberbauer, George B. (1981) *Hunter and Habitat in the Central Kalahari Desert.*

SETTLEMENT PATTERNS

Settlement patterns are the "characteristic manner in which household and community units are arranged spatially over the landscape" (Vogt and Albert 1966:162). There is considerable variation across cultures and within cultures in settlement pattern features and each pattern in some way reflects differences across cultures in peoples' relationships with and beliefs about the environment.

Settlement Pattern Features

Settlement patterns across cultures can be described and compared in terms of a number of general features: fixity, compactness, size in space and population, population density, types of buildings, plan, orientation, and shape.

Fixity of settlement refers to whether the society is typically nomadic or sedentary. A survey of 186 cultures with information for their ways of life mainly in the nineteenth and early twentieth centuries indicates that (1) 15 percent were nomadic throughout the year; (2) 11 percent were seminomadic, migrating for most of the year, but living in settled communities for at least one season (usually winter); (3) 3 percent rotated between two or more settlements on a seasonal basis; (4) 8 percent were semisedentary, living most of the time in a central settlement from which groups would migrate for periods in order to hunt, fish, or herd; (5) 15 percent lived in impermanent settlements that were relocated every few years when local resources became scarce or the population too large, epidemics made the village unsafe, or custom required that a village be abandoned when the leader died; and (6) 54 percent lived in permanent settlements established for long and indefinite periods of time. If this same survey of 186 cultures were conducted in the 1990s, the percentage of cultures with permanent settlements would be much higher—close to 100 percent—as most peoples who previously utilized the five other less-than-permanent settlement patterns have now been settled in permanent villages by the governments that rule the nations in which they live.

Compactness refers to the degree in which the buildings and natural features comprising the settlement are dispersed over or concentrated in space. The same survey of 186 cultures noted above indicates that (1) 54 percent of cultures have settlements that are mainly compact, that is, nucleated villages or concentrated camps; (2) 24 percent have settlements that are mainly dispersed, that is, composed of isolated homesteads or dwellings strung out some distance from one another; (3) 11 percent have settlements composed of a number of dispersed subsettlements, each with a number of dwellings within it; and (4) 11 percent have partially dispersed settlements, that is, a central village with dispersed settlements linked to it although spatially separate.

The size of a settlement includes its physical size—the amount of land within its boundaries, measured both linearly and vertically; the number of inhabitants; and the population density—the number of inhabitants per some standard unit of space such as per city block, per mile, or per square mile. Settlement size is directly related to fixity and compactness; permanent and compact settlements nearly always have larger, denser populations than do impermanent and dispersed settlements.

The plan of a settlement refers to the actual location of buildings, open spaces, and other features of the settlement relative to one another. The plan includes how close the buildings and other elements are to one another, how they are orientated to one another, and how they are oriented to the surrounding environment. Settlement plans across cultures can be divided into five very broad types, with hundreds of variations of these types found around the world. First are dispersed settlements in which houses and other buildings are located relatively far apart from one another. A sense of a unified settlement is created by a centrally located town, store, government office, mission station, or landowner's estate that draws residents from the surrounding homesteads. Second is the compound settlement composed of a number of extended family households, with each family occupying a single, often walled, compound some distance from other compounds, although not as far as homesteads in the dispersed pattern. A sense of community is maintained through kinship ties among residents of different compounds and is established mainly through marriage; community buildings such as the elder's meeting house; and the sharing of land, usually grazing land for cattle. Third is the circular village plan, found mainly in the Amazon region of South America in which all members of the settlement live in one large, circular building, usually with open sides and a palm-thatch roof. Each family has its own living area within the dwelling and the center is usually an uncovered communal space. Fourth is the nuclear town usually surrounded by a wall, with entrance gained through a gate or gates and individual houses or compounds within the walls aligned in some sort of grid arrangement on paths or streets. In larger towns, one or more streets may serve a specialized function as the location for shops, government buildings, and the church. Fifth is the linear settlement plan in which dwellings, communal buildings, stores,

A village in Morocco

and so forth are aligned in single or double rows along the course of some physical feature such as a river or road.

The final major feature of settlement patterns is orientation of the settlement. The direction in which the settlement faces or direction in which elements of the settlement, such as gates, doors, dwellings, or certain buildings, are oriented is a major concern in many cultures. Pueblo Indians in the Southwest, for example, prefer that their ceremonial chambers—called *kivas*—be located in the center of the settlement. In many cultures the leader's dwelling is located in the center of the village. Direction is often considered in the placement of dwellings. For the Quechua of Ecuador, the concern is mainly practical as houses are built facing west to protect the front from the strong southeast winds

of the July to September dry season. The Plains Indians in traditional times were less concerned with practical matters than with symbolism when they used the concepts of center, axis, and direction in erecting tipis and orienting each tipi. In general, the camp opening and each tipi entrance faced east as did openings of other structures such as sweat lodges. But in special situations, the orientation might be different as among the Osage who placed the entrance to the west when on an expedition that involved killing. The west was the direction of the sunset and the land of the dead.

Settlement Types

A key feature of settlement pattern elements such as degree of fixity, compactness, size, and plan is that they are closely related to one another in predictable ways across cultures. For example, settlements that are large and densely populated are most likely to also be permanent and follow a nucleated plan, regardless of the cultural context. Similarly, settlements that are small and lightly populated are more likely to be semipermanent or temporary and to follow the dispersed or molecular plans. Settlement pattern features are not only related in predictable ways to one another, they are also related to other aspects of cultural systems such as the economic system, social organization, politics, and religious beliefs and practices. These sets of complex interrelationships have led many social scientists to conclude that settlement patterns are perhaps more profitably described in terms that also include these other factors than by simply looking at the patterns in isolation. Following this approach,

settlement patterns across cultures are of five major types: band, village, town, city, and state.

The band pattern is characterized by either nomadic movement in a defined territory throughout the year or seasonal excursions from a home settlement. Communities are small and composed of related or friendly nuclear families with leadership in the hands of men who are known for their skill or ability. There is no ownership of property, although the group may restrict access to its territory by outsiders, and individuals own their own personal property—mainly tools and equipment used in subsistence activities. Status differences between individuals and between groups are either absent or are based on skills and abilities. Religious activities are managed by the part-time shaman whose work is mostly concerned with curing illness,

A village in Karkar, New Guinea

bringing good luck, and predicting the future. The hunting-gathering societies discussed in the following section are all examples of societies with a band level settlement pattern as they have existed in recent times.

The village settlement is characterized by communities of several hundred people living in the villages on a semipermanent basis and moving to build a new village when environmental resources around the existing village are exploited to the point where they can no longer support the village population. In some cultures the village might be abandoned before the local environment is fully exploited because of warfare with other groups, if a chief dies, or because of a disease epidemic. The economy centers on horticulture supplemented by hunting, fishing, gathering, and trade with other communities. If trade is important, some members of the community might engage in the full-time production of items such as baskets for trade. The society is organized on the basis of kinship, with each member belonging to a specific, although large, kinship group such as a clan. Members of each clan live in different villages, thus creating cohesion among villages in the society. Leadership of each village is vested in the headman, who usually comes from the most powerful kinship groups, and other kin group leaders. Societal cohesion is achieved through intermarriage of men and women from different villages and kin groups, joint calendrical ceremonies, and trade. Status differentials among individuals and families are based on the accumulation of wealth either in the form of money or real property such as pigs, yams, or land.

In the town settlement pattern the settlement is permanent and is moved only in unusual circumstances such as an environmental disaster or warfare. The settlement might be (1) self-sufficient economically, based on a combination of farming, herding, and occupational specializations such as pottery making, weaving, and curing; (2) a ceremonial center for surrounding communities and thus the location of ceremonial buildings and the home of the clergy; or (3) a regional trade center for the distribution of goods that flow in from rural communities and out to urban centers. Economic wealth, social status, and political leadership depend mainly on the ownership of land and the accumulation of wealth, although kinship ties are important as well. In some societies, the religious practitioner plays a major role in village affairs.

The city settlement is characterized by a substantial percentage of the population living in large, densely populated cities, with the cities often serving as administrative centers for a region. The economic system is diverse and market-driven with status distinctions based on wealth, which, in turn, are a source of political power and influence. In societies with city-type settlements, kinship ties are no longer important and are replaced by a formal set of laws enforced by the coercive power of a king or royal family. The political system is often a theocracy, with the priests playing a major role in political as well as religious matters.

A state-level settlement pattern is characterized by a number of cities under the control of a central state government that often administers the cities through regional administrative structures. The economic system is based on the internal production of goods and products and their distribution to villages, towns, and cities; external trade; and the collection of taxes by the central government through its regional and local agents. Labor is provided by slaves or a large lower class that is exploited by the rulers. There is often a distinct professional class of clerks, soldiers, tax collectors, craft specialists, and priests.

Determinants of Settlement Patterns
As the above typology suggests, the factors that determine where and in what characteristic

pattern a culture or community builds its settlements are complex and interrelated and include the physical environment, economic considerations, the need to defend the settlement from invasion, and sociocultural beliefs and practices.

Environmental factors that shape settlement patterns are the physical landscape itself, underground geological features, the climate, and the availability of plants and animals. While environmental factors influence settlement patterns in all cultures, their influence is most profound in hunter-gather cultures where the people rely on direct contact with the environment to collect food and other resources for their survival. In horticultural, pastoral, and agricultural societies, people mostly produce rather than collect food and thus have more control over the environment and therefore a greater capacity to alter the environment to meet their settlement needs. Except in the modern industrialized world, however, the environment is always a major determinant of settlement patterns. Hunting and gathering societies described by outsiders in the last two centuries have lived almost exclusively in harsh, marginal regions representing a variety of environmental types. The patterns of adaptation of these peoples to these environments provide a clear example of how the environment influences settlement patterns, although even in these societies other factors such as fear of spirits or ghosts in certain places, relations with kin, and trade with other societies and communities can and do influence settlement patterns. Before summarizing the different settlement patterns used by different hunter-gatherer cultures in different environments, it is important to note that these settlement patterns are no longer used in most cultures, who, through contact with or under the control of the national governments in whose territory they reside, have adopted "Western" settlement patterns characterized by permanent structures aligned in square or rectangular blocks and located in villages or towns.

Hunter-gatherer societies in seven different environments—evergreen tropical forest, semideciduous tropical forest, tropical savanna, desert, grassland, mid-latitude forest, and boreal forest and tundra—tend to have different types of settlement patterns, determined in large part by the availability of food and other environmental constraints and opportunities that influence the food quest. Hunter-gatherers in evergreen tropical forests such as those in central Africa and southern Malaysia mainly employ a restricted nomadic settlement pattern in which small groups composed of a number of nuclear families travel all year, relocating each time to exploit plants and to a lesser extent animal foods available in particular locales. The evergreen tropical forest environment is unique among environments in that there are no seasonal variations marked by changes in air temperature, length of the day versus the night, or precipitation. But, at the same time, animals do have breeding cycles and plants bloom and flower at different times, although the variety of plants of a given species is often quite limited. These factors create diversity in the environment, and the people must move about to exploit these limited resources that become available in different locales throughout the year. A society that traditionally followed this pattern is the Semang of Malaysia. The Semang lived in camps of from 6 to 60 people for periods ranging from a few days to up to six weeks, depending on the availability of plant foods such as wild yams, bamboo shoots, nuts, and honey and animals such as monkeys, rats, gibbons, and birds. Each settlement was composed of palm-thatch lean-to huts aligned in two facing rows with openings at either end of the row. The composition of the settlements might change as people chose to move to other camps or to join other groups and would decrease or increase in population depending on the availability of local resources.

Societies in semideciduous tropical forests in South America, Africa, Australia, and South

Thatched huts in Cameroun

Asia are typically semisedentary, living in settled communities during one season and then living in smaller, dispersed subgroups during the other season. The Andaman Islanders of the Bay of Bengal, for example, lived on the coast in settlements of a few families each during the dry season from October to February. During the wet season, from May to September, they would migrate inland and form smaller villages, although the actual alignment was the same with the huts arranged in a circle around a central clearing. Near the end of the rainy reason, each family would move to the permanent clan house that it shared with up to 20 related families. While the dry and wet season huts were dismantled after use, the clan house was permanent and maintained by male members of the clan during the year. Site selection was determined for all settlements by the availability of freshwater; firewood; plant foods such as yams, fruits, and berries; and animal food such as turtles, pigs, turtle eggs, and honey.

Tropical savanna lands were inhabited by hunter-gatherers in Africa, Australia, and South America. These groups were usually semisedentary with their pattern of movement dependent on the availability of water. When rain was heavy and caused floods that made travel difficult, they lived in villages in the rainy season and moved about in the dry season. But if the dry season was harsh and water scarce, they remained instead in settlements near water. The Wik Mungkan of the Cape York region of Australia, for example, lived in small camps on high ground in the rainy season. In the dry season they moved to semipermanent settlements near lagoons and lakes where they fished, collected plant foods, and hunted birds and moved more readily to form larger settlements to hold rituals, to trade, and to maintain social and kin-based relationships.

Hunter-gatherers in deserts such as those in southeast Africa, western and central Australia, and the Southwest of the United States were mainly semisedentary, living during the rainy season in areas with heavy rainfall that promoted plant growth and attracted game animals. These settlements, like those of the Ngatajara of Australia might be quite large and number over 100 people but were often of short duration, as the rainy season was often short and the pools of water disappeared quickly. When the water dried up, the group split into smaller units composed of extended families of about 10 to 15 persons and moved about, settling for short periods at water sources. Settlements were generally of shelters built around a central hearth.

Hunter-gatherers in grassland environments exhibited two different types of settlement patterns depending on the certainty of local food resources. Those who lived on the open plains, such as the Arapaho Indians in the United States, depended on one major resource such as the bison for most of their food and material needs and therefore migrated in the summer following the herds but lived in settled communities in the winter months when travel was difficult. Others, such as the Chiricahua in the United States, lived in areas with a variety of resources, primarily small game such as rabbits and deer and plant food such as nuts. They tended to be more mobile but were likely to stay in one location for as long as local food sources were reliable.

Hunter-gatherers living in mid-latitude forests displayed a mix of settlement patterns, depending on local conditions. Some such as the Kutenai in North America and Yahgan in South America lived near the sea and thus were relatively sedentary. Others, such as the Hupa and Yokuts in the western United States lived in diverse river valleys, and their movements were directed at exploiting different economic niches at different times of the year.

Finally, hunter-gatherers of the north live in boreal forest and tundra environments with long, harsh winters and short summers. These groups such as the Ket in Siberia, Cree in Canada, and Ainu in northern Japan settled in larger villages living off food collected in the summer or that which could be obtained from local fishing holes or breaks in the ice. The village might relocate periodically as local resources became scarce. In the summer, they migrated in smaller groups to hunting grounds, and for a short period of several weeks or so before the winter the small, nomadic family groups would join together in a single settlement often near a large water source to socialize, engage in religious activities, trade, and arrange marriages. Many of these societies varied their dwelling form by the season, using snow or stone or semi-subterranean lodges in the winter and tents or other portable housing in the summer.

This quick survey points to the role the environment plays in shaping settlement patterns, particularly the fixity, compactness, and size of the settlement. However, the environment is not the only factor. A second major determinant is economic consideration. Throughout human history, where people choose to settle and the pattern of the settlement have often been determined by economic considerations such as availability of economic resources and access to trade routes. As indicated above, for people who live by directly exploiting the environment, locating their settlements, whether permanent or migratory, near subsistence resources is a major decision factor in both settlement location and pattern. People who subsist on marine resources prefer to locate their settlements near or on the beach, with the houses in a row or two rows opening toward the sea. Canoes, boats, nets, and other equipment are stored alongside the dwelling or on the beach. For example, the Aleut in southwestern Alaska considered prime sites to be ones with safe access to the sea; access to a mix of food resources such as seals, sea lions, clams, mussels, birds, cod, and halibut; and with a clear view of both the sea to spot these resources and inland to spot intruders. Haida villages on the Northwest Coast of North America were constructed of two rows of plank houses facing the ocean with boats and gear stored in front or nearby. And in Oceania, the single or two-row pattern on or near the beach is preferred in many cultures. Farmers prefer to locate their farms and settlements near fertile soil, and thus we find farms in river valleys and deltas such as the Mississippi in the United States, the Ganges in India, and the Yellow in China. For pastoral cultures such as the Cotopaxi Quichua of Ecuador the settlements are dispersed, with the households located in the pastures near corrals holding the sheep and llama. Similarly, cultures that must exploit limited resources often use a dispersed pattern, such as Matsigenka settlements in Peru that are scattered to avoid competition with other settlements for scarce resources.

Most cultures are involved in trade relations with other cultures, and thus some communities are either temporarily or permanently located at places that can be easily reached by the traders. These locations include river deltas, points where two or more rivers converge, valleys and mountainous regions, natural harbors on the seacoast, and along highways or railroad tracks in industrialized nations.

Across cultures and throughout human history, all cultures have considered safety from enemies when choosing a settlement site and designing the settlement. For example, the Catawba built palisaded towns with open courtyards and a large ceremonial house in the center. Similarly, the Iroquois in New York built palisaded villages on elevated terraces near streams or lakes. Each village contained residential longhouses for 300 to 600 individuals and several acres of gardens. Additional gardens were planted on cleared land around the village that also afforded the Iroquois a clear line of sight to the distant forest. Iroquois villages across the region were located on an east-west gradient and were connected by a system of trails across the region that could be covered in several days by messengers. In northern Burma, villages are also palisaded or are enclosed by a fence, with a gate staffed by guards and houses clustered within. And the European countryside is dotted with walled villages and towns with towering stone and earth ramparts that show the earlier concern with protecting one's settlement from invading armies. Not all cultures build defensive settlements; some instead rely on natural features for protection. The Ifugao in the Philippines, for example, traditionally built their villages on fairly inaccessible lower mountain ridges. And the Hopi built their villages on mesa tops in Arizona to deter attacks from the canyon floor below.

Sociocultural forces also play a role in settlement patterns. The tightness or looseness of the social structure of a society partially determines the settlement plan: tightly knit communities will have compact settlements; loosely knit communities will have dispersed settlements. Kinship relations also influence settlement plans—a settlement might be divided into two sectors, with each kinship group occupying a different sector. Settlements are also influenced by and reflect differences in social status, wealth, and power among the groups living in the settlement. In South Asia, East Asia, Africa, and Europe, groups who were considered inferior such as "Untouchables," blacksmiths, Jews, or Gypsies generally lived in their own sector or on the edge of the settlement. Similarly, communities with a mix of different ethnic groups will often be organized by ethnic neighborhood, with a particular group being the majority population in a specific area often called a "ghetto" or "barrio." Conversely, the wealthy or powerful often occupy homes or compounds in the center of the

Aerial view of Marsh Arab village in South Iraq

settlement. The role of sociocultural factors in shaping settlement patterns is suggested by the Taos Indians of New Mexico. Taos Pueblo (village) is divided into north and south side house blocks of five and four stories each, separated by a large dirt plaza and bisected by Rio Pueblo de Taos. The north and south side groups, while not different kin groups, do maintain reciprocal ritual obligations toward each other. The Pueblo symbolizes traditional Taos culture in the modern world and thus only Taos are allowed to reside there, no running water or electricity is available, and visits by tourists are allowed but restricted. Newer houses on the reservation are outside the low pueblo walls and mostly out-of-sight. The Roman Catholic church (and the ruins of a previous church) and the kivas in which the traditional Taos religion is practiced are within the pueblo walls, but the tribal government office is outside. Major Taos ceremonial

events are performed in the central plaza, with non-Taos allowed to observe some events but not others. Access to the Pueblo is controlled by the tribal police force.

The key point about the forces that shape settlement patterns is that no single factor is all important, but, rather, patterns are shaped by a complex and changing mix of factors. This complexity is suggested by the different settlement patterns found among five different culture groups in the same environmental region of New Mexico. Over the past 1,000 or so years, the region has been settled first by the Zuni, then the Navajo migrating south from the Plains, then the Spanish, the Mormons, and, most recently, homesteaders from Texas. These groups have developed three different types of settlements. The Zuni, Mormons, and Hispanics prefer to live in compact settlements with a central plaza, houses arranged around the plaza, and fields located some distance from the settlement. The Navajo live mainly in dispersed homesteads in mountain valleys with their flocks grazing on communal land. The homesteads are organized in accordance with matrilineal kinship and matrilocal residence rules and thus, a mother, her husband, and unmarried daughter will live within shouting distance of at least one married daughter, her husband, and their children. The Texans live in isolated nuclear family homesteads and purchase supplies and services from businesses located in small crossroad service centers. This variation in place of settlement is a product of a number of factors including time of settlement, availability of water and arable land, and the relative political power of the groups. The Zuni were there first and settled near water and land that was suitable for farming. The Navajo herded sheep and chose mountain valleys near springs or other water sources. The Spanish and later the Mormons had more political power than the Navajo and were able to push them off the better land, forcing the Navajo to move further into the valleys. Finally, when the Texas homesteaders arrived, economic factors, property ownership laws, and government regulations meant that the only land available was dry land. The differences in settlement patterns (compact versus dispersed) are a result of different value orientations among the five cultures. The Zuni have a preference for living in tight-knit communities near kin and therefore built a clustered village; even those with homes outside the village also keep a home in the village. The Mormon grid-style settlements are based on the Mormon model for all Mormon communities—"The Plan of City of Zion" invented in 1833—that is meant to prepare a place for the Savior at "His Second Coming." The Hispanic cluster settlement pattern is based on the typical settlement pattern in Spain and is thus a diffusion from one region of the world to another. The Navajo dispersed homestead pattern reflects the importance they place on the extended family and

on "familistic individualism." Finally, the Texas homesteader's pattern of isolated single-family farms reflects the western United States core values of individualism, autonomy, and self-reliance.

See also DIRECTION; GEOMANCY; MOBILITY AND SEDENTISM; SPACE; TERRITORY AND TERRITORIALITY.

Endicott, Kirk. (1979) *Batak Negrito Religion.*

Fraser, Douglas. (1968) *Village Planning in the Primitive World.*

Gould, Richard A. (1969) *Yiwara: Foragers of the Australian Desert.*

Jordan, Ann Turner. (1979) *A Comparative Study of the Settlement Patterns of Hunting and Gathering Groups.*

McNett, Charles W., Jr. (1973) "A Settlement Pattern Scale of Cultural Complexity." In *Handbook of Method in Cultural Anthropology,* edited by Raoul Naroll and Ronald Cohen, 872–886.

Murdock, George P., and Suzanne F. Wilson. (1972) "Settlement Patterns and Community Organization: Cross-Cultural Codes 3." *Ethnology* 11:254–295.

Oliver, Paul. (1987) *Dwellings: The House across the World.*

Levinson, David, ed. (1991–1994) *Encyclopedia of World Cultures. Volumes 1–7.*

Vogt, Evon Z., and Ethel M. Albert. (1966) *People of Rimrock: A Study of Values in Five Cultures.*

SHADOW

A shadow is a dark image formed by a solid or translucent object blocking rays of light. The shadow takes the form of the object blocking the light and will be distorted depending on the angle at which the light strikes the object. While in some cultures a shadow of the human form is seen as separate from the person casting the shadow, in others it is seen as an appendage of the person or as an image of his or her soul—the person's inner being. In some cultures, shadows are believed to have an existence of their own. For example, Peter Pan (in the famous English story by J. M. Barrie) left his shadow behind when he returned to Never Land and had to return to retrieve it because he had to have his shadow. In still other cultures, a shadow can take on a life of its own, separate from that of the individual or the object casting the shadow. For example, among rural Jamaicans the shadow is thought to live on after death, even after the body goes into the earth and the soul becomes a ghost. Thus, even when a tree is felled, its shadow is thought to continue existing somewhere. The Senoi of Malaysia have a similar belief in which the shadow-form, associated with both the exterior and interior image of the person, can detach itself, usually with the guidance of a spirit medium, as reflected in the following song:

Mother

Mother, the body feels cool and refreshed [as the song passes through]

The shadow-form [separates from the body and travels around]

Consistent with this belief, the Senoi view photographs as the equivalent of shadows. The Senoi also believe that a tiger can see a wandering shadow-form at night and follow it back to its owner. Thus, when out hunting, the Senoi build a fence around their sleeping place to keep tigers out. In many cultures, as with the Senoi, shadows are seen as a source of misfortune, especially if customs about shadows are violated. Among the Serbs, if a man walks on his own shadow, another person walks on it, or it falls on a ritually unclean spot, he may become mentally or physically ill. Similarly, Serbs also believe that

women and children should not see their own reflection because one can catch the evil eye by seeing its reflection in water and that a reflection from pure water is curative. In rural Jamaica, if a person fools with his shadow the shadow will prevent him from sleeping and worse yet, sorcerers will attempt to catch a shadow in order to turn it into a ghost.

In a number of cultures, one's shadow is equated with one's soul. Like the Zulu of South Africa, the Shona of East Africa believe that all individuals have two souls. The black, or dark, shadow reflects the individual's physical being while the white shadow—called *munhu*—reflects the inner person and is equated with the soul that transforms into a spirit after death. In order not to displease and anger the white shadow, the relatives of the deceased take care to follow burial customs carefully and to honor the deceased. If anyone sees the white shadow it is a sign that it is angry, and a healer must be consulted to placate the shadow so that it will depart. The Aymara of Bolivia and Peru also equate the soul with the shadow, and a person's shadow is clear if he is healthy but it becomes dark if he is sick. The Senoi of Malaysia believe that a person's shadow-form lingers after death and burial, often near the grave. Restrictions on contact with shadows are also an important component of Senoi healing practices. Patients are isolated so that another's shadow will not fall on them, thereby protecting the patients internal shadow. Shadows from inanimate objects are considered harmful and patients are restricted from reading because the dark print on the page is considered a form of shadow.

While beliefs about the shadow are heavily imbued with symbolism in many cultures, they are not entirely distinct from the realities of day-to-day life. Zulu shadow beliefs and practices, for example, closely reflect the social organization and customs of Zulu society. A long shadow is associated with life and a short one with death. Zulu rulers are thought to have longer shadows than commoners while the ruling clan has the longest shadow of all—a shadow that is endless like that of the sun. A king's ancestors are referred to as "shadows," and a commoner may not cross a ruler's shadow just as a son should not step across his father's. Similar customs govern who may step over one another. Thus, customs about behavior involving shadows reflect customs about behavior involving actual individuals and are in accord with the hierarchical nature of social relations among the Zulu. In times of war, a Zulu wife would place her husband's sleeping mat in front of the home—a long shadow caste by it indicated that he was alive, a short one that he was dead.

The symbolic role of shadows is displayed also in their use as entertainment in some cultures. In the United States and elsewhere, children are often entertained by hand shadows depicting various animal shapes. In Java, Bali, China, and Turkey, shadow plays are a major form of drama, often drawing large crowds who watch the performance of important cultural and religious texts for hours. In Bali and Java, where this art form is most highly developed, shadow plays are performed by highly skilled and trained puppeteers (called *dalang*). The puppeteer holds colored flat cutouts over his head on a pole between an oil lamp or electric light and a blank screen on which the shadow is cast. The drama is accompanied by a small orchestra and the audience either sits behind the puppeteer and sees both the puppets and the screen or behind the screen where it sees the screen alone. Viewing from the back side is considered superior, and these seats are often reserved for those of the Javanese upper class.

Aschwaden, Herbert. (1982) *Symbols of Life: An Analysis of the Consciousness of the Karanga*, translated by Ursula Copper.

Beckwith, Martha W. (1929) *Black Roadways: A Study of Jamaican Folk Life.*

Covarrubias, Miguel. (1938) *Island of Bali.*

Geertz, Clifford J. (1964) *The Religion of Java.*

Kemp, Phyllis. (1935) *Healing Ritual: Studies in the Technique and Tradition of the Southern Slavs.*

Métraux, Alfred. (1934) "Contribution au Folk-Lore Andin." *Société des Amérocanistes de Paris Journal,* n.s. 26:67–102.

Raum, Otto F. (1973) *The Social Functions of Avoidances and Taboos among the Zulu.*

Roseman, Marina L. (1986) *Sound in Ceremony: Power and Performance in Temiar Curing Rituals.*

Webb, Phila H., and Jane Corby. (1990) *The Little Book of Hand Shadows.*

SNOW

See PRECIPITATION.

SPACE

Space is a cultural universal in that all cultures use and organize physical space. This fact is true even for cultures such as the Aranda of Australia who have no "buildings" but still have concepts of space, boundaries, and space markers that enable them to organize their physical and social landscapes. There are various types of space—physical, social, personal, sensory, symbolic, and ritual to name only a few. While it is possible to discuss space by itself, in reality, concepts about and the use of space are closely related to concepts about the use of time, meanings associated with space, and communication. In all cultures, people hold certain beliefs about space or a particular space, and use that space in specific ways because of the meanings that space has for them; they communicate those meanings to other people as a way of controlling the use of the space. In addition, the meanings associated with a physical space and how that space is used often vary greatly at different points in time. For example, during the day a public park may be heavily used by older people sitting on benches, children playing in the playground, teenagers playing on the basketball court, and so on. At night, however, the park may seem dangerous rather than safe and friendly and will be unused save for homeless persons sleeping in secluded spots, a few brave souls cutting through it as a shortcut, and muggers awaiting the brave souls.

In every culture, the organization of space always involves classification of the space into culturally meaningful categories, rules about access and use of the space, and communication of these meanings and rules. Space is generally marked along horizontal and vertical planes and also in some cultures in concentric rings as well. The vertical marking of space often indicates relative differences in status among the persons, objects, or events associated with each level of space. The Central Thai, for example, live in houses of at least two and often three or more floors, with more important people, objects, and events located on the upper floors. The same meaning and rules associated with vertical space also apply to the relations between people and objects. For example, a younger person should also be in a lower position when talking to an older person, and when passing an older person, the younger person's upper body should not be above the head of the older person. The arrangement of objects in the Central Thai home is governed by the same rules. The shelf of the ancestors in each home, which holds an urn with ashes of the ancestors, ritual objects, and daily offerings such as candles, is often set about 5 feet up on a wall. Secular objects such as pictures or calendars must be hung on a different

wall and at a lower height. Similarly, the picture of a Buddhist priest is hung higher than pictures of other people, including the royal family of Thailand who are ritually inferior to a priest. Similarly, in the Andes in South America, entire villages might be socially divided into lower and upper sections, with the upper section thought to be associated with masculinity, strength, and order and the lower section by femininity, weakness, and disorder. The use of concentric circles in conceptualizing space is often based on people, objects, and events in the center of the circle being more important and those further out progressively less important. For example, Tibetan refugees in a village in Nepal conceptualize the space they use as composed of four zones: (1) the interior of the house where they sleep, cook, eat, and entertain guests; (2) the veranda, roof, and ground adjacent to the house bounded by the wood pile or vegetable garden where they work and engage in talk with neighbors; (3) the village square where rituals and political meetings are held; and (4) the village, with a wall separating the Tibetan from the Tamang sections. Similarly, the Tibetans view farmland as composed of three zones: (1) private vegetables used by the family, (2) communal land used by the village, and (3) sharecropped land controlled by the Tamang.

Across cultures, four general criteria are commonly used in organizing physical space—sex, age, social status and role, and kinship. In most cultures, sex, age, and social status are commonly used while kinship is most marked in cultures whose social organization is kin-based. The above example of the Central Thai points to the importance of age in organizing and allocating the use of space. The rural Highland Scots also consider age, along with sex and status, in determining who uses which space in the home. When entertaining guests, the senior male in the household and the senior male guest sit nearest the stove, the place of honor and the warmest spot in the dwelling; the oldest women—the senior woman in the household and the senior female guest—sit nearby but not as close to the stove; the daughter and eldest son of the dwelling owner sit in the next sector; and the youngest son sits across the room.

As with age, sex is a common organizing criteria for the use of space across cultures. Exactly why space is commonly divided between men and women is not clear, although some factors related to this pattern are the division of labor by sex common in many cultures, the fact that people often feel more comfortable with members of the same sex, to prevent conflict that often arises when men or women compete for the attention or affection of the same woman or man, and the belief in some cultures that women are polluting and that men should avoid contact with them. The organization of space on the basis of sex plays itself out in a variety of ways around the world. Among Rom Gypsies there is a strict segregation of the sexes based on the strong belief that women—and especially their genitalia—are polluting to men and male objects. Thus, participation in all daily and ritual activities is segregated by sex. At public gatherings, men and women sit, eat, drink, and converse apart from one another and never sit together or even near one another. When traveling by automobile, men sit in the front, women in the back. Rom men occupy places of status and comfort such as the head table at a feast (women sit at side tables), at the table if there is only one table, and in the most comfortable room and chair in the home. Rom segregation by sex extends to vertical space as well as horizontal space. Again, because of the belief that female genitalia are polluting, women never sit on a man's lap (in a crowded car, women will sit only on other women's laps) and women always walk around rather than step over male objects.

A fairly common form of sex segregation in the organization of space is the delineation of specific places or buildings for exclusive use by only men or women. In the United States, such segregation has been common in many social and fraternal organizations that either ban women from the premises or permit them to enter only in the company of a man, for special events, or at certain times. Across cultures, the equivalent of this form of sex-based organization of space are men's houses. A men's house is a communal building that is used exclusively by men and boys. Such buildings are used in 45 percent of cultures in a worldwide sample of 120 cultures. There are differences across cultures in the extent to which men use men's houses. In 29 percent of cultures, men congregate there only to gossip during their spare time, eating and sleeping at home with their wives and children. For example, for Lamet men in Southeast Asia, the men's house is really a meeting house where they gather before and after work each day to discuss the day's activities. In 38 percent of cultures with men's houses, men sometimes eat and sleep in the house as well as using it as a meeting hall. For example, among the traditional Yokuts of California, men used the communal sweat lodge as a place to relax and to occasionally sleep as well. In 33 percent of cultures with men's houses, the houses serve as the permanent living quarters for the male population of the village. For example, traditional Mundurucu men in Brazil slept and ate in the *eksa*. They would provide their wives with food that the women cooked and brought to the men at the eksa. In some cultures only adult men live in the houses while in other cultures, such as the Mae Enga in New Guinea, boys as young as five years of age will live there as well. And in some cultures, separate quarters for unmarried men—bachelor's houses—are used by adolescent boys. Across cultures, there are no similar houses for the exclusive use of women, save for menstrual huts where women are segregated during their menstrual cycle.

The organization of space is an important marker of status differentials among the members of a community and also a marker of ethnic identity for members of different ethnic groups. For example, differential access to places marks status distinctions among managerial employees, workers, and Quechua Indians in Ecuador. Managers and workers live in separate residential sections. Indians rarely enter beyond the threshold of a manager's home, while managers sit in the best or the only chair when visiting an Indian's home. Similarly, Indians move off the sidewalk to let a non-Indian pass, while non-Indians push, pull, and kick Indians aside. In the presence of a non-Indian, the Indian will sit in a lower position, usually on the floor, but they will only rarely share food or drink with non-Indians, as such behavior will cause ostracism from the Indian community.

In rural Taiwan, where people sit or stand while attending the opera in a village plaza tells much about their status and role in the community. At the end of the plaza, furthest away from the performance, stand those in the village interested in and eager to discuss local politics. Seated at the front are older people who are interested in the performance and not in politics. In between stand the younger members of the community and those who are unimportant. And on the edge of the crowd stand people from other communities who are visiting to attend the performance.

Space is also organized in some cultures to keep separate different ethnic, social, or occupational groups. For example, in Europe during the Middle Ages through the seventeenth century, Jews were commonly required to live in their own sections of a city (called ghettos) or on streets occupied only by Jews in towns and villages. The Jews were required to sleep in the ghettos, and in some cities they were locked in at night, although during the day they were permitted to leave the ghetto and interact openly with non-Jews. In Hindu India, distinctions among different castes are marked in part by the organization of space. In Tamil villages, for example, members of the Nadar caste of toddy-

tappers (considered an unclean and polluting occupation) are not allowed to enter Hindu temples, are forbidden from drinking water from public wells, must live in houses on the edge of the main village, and must keep a few paces distant from a person of a higher caste. These space requirements are even more severe for Untouchables in the village who must live even further outside the village and must keep even further away from higher-caste persons. As with the segregation of women and men, the organization of space to keep ethnic or social groups apart is often based on the belief of the more powerful group that the other group is impure. In addition to marking status, space can be organized also to mark the social role played by certain groups in a society. For example, Zulu soccer team members in South Africa typically engage in highly ritualized behavior the night before and day of a match, some of which involves the organization of space. The night before the match the entire team, managers, and loyal supporters sleep naked together around a fire in a "camp." The team travels together on the same bus to the match the next day and enters the soccer stadium together in a tight formation, with each man touching the men in front, behind, and adjacent to him. This ritualized use of space along with other ritualized behavior is meant to segregate the men from women, alcohol, and members of the other team.

Across cultures, there is a marked difference between the use of the same space by persons who are related to one another in comparison to the use of the same space by persons who are not related. In virtually all cultures, kin, and especially kin related by blood, are more likely to share the same space, allow one another into personal space, and more often touch each other than do nonkin. For example, among the San of Botswana, blood kin sit and stand closer to one another and more often touch each other than do nonkin or nonblood kin. Across cultures, a common form of systematized organization of space involving relations among kin reflects what are called avoidance relationships. In avoidance relationships certain categories of kin are required to avoid each other on a day-to-day basis. These individuals may be prohibited from eating together, from being in the same house or room together, from talking to each other, from making eye contact, or from touching one another. Thus, at some level, one person is forbidden to enter the space occupied by the other. The most common avoidance customs are those attached to the relationship between a man and his wife's mother (his mother-in-law) and a woman and her husband's father (her father-in-law). For example, the San require that these sets of in-laws should stay at least 3 feet apart from one another and one should never enter the home of the other. Another form of avoidance is brother-sister avoidance, which applies mainly to adult brothers and sisters. In general, avoidance rules serve to minimize contact between individuals when that contact might lead to conflict in the family. For example, a husband is often required to avoid his mother-in-law in societies where the husband goes to live with the wife's family after marriage. The avoidance rule prevents conflict by keeping apart the wife's mother and husband, the two people who expect to have some control over her daily activities.

The organization of personal space involves customs about how close people stand or sit to one another, how and in what ways they touch one another, and the amount of eye contact that is considered acceptable. As noted above, factors that influence the organization of space, including personal space, in many cultures are age, sex, status, and role differences among individuals and their status as blood kin, nonblood kin, or nonkin. Keeping in mind that there are internal differences within cultures regarding personal space, there is also some consistency within cultures and variation across cultures. At one extreme are cultures like the San where individuals routinely sit shoulder to shoulder and

knee to knee, with their ankles crossed over each other's and where people touch each other in grooming, arranging ornaments, and rubbing each other's bodies down with fat. Toward the other extreme are cultures like the Javanese in Indonesia where touching by men and women is not allowed in public and where money is exchanged in markets by the buyer placing it on the counter and the merchant picking it up, so that the money does not pass from hand to hand. However, the Javanese do not restrict touching by friends of the same sex who freely lean on one another in informal settings.

In many cultures the concept of personal space centers not just on one's physical person but also on one's home. For example, Quechua Indians in Ecuador define their personal space as their house and the area within the walls around the yard. A passerby seeing someone in the yard will stop and ask, "Let me pass," to which the homeowner responds "Pass please." Similarly, a visitor will stop at the gate and ask "Give me orders," and the owner will respond with "Please come ahead." However, the visitor remains on the veranda as few visitors are actually invited into the house.

Related to the concept of personal space is the amount is space in the home. Cultures vary widely in the amount of space that is considered appropriate for a household ranging from those like the Ganda in Uganda, Tiv in Nigeria, and Khasi in India whose typical houses average less than one occupant per room to cultures at the other extreme such as the Klamath in North America and Mataco in South America whose single-room houses are home for over a dozen people at a time. Klamath homes were traditionally large wooden structures with areas allocated to different individuals while Mataco houses were small, grass, single-room huts. In general, however, people across cultures seem to prefer more rather than less space in the dwellings, as 40 percent of cultures in a worldwide survey of 50 cultures have dwellings that typically house one or less persons per room. While crowded living conditions are associated with antisocial behavior in some animals such as rats, across cultures living in a dwelling with many other people is not associated with a higher frequency of behaviors such as suicide, homicide, or divorce than in cultures where only a few people live in a household. And it seems that in cultures with many people living in the household, infants and children are more indulged and better cared for. Related to the issue of crowding is the value placed on personal privacy. A concern with privacy is reflected across cultures in the amount of effort people make to place physical barriers such as solid walls, closeable windows and doors, shutters, and partitions between rooms between themselves and other people. A survey of 42 cultures indicates that in 56 percent privacy is not a major concern as people can usually see or hear one another, in 20 percent people make some attempt to keep separate from others, and in 24 percent privacy is considered important. Cultures where privacy is important tend to be large, socially complex ones such as modern industrialized societies as well as societies that rely heavily on agriculture or pastoralism. A concern with personal privacy probably appeared only in the last 10,000 years, and probably first in the Near East in settled agricultural and pastoral societies where differences in wealth and status among the members of a society and the construction of permanent dwellings and other buildings would have made privacy possible.

See also Built Environments; Geomancy; Mobility and Sedentism; Place Names; Settlement Patterns; Territory and Territoriality; Universe.

Arterburn, Yvonne J. (1977) *The Silk Weavers of Kanchipruam: A Case Study of the Indian Cooperative Movement.*

Bourque, L. Nicole. (1994) "Spatial Meaning in Andean Festivals: Corpus Christi and Octavo." *Ethnology* 33:229–244.

Broude, Gwen. (1994) *Marriage, Family, and Relationships.*

Butler, Barbara. (1981) *Indigena Ethnic Identity and Ethnic Identity Change in the Ecuadorian Sierra.*

Coleman, Jack D. B. (1976) *Language Shift in a Bilingual Hebridean Crofting Community.*

Corlin, Claes. (1982) "The Organization of Social Space in a Tibetan Refugee Settlement." In *The House in East and Southeast Asia*, edited by K. G. Izikowitz and P. Sorenson, 173–180.

Crespi, Muriel K. (1968) *The Patrons and Peons of Pesillo: A Traditional Hacienda System in Highland Ecuador.*

Eban, Abba. (1984) *Heritage: Civilization and the Jews.*

Keeler, Ward. (1975) "Musical Encounter in Java and Bali." *Indonesia* 19:85–126.

Levinson, David. (1979) "Population Density in Cross-Cultural Perspective." *American Ethnologist* 6:742–751.

Marshall, Lorana. (1976) *The !Kung of Nyae Nyae.*

Rapoport, Amos. (1994) "Spatial Organization and the Built Environment." In *Companion Encyclopedia of Anthropology*, edited by Tim Ingold, 460–502.

Roberts, John M., and Thomas Gregor. (1971) "Privacy: A Cultural View." In *Privacy*, edited by Roland Pennock and John W. Chapman, 199–225.

Rohsenow, Hill G. (1974) *Property Settlement: The Politics of Paipai in Taipei, Taiwan.*

Scotch, Norman A. (1970) "Magic, Sorcery, and Football among Urban Zulu: A Case of Reinterpretation under Acculturation." In *Black Africa: Its Peoples and Their Cultures Today*, edited by John Middleton, 248–252.

Silverman, Carol T. (1980) *Expressive Behavior as Adaptive Strategy among American Gypsies.*

Sugawara, Kazuyoshi. (1984) "Spatial Proximity and Bodily Contact among the Central Kalahari San." *African Study Monographs* 3:1–43.

STARS AND PLANETS

The solar system or at least some of its components are recognized in all cultures around the world. Across cultures, the sun and the moon are the components that draw the most attention because of their proximity to earth and their obvious effects or association with changes in the seasons and the weather and therefore their influence on the environment. Interest in the stars and planets varies more widely across cultures, with the stars always given more attention than the plants, probably because the stars are more numerous, more predictable, and are arrayed in ways that lend themselves to interpretation. But even with the stars, cultures vary widely in the number that are named and assigned meanings and in their beliefs about the influence of stars on human concerns. At one extreme are cultures that pay little attention to the stars, such as the Western Shoshone of Utah who consider such matters unimportant. Similarly, the Miao of Thailand know of and name certain stars but do not considering them as having any sort of influence on human affairs. The Toba of Argentina do not assign special status to any objects in the sky although the sun and moon are used for counting time and as weather omens. In contrast, the following cultures are those that do attach some importance to the stars. The Chukchee of Siberia, for example, consider stars and constellations to be benevolent spirits. Various Plains Indians groups such as the Blackfoot used the stars for navigation and paid special attention to certain stars whose importance was noted in the decorative art on the tipi covers, rattles, and other objects. For the Blackfoot the most important stars and planets (although the Blackfoot themselves did not distinguish between stars and planets) were Ursa Major, the Pleiades, Venus (called the "Mistaken Morning Star"), Jupiter ("Morning Star"), and Mars ("Big-Fire Star"). Beyond cultures like the Blackfoot are those that consider stars and other heavenly bodies to be quite important and that devote considerable resources to their identification, naming, veneration, and study. In ancient civilizations such as Babylonia, this level of attention often manifested itself in complex astrological systems that were used to predict the future by ritual specialists called astrologers. Although dating back some 3,500 years, astrology remains in use today in nations such as China and in the Western world as well, especially in what is called the New Age movement. As astrology pertains to individuals rather than cultures and is more about religion than human-environment relationships, it is beyond the scope of this article. However, not all cultures that view the solar system as important are ones with beliefs in astrology; for many, the solar system, however defined, is a major component of the universe along with the underworld and the earth. In some cultures, elements of the solar system are seen as playing a major role in their culture and are seen as environmental forces that influence the lives of people on earth and therefore must be noted and reckoned with on a daily basis. One such culture is the Pawnee of the North American Plains. The importance of the stars in particular is seen in Pawnee religious beliefs and practices, arts, customs, and mythology. The following story highlights the centrality of the stars in Pawnee culture.

The Morning Star and the Evening Star

Over all is Tirawa, the One above, changeless and supreme. From Tirawa comes all things: Tirawa made the heavens and the stars.

The Pathway of Departed Spirits parts the heavens. In the beginning, east of the path was Man; west of the path was Woman. In the east was creation planned; in the west was creation fulfilled. All that the stars did in the heavens foretold what would befall upon the earth, for as yet the earth was not made.

In the west dwelt the White Star Woman, the Evening Star, who must be sought and overcome that creation might be achieved. From the east went forth the Great Star, the Morning Star, to find and overcome the Evening Star, that creation might be achieved. The Morning Star called to his younger brother: "Take the Sacred Bundle, bear it over thy shoulder and follow." And the Morning Star journeyed to the west. And ever as he journeyed, the Evening Star moved, came, and drew him towards her. (For men may see how the Evening Star moves nightly. One night she is low in the heavens, another night she is high in the heavens. Even so she moved and drew the Morning Star.) Yet when the Evening Star beheld the Morning Star draw near, she placed in his path Hard Things to hinder his approach. Thus, even as the Morning Star first saw the Evening Star, she rose and looked on him and beckoned him. He started towards her, but the earth opened and waters swept down, and in the waters was a serpent with mouth wide open to devour.

The Morning Star sang, and drew from his pouch a ball of fire and threw it at the serpent; and straightway the monster vanished, the waters dried, the ground was level, and the Morning Star passed on.

Even so, each time the Evening Star placed in the path of the Morning Star Hard Things to hinder his approach, the Morning Star sang, and drew from his pouch a ball of fire and threw it at the hinderance; and straightway the hinderance vanished and the Morning Star passed on. After each triumph he spoke, saying, " I have overcome my Grandfather," or, "I have overcome my Grandmother," and again, "I have overcome my Father," "I have overcome my Mother," and again "I have overcome my Brother," "I have overcome my Sister."

Ten were the hindrances, and ten times spoke he thus, each time naming a kinship, in prophecy of kinships on the earth; for of human kinships is the number ten. Cactus, thorns,

and thick woods, monsters, and evil animals—of such forms were the hindrances. So were they the prophecy of what should be Hard Things for man upon the earth.

So passed the Morning Star in victory, and journeyed westward ever, and reached the lodge of the Evening Star.

To the Evening Star had Tirawa given the Powers of the West. Also had he placed, to guard her, four beasts—Black Bear, Mountain Lion, Wild-Cat, and Wolf. These Beasts, placed by Tirawa in the heavens, were stars—Black Star, Yellow Star, White Star, and Red Star. They were beings who should send to earth beasts like themselves. They were the prophecy of animals to be upon the earth. Also were they Autumn, Spring, Winter, summer; thunder, lightning, clouds, winds; and they betokened four kinds of wood to be upon the earth—cottonwood, elm, willow, box-elder; and four kinds of corn—black, yellow, white, red. Great was the power of the four beasts; great was their power to guard the Evening Star; yet were they vanquished by the Morning Star.

And the Morning Star spoke and said, "I have conquered, and ye shall obey my command. Thou, Black Star, shalt stand in the northeast, whence cometh night. Thou art Autumn. Thou, Yellow Star, shalt stand in the northwest, where is the golden setting of the sun. Thou art Spring. Thou, White Star, shalt stand in the south, facing north, whence cometh the snow. Thou art Winter. Thou, Red Star, shalt stand in the southeast. Thou art Summer."

Now are the four stars known as the four World-Quarter Gods. At the four world-points they stand to hold up the heavens, and they obey the Morning Star.

Then the Morning Star approached the Evening Star to overcome her. Yet might the Evening Star not yield until the Morning Star should bring to her the cradle-board for the child that was to be born. The board should be of the cottonwood; the covering, a speckled wild-cat-skin, emblem of the starry heavens. With strips of otter-skin should the child be bound upon the boards; for the otter lives in the water, and betokens the rain-storms.

Above the board, over the head of the child, should be stretched a hoop, cut from the willow-tree. This too betokens the rain-storm, also the Arch-Above-the-Earth—the Rainbow.

The Morning Star went for to seek the cradle-board. The Star Beasts helped him, and the Morning Star found, and won, and brought the cradle-board to the Evening Star. But still, ere she yielded, the Evening Star bade the Morning Star seek and bring to her a mat for the child to lie upon. And the Morning Star went to the south and killed a buffalo, and brought the softest part of the hide to be a mat for the child to lie upon.

Then said the Evening Star, "Yet must thou seek and bring to me water wherewith to bathe the child." And the Morning Star sought and won and brought to the Evening Star water wherewith to bathe the child. The water was sweet and fragrant, for it came from a spring around which grew sweet-smelling grasses. The water was the rain, and it was part of the garden of the Evening Star—her garden, ever growing and ever green. This water, brought by the Morning Star to the Evening Star, was the rain, which from henceforth should go to the people of the earth.

Now could the Morning Star approach the Evening Star and overcome her. And when the Morning Star overcame the Evening Star, he gave to all that he had. And when the Evening Star yielded to the Morning Star, she gave to him all that she had; each gave unto the other of their Power for the sake of the people; for all that they gave should henceforth go to men upon the earth. The Power of the Morning Star is in the bed of flint on which he stands. And the Morning Star gave to the Evening Star his Power. To the Evening Star belongs the Powers of the West; the Power of the Storms is hers. But into the Storms the Morning Star put his Power of Flint, and placed it in the clouds to strike as lightning from the rain-storms. This Power of Flint from the Morning Star would give knives, axes, and weapons to the people of the earth.

Now when the Morning Star had overcome the Evening Star, he received from her a pebble, and he let fall the pebble into great waters. After a long time (so tell the songs) the pebble became the earth. Then the Morning Star threw into the air his ball of fire, and said, "Stand there, and give light to the earth!" And the ball of fire became the Sun. The Power of the Sun is from the Morning Star.

Now when the pebble under the waters had become the earth, the four World-Quarter Gods struck downward, with closed hands, and on each side of the waters the earth rose up. (Thus in the Bundle of each World-Quarter God is a war-club to mean the downward stroke that made the earth to rise up on each side of the waters.)

The Evening Stare bore a daughter. And she placed the little maiden on a cloud to send her to the earth. Now in the garden of the Evening Star were seeds of all kinds that should go to the people of the earth. Here grew the Mother-Corn. And the Evening Star gave to the maiden the Mother-Corn and said, "Plant this upon the earth!" Then she sent her daughter downward.

The maiden dropped from the cloud upon the earth like rain, and to this day the name for the maiden in the Pawnee tongue is "Standing Rain." The little maiden knew not where she was. She turned her ear this way and that, listening, till at last there came towards her a boy, child of the Sun and the Moon, even as was the maiden child of the Morning Star and the Evening Star. From the union of these two sprang the people of the earth.

To the Stars did Tirawa give powers to watch over the people. If the people were evil, the Stars might send storms to destroy them. But Tirawa himself is ever without anger. He is feared by none. Tirawa is changeless.

Stars

While only in the modern world and with the aid of powerful telescopes is it possible to see and know something about the thousands of stars in the solar system, some stars are visible to the naked eye in all parts of the world every night of the year. Thus, even though not all cultures agree on how important stars are, in all cultures people do wonder about where stars came from and what they are. In most if not all cultures, people distinguish among different stars on the basis of a number of criteria. The Western Shoshone, for example, distinguish among big, regular, and shooting stars. The Tonga classify stars by direction and consider the five southward, ten northward, and eight northern stars to be the most important ones. The Ifugao of the Philippines categorize stars in terms of the star's location relative to the moon (near, surrounding, accompanying, in line with), size, and alignment relative to each other (row, cluster, triangular constellation, twin). And the Teda of the Sudan distinguish by large, bright stars that are the stars of rich and powerful people and those that are small and dim that are the stars of the poor. Thus, across cultures, stars are identified by their size, brightness, location in the sky, movement, alignment with one another, and alignment with other objects such as the moon.

In all cultures, people are interested in where the stars came from—what caused them to appear. And, again, there is considerable cross-cultural variation in explanations for the stars. In cultures like the Pawnee that consider stars to be very important, there is often a long and complex creation myth like the Pawnee one recorded above that not only explains the origin of stars but also notes their place in the universe. In other cultures, explanations are less elaborate and often link specific stars or constellations to human beings or animals. The Copper Inuit believe that all stars were either humans or animals before they ascended into the sky. The Western Shoshone call stars "Coyote's Children" after the animal that figures heavily in Native American mythology. The Teda believe that when a person is born, an angel places a stone in the sky that then becomes a star and when the person dies, the star falls. The Aymara of Bolivia also believe that each person has his or her own star that falls when they die. Finally, there are other cultures that attribute the stars to non-human or animal sources. For example, the Ifugao believe that the stars are the children of the sun and moon and the G/wi San of Botswana explain the stars as the work of N!adima, the Creator, a belief quite like that found in the Judeo-Christian tradition.

Names of Stars, Clusters, and Constellations

Across cultures, people perceive stars and clusters and groupings of stars in ways that are consistent with their social and natural environments and their belief systems. Thus, there is much cross-cultural variation in the shapes people customarily see in the stars and in the names they give those shapes. At the same time, though, there is considerable cross-cultural similarity in that in all cultures people name many stars and constellations after animals important in their environments or persons or activities having to do with getting food. The following is a list of some stars and constellations well known in Western culture and the names or meanings assigned those same stars or constellations in other cultures.

Arcturus (brightest star in the Boötes [Herdsman] constellation)

Chukchee (Siberia): "Front Head" paired with Vega, which is called "Rear Head" because they are brothers or cousins

Copper Inuit (Canada): "The Leader" because when it is high in the sky it signals the opening of the seal hunting season

G/wi San (Botswana): "Firewood Finisher-Child"

Big Dipper or Plough

Blackfoot (United States): "Seven Brothers" because four brothers who fell from a tree are the four lowest stars

Ifugao (Philippines): "The Turner"

Teda (Africa): "Wild Donkeys" because it stands apart from other constellations

Western Shoshone (Utah): "Is Driving Rabbits" or "Has a Tail"

Crux (Southern Cross)

G/wi San: "They Are Big, Like Giraffes"

Teda: "Udder of Wild Donkey" because of its shape

Toba (Argentina): "Rhea" with nearby stars called dogs that are chasing but never catch it

Gemini (Castor and Pollux—The Twins)

Chukchee: two elks running from two hunters

Garo (India): "Chapchore and Nonje Janje," two beautiful women turned into stars

Leo (Lion)

Chukchee: "Standing Woman"

Lynx

Blackfoot: "Person's Hand"

Chukchee: "Mouse-Driver"

Milky Way

Aymara (Bolivia): "River of the Sky"

Chukchee: "Pebbly River"

Garo: "The footprints of the Buffalo" because it was made by a buffalo who broke away while being led to sacrifice

G/wi San: "Night's Backbone"

Ifugao: "Twinkling and Twinkling"

Toba: a road once walked upon by young girls or a road the rhea runs along pursued by dogs or hunters

Western Shoshone: "Dust Road" because it is smoke from a fire made by a woman cooking pine nuts; also "Streak," "Sky Path," "Ghost Road," "Soul Road"

Orion (The Hunter)

Aymara: right angle is "The Farm" or "The Field"

Chukchee: "Archer with a Crooked Back"

Copper Inuit: "The Little Hunters" as they were formed from three bear or seal hunters who suddenly rose from the earth to the sky

G/wi San: "Man Shoots Steenbok"

Pleiades (cluster of seven stars in the Taurus [Bull] constellation)

Blackfoot: "Poor Children"

Chukchee: "Group of Women"

Copper Inuit: a star cluster called "The Bear"

Ifugao: "The Mauler" because it looks like a wooden maul

Toba: "Our Ancestor," "The Chief"

Western Shoshone: "Many"

Polaris (Pole Star)

Chukchee: "Motionless Star," "Nail Star," "Pole-Stuck Star"

Ursa Major (Great Bear)

Chukchee: "Sling-Throwers," men shooting with strings

Copper Inuit: a constellation called "The Caribou"

It is common across cultures for people to identify a specific star or to conceptualize groups of stars as constellations and to assign them meanings and names, with these same stars and constellations going unrecognized in other cultures. Thus, not all peoples recognize Western constellations and not all constellations recognized elsewhere are noted in Western cultures. For example, the Toba of Argentina in addition to naming what Westerners call the Milky Way, Pleiades, and Southern Cross as noted above, also see constellations called pigeon, iguana, crow, rabbit's burrow and playing ground, armadillo, dear, three old women and their house, and stretched skin. And the Garo in India have 14 named stars and constellations, including those of interest in the West such as Sirius, Pleiades, and Gemini, and also others such as constellations called "The Walking Stick," "Fighting Cocks," and "Carrying the Cat."

Planets

Because planets are fewer in number and less visible to the naked eye, they do not draw the same level of interest as do stars in traditional cultures. Those planets that are named are often classified as stars and not as a separate category of heavenly bodies. The planet that draws the most attention across cultures is Venus, which is often called the Morning and Evening Star, as among the Western Shoshone, Toba, Chukchee, and Garo who believe that they are two stars rather than one. The Chukchee are one culture that does see the planets as being objects that differ from the stars in that the planets move in irregular paths and are called Crooked-Way Stars and Venus is said to have "many clothes" because it changes color.

Moving Objects in the Sky

In many Western cultures, moving objects in the sky such as shooting stars and meteors or comets are of considerable interest. In many cultures people believe that a shooting star will bring good luck if one makes a wish before it disappears. This view is not shared in many non-Western cultures where such objects are often considered to be star excrement. For example, the Ifugao call tektite, a mineral residue of meteorites found near Manila, star dung. However, this view is not universal. The Chukchee consider meteors to be fire and the Toba consider them to be spirits. In general, however, in most cultures objects moving across the sky are not considered of much importance and most people are like the G/wi San who wonder and worry about new comets and satellites but quickly forget them once it is clear that they will cause no harm .

Religion

Beliefs about the stars are a component of the religious belief system in many cultures, although the exact beliefs differ widely from culture to culture. For example, a star festival is an important holiday for the Mongols of Inner Mongolia and is celebrated by all tribes on 8 January, the time of year when the sky is filled with bright stars. The religious leaders arrange fire pots in a pattern of nine stars; the assembled villagers each offer coins equal in number to their ages to the pots and then burn incense and worship at the pot representing their star and then to the gods of the four directions. The Ifugao believe that the star deities have considerable influence on human affairs and can cause fights and sickness. Thus, considerable ritual activity of the religious practitioners is devoted to pleasing the star deities or reversing the harm they have caused.

As with the Ifugao, the stars are linked in a variety of ways with death in many cultures. In traditional Korea, stars play a role in funerals, as the body of the deceased is tied in seven places with hemp rope, with the ties oriented to the positions of the stars in the Ursa Major constellation, as it is considered lucky. For the Dogon of West Africa, the stars also play a role in death as in the following lament in which the dead wife is symbolized by the moon and her surviving children by the stars (Paulme 1940:490):

> the moon has gone down, the stars (remain alone)
>
> the pretty calabash, the moon, has gone down,
>
> the stars remain alone,
>
> who (henceforth) will come to wash my bowl,
>
> the pretty calabash, the moon (has gone down),
>
> who will come to wash my bowl.

And for Mbuti Pygmies of central Africa, when a person dies, his or her soul is believed to return to God (Tore) and then to turn into a star. The Pawnee also relate the soul to stars, although for them it is the stars that control the destiny of the soul. The souls of people who die from an illness resulting from being seen by the Star of Disease are taken by the South Star to his home in the south. The Morning Star decides on the destiny of all other souls—bringing them back to life or sending them to the east or the south.

Navigation

The primary practical use of the stars is as a guide in navigation at night. For people traveling on the land, the stars are of limited use as other guides, such as the moon, or visible markers in the environment, such as prominent mountain peaks or bodies of water, are easier to use and more reliable. The stars are most important for people who had to travel over large bodies of open water without the use of navigational devices such as sextants or compasses. Nowhere were stars more important than in Oceania. The islands of the Pacific Ocean were settled over a period of some 4,000 years beginning about 5,000 years ago by peoples moving off of farms near the coast of southern China. Much of this region is open water dotted by thousands of islands, some inhabited and some not. People in Oceania traditionally sailed across the open sea from island to island in canoes, usually in the form of single-hulled canoes with an outrigger for stability or double-hulled canoes. The canoes were powered by the wind caught in triangular mat sails. Travel from one island to another often required navigation without the benefit of sighting islands along the way. Throughout Oceania people traditionally relied on the sighting of known islands, the position of the sun, the direction of ocean swells, and other directional indicators such as the flight paths of land-nesting

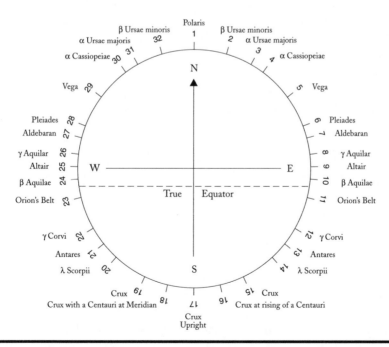

FIGURE 2   THE SIDEREAL COMPASS OF THE CENTRAL CAROLINES

birds for navigation during daylight hours. At night, they relied heavily on star-path navigation to stay on course. Open-sea navigation is a serious undertaking for Oceanic cultures, and navigators enjoyed considerable prestige, with knowledge of navigation passed from fathers to sons or from mother's brothers to sister's sons. The importance of star and sun navigation is suggested by the fact that most Oceanic peoples were little interested in explaining or the religious use of heavenly bodies; they were most concerned with the practical application of these bodies. Probably the most complex star-path navigation system was developed by the navigators in cultures located on the Caroline Islands who developed a sidereal compass (see Figure 2 on page 205) and kept detailed almanacs and calendars that enabled them to navigate during the day or night from island to island.

The sidereal compass and other star-path navigation systems used in Oceania were based on the principle that each star (with the exception of the Pole Star) rises at the same place on the eastern horizon, follows the same path across the sky, and then sets at the same place on the western horizon. (The stars don't actually rise or set; the rotation of the earth makes them appear to rise and fall.) These risings and settings of the stars were seen as paths by the navigators that they could follow to locate islands along the paths. These paths were then followed in the future to move from island to island, with several often followed in a night to reach the desired destination. While this practice seems quite straightforward, such a navigation system required the acquisition of considerable knowledge and much skill as paths must be chosen throughout the night to account for changes in wind and sea conditions. While the traditional navigation system was replaced by instrument-based systems following Western colonization, recent voyages of thousands of miles using only the traditional methods point to their ingenuity and continuing viability.

See also AURORA BOREALIS; RAINBOW; SUN AND MOON; UNIVERSE; WEATHER CONTROL.

Barton, Roy F. (1946) *The Religion of the Ifugaos.*

Bernatzik, Hugo A. (1947) *Akha and Miao.*

Bogoras, Waldemar. (1904–1909) *The Chukchee.*

Chamerlain, Von Del. (1982) *When Stars Came Down to Earth: Cosmology of the Skidi Pawnee Indians of North America.*

Collocott, Ernest E. V. (1922) *Tongan Astronomy and Calendar.*

Dorsey, George A., and James R. Murie. (1940) *Notes on Skidi Pawnee Society.*

Finney, Ben. (1994) *Voyage of Rediscovery.*

Goodenough, Ward H. (1953) *Native Astronomy in the Central Carolines.*

Hungry Wolf, Adolph. (1977) *The Blood People: A Division of the Blackfoot Confederacy: An Illustrated Interpretation of the Old Ways.*

Jenness, Diamond. (1922) *The Life of the Copper Eskimos.*

Karsten, Sigfrid R. (1923) *The Toba Indians of the Bolivian Gran Chaco.*

Kronenberg, Andreas. (1958) *The Teda of Tibesti.*

La Barre, Weston. (1948) *The Aymara Indians of the Lake Titicaca Plateau, Bolivia.*

Lehmann-Nitsche, Robert. (1923) "La Astronomía de los Tobas." *La Plata, Universidad Nacional, Museo de La Plata, Revista* 27:276–285.

Malouf, Carling. (1947) "Some Gosiute Mythological Characters and Concepts." *Utah Humanities Review* 1:369–377.

Metraux, Alfred. (1946) *Myths of the Toba and Pilaga Indians of the Gran Chaco.*

Oliver, Douglas L. (1989) *Oceania: The Native Cultures of Australia and the Pacific Islands.*

Osgood, Cornelius. (1947) *The Koreans and Their Culture.*

Paulme, Denise. (1940) *Social Organization of the Dogon (French Sudan),* translated by Frieda Schutze.

Playfair, Alan. (1909) *The Garos.*

Rasmussen, Knud J. V. (1932) *Intellectual Culture of the Copper Eskimos.*

Ronan, Colin A. (1992) *The Practical Astronomer.*

Rongmuthu, Dewan S., comp. (1960) *The Folk-Tales of the Garos.*

Silberbauer, George B. (1981) *Hunter and Habitat in the Central Kalahari Desert.*

Steward, Julian H. (1941) *Culture Element Distributions: XIII. Nevada Shoshoni.*

Turnbull, Colin M. (1965) *The Mbuti Pygmies: An Ethnographic Survey.*

STORMS

A storm is a weather condition that is disruptive or destructive. There are four major types of storms. Thunderstorms are the most common type in that they occur in all environments (although more often in tropical environments) and occur very frequently—in some locales such as peninsular Southeast Asia every afternoon for about 200 days of the year while in the northeast United States, high heat and humidity make thunderstorms a threat on many days in July and August. They are characterized by thunder, lightning, heavy rain, wind, and sometimes hail. Because they are so common and have a worldwide distribution, they are of interest and concern in many cultures and are covered in detail in the article "Thunder and Lightning." Windstorms are storms characterized by high winds but without the precipitation that is typical of other types of storms. Sandstorms are windstorms in which sand is lifted into the air and blown around by high winds. They occur mainly in deserts. Dust storms are another form of windstorm and are characterized by blowing winds that lift dry soil into the air and blow it around. They occur most commonly in agricultural or pastoral regions where vegetation has died and the land has dried out because of a lack of water. Cyclones and tornadoes, although often confused with one another, are different types of related storms. Cyclones are winds blowing in a spiral toward an area of low pressure and may cover hundreds of miles. Tornadoes are winds whirling around an area of low pressure creating a powerful sucking effect over a small area. A tornado over water is a waterspout. Hurricanes are cyclones that develop over warm tropical water and often cause more damage once they reach land than do other types of storms. Hurricanes are called typhoons in Oceania, cyclones in South Asia, willy-willies in Australia, and baquios in the Philippines. Hurricanes tend to be seasonal—in the Caribbean and the southern and eastern United States, late summer and early fall is the hurricane season, with hurricanes forming in the Atlantic Ocean and then gaining strength as they pass over the Caribbean Sea. Many cultures in the Caribbean such as Jamaicans and the Garifuna in Belize know the hurricane season well:

> June too soon
> July stand by
> August it must
> September remember
> October all over

"September remember" refers to previous destructive huuricanes in that month such as the 31 September 1931 hurricane that killed about 1,000 people in what is now Belize.

With the exception of thunderstorms, destructive storms seem to draw less ongoing attention than do other weather phenomena across cultures. Perhaps this is because these storms are uncontrollable even when predictable and therefore people everywhere react mainly by taking protective action. In most cultures, people flee approaching storms and seek shelter either away from the path of the storm or in buildings that have withstood storms in the past. In some cultures regularly hit by damaging storms, the built environment is construced to provide protection or to withstand storms. In the Great Plains of the United States where tornadoes are frequent, rural homesteads have underground tornado shelters in which families take shelter when a tornado approaches. And the Seminole of Florida built their houses on poles with open sides, mainly to keep cool in the heat, but these dwellings also withstood hurricane winds and rain with damage only to their palm leaf roofs. Most efforts across cultures, however, are directed at recovering from the destruction and disruption caused by storms, a topic covered in the articles "Environmental Disasters" and "Environmental Uncertainty and Risk."

As with the lack of day-to-day attention paid storms except when they are approaching and when they hit, in most cultures storms are not attributed to supernatural forces nor are supernatural means used to control them. There are exceptions, however, although even in these cultures the supernatural explanations seem somewhat superficial compared to explantions for other weather phenomena. Even though hurricanes are predictable, in rural Jamaica people often attribute crop failures clearly caused by drought or hurricanes to sorcerers hired by jealous neighbors. Similarly, the Senoi of Carey Island in Malaysia believe that the most powerful storms are caused by spirits but that somewhat weaker storms are caused by witches in other communities. Finally, the cross-cultural pattern of people being less than concerned with storms except when they threaten or hit is indicated by the Andaman Islanders of the Indian Ocean who believe that storms are caused by human behavior that angers the spirit, Biliku. Actions that most anger him are burning or melting bee's wax, killing a cicada or making noise while it is sing-

ing, and eating forbidden foods such as certain seeds or roots. However, these are things the Andamanese regularly do, regardless of their belief that storms will result, although they might be more careful in the stormy months of October and November.

See also ENVIRONMENTAL DISASTERS; ENVIRONMENTAL UNCERTAINTY AND RISK; PRECIPITATION; THUNDER AND LIGHTNING.

Cohen, Yehudi. (1966) *A Study of Interpersonal Relations in a Jamaican Community.*

Edwards, David T. (1961) *Report on an Economic Study of Small Farming in Jamaica.*

Fairbanks, Charles. (1973) *The Florida Seminole People.*

Radcliffe-Brown, Alfred R. (1922) *The Andaman Islanders: A Study in Social Anthropology.*

Wazir-Jahan, Begum K. (1985) *Ma' Betisek Concepts of Living Things.*

SUBSISTENCE SYSTEMS

A subsistence system—also commonly called subsistence economy, subsistence strategy, or subsistence technology—is the means used in a culture to exploit the environment to meet people's basic food needs. Across cultures, there is actually no such thing as a pure subsistence system, as the subsistence system of every culture at least sometimes produces a surplus of food or other material items that are saved for future use, traded to other groups, or used ritually. Additionally, while cultures are often described in stereotypical terms as utilizing a specific subsistence system such as San hunter-gatherers or Turkana pastoralist or Yanomamö horticulturalists, no culture depends entirely on one type of subsistence system.

Developing a typology of subsistence systems across cultures has been a focus of social science research for a number of years. This interest has been motivated by two major factors. First, subsistence systems are predictably related to other features of culture. That is, by and large, cultures that share the same type of subsistence systems tend to also be alike in other ways and systematically different from cultures with other types of subsistence systems. For example, cultures that subsist primarily by hunting and gathering such as the San of Botswana and the Copper Inuit of Canada, although living in very different environments, both have small populations and settlements, move about in search of food, have small families as the basic social units, divide up work responsibilities mainly on the basis of sex, and have an egalitarian form of community leadership. Thus, knowing the subsistence system of a culture helps us predict the presence or absence with some degree of accuracy of other features of that culture. Second, social scientists have long been interested in the evolution of human societies since humans first appeared about 3 million years ago. And since subsistence systems differ from one another in the degree of control they allow over the environment and the sources of energy with which to exploit the environment, knowledge of a culture's subsistence system can be used to rank that culture with others on a scale of cultural evolution. Greater control of energy resources such as animal, fossil-fuel, or nuclear power and the resulting greater control of the environment are key indicators of the level of cultural complexity of a culture on an evolutionary scale.

With these two purposes in mind, anthropologists and sociologists have developed a number of typologies of subsistence systems. Anthropologist George Peter Murdock defined subsistence economy as relating to the acquisition, transport, storage, and preservation of food and delineated five major types: agriculture, animal husbandry, fishing, hunting, and gathering

for a sample of 186 cultures. In a later refinement of this classification, cultures are rated as intensive tillers (agricultural peoples who use irrigation, artificial fertilizers, or crop rotation), extensive tillers, pastoralists, hunters (hunt or trap animals), fishers (fish, collect shellfish, or hunt sea mammals), and foragers (both hunt and fish). A survey of 563 cultures shows the following percentage distributions of these subsistence types before the economies were changed by extensive contact with Western cultures:

Intensive Tillers	27 percent
Extensive Tillers	36 percent
Pastoralists	6 percent
Hunters	6 percent
Fishers	8 percent
Foragers	17 percent

There is a marked regional pattern to the geographic distribution of these cultures. Intensive tillers were found mainly in Africa, the Mediterranean region, and East Asia. Extensive tillers (essentially the same as horticulturalists in other typologies) were concentrated in Africa, on islands in the Pacific Ocean, and in South America. Pastoralists were essentially an Old World phenomenon while hunters, fishers, and foragers predominated in the New World.

Another classification system developed by anthropologist Yehudi Cohen stresses the function of subsistence as an adaptive strategy related in a patterned way to other features of culture rather than as a technique or bundle of techniques for simply extracting food from the environment. This classification proposes six systems of economic production, four of which—foraging, horticulture, agriculture, and pastoralism—pertain to nonindustrialized cultures and the other two—trade and industrialism—to more economically complex cultures.

A more clearly evolutionary typology is suggested by sociologist Gerhard Lenski who sets forth a scale of four general types and three specialized types. At the bottom of the evolutionary scale are hunting and gathering societies (who were the only type up to about 12,000 years ago) including both simple hunter-gatherers and advanced hunter-gatherers. Simple hunter-gatherers were prehistoric societies; advanced ones include contemporary hunter-gatherers and are characterized by the use of specialized tools such as the spear-thrower or bow and arrow. Next on the scale are horticultural societies, again of both simple and advanced types. Simple horticulturalists subsist by gardening without the use of metal tools while advanced horticulturalists use metal tools. At the third stage are agrarian societies, again of the simple and advanced types. Simple agrarian cultures grow crops and use metal tools and the plow. Advanced agrarian cultures have all the characteristics of horticulturalists and simple agrarian cultures but also manufacture iron tools and weapons. At the top of the scale are industrial societies that exploit the environment by using nonhuman forms of energy such as water, wind, fossil fuels, and nuclear energy. In addition to these four subsistence types, there are three other types that do not fit neatly on the evolutionary scale—fishing, herding, and maritime societies. As a group, these societies use subsistence systems that heavily exploit specific resources in their environment. Fishing societies exploit fish, shellfish, and sea mammals. While being food collectors like hunter-gatherers, regarding other cultural features such as population size and settlement patterns these societies more closely resemble agrarian societies who also draw on a large food base that often produces a sizeable surplus. Native Americans of the Northwest Coast, such as the Tlingit, were of this type. Herding societies or pastoralists subsist mainly by herding stock such as goats, cattle, camels, and sheep on open graze land. Maritime societies, such as the ancient Phoenicians and Venetians who subsisted by trade on the seas, were common in antiquity but no longer exist.

Another evolutionary scale is suggested by anthropologists Alan Lomax and Conrad Arensberg. They suggest an evolutionary development sequence running from food extraction to food production to industry. Food extractors include collectors who are found all over the world and hunters and fishers found mainly along the Pacific Rim. Food producers, in evolutionary order, begin with incipient producers of the New World who grew mainly cereals and vegetables, animal husbanders of the Old World who combined gardening with keeping domesticated livestock, pastoralists of Asia and Africa, and plow agriculturalists of Europe and East Asia.

These various attempts to identify different cultures as utilizing a specific subsistence system provide stereotypical snapshots of these cultures as they existed prior to extensive and intensive contact with Western societies. Western contact by the start of the twentieth century had markedly influenced the subsistence systems of most cultures around the world and that change has accelerated throughout the century. A survey of 87 cultures shows that the subsistence economies of 75 percent had been changed partially by Western contact, the economies of 9 percent changed completely, and the other 16 percent not changed at all. The major changes across cultures were increased acquisition of goods through trade (45 percent of cultures), greater reliance on agriculture including more intensive growing of existing crops or the introduction of new crops (40 percent), increasing work and wage labor and the use of wage laborers (37 percent), a major decline of some traditional subsistence activity such as hunting or the loss of a major subsistence resource such as grazing land (36 percent), and the introduction of new crops (22 percent). Specific details about different subsistence strategies and how they have changed over time across cultures are provided in the relevant entries in this volume.

See also AGRICULTURE; FISHING; HORTICULTURE; HUNTING-GATHERING; IRRIGATION; PASTORALISM.

Bradley, Candice, et al. (1990) "A Cross-Cultural Historical Study of Subsistence Change." *American Anthropologist* 91: 447–457.

Cohen, Yehudi, ed. (1974) *Man in Adaptation: The Cultural Present.* 2d ed.

Lenski, Gerhard. (1970) *Human Societies.*

Lomax, Alan, and Conrad M. Arensberg. (1977) "A Worldwide Evolutionary Classification of Cultures by Subsistence Types." *Current Anthropology* 18:659–708.

Murdock, George P. (1981) *Atlas of World Cultures.*

Murdock, George P., and Diana Morrow. (1970) "Subsistence Economy and Supportive Practices: Cross-Cultural Codes 1." *Ethnology* 9:302–320.

SUN AND MOON

People across cultures have long recognized that both the sun and the moon exert influence on the earth. However, most people around the world have not, until recently, had access to scientific information that helps explain how these bodies influence nature. It is, therefore, not surprising that both celestial bodies have invoked considerable wonder and questioning and have been the subject of much speculation throughout human prehistory and history. The creation myths of nearly all cultures account for not just humans and the earth but also for the sun and the moon and therefore tell much about how different peoples view these two celestial bodies. It is no surprise that people in all cultures are interested in the sun and moon, as the movement of these bodies and their positions relative to earth are of considerable practical importance due to the fact that they influence plant life and animal behavior and therefore human subsistence activities.

The sun and moon were the objects of worship in a number of major civilizations such as the Inca, Maya, and Aztec in the New World and the Egyptian and ancient Hindu civilizations in the Old World. For the ancient Egyptians, Ra the Sun God, Horus the Sky God, and Orisis the God of the Dead were the major supernatural forces in their large pantheon. Egyptians believed that Ra sailed across the sky each day in his boat, disappearing into the underworld each night. In the underworld, Orisis, the God of the Underworld, pulled the boat along the underground River Nile and then it rose again. The Egyptians also worshipped Thoth, the Moon God, who was believed to be the inventor of writing and the scribe of the pantheon of Egyptian gods. In ancient times in northern India, Hindus looked upon Surya as the Sun God. He was the son of Dyaus, the Bright Sky, and Ushas, the Dawn, and was pulled across the sky each day by seven mares. About A.D. 1000, there were six sects devoted to sun worship, although the Sun God and sun worship are now no longer a major part of Hinduism. Perhaps sun worship reached its highest form and greatest level of devotion among the Aztecs of Mexico. The sun was created by the two Aztec creator gods through the sacrifice of other gods. To keep the sun in the sky, the earth illuminated, and to forestall the end of the world, the sun needed to be fed with human blood. This was accomplished through the regular sacrifice of humans (usually those taken captive from other groups by Aztec warriors) and the offering of their hearts to the sun by Aztec priests. The moon played a less dramatic role in Aztec life, but its relationship to agriculture was known and its phases and eclipses were carefully monitored. Spanish conquest destroyed the Aztec empire and civilization; their beliefs and practices related to the sun and moon are now mainly only a part of prehistory and history.

In more recent times, the worship of the sun has not been a major feature of world religions nor has the worship of either the sun or moon been a major feature in the religious systems of most non-Western cultures. But people in most cultures have often sought answers to two questions about the sun and moon: Where did they come from? and What are they? The answers are usually found in myths passed down orally from generation to generation. For the Toba of Argentina, the sun is a woman who walks across the sky, disappearing in the evening when she enters an opening between the sky and the earth. In the winter, when days are short, she is a young, lithe girl who moves quickly. In the summer, when days are long, she is an old woman walking slowly across the sky. The moon is a pot-bellied man, at war with the jaguar, a spirit of death. The moon defends himself with a spear and club, but as the jaguar tears at his body, pieces fall away and are seen as meteors. Humans must intervene by making noise to scare the jaguar away and the moon then grows again to its full form.

For the Yanomamö of Venezuela, the sun and moon are both men and enemies of each other. Their animosity goes back to a time when a man searched for wood for the moon. Upon realizing that the moon's real intent was to devour him, the man sought protection from the sun who hid the man and burned the moon, producing the uneven surface visible from earth. The sun became the friend of humans while the moon became their enemy. When the moon is rose-colored it is because it is eating human flesh.

The Mbuti of central Africa explain why the sun shines during the day and the moon at night. According to their mythology, the sun and moon were friends who agreed to stay high above the earth and to stand apart—the sun to the east and the moon to the west. They further agreed that their paths should never cross, so that is

why the sun shines during the day and the moon at night.

The Hopi of Arizona take direct responsibility for creating the sun and moon. In their version of the creation of the sun and moon, the Hopi people made a man from flowers and water and then covered him with a hoop made from wood and buckskin and supplied him with feathers and prayer sticks. He was then sent off to be the sun. However, since he was not fully painted, he became the moon instead of the sun. To correct their mistake, the Hopi then covered another hoop with a woman's wedding blanket and painted it blue and decorated it with red hair. They placed it over another flower-and-water man and told him to live forever and supply humans with heat and rain. He then rose up in the east as the sun.

As these above examples indicate, the sun and moon are often associated with supernatural forces or are thought to possess such force themselves. In some other cultures they are thought to be supernatural. For Hindu Bengalis in West Bengal, the Sun, Siva, and Durga are the three primary deities, although the Sun is not worshipped. Instead it is seen as a regulating force that sheds light on the universe and therefore "everyone wants the sun."

The Serbs believe that the moon is filled with energy and out of respect refer to it as Father or Grandfather. The moon can make one feel young and be fertile. The association of the moon with fertility is not particular to the Serbs but is also believed to be true elsewhere—and widely so among many cultures such as the Abelam, Trobriands, and Enga in New Guinea. In some of these cultures, a newborn is held up to the first full moon to help it grow quickly and speak at an early age. But for the Serbs, the moon is also dangerous and can shoot arrows that kill and can weaken children. Thus, it is unwise to sleep in the moonlight. But while the moon can harm, it can also heal and its power can be invoked through prayers such as the following to cure an enlarged spleen: "Young moon, the old one has greeted you that you may not eat crabs or fish but my spleen." The sun is also seen as powerful by the Serbs who say that a "House that has no sunlight will breed disease."

As these myths and beliefs show, across cultures it is common to assign a sex to the sun and moon. However, there is no apparent patterning to this practice. In some cultures the sun is considered male and the moon female, in others it is the reverse, and in still others both are considered male. Sometimes, one can be both male and female as is the moon for the West Bengalis who conceptualize the waxing moon as male and the waning moon as female. Also, in some cultures the sun and moon are seen as kin, most commonly as husband and wife or brother and sister.

In most cultures, the traditional calendar that marks the monthly and annual subsistence cycles is a lunar one. Thus, it is common across cultures for people to look to the moon for signs that govern their subsistence activities. Mountain Whites in rural Appalachia traditionally scheduled various activities such as when to plant crops, when to hunt, when to roof a cabin, or when to give birth by the phases of the moon. Agricultural peoples who often tie their activities to the lunar month are especially sensitive to the phases of the moon. In rural Haiti the preferred time for planting is the period beginning eight days after the new moon and ending with the full moon. Anything planted at other times will spoil. Rural Jamaicans also look to the moon for guidance and routinely consult planting almanacs based on the phases of the moon. The Yucatan Maya believe that three days after the full moon is the best time for planting fruit trees and root crops because the moon "has been in the ground for three days." The sun, although it has more effect on crops than the moon, is rarely consulted as a guide to subsistence activities, mainly because it does not have the clear phases over the course of a month as does the moon.

Other peoples use the moon and sun to help manage human affairs. The Latinos of southern Texas use the phases of the moon in black magic to counteract the evil deeds of witches: a full moon is a good time for aggressive acts, a quarter moon for destructive acts, and a barely visible moon for murder. And the Blackfoot of the North American Plains traditionally invoked the sun in oath-taking to settle disputes: "Now, we will talk to the sun. If what I say is not true, may I never live to put my foot into another snow."

Eclipses

In most cultures people become worried when they witness a solar or lunar eclipse, probably because eclipses are unnatural natural events. That is, they are unpredictable events (for peoples without access to predictions based on modern astronomy) that disrupt the predictable cycle of light and darkness caused by the appearance and disappearance of the sun and moon. And because human life depends on this cycle and especially the sun, any disruption to the cycle raises concerns about one's own survival. However, even in modern cultures with access to rational, scientific explanations for eclipses, such events cause considerable interest, perhaps because they disturb the natural order of daily events. An eclipse of the sun is caused by the moon passing between the earth and sun blocking one's view of the sun from the earth. An eclipse of the moon is caused by the earth moving between the moon and the sun and blocking sunlight from being cast onto the moon.

As noted above, in most cultures, people react to eclipses with trepidation or fear—they believe them to be harmful or signs of trouble in the future. The Tonga of Oceania call both solar and lunar eclipses *mate*, meaning "dead," and consider lunar eclipses as especially ominous. They are less concerned about and generally ignore an eclipse of the sun, perhaps because the Tonga use the moon rather than the sun to set their calendar. The Taos Indians of New Mexico fear eclipses of both types, believing them to cause illness and harm to unborn children. For this reason, during an eclipse a pregnant woman carries a protective object such as an arrowhead or stone knife and religious ceremonies are conducted following an eclipse. The Hopi of Arizona also fear eclipses, particularly those of the sun that are associated with death: an eclipse immediately after sunrise will cause people to the east to die; one in midmorning will cause Hopi to die; and one at noon will cause people to the southwest to die. Various measles, smallpox, and pneumonia epidemics of the past are blamed on eclipses that preceded them.

In the absence of the scientific explanations for eclipses, various other explanations are invoked in different cultures around the world, most centering on the actions of evil or destructive forces. Various American Indian groups in South America such as the Toba, Guarani, and Chiriguano believe that both solar and lunar eclipses are caused by attacks of the devil or jaguars on the sun or moon. The Aranda of central Australia associate a solar eclipse with evil forces and fear their occurrence, reasoning that because the sun is close to the earth, so too must be the evil during an eclipse. The Aranda believe that the evil force wants to inhabit the sun but can be driven away by an Aranda shaman who extracts stones from their bodies and hurls them at the sun. The evidence that this ritual drives off the evil forces is the inevitable reappearance of the sun. The Yucatan Maya believe that an eclipse is caused by an evil animal (perhaps an ant) trying to eat the sun or moon and therefore an eclipse is a time of great danger. The Maya words for solar and lunar eclipses—*chibal-kin* and *chibal-luna*—literally mean "biting of the sun" and "biting of the moon." The Maya fear that if the sun or moon fails to reappear then furniture and other objects will become devils or beasts and will turn on and kill their owners.

To prevent this calamity, Maya men fire guns at the sun or moon during an eclipse to drive off the animals. Because eclipses do not occur often and because they end rather quickly, in most cultures these efforts to drive off the evil forces causing the eclipse are thought to be effective.

See also ANNUAL CYCLE; CALENDARS; SEASONS.

Beaglehole, Ernest. (1937) *Notes on Hopi Economic Life.*

Cohen, Yehudi A. (1966) *A Study of Interpersonal Relations in a Jamaican Community.*

Collocott, Ernest E. V. (1922) *Tongan Astronomy and Calendar.*

Crooke, W. (1986) *The Popular Religion and Folk-Lore of Northern India.*

Fetterman, John. (1967) *Stinking Creek.*

Herskovits, Melville J. (1937) *Life in a Haitian Valley.*

Kemp, Phyllis. (1935) *Healing Ritual: Studies in the Technique and Tradition of the Southern Slaves.*

Kiev, Ari. (1968) *Curanderismo: Mexican-American Folk Psychiatry.*

Metraux, Alfred. (1946) *Myths of the Toba and Pilaga Indians of the Gran Chaco.*

Östör, Akos. (1980) *The Play of the Gods: Locality, Ideology, Structure, and Time in the Festivals of a Bengali Town.*

Parsons, Elsie W. C. (1936) *Taos Pueblo.*

Redfield, Robert, and Alfonso Villa Rojas. (1934) *Chan Kom: A Maya Village.*

Soustelle, Jacques. (1962) *The Daily Life of the Aztecs on the Eve of the Spanish Conquest.*

Spencer, Walter B., and F. J. Gillin. (1927) *The Arunta: A Study of a Stone Age People.*

Turnbull, Colin M. (1965) *The Mbuti Pygmies: An Ethnographic Survey.*

Wilbert, Johannes. (1963) "Los Sanema." In *Indios de la Región Orinoco-Ventiari*, 177–236.

Wissler, Clark. (1911) *The Social Life of the Blackfoot Indians*.

Copper Inuit men make, own, and maintain their own seal-hunting equipment. But they hunt in teams, conduct rituals before and following the hunt, and the product of the hunt is butchered by women using their own tools and divided among members of the community following a rigid set of allocation rules. Thus, in no society does technological activity exist in isolation.

Tools

Although other species use tools and engage in limited tool-making behavior, human beings are differentiated from all other species by their reliance on tools to exploit the environment, the variety of tools used, and their ability to invent new tools. Tools can be classified in a variety of ways using a number of different criteria:

1. Material they are made from—wood, stone, bone, iron, bronze, steel—and tools made from one material such as stone knives versus composite tools made from two or more materials such as a hammer with a steel head and a wood shaft and handle.

2. Shape—round, curved, straight, and so forth.

3. Use—striking, cutting, piercing, scraping.

4. Relation to the work being done. Primary tools produce a product that can be used without any further work. Secondary tools are used to make primary tools. Tertiary tools are used to make secondary tools.

5. Natural or human-altered or produced. Natural tools are features of nature either used in place by humans or removed from nature and used without modification. They include a rock to hide behind while hunting, sticks to extract honey from a comb, a stone to kill snakes, or a shell for scraping sap from a tree trunk. Other natural tools are used with only slight modification such as a leaf bent to form a drinking cup or a

TECHNOLOGY Technology is the "means by which man seeks to modify or control his natural environment" (Spier 1970:2). The goal of technological activity is to alter the physical state of an object. Technological activity is always enmeshed in a wider system of social structure and sometimes religious belief that together form the sociotechnical system of a society. One key difference between the sociotechnical systems of nonindustrialized societies (the focus of this article) and industrialized societies is the use of tools in the former and machines in the latter. The use of tools is believed by some social scientists and environmentalists to represent a greater degree of personal independence and closeness with nature than is the use of machines. Additionally, reliance on machines is thought to create a social order based on anonymity, distant economic relations, and social stratification. While there are many differences between societies that rely on tools and those that rely on machines, it is also clear that cultures that rely on tools also develop complex sociotechnical systems. For example,

twig with leaves used as a broom. Human-altered or produced tools used in food-getting include instruments, weapons, tended facilities, and untended facilities. Instruments are tools used to gather food from sources that are not hostile to humans and include digging sticks, seed beaters, hoes, axes, paddles, porcupine spears, among others. A weapon is a tool used to kill or harm an animal capable of movement and includes spears, clubs, knives, slings, bolas, bows and arrows, boomerangs, and harpoons, among others. A facility is a tool or structure that controls an animal's movement. Facilities tended by people include lures, poisons, nets, pits, surrounds, deadfalls, musical scares, weirs, blinds, and seines, among others. Untended facilities include some of the same ones as tended such as pits and traps and also items such as cowbells, corals, hobbles, and scarecrows, among others.

Tools are so central to human survival and the evolution of human culture that the major eras of human cultural evolution are marked by differences in tools and tool innovations as shown below.

Lower Paleolithic: 2 million to 300,000 B.P.—stone tools made by percussion flaking, use of flakes and core tools (choppers, scrapers, hand axes), wooden spears, fire-hardened spear points

Middle Paleolithic: 300,000 to 50,000 B.P.—percussion flaking, retouching of flake tools, production of same size flakes from a single core, pointed tools, greater variety of flake tools

Upper Paleolithic: 50,000 to 14,000 B.P.—stone tools made by pressure flaking, bone and antler tools, greater variety of tools (awls, pins, saws, spear-thrower, shovels)

Mesolithic: 14,000 to 10,000 B.P.—composite tools made with bone or wood handles, microliths widely used (small, thin blades), nets, baskets, a variety of stones used for tools

Neolithic: 10,000 to 5500 B.P.—ground stone tools, pottery, greater variety of finer tools

Bronze Age: 5000 to 3000 B.P.—use of bronze, an alloy of copper and tin, for tools and other objects

Iron Age: 3000 B.P.—use of iron for tools and other objects

It is important to note that these tool use patterns and dates pertain to cultural evolution in the Old World and do not indicate regional variation within the Old World. For example, in the years 31,000 to 16,000 B.P., there was no tool use in the New World because it was not yet inhabited by humans; in East Asia and Australia hand axes made by grinding the edges of stones were widely used; in the Middle East and South Asia blade tools such as knives, points, and scrapers were used; in Europe flint blades and bone and antler tools were used; and in Africa small, fine quartz blades were mounted on wood or bone handles.

Materials

People in traditional societies make things from natural materials. Four categories of natural materials are used alone or in various combinations:

1. *Liquids:* blood, plant juices, milk, mucus, oil, saliva, urine, water

2. *Plastics:* asphaltum, clay, resin, gum, sap, wax

3. *Flexibles:* bark, roots, brush, vines, feathers, grasses, hair, intestines, leaves, sinew, skin

4. *Solids:* antler, horn, nails, bone, copper, shell, spines, stone, teeth, turks, wood, seeds, coral

In many cultures, a single source of raw material resources may be used for a variety of materials. For example, indigenous peoples in the sub-Arctic region of North America traditionally used different parts of the spruce tree for different tools and objects. Mauls, wedges, and canoe paddles were cut and shaped from planks of trunk wood. Sap on the bark was chewed as gum. A simple drawing compass was made from two straight sticks lashed together with twine. A bridge for crossing a stream was fashioned from straight branches lashed together with twine. A breath protector was made of clumps of spruce shavings. A funnel was carved and bored from the spruce roots. Spruce gum on the trunk and that dripping off the branches was boiled with fish oil to make a waterproof glue. And spruce needles were boiled in water to make a potion for curing a stomachache.

Technological Activities

In all cultures people engage in technological activities to collect or produce food; to prepare food; to make fire; and to make tools, objects in which to store food and water, and clothing. In addition, people in all cultures engage in many other technological activities. A cross-cultural survey of 185 nonindustrialized cultures indicates the following 50 technological activities across cultures.

Food Collection

Gathering plant foods

Gathering insects, eggs, and/or small land animals

Gathering shellfish and/or small aquatic animals

Collecting wild honey

Hunting birds

Fishing

Trapping

Hunting of large land animals

Hunting of large aquatic animals

Food Production

Clearing land

Preparing soil

Planting crops

Weeding and irrigating crops

Harvesting

Caring for small domestic animals

Tending domestic animals

Milking

Food Preparation

Preparing vegetal foods

Butchering

Preserving

Preparing drinks

Making dairy products

Cooking

Extractive Industries

Mining and quarrying

Gathering fuel

Lumbering

Fetching water

Processing of Raw Materials

Tanning and scraping skins

Spinning

Weaving

Smelting

Manufacturing

Mat making

Net making

Basket making

Making cordage

Leather working

Making clothing

Pottery making

Manufacturing *(continued)*

Woodworking

Bone working

Stoneworking

Metalworking

Making musical instruments

Miscellaneous Activities

Fire making

Laundering

Body mutilation

Surgery and bonesetting

Burden carrying

Boat building

House building

Some activities are found across many cultures and have been intensively described.

Fire making. The ability to make and use fire is valued in all cultures. Fire provides heat for warmth and cooking, light, and protection from predators. Fire also is used in rituals in many cultures and is vital in the manufacture of metal tools and objects. Fire is produced across cultures by three major methods—friction, percussion, and compression. Fire produced by friction is either by rotation as in drilling or by reciprocating motion as in the use of fire saws and plows. A fire drill is the most often used fire-making tool around the world. The Yao of Mozambique use a drill consisting of a flat platform (a log with one side cut flat) with a depression drilled in the center and a groove down one side. Tinder is put at the bottom of the groove and when a drill stick is rotated rapidly in sand in the depression, the sawdust that results starts to smolder and then falls on and ignites the tinder. Fire saws and plows like drills also require two pieces of wood. With the saw, one piece such as a sturdy vine is used to cut into the other; the friction causes the sawdust to smolder and ignite the tinder. With the plow, a piece of hardwood is sawed across a piece of softwood, again dropping smoldering sawdust into the tinder. Percussion involves striking materials such as flint, pyrite, quartz, or sulfur together or against other materials to produce a spark that will ignite tinder placed underneath. Percussion is especially important in the Arctic where wood for plows, saws, or drills may not always be available or always be dry. The use of compressed gas to produce fire is less widespread than the other methods and is used mainly in Asia. The tool for producing fire by compression is the fire piston, consisting of a wood cylinder, a wood piston, and tinder. Heat generated by driving the piston into the cylinder in turn ignites tinder tied to the bottom of the piston.

People who live in permanent communities either keep fires burning all the time or can use hot charcoal from yesterday's fire to start a new fire. People in nomadic communities, however, face the problem of starting new fires each time they move. Rather than start fires from scratch, many nomadic peoples carry their fire with them in the form of smoldering cordage or plant matter or as hot charcoal in fireproof containers such as gourds, shells, pottery, or sand-lined boxes.

Stoneworking. Because wood does not survive the elements nearly as well as stone, it is not known whether stone or wood tools were used first by humans. Although stone tools were the primary type of tool for almost all of human history, they are now essentially extinct. Even cultures using stone tools in the modern era such as Australian aboriginals have now switched to mass-produced iron or steel tools first brought to them by missionaries, traders, or colonial officials. Today, however, people do work stone for other purposes, such as to build walls around fields, for dwellings and other buildings, and for ceremonial or art objects. The Ifugao of the Philippines, for example, break and shape boulders and pieces of mountain outcroppings into sizes and shapes suitable for walls for their terraced rice ponds and irrigated fields.

A rural machine shop in India

In the past, stone tools were produced by two major techniques. The first to be used by prehistoric humans was percussion flaking that involved striking a flake off a core stone. Both the flake and the core were used as blades and scrapers, and the core was used as a hand axe. Later, percussion flaking was replaced by pressure flaking in which flakes were knocked off by putting pressure on a core with a tool such as a stick or piece of bone. Pressure flaking afforded the tool maker more control over the process and a greater variety of tools were produced. Later, humans learned to improve flakes by retouching them by pressure flaking and by grinding edges.

Woodworking. As noted above, several million years ago the first tools used by humans were made either of wood or stone and wood. Since then, wood has been used routinely for tools and other objects in cultures around the world.

In making wooden tools and objects, people working without the benefit of modern tools must complete a number of steps: (1) fell the tree usually by controlled burning around the trunk; (2) cut and split the wood to length; (3) transport the wood to the construction site, often by water if possible; (4) reduce the wood to useable size by sawing and splitting; (5) shape the wood by burning, chiseling, heating, steaming, cutting, and chopping; (6) finish the wood by scraping and abrading; and (7) fasten the object together if necessary by lashing, pining, pegging, notching, forking, sewing, or gluing.

Basketry. A basket is made when relatively stiff elements are intertwined or interwoven by hand. Baskets range in shape from those that are flat to those that are round with a small opening resembling a bottle. Various materials are used for baskets across cultures including tree bark, tree roots, plant fibers, and grasses. In most situations, these natural materials must be scraped or split, cut to length, and then softened by soaking in water before the basket is made. Baskets are either coiled or woven. Coiled baskets are built from the bottom up beginning with a foundation that is then coiled upward in a spiral. Material is sewed or stitched so that it holds the coils in place. The stitching is done precisely to create a visible pattern based on the distance between the stitches and the coils and the number of stitches used. Woven baskets take a variety of forms, based on the technique used including checkerboard, diagonal, wickerwork, wrapped weft, and twined. Baskets are used for a wide range of purposes across cultures including collecting fish, carrying foodstuffs, winnowing grains, storing food and other items, and carrying water.

Weaving. With the exception of finger weaving, all weaving as a technological activity is based on the use of a loom. Although looms vary widely in style and complexity across cultures, all are characterized by the use of a heddle that separates warp yarns between which the wefts pass. The major fibers used in weaving around the world are cotton; flax; and animal hair from sheep, goats, camels, horses, cows, llamas, yaks, and so forth. Before weaving can begin, the fibers must be separated from other matter such as seeds, cleaned, aligned, and then spun into yarn.

Pottery making. Pottery is produced when shaped clay is heated and the water in the clay is driven out. Pottery was first made by humans in the Middle East in about 6000 B.C. It evidently was invented independently in the New World, with the oldest pottery dating to about 3000 B.C. in northwestern South America. Pottery is made almost exclusively by peoples living in sedentary communities mainly because they had items including surplus food to store, sedentary life is amenable to the building of kilns, and pottery is breakable and therefore not suitable as a storage container for nomadic peoples. Not all sedentary peoples, however, used pottery. For example, many groups in Oceania lacked suitable clay deposits on their islands or had better containers such as coconut shells readily at hand. Pottery is made with clay soil; in some cultures clay

Human, animal, and fossil-fuel energy in Jaipur, India

alone is used, in others it is mixed with tempering materials such as straw, mica, or bone that make it easier to fire. Many potters have their own secret sources of clay that may be passed on to potters in succeeding generations. Before clay can be shaped and fired, moisture must be distributed through it evenly by kneading, pounding, rolling, and adding and removing water. Pottery is shaped by digging it out, modeling, coiling, paddling, and molding. Most pottery is decorated by texturing, painting, glazing, impressing, and encrusting. Pottery can be fired in or around an open fire or in a kiln where the temperature and flow of hot air can be better controlled.

Leather working. Animal hides are used as clothing, bedding, roofing, house siding, shields, and as containers. In some situations, such as for clothing or bedding, hair is left on the skin; the process to produce leather with hair left on generally produces a product of limited life span. Before tanning, hides must be stripped from the animal, cleaned, pounded, dehaired by sweating or liming, scraped, and washed. The final step is tanning either with oil, minerals, or plant tanning materials such as solutions made from oak bark or chestnut wood.

Division of Labor

An important feature of technological activities across cultures is the sexual division of labor in which men perform some tasks, women do other tasks, and both share in performing others. There is a marked patterning in the division of labor by sex across cultures. Men usually or always perform the following in all or most cultures—hunting large aquatic and land animals, smelting ore, metalworking, lumbering, woodworking, hunting birds, manufacturing musical instruments, trapping small land animals, boat building, stoneworking, bone working, mining, surgery, butchering, collecting wild honey, clearing land, fishing, and tending large domestic animals. Women usually or always perform the following in all or most cultures—preparation of plant foods, cooking, fetching water, laundering, spinning, dairy production, and gathering wild plant foods. Other tasks are performed by either sex, but only four—preparation of skins, gathering of small land animals, crop planting, and leather working are performed equally by men or women across cultures.

Why is there a division of labor by sex? There are two related reasons. First, women perform tasks that are compatible with child rearing—tasks that can be done with children at hand, near or in the home, and away from hazards. This leaves the more dangerous tasks such as hunting to the men. Second, economies of effort encourage each sex to perform tasks related in time, space, or work sequence to other tasks they already perform. For example, men make nets because they more often fish, while women clean house because they cook in or near the house.

Cultural Evolution

Cultural or sociocultural evolution is the worldwide developmental process characterized by (1) the growth in size and complexity of societies, (2) increasing diversification and specialization of features of culture across and within societies, (3) an accelerating rate of change, and (4) increased human control of the environment. Changes in the technological system of a society and across societies are the driving force of cultural evolution because technology is the means that humans have used for several million years to exploit and control their physical environment. Especially important in regard to environmental control are technologies that produce more efficient flows of energy into societies. Thus, the evolution of human cultures is very much the product of shifts to more efficient sources of energy—human, animal, steam, fossil fuel, hydroelectric, and nuclear. Additionally, the technology used in any society sets limits on how much of the environment the society can effectively exploit and also influences the choices the society has in exploiting features of the environment.

Societies around the world can be ranked on a scale of cultural evolution based on the level of complexity typical of the culture. Nomadic hunter-gatherer societies such as the Mbuti or Copper Inuit are ranked near the bottom of the scale, pastoral societies like the Masai and horticultural societies such as the Trukese near the middle, and agricultural societies like the Thai or Chinese at the top. Fishing societies, however, do not neatly fit on the scale as they often use low-level forms of technology to exploit a rich environment that produces considerable sociocultural complexity. These rankings on a evolutionary scale do not mean that one society is better than another, only that one is more complex because it uses more efficient energy sources in exploiting its environment.

Evolutionary change in sociocultural systems occurs in three ways: first, through discovery, which is an innovation that provides new information not previously used in the culture; second, through invention, which is an innovation that is a combination of existing information; and third, through diffusion, which is the transfer of information from one culture to another, either through peaceful contact or warfare. Additionally, many cultural features are also altered after they are discovered, invented, or diffused; however, these alterations are usually ones of style and not ones of use and therefore rarely have any impact on cultural evolution.

Ember, Carol R., and Melvin Ember. (1993) *Anthropology*. 7th ed.

Lenski, Gerhard, and Jean Lenski. (1974) *Human Societies: An Introduction to Macrosociology*.

Levinson, David, and Martin J. Malone. (1980) *Toward Explaining Human Culture*.

Levinson, David, and David Sherwood. (1993) *The Tribal Living Book*, 2d ed.

Murdock, George P., and Caterina Provost. (1973) "Measurement of Cultural Complexity." *Ethnology* 12:379–392.

Oswalt, Wendell H. (1976) *An Anthropological Analysis of Food-Getting Technology*.

Pfaffenberger, Bryan. (1992) "Social Anthropology of Technology." *Annual Review of Anthropology* 21:491–516.

Scarre, Chris. (1993) *Smithsonian Timelines of the Ancient World: A Visual Chronology from the Origins of Life to A.D. 1500*.

Spier, Robert F. G. (1970) *From the Hand of Man: Primitive and Preindustrial Technologies*.

TERRACES

In a few cultures around the world, crops are grown on terraces constructed on mountain- and hillsides or on gently sloping terrain. These terraces, which generally resemble steps, are supported by stone walls and create a flat field in which crops can be grown and irrigated. In its natural state, such land is often unsuitable for agriculture because the rains would regularly wash the soil away. Terracing makes the land suitable for agriculture by turning slopes into flat fields and by controlling and channeling water flow into an irrigation system to water the crops. Thus, terracing creates additional agricultural land that can support a larger population than would otherwise be possible and allows people to use available water in an effective manner. Extensive terracing also turns the irrigated terrace fields into microenvironments that serve many purposes other than as fields for growing crops. The Ifugao of northern Luzon Island in the Philippines, who have the most extensive and complex terracing system known to humankind, for example, use the wet topsoil layer of their wet rice terraces for a variety of other purposes: as a pond for fish and shellfish, as a breeding ground for edible insects, as a soaking vessel for plant fibers to be worked into cordage, as a play area for children, and as a source of mulch.

Terracing is not common around the world but is used by people living in a number of different environments. The Inca of Peru built large stone terraces on which to grow corn. Called *andene*, these terraces had three stone walls slanted slightly inward to support the earth behind them and were irrigated as needed with water brought in irrigation channels. The Inca terraces fell into disuse with the fall of the empire, but ruins are still visible in Peru. The Amhara of Ethiopia build simple terraces on hillsides to create additional agricultural land and to control erosion. The terraces consist of a stone wall, with the slope behind the wall sometimes filled with earth by hand but more often allowed to simply fill with soil from above as it washes down the hillside in rainstorms. The Marquesas Islanders in Polynesia traditionally used two types of terraces to grow taro, a crop requiring wet conditions. One type of terrace was built in valley bottoms at a right angle to a stream. The second type was built on ground above the stream and parallel to it, with water channeled to the fields in stone-lined irrigation ditches.

One set of terraces might have a series of stone walls each about 3 feet high, stretching in rows about 150 feet alongside the stream. The Betsileo on Madagascar build terraces up the sides of mountains to support their large population. The terraces are watered by an irrigation system fed by springs flowing out of the mountainside above the terraces. Finally, terraces for agriculture are also used in Central America—in some communities fairly extensively and in others only to provide additional land for secondary crops.

The greatest use of terraces is by the Balinese on the Island of Bali in Indonesia and the Ifugao in the Philippines—in both situations primarily for wet rice agriculture. In Bali the terraced fields have been integrated into the modernizing agricultural economy and are often now farmed with machines and treated with chemical fertilizers. The Ifugao, however, have maintained their traditional terrace-based agricultural system and traditional labor methods

and tools, despite the promotion of the spectacular terraces as a tourist attraction by the Philippine government. The Ifugao have lived in their region of northern Luzon Island for at least 300 years; the terracing system has been used there for at least that long as well. In terms of scale, complexity, and productivity, the Ifugao terraces represent a unique achievement in human-environment interaction.

Wet rice grown in the terrace pond fields is the major subsistence crop for the Ifugao, although they also grow sweet potatoes and other crops in the dry clearings slashed and burned on the hillsides and hunt and collect in the forest. Thus, for purposes of acquiring food, the Ifugao are reliant on three types of land—wet terrace ponds, dry clearings, and the forest. Although the forest is the dominant type of land, by the 1960s, the Ifugao had converted about 16 percent of the land in the region studied by anthropologist Harold Conklin into terraces. The

Slope being cleared and terraced in eastern Taiwan

Ifugao distinguish among three distinct types of terrace land: (1) house terraces that are flat, smooth terraces used for houses, other buildings, and laying out crops to dry; (2) drained fields that are terraces used for dry crops such as sweet potatoes; and (3) pond fields that are terraces walled to hold water and irrigated to create permanent puddles of topsoil and used to grow rice and taro. Although the terraces cover thousands of acres of mountainside, no two are identical; some are like narrow pathways on steep mountainsides, others look like amphitheaters rising up a gently sloping hillside. Still others are concave and others convex. Despite their different appearances, all are part of a complex agricultural system consisting of the terraces and also of water sources, channels, aqueducts, sluice gates, and dams. The construction, maintenance, and repair of the terraces are entirely by hand with hand tools and use local construction materials such as round river stones, angular rocks broken from outcroppings, boulders, and earth. Expanding, maintaining, and repairing the system requires a major investment of labor throughout the year. As with the Ifugao, terracing in all environments around the world requires vast quantities of raw materials and a major investment of human labor; these may be two reasons why terracing on the Ifugao scale is rare.

Although time and resources are devoted to other activities, the Ifugao annual cycle centers on wet rice growing in the pond fields and work on the terraces and irrigation system. In the off-season—from August through November—the men collect, channel, and sluice the water and repair and expand the fields. These tasks are complex and require the preparation and movement of tons of earth and stone, the building of temporary waterways and rigs to move the earth and stone, and the building of the stone walls. Women use this season to repair waterways and to exploit the ponds for secondary purposes such as catching shellfish and mulching plant matter. In the planting season from December through

March, the soil is prepared and manured, the rice seedlings planted and then transplanted, and the terraces repaired and maintained as needed. In the dry season that follows from the end of March to mid-June, agricultural activity centers on the dry clearings while the irrigation system is improved and maintained to ensure a water supply during the season. The harvest season runs from mid-June to the end of July and is a period of intense activity during which the rise is harvested, bundled, dried, and stored—an undertaking celebrated with much ritual activity.

See also AGRICULTURE; IRRIGATION; PRECIPITATION; WATER.

Buxton, D. R. (1949) "The Shoan Plateau and Its People: An Essay in Local Geography." *Geographical Record* 114:157–172.

Conklin, Harold C. (1967) "Some Aspects of Ethnographic Research in Ifugao." *Transactions of the New York Academy of Sciences*. Series II, Vol. 30:99–121.

———. (1980) *Ethnographic Atlas of Ifugao*.

Garcilaso de la Vega (El Inca). (1869–1871) *First Part of the Royal Commentaries of the Incas*, translated and edited by Clements R. Markham.

Handy, Edward S. C. (1923) *The Native Cultures of the Marquesas*.

TERRITORY AND TERRITORIALITY Human beings express their concern with territory and territoriality in a number of ways. In all cultures, individuals have a sense of personal space, marked by the customary distance different categories of individuals keep apart from each other. In all cultures, people also recognize that land is a form of property, and in most cultures, there are rules that govern land ownership. People across cultures are also willing to defend land they consider their own and often fight to take land away from others. There are limits on how far people will travel in a day, year, or their lifetime. In economic terms, territoriality expresses itself through willingness to defend an economic niche or a market territory. And the ideology and political reality of nationalism make all residents of the world citizens of a particular nation-state, whose status as such is defined by a boundary that separates its territory from that of neighboring nation-states. As with other species, humans adjust their territorial behavior in reaction to environmental circumstances, including conditions set by the physical environment. For humans, territorial behavior is linked to the ability and the goal of controlling resources over time. Thus, for humans, territoriality involves the control and use of space, the use of resources found in that space, and access to the space and the resources over a period of time. From the perspective of environmental uncertainty, under certain conditions territorial behavior can reduce both uncertainty and risk.

A territory is an area that an individual or group uses exclusively or almost exclusively and that the individual or group will defend against intruders. Territoriality is a strategy used by humans to influence and control others. Territoriality refers both to individual behavior that has to do with defining personal space and cultural mechanisms that distribute groups across an area. The tendency to defend one's territory is based on both hostility to some other group such as another band, culture, ethnic group, or nationality and one's own attachment to the territory. Attachment may be instrumental in that the territory is the source of vital resources such as food; territorial in the sense of ownership of the land whether it is used or not; sentimental in the sense of emotional attachment to it; or symbolic in

the sense of moral, ethical, or religious significance associated with the territory or features of it. Across cultures, territories are defended in a variety of ways including fighting, threatening intruders, erecting barriers such as fences or moats to prevent entry, providing visible signs that the territory is occupied or in use, and by advertising such as marking the boundary.

Territoriality can provide a number of general benefits for human societies, all of which in some way are derived from controlling space and resources over time. Benefits include spacing groups out over a territory to make maximum use of resources, regulating population size, reducing fighting between groups, limiting the spread of disease, and stimulating reproductive behavior. However, across cultures, these benefits can also be gained in a wide variety of means other than territoriality including migration, nomadism, flexible group membership, killing unwanted infants, exchange, and marriage prohibitions and prescriptions. Thus, as discussed below, territorial behavior varies across cultures and people tend to behave territorially or more territorially under certain environmental conditions.

Related to territoriality are a number of other forms of spatial organization, some of which are used mainly in reference to the behavior of non-human species. A home range is the area in which one normally travels within and carries out routine activities. A core area is the space within a home range that is most regularly used, such as the area around a waterhole. An annual range is the area covered in a year. A lifetime range is the area covered in a lifetime. In addition, territories can be seasonal or permanent, exclusive or overlapping, or used for all purposes or only for specific purposes such as getting food. Territories can also be movable as in the sense of one's personal space that moves with the individual.

Is Territoriality Innate?
Interest in human territoriality was preceded by much study of territoriality in ants, birds, and

nonhuman primates such as baboons and gorillas. While there is variation both within and across these species in territorial behavior, a central question was raised about the basis of human territoriality—is it inherited and therefore innate or is it a learned cultural behavior? There are three possible answers to this question: (1) territoriality is instinctual and humans are by nature territorial; (2) territoriality in cultures in the contemporary world is a product of millions of years of human biological and cultural evolution; and (3) territoriality is cultural and humans behave territorially only under certain environmental conditions.

The instinctual view holds that humans are born with a drive to "defend one's property." This drive, along with the accompanying drive to fight, are motivated by the human needs for security and stimulation and the need to identify with a larger group. Thus, given that humans are by nature territorial and aggressive, much of human conflict is based on inevitable disputes over space.

The second answer, which might be characterized as a sociobiolgical explanation, emphasizes the combined influences of human biological and cultural evolution over several million years. For much of human history, up to about 100,000 years ago, humans were territorial in the sense that they defended for exclusive use rich hunting and gathering territories and protected their dwellings and camps from animal and human predators. At the same time, some hunting took place in open ranges or for migratory animals that required little territoriality. With the emergence of agricultural and settled communities some 8,000 years ago, resources and settlements became relatively permanent and dense and territorial assignment of space and access to resources became more pronounced. As larger settlements and cities developed, territoriality focused more and more on relations between those in the communities rather than in protecting land from outsiders.

Territorial boundaries played a role in controlling conflicts and indicating social roles and statuses within the community. The evolution of territoriality was accompanied by other evolutionary developments such as the use of language, writing, and centralized political control.

The third answer to the question of the basis of human territoriality suggests that the issue of nature versus culture can be ignored entirely and that the emphasis should be on the variation of territorial behavior within and across cultures and the environmental and social conditions that encourage territoriality. This answer proceeds from the assumption that territoriality is social behavior that is basically motivated by a desire to control the actions of others. At this time, there is no clear evidence that any of these answers fully accounts for territoriality in humans or across cultures. As discussed below, the most plausible explanation combines elements from answers two and three.

Cross-Cultural Patterns

In general, across cultures territoriality occurs when the benefits of exclusive use and defense of a territory are greater than the costs of defending it. Regarding exploitation of the physical environment for food, benefits tend to outweigh costs in environments where food resources are both predictable and dense. Thus, territoriality is found commonly in agricultural societies where it serves to keep farmers out of each other's way; controls predation by animals; and keeps land for the exclusive use of the individual, kinship groups, or community by denying outsiders access to and use of the land. Agricultural communities are territorial regarding their relations with other communities and also internally, as plots of land are controlled by individuals or families. For example, among the Karimojong of East Africa, sorghum is a predictable and dense food resource. The land where it is grown is owned by the people living near it and individual plots are owned by the women who farm them. The fields are protected by fencing and when ripe, the field owners stand guard day and night to chase away birds and human thieves. Stored sorghum is kept by each woman, and all sorghum stored in a settlement is guarded by older members of the community. On the other hand, Karimojong cattle herders are not as territorial; the cattle are herded on open graze land and moved to water and food resources. This difference is because cattle for the Karimojong are not as predictable and dense a resource as is sorghum; therefore, fewer benefits would accrue to the Karimojong relative to costs from rigid, territorially controlled herding.

The benefits of territoriality when resources are predictable and dense are indicated by the experience of lobstering off the coast of Maine. While waters fished for lobsters are open to all, access to the waters have been traditionally controlled by local territorial practices that assign specific areas of water to particular communities and men. One form of territory is perimeter-defended territory in which specific men have rights to fish for lobster in clearly bounded areas of water often near islands on which they own property. Even when they do not fish the water, they still control the rights to it and others must "rent" the water from them. Poachers are kept out by warnings, threats, and ultimately the destruction of their lobster pots. This perimeter defense controls access to the lobster grounds and therefore results in each lobsterman taking more and larger lobsters that command a higher market price and thus earning more than lobstermen in nonperimeter-defended areas.

At the other extreme from societies that subsist on predictable and dense food resources are many hunter-gatherer societies whose traditional way of life displays little rigid territorial organization. Hunter-gatherers rarely have dense, predictable resources to exploit. Instead, their primary adaptive requirement is matching group size to available resources that often vary from season to season and location to location. Many hunter-gatherers such as the San and Hadza in Africa, the Birhor in India, and Australian aboriginals define and defend group boundaries rather than territorial ones. For example, for the San of Botswana an individual's ties to the land are through his or her ties to the community. The band controls the rights to use an area when it first moves there and that right ends when the band moves away. Persons who move to other bands have rights to the territory controlled by that band. Thus, the San adjust and meet their resource needs by moving to new locations and adjusting the size of their groups through flexible group membership in which people are free to leave one band and move to another.

Among the Northern Algonkian peoples of Canada, such as the Cree, Montagnais, and Ojibwa, territoriality was not an indigenous practice but developed only after the arrival of Europeans and the involvement of these groups in the fur trade. For example, once the Montagnais were involved in the fur trade they became dependent on trade foods and goods and began competing with one another for beaver pelts. One manifestation of this competition was the replacement of communal hunting by individual trapping and the establishment of trapping territories. For the Northern Ojibwa, the depletion of large game animals that were hunted in groups and a shift to hunting small, nonmigratory animals such as the hare led to the establishment of hunting and trapping territories.

A world survey of pastoral cultures indicates that they use six general types of territorial organization in assigning or claiming land for grazing their herds, depending on the local environmental conditions. One important environmental condition is the amount of rainfall that determines when and how long land can be used for herding livestock. In the first three situations, rainfall is sparse, unpredictable, or seasonal and not all pastureland is used each year. In the last three, rainfall is more predictable and all land can be used each year.

1. One or more cultures use the same area, with rights granted to herders on a first-come basis.

2. One group uses the same area with subgroups such as clans, lineages, or tribes using specific areas that they may defend against other subgroups or members of other cultures while the entire group might band together to defend the entire area.

3. The clan or some other subgroup controls the right to land use and assigns the right to individuals usually on a first-come basis.

4. Pastureland is owned by corporate organizations such as syndicates or communes that assign rights to individual herders who generally rotate to new pasturelands over the course of a season.

5. The land is owned or controlled by individuals, the government, or a corporate body such as a village that rents it to individuals.

6. Land is owned by the individual who can use it, not use it, lease it, or sell it.

In all of the above situations, territory and territoriality are discussed in terms of access to, ownership or, control of, defense of, and use of resources on the land or in the sea. However, territoriality can also exist in the absence of actual control of the land. Instead, the focus is on access to and defense of resources in a territory. For example, for Gypsies in many places a key resource is the "goodwill" of non-Gypsies because non-Gypsies allow them to stay in the area and also buy their services. To exploit this resource, the Gypsies must accommodate the non-Gypsy world and compete with other Gypsy groups interested in exploiting the same resource. Gypsies accommodate the non-Gypsies by forming relationships with powerful non-Gypsies, when possible obtaining licenses to provide services such as fortune telling, and gen-

erally remaining invisible. Competition with other groups is controlled by informal rules that assign rights to the group there first, periodic ritual events that bring all groups together, and occupying the best locations for business, thus forcing other groups to move elsewhere. These mechanisms allow Gypsy groups to control and exploit an economic territory that the surrounding non-Gypsy population is unaware of.

Territoriality and Ethnic Relations

In the contemporary world, beliefs and behaviors that are similar to territoriality are a key feature of ethnic relations and especially ethnic conflict. Ties to the homeland (one's own birthplace or the birthplace of one's ancestors) are an important component of feelings of ethnic identity. Homeland ties may be primordial in the sense of reflecting some very basic human condition akin to innate territoriality or more rational in the sense of being purposeful behavior that benefits the individual or group in some way, or a combination of both. In multicultural societies such as the United States, homeland ties can create tensions between the host society and the ethnic minority who might be accused of divided loyalties. That is, in the host nation, the ethnic group might be suspected of placing the interests of its homeland ahead of the interests of the host nation. This is one reason ethnic groups are sometimes denied citizenship in their host nation or are made to be scapegoats in times of political or economic unrest.

Land, homeland, and territorial issues are also a major consideration in relations between nations and indigenous peoples resident within their borders. In nations such as the United States, Canada, Mexico, Ecuador, Australia, and Finland, indigenous peoples are demanding the following:

1. Ownership and control of their ancestral land and the resources on it

2. Return of land taken illegally

3. Control of access to the land by outsiders

4. Right to prevent the destruction of the land or resources on it

5. Right to use the land in accord with their cultural traditions

Virtually all indigenous peoples believe that their survival rests on their success in regaining control of their land and their right to live there free from outside control.

Homeland ties and the desire to regain or control territory traditionally associated with an ethnic group is a major cause of ethnic conflict around the world today. Ethnic conflicts are of a number of types, three of which involve issues of territorial control. Separatist movements are efforts by one group to free itself from the control of another group or a national government. These conflicts, such as those involving the Catholics in northern Ireland, the Basques in Spain, the Tamils in Sri Lanka, and the Kurds in Turkey, Iran, and Iraq, often involve a desire by the separatist group for a separate nation, defined in part by a territorial border under control of the ethnic group. Another type of ethnic conflict centers on rivalry for political, economic, or territorial control in a nation. Again, territory is often a key issue, as for the Hungarians in Romanian Transylvania, Serbs in Bosnia, the Zulu in South Africa, and the Chakma in Bangladesh. Some of these conflicts are labeled irredentist because one group seeks to join together territory that was once but is no longer under its control. For example, Hungarians would like the return of the Transylvania region of Romania to Hungary because it was once Hungarian territory and continues to be home to a large Hungarian population. A third type of ethnic conflict is that which involves efforts by one group to take territory controlled by another group. The situation in the former Yugoslavia is of this type.

The issue of homeland and territory in ethnic conflict situations suggests that people across cultures often will fight to defend or acquire territory because they derive considerable economic, political, and emotional security from control and exclusive use of a territory.

See also EARTH, LAND, AND SOIL; ENVIRONMENTAL UNCERTAINTY AND RISK; HUNTING-GATHERING; MOBILITY AND SEDENTISM; RANCHING; SPACE.

Acheson, James M. (1975) "The Lobster Fiefs: Economic and Ecological Effects of Territoriality in the Maine Lobster Industry." *Human Ecology* 3:183–207.

Ardrey, Robert. (1966) *The Territorial Imperative.*

Bishop, Charles A. (1970) "The Emergence of Hunting Territories among the Northern Ojibwa." *Ethnology* 9:1–15.

Cashdan, Elizabeth A. (1983) "Territoriality among Human Foragers: Ecological Models and an Application to Four Bushmen Groups." *Current Anthropology* 24:47–66.

Casimir, Michael J. (1992) "The Determinants of Rights to Pasture: Territorial Organisation and Ecological Constraints." In *Mobility and Territoriality,* edited by Michael J. Cisimir and Aparana Rao, 153–177.

Casimir, Michael J., and Aparana Rao, eds. (1992) *Mobility and Territoriality: Social and Spatial Boundaries among Foragers, Fishers, Pastoralists, and Peripatetics.*

Cohen, Erik. (1976) "Environmental Orientations: A Multidimensional Approach to Social Ecology." *Current Anthropology* 17:49–70.

Dyson-Hudson, Rada, and Eric A. Smith. (1978) "Human Territoriality: An Ecological Reassessment." *American Anthropologist* 80:21–41.

Leacock, Eleanor. (1954) *The Montagnais "Hunting Territory" and the Fur Trade.* American Anthropological Association, Memoir 78.

Lee, Richard B., and Irven DeVore, eds. (1968) *Man the Hunter.*

Levinson, David. (1994) *Ethnic Relations.*

Mirga, Andrzej. (1992) "Roma Territorial Behaviour and State Policy: The Case of the Socialist Countries of East Europe." In *Mobility and Territoriality,* edited by Michael J. Casimir and Aparana Rao, 259–278.

Olson, Paul A. (1989) *The Struggle for the Land: Indigenous Insight and Industrial Empire in the Semi-Arid World.*

Peterson, Nicolas. (1975) "Hunter-Gatherer Territoriality: The Perspective from Australia." *American Anthropologist* 77:53–68.

Sack, Robert D. (1986) *Human Territoriality.*

Sheffer, Gabriel, ed. (1986) *Modern Diasporas in International Politics.*

Silberbauer, George B. (1981) *Hunter and Habitat in the Central Kalahari Desert.*

Taylor, Ralph B. (1988) *Human Territorial Functioning.*

Wilmer, Frankie. (1993) *The Indigenous Voice in World Politics: Since Time Immemorial.*

THUNDER AND LIGHTNING

Estimates suggest that at any given moment about 1,800 thunderstorms are occurring in various places around the world and that these storms produce more than 100 bolts of lightning every second. Although most frequent, violent, and damaging in tropical regions, thunderstorms are experienced in all cultures and therefore are of concern to all peoples. While variability exists in beliefs about thunder and lightning across cultures, in the majority of cultures both thunder and lightning and the storms they are part of are seen as supernatural forces or are under the control of the supernatural forces and are feared.

At the same time, there are a few cultures where thunder and lightning are of little consequence and a few others where they are thought of as beneficial to humans.

The San of Botswana, for example, although much concerned about rainfall, have no fear of thunder or lightning even though violent storms often produce bolts that hit trees. The San prefer a soft, steady rain to the heavy rain that falls during thunderstorms, but believing that the weather changes at the whim of the supernatural spirit N!adima, they do not try to directly influence it. The Pawnee of North America and the Aymara of western South America are two cultures in which thunder and lightning are seen as beneficial. For the Pawnee the first thunder of the spring was an auspicious sign that signified the return of the gods from their winter resting place and that the gods' attention would turn again to matters on earth. When they heard the thunder, the religious leaders would quickly gather together to begin the Thunder Ceremony, the first ceremony of the annual cycle. Accompanied by their rattles, the leaders would sing the following verse 56 times, changing one word each time. At the conclusion they would grunt four times, symbolizing the thunder in the wind, clouds, lightning, and thunder.

> They sang this song above, they have spoken.
> They have put new life into the earth.
> Puruxti speaks through the clouds,
> And the power has entered Mother Earth.
> The earth has received the powers from above.

The Aymara view of thunder and lightning is complicated and has changed through the influence of the Inca Empire prior to Spanish conquest and then again under Spanish rule when indigenous beliefs were merged with Christian ones. Today, these beliefs vary from community to community. In Inca times, thunder was believed to be a major deity who, following the Spanish Conquest, was merged with Santiago, the patron saint of Spain. Lightning has evidently long been feared by the Aymara who put

T 233

protective devices such as crosses on their roofs to ward it off and refuse to eat the meat of an animal killed by lightning. At the same time, however, lightning is seen as power-giving, and to become a magician one must be struck twice by lightning—first to be killed and then to be brought back to life. The rationale for this belief is straightforward (Tschopik 1951:225):

> A man can only be a magician after he has been struck by lightning. God is in the lightning bolt. If it were not for God in the lightning, it would kill him for good; he would never come back to life. That is why we say a magician is a man chosen by God.

These cultures are the exception. In most cultures, thunderstorms and lightning are seen as causing damage to humans, their animals, buildings, crops, and the environment, and both are feared. One manifestation of this fear is the association of thunder or lightning with evil supernatural forces. The Khasi of India believe that thunderstorms are caused by devils; when lightning strikes they sacrifice a fat pig to propitiate the spirits to prevent another strike. For the Mbuti of central Africa, lightning is a sign of misfortune and if a storm approaches at night, they cover their campfires so it will pass. Mongolians believe that thunder is the voice of a dragon and lightning is sparks caused by the swishing of its tail.

In other cultures, thunderstorms are believed to be caused by angry deities. The Andaman Islanders of the Indian Ocean believe that both thunder and lightning are caused by deities who have a human form. Lightning is the deity Ele who when awakened by another deity, Lato, shakes his leg in anger and it is this leg shaking that is experienced as lightning on earth. Thunder is the deity Korude who makes thunder by rolling a large stone in the sky. Sea Islanders off the coasts of Georgia and South Carolina traditionally believed that thunderstorms were manifestations of God's anger and sang the following song during thunderstorms (Parrish 1942:148):

Oh sister, yo'r robe don't fit you like mine
Oh sister, yo'r robe don't fit you like mine
Oh sister, yo'r robe don't fit you like mine
In that mornin' when I rise cryin' Holy.
Oh Gabriel, blow yo'r trumpet loud
Oh Gabriel, blow yo'r trumpet loud
Oh Gabriel, blow yo'r trumpet loud
In that mornin' when I rise cryin' Holy.
Oh Jesus, don't come that angry way
Oh Jesus, don't come that angry way
Oh Jesus, don't come that angry way
In that mornin' when I rise cryin' Holy.

In some other cultures, thunder is believed to be a deity, although thunder itself is not necessarily a sign of his anger. In western Africa many cultures, such as the Hausa, Yoruba, and Ashanti, believe in a thunder deity who hurls stones to earth with the thunder. The stones, called thunder stones and generally of a smooth and polished appearance, are believed by the Ashanti to be the axe or hoe of the deity and when found are given to the priest for proper disposal. In eastern North America, native peoples such as the Iroquois and Cherokee traditionally believed in supernatural holy people called Thunderers and believed that thunder was caused by holy people at war above the clouds, with the level of the noise reflecting the level of the violence.

As noted above, it is common across cultures for people to fear thunder and lightning and also to take protective or preventive action. In cultures where thunder and lightning are linked to the supernatural, such actions go well beyond the typical advice of staying out from under a lone tree, lying down in a field, going indoors, and so forth. Two cultures where thunder and lightning are major concerns are the Senoi of Malaysia and the Zulu of South Africa.

Thunderstorms in southern mainland Malaysia where the Senoi live are especially dramatic—black skies, bright flashes of light, roaring thunder, torrential rain, and high winds pound the houses and tear off the roofs. For the Senoi these frequent events are a violation of the "natural order." Thunderstorms are controlled by the thunder deity Enku who causes the storms as a way of punishing those who violate rules of behavior and thereby disrupt the natural order of the universe. Acts likely to lead to such punishment are laughing too loudly, playing in the dark, harming or making fun of insects such as dragonflies and butterflies, or eating taboo foods. The Senoi are terrified of the storms and often flee their homes to seek refuge in the most secure homes in the village. To stop the storm they conduct rituals to propitiate Enku that include blood offerings, cutting one's hair, as well as cursing the storms or flailing at the wind with a spear. The Senoi beliefs about, reaction to, and methods of dealing with thunderstorms point to the interrelationships among the physical environment, social behavior, and religious beliefs and practices found in many cultures. For the Senoi, terrifying thunderstorms are believed to come from the supernatural world with their cause attributed to human misbehavior. These two related beliefs then encourage people to follow social norms to avoid supernatural punishment in the form of thunderstorms. Since the entire community and not just the individual wrongdoer suffers the effects of thunderstorms, members of the community are motivated to both follow the rules themselves and see that others follow the rules as well.

Like the Senoi, the Zulu of South Africa take thunderstorms and lightning very seriously. Zulu efforts to prevent lightning strikes from causing harm and to correct the harm they do cause are managed by a ritual specialist—the lightning doctor—whose experience, training, and personal lifestyle qualify him for this position. The lightning doctor's practice is aimed at influencing the supernatural forces that control the lightening through various rituals, potions, protective devices, avoidances, and taboos. For protection of people and their homesteads, the doctor supplies specially treated pegs to be placed and buried in and around the homestead and lightning rods to be erected when a storm approaches, and injects individuals with a special lightening mixture whose effectiveness is enhanced by a series of rituals. In addition, the doctor might prescribe special measures for certain homesteads such as a requirement that all fuel be brought in only through the main entrance.

The behavior of the doctor during the storm involves the intensification of certain taboos he normally follows as well as waging war with the storm by burning potions to ward it off, fighting it with spears, and scolding it. The doctor is supported by members of the community who also must restrict their movements, limit social interaction to only certain categories of relatives, avoid sexual relations, and follow certain food taboos such as not drinking sour or fresh milk.

The effects of lightning are considered harmful to all except the doctor. He uses the bark of a tree struck by lightning to cure people knocked unconscious, treats the meat of dead cattle so that it may be eaten by others, cleanses struck homesteads by prescribing behavior restrictions for the residents, and performs cleansing rituals. The doctor, however, cannot bring back those struck and killed by lightning, and their relatives mourn and say: "The Lord has found fault with him; the Lord has struck; the Lord is angry."

See also PRECIPITATION; STORMS.

Dentan, Robert K. (1978) *The Semai: A Nonviolent People of Malaya.*

Greenburg, Joseph H. (1947) *The Influence of Islam on a Sudanese Religion.*

Lattimore, Owen. (1941) *Mongol Journeys.*

Linton, Ralph. (1922) *The Thunder Ceremony of the Pawnee.*

Mooney, James. (1982) *Myths of the Cherokee and Sacred Formulas of the Cherokees.*

Parrish, Lydia. (1942) *Slave Songs of the Georgia Sea Islands.*

Radcliffe-Brown, Alfred R. (1922) *The Andaman Islanders: A Study in Social Anthropology.*

Raum, Otto F. (1973) *The Social Functions of Avoidances and Taboos among the Zulu.*

Silberbauer, George B. (1981) *Hunter and Habitat in the Central Kalahari Desert.*

Stegmiller, P. F. (1921) "The Religious Life of the Khasi." *Anthropos* 16:407–441.

Tschopik, Harry, Jr. (1951) *The Aymara of Chucuito, Peru: 1. Magic.*

Turnbull, Colin M. (1965) *The Mbuti Pygmies: An Ethnographic Survey.*

TIME ·

For most Americans time is a precious commodity to be used as efficiently as possible. People use their time carefully, monitor how they spend their time, and try to spend as much time as possible involved in activities they prefer. "Time is money" sums up the view of time held by many. Corporations routinely send their employees for time management training, most households have a family calendar prominently displayed in a public place, and various computer programs enable people to schedule their time down to the minute. Americans also see time as a linear progression from the past to the present to the future, with the past having relatively little impact on the present and future. For each individual, time begins with their birth and ends with their death. This linear-precious commodity conception of time is just one of a variety of different conceptions of time found across cultures. Ideas about time, what it is composed of, when it began, how it moves, how it is measured, and how it is used vary across cultures. Thus, time is culturally defined. Perhaps the only three cross-cultural universals about time are that time is recognized in all cultures; all cultures distinguish between night and day (or dark and light periods); and all cultures use the notion of generation to classify people, structures, and the relations among people of different ages. This generational structuring might reflect a human universal need to "tame time."

In other cultures, conceptions of time are very different than the shallow, linear one found in many European societies. For Hindus, time is not linear but circular, with most individuals endlessly reincarnated into various animals or human forms. Thus, one's life on earth is not just about the present but also about the past and future. One's behavior in their past life has determined their current fate while one's behavior in their present incarnation determines their future fate. Latinos are stereotypically described as being primarily concerned with yesterday and today with little interest in tomorrow. They are described as "living every moment twice—first as present, then as past." Latinos are also considered to be less punctual than middle-class Americans; there is some truth to the generalization that for some Latinos the social interaction is of primary importance while for white Americans, being on time is more important. The San of Botswana pay little attention to time as an organizing framework and see it as a linear series of events with no event occurring twice; therefore, the past is of little importance for the present or future.

For many aboriginal peoples of Australia, the conception of time and its role in one's life is of major importance. The Mardudjara and other aboriginal cultures have a deeply spiritual view of the world, with their conceptualization of time a central element. The Mardudjara believe deeply in what is called the "Dreamtime," a period of time long ago when the world was transformed into its present form by ancestral beings who were part human and part animal in appearance. These beings hunted animals and collected wild plant foods as do the Mardudjara today, but their actions shaped the landscape. For example, a streambed is the result of the movement of an ancestral snake while a gap in the hills was caused by the axe of a lizard-man. These ancestral beings possessed a life power that was eventually transferred to their children who became human beings. Thus, every Mardudjara is linked directly to the ancestors and to the Dreamtime. While these ancestral beings died, their spiritual power remains and the Dreamtime itself is without a clear beginning or end point. For the Mardudjara and other Australian aboriginals, the Dreamtime is about the past, the present, and the future and is a daily source of guidance and knowledge about their world and the central focus of ritual and artistic activity.

The Hopi of Arizona also have a nonlinear, complex conception of time, one resting on a belief in the dual organization of time and space between the upper world of the living and the lower world of the dead. This duality is reflected in the sun's daily cycle (night and day), the sun's annual cycle (summer and winter), and the human cycle of life and death (the dead acquire supernatural powers). In Hopi rituals, time is controlled by the number four, reflecting the Hopi's fourfold model of the universe—color-number, space-time. Thus, a ritual might take place over a 20-day period, with 16 days for preparation and 4 days of ritual observance and the dances performed in sets of four.

As with the aboriginals, the beginning of time is often found in the creation myths of cultures, although no date is generally assigned. In Judeo-Christian cultures, the Book of Genesis sets forth the beginning of time. The Tzeltal in Mexico believe that time began "when k'os, the youngest son of our Grandmother the moon, took the sun from his elder brother and carried it around the world so that there was a succession of day and night."

In most cultures, ideas about time and the measurement of time are linked to natural events, mainly the appearance and disappearance of the sun causing light and dark, the appearance and disappearance of the moon, and seasonal changes. The Tzeltal in Mexico, as in many other cultures, reckon time by the position of the sun during the day and the moon and stars at night. Time is reckoned in other ways as well. The Tonga of Oceania reckon past times by notable events or the generation of a specific person. For example, an event might be placed in time by saying it occurred at the time of a particular hurricane or at a specific life-stage of the speaker—"When I was a child." The distant past is expressed in reference to a specific ruler such as "When Momo was king," a similar practice to speaking of the Antebellum period in American history, the Victorian Age in British history, or the Soviet period in Russian history.

The Miao in Thailand measure time by the length of time it takes to travel a specific route or to complete a specific task. This is similar to the custom of many people who live in urban areas of measuring distance in time—if asked how far they live from work, they often answer in units of time such as 30 minutes or two hours. Thus, time is used in this way to classify other aspects of culture or behavior. For an urban dweller, time is more important than distance. Similarly, the Javanese use time to classify the importance of dreams. Dreams occurring between 7:00 and 10:00 P.M. and 11:00 P.M. and 2:00 A.M. are considered to have no significance. Those occurring between 3:00 and 6:00 A.M. are considered to be harbingers of the future.

Cultures vary widely in the number of words in their languages for concepts of time. The San, for example, have at least 14 terms about times of the day—morning, first light, midnight, noon, dawn, false dawn, sunrise, midmorning, midafternoon, midevening, sunset, dusk, late afternoon, and after 10:00 P.M. The Yanomamö of Venezuela, on the other hand, have only five—morning, night, first light, evening, and day ends. This variation might reflect the relative importance of different times of the day in a culture.

Cultures also vary in how much time is allocated to different activities. Recent detailed studies of how people around the world spend their time have produced some surprising results. For example, the common assumption that hunter-gatherers spend all their time searching for food seems wrong. Hunter-gatherers generally spend less time foraging for food than Western peoples do working. All over the world, however, adults generally spend at least some time in the same general activities: food production, commercial, manufacturing, food preparation, housework, eating, social, and individual.

See also ANNUAL CYCLE; CALENDARS; SEASONS.

Albert, Steven M., and Maria G. Cattell. (1994) *Old Age in Global Perspective.*

Becher, Hans. (1960) *The Surara and Pakidai, Two Yanoama Tribes in Northwest Brazil.*

Bernatzik, Hugo A. (1947) *Akha and Miao: Problems of Applied Ethnography in Farther India.*

Collocott, Ernest E. V. (1922) *Tongan Astronomy and Calendar.*

Hieb, Louis A. (1972) *The Hopi Ritual Clown: Life as It Should Be.*

Johnson, Allen, series ed. (1988–) *Cross-Cultural Studies in Time Allocation.*

Nash, June C. (1970) *In the Eyes of the Ancestors: Belief and Behavior in a Maya Community.*

Shorris, Earl. (1992) *Latinos: A Biography of the People.*

Silberbauer, George B. (1981) *Hunter and Habitat in the Central Kalahari Desert.*

Tonkinson, Robert. (1978) *The Mardudjara Aborigines: Living the Dream in Australia's Desert.*

Weiss, Jerome. (1978) *Folk Psychology of the Javanese Ponorogo.*

TOTEMISM

Totemism is the customary belief that one's social group has a special relationship with some element of nature such as an animal, bird, plant, or physical feature. A totem is the specific feature of nature that is the object of the special relationship. Usually the totem is an animal or bird and less often a plant or feature of the landscape that is very common, of considerable importance to the people, or one that possesses certain qualities considered desirable by the people. The word *totemism* itself is from the Chippewa Indian word, *ototeman*, the stem of which (*ote*) referred to a specialized form of relation among relatives. Totemism has drawn the attention of various social theorists from Emile Durkheim, the founder of sociology, to Sigmund Freud, the founder of psychoanalysis, to the French anthropologist Claude Levi-Straus, all of whom have stressed the key role played by totemism is the evolution, structure, and functioning of human societies. While totemism does exist in different cultures around the world, there is no one type of totemism and, across cultures, it takes a wide variety of forms. Totemism in somewhat different forms is most common in Australian aboriginal societies and among Native American cultures in North and South America.

The major beliefs and practices associated with totemism in these cultures (although the distribution of these beliefs and practices varies widely across cultures) are the association of a specific group with a specific animal, bird, plant, or natural feature; a belief that the group is descended from its totem; the group naming itself after its totem; a belief that a supernatural spirit appears in the form of the totem; a rule that people show respect for their totem and not kill or harm it; various taboos associated with the totem such as not eating it; the carving and display of symbols of association with the totem; and the requirement that people marry outside their totem group—that is, one must marry someone who comes from a group associated with a different totem. Across cultures, the only three features shared by all cultures with totemic beliefs are (1) an association with a specific feature of nature, (2) the totem is the object of association for a specific social group such as a clan (a kinship group composed of people descended from a common ancestor) or a fraternal organization, and (3) totemism has a strong emotional component for members of the group.

Totemism is especially common among the aboriginal peoples of Australia and takes a variety of forms. Individual totemism involves one person and his or her ties to a feature of nature. In sex totemism the male and female members of a culture each have different totems, which tends to reinforce a rigid division between men and women. In moiety totemism the entire culture is divided into two groups, with each group having its own totem. In section totemism, each of the primary kin groups in the culture has its own totem. In clan totemism, which is also common among native peoples of the New World, all members of each clan share the same totem—hence the names Bear Clan, Wolf Clan, Raven Clan, and so forth. In local totemism people who reside in the same territory and share a spiritual attachment to it share the same totem. Finally, some cultures are characterized by multiple totemism in which a number of the above types coexist.

The most important types in traditional aboriginal cultures were those such as section and clan totemism in which their identification with the same totem united smaller groups into larger ones for ritual and other purposes. Traditional aboriginal societies were composed of small, nomadic bands, a number of which through ties of kinship and marriage formed larger groups known as clans. Each clan had a unique totem—an animal or plant, took its name from the totem, and could not harm the totemic plant or animal. The totem represented the relationship among the supernatural, nature, and human beings. In addition, each totem was each clan's

emblem and the totemic design was carved on sacred stone or wood slabs. Some members of the clan scarified their bodies with the design to enhance their own ties to the supernatural and the group.

In North America, many native cultures also had totems that were thought of as guardians or protectors of the person or group who adopted the totem. In addition, in some cultures such as the Iroquois in New York State, clans were identified by totemic names, and persons were required to marry persons from outside their own clan. In some cultures, persons were born into the totemic group while in others affiliation was by individual choice. For example, among the Omaha, anyone who had seen a bear during their personal vision quest became a member of the Bear Society. Some groups in the Northwest such as the Haida and Tlingit displayed their totemic emblems on totem poles, which when placed in front of their houses identified the residents as members of a particular totemic group.

Another form of totemism is cult totemism, which is more individualistic and involves an individual's personal choice to associate him- or herself with a particular totem. Cult totemism reflects an individual's desire to bring some aspect of nature into their life and in the contemporary world is reflected in the use of the names of animals or birds in the names of fraternal organizations such as the Loyal Order of Moose or the Elks Lodge and in the names of sports teams such as the Chicago Bears, Seattle Seahawks, or Michigan Wolverines.

Child, Alice B., and Irvin L. Child. (1993) *Religion and Magic in the Life of Traditional Peoples.*

Hodge, Frederick W. (1959) *Handbook of American Indians North of Mexico.*

Lessa, William A., and Evon Z. Vogt, eds. (1965) *Reader in Comparative Religion: An Anthropological Approach, 2d edition.*

Malefijt, Annemarie de Wall. (1968) *Religion and Culture: An Introduction to the Anthropology of Religion.*

TRAGEDY OF THE COMMONS

The "tragedy of the commons" is the idea popularized by biologist and ecologist Garrett Hardin that all resources used in common will eventually be overused and degraded. These resources include bodies of water such as the oceans, lakes, and rivers; parks; highways; wildlife; marine resources; rangeland; and air. Common property resources are "a class of resources for which exclusion is difficult and joint use involves subtractability" (Feeney et al. 1990:4). Thus, common property resources such as those listed above have two key characteristics: *excludability,* which means that it is too expensive or impossible to control access to the resource, and *subtractability,* which means that each use by each user is capable of reducing the benefit other users will gain from the resource. The combination of the unrestricted access and competition among users produces the "tragedy" of the commons. Open access means that an unlimited number of users can exploit the resource; competition between users means that users derive the greatest gain from the resource by exploiting it to the fullest while they derive little benefit from maintaining it because other users will also benefit from the user's investment in maintenance. In areas of high population density, this combination of open access and competition leads to environmental degradation and is often cited as a primary cause of the high levels of water, air, and soil pollution found around the world today. The tragedy of the commons is not confined to one region and, in fact, actions that damage the environment in one location can have far-reaching effects on common resources around the world as is the case with the depletion of the ozone layer, water pollution, and deforestation.

An example of the tragedy of the commons typical of many such situations around the world is the experience of the western Malaysian coastal fishery in the Indian Ocean. Prior to the 1960s, the fishery supported the local fishing communities along the coast. In 1960 motorized trawlers began fishing the region and the stock of high-value fish and shrimp declined rapidly, leading to the ruin of many fishing communities. The combination of overfishing, pollution, and landfill in the mangrove swamps essentially destroyed what had been a reliable common resource. In an attempt to control the situation, the government passed laws restricting fishing and forming fishing cooperatives. Because the laws were ineffective and weakly enforced, neither measure was effective.

Across cultures, four types of property rights are used in reference to common property resources:

Open access property rights: the absence of or a very limited system of property rights

Private property rights: individual or corporate ownership

Communal property rights: ownership by a group of individual users who control access by nonmembers of the group and allocate use rights among themselves

State property rights: ownership by the government, which controls access and use

These four types of property rights have different effects across cultures on the tragedy of the commons. Open access is predictably associated with uncontrolled access and degradation and therefore does not control the overexploitation and degradation of common resources. Private ownership is an effective control on access and also leads to economically rational use of the resource, meaning that the resource is not overexploited and thereby depleted. Communal ownership is an effective control in some small communities and allows for the exploitation of resources by individuals. In communal ownership situations with rights allocated to individuals or small groups such as villages or kin groups, resources are used and maintained in ways that control the amount of resource taken and prevent its decline. Finally, when the state owns the resources, access can be controlled although the bureaucratic control apparatus is often ineffective; poaching is common and use is often regulated.

Of these four general types of property rights, three are used across cultures to control the tragedy of the commons. Modern industrialized nations often use some combination of private ownership and state control to protect common resources while in many small-scale societies or communities, communal approaches were traditionally used and, when not impinged upon by private or state control, continue to be used today. Communal control takes a variety of forms across cultures. For example, lobstermen effectively control the tragedy of the commons through a traditional, informal system in which rights to take lobster from a specific section of water are allocated to specific lobstermen. These rights are an extension of onshore land rights and are enforced first by issuing a warning to the encroaching lobstermen and then by destroying their lobster pots. On Belau in Oceania, fishing rights are controlled by villages; the village leader is also responsible for controlling poaching by members of his community. Often, communal control is used in combination with other forms of resource control that also serve to control the tragedy of the commons. For example, the Cacmilla of the Upper Amazon in eastern Peru control resources through a combination of out-migration, flexible group membership, customary beliefs such as a taboo on using dying lakes, the banning of commercial fishing by outsiders, and land ownership rights that they enjoy as an officially recognized native community. In general, across cultures, communal control is effective when the community is small, when the resources are near the residential village, and when they can be carefully watched.

Feeney, David, et al. (1990) "The Tragedy of the Commons: Twenty-Two Years Later." *Human Ecology* 18:1–19.

Gerlach, Luther P. (1990) "Cultural Construction of the Global Commons." In *Culture and the Anthropological Tradition,* edited by Robert H. Winthrop, 319–343.

Hardin, Garrett. (1968) "The Tragedy of the Commons." *Science* 162: 1243–1248.

Hardin, Garrett, and J. Baden, eds. (1977) *Managing the Commons.*

McCay, Bonnie J., and James M. Acheson, eds. (1987) *The Question of the Commons: The Culture and Ecology of Communal Resources.*

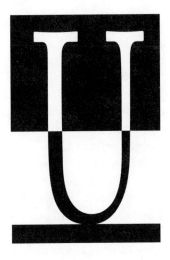

dictate their annual cycle of economic and ritual activities.

Although it is impossible to generalize completely about the differences between Western and non-Western ideas about the universe, much attention has been given to both. Attention has been given to the assertion that non-Western peoples live with nature while Western peoples exploit and damage nature. While in some broad sense this assertion is true for some cultures, more important are the various ways human beings have come to see the universe and their relationship with it. However, before reviewing these differences, it is also important to note that some basic similarities exist across cultures, both Western and non-Western. Three beliefs about the nature of the universe are typical of people in many cultures: (1) that the universe consists of multiple layers or phenomena, (2) that a set of core elements comprise the universe, and (3) that some elements of the universe are polluting.

In nearly all societies people believe that the universe is composed of two or more layers or phenomena. The Copper Inuit, for example, view the universe as composed of (1) the earth, a vast expanse covered by snow and ice, and (2) the sky, inhabited by animals such as the caribou, which are also found on earth, and spirit beings such as the sun and moon. The Amhara of Ethiopia also have a dualistic view of the structure of the universe, although they differentiate between the physical world and the world populated by all living things. The Western Apache of Arizona view the universe as composed of three categories: (1) *hindfa*—animals and objects capable of generating their own movement; (2) *desta*—immobile objects such as environmental features; and (3) *godiyo*—items and thoughts of religious significance.

Since the time of the classical Greek philosophers, the idea found in the Western world that the basic elements of the universe are earth, air, fire, and water is common across cultures, although in some such as in China, a fifth category,

UNIVERSE Across cultures, people's ideas about the origin and structure of the universe (called cosmology) and about human beliefs about their place in the universe (called worldview) vary widely. In Western and Asian civilizations, ideas about the universe can be quite complex and encompass the supernatural and natural worlds, their origins and structures, human place in these worlds, and ethics and morals that govern human action. In other cultures, notions of the universe are more restrictive. The Tlingit of the Northwest Coast of North America, for example, have no clear set of ideas that explain the universe, although they do have clear notions about its structure and the human place in it. Australian aborigines are more concerned with the immediate features of nature and their functioning than with their origins. The Copper Inuit of northern Canada also concern themselves mainly with the physical features of their environment such as snow and ice and the sun and moon. And agricultural peoples tend to see their universe in terms of the seasons because seasonal changes

wood, is added. Cultures vary on the degree of importance they attach to these elements and the influence they see them exerting on the human world. The Javanese, for example, believe that individuals require a sufficient quantity of each element to maintain balance in their lives. This view rests on the broader Javanese belief that the universe is composed both of individual organisms and the natural universe, with the former a miniature version of the latter. Thus, for the Javanese water-air-fire-earth are the basic elements of both the physical universe and of each living organism.

The third general commonality across cultures is a belief that certain features of the universe are polluting. Pollution in this sense refers to both physically polluting and also or only to ritually polluting in that contact with the polluted substance, object, or person will disrupt the natural order of relations among elements of the universe. To maintain this order, special rules exist to prohibit contact with polluting substances. Hindus believe that cattle and cattle products are polluting and those who work with cattle and leather are considered to be untouchable—outside the four-level hierarchical structure of Hindu society. Jews and Muslims believe that pork is polluting and a taboo exists on its consumption. Gypsies consider various parts of the body and bodily functions as polluting and attend to such matters with considerable ritual. Gypsies also find contact with non-Gypsies polluting and thus minimize such contact. And in traditional Polynesia, chiefs occupied a special social category and they as well as objects and places associated with them were taboo to commoners.

Western Views of the Universe

From the viewpoint of Western science, the visible universe consists of stars, galaxies, planets, asteroids, and comets. Earth is part of the Milky Way galaxy that also contains the sun, eight other planets, moons, asteroids, and comets. The age of the universe is placed by astronomers at from 10 to 20 billion years, with the majority favoring a figure of about 12 billion years, and that the universe came into existence all at once through a "Big Bang." The Judeo-Christian perspective is set forth in the Book of Genesis in the Bible in the story of creation that placed man in charge of the world, superior to other living things and subject only to God.

One key feature of the Western conception of the universe is a dualism in which various phenomena are placed in contrasting pairs. These pairs include light-dark, sacred-profane, animate-inanimate, living-dead, body-soul, and nature-culture. In addition to their being contrasting, some of these pairs are often seen in terms of superiority-inferiority with light being better than dark, sacred better than profane, and living better than dead. Other pairs such as animate-inanimate, body-soul, and nature-culture are seen as mutually exclusive alternatives. A second feature of Western views is that Westerners often feel alienated from nature and see nature as something to be used or be transformed for human use rather than to be lived with. And third, Western philosophy and science take a basically linear view of time and the relationship between the components of the universe. That is, attempts to explain features of the universe or events usually cite one factor or set of factors as the cause and another factor or set of factors as the effect, rather than conceptualizing the supposed causes and effects as part of a broader, more complex pattern of interrelationships.

Non-Western Views of the Universe

As noted above, there is much variation across cultures in how the origin and structure of the universe is conceptualized. At the same time, however, there are some cross-cultural patterns that apply to many cultures and differ markedly from Western conceptions. First, in many cultures, people customarily feel a oneness and closeness with nature different from the more distant human-nature relationship characteristic of the Western world. For the Native Americans, this relationship is described as follows (N. Scott Momaday quoted in Todd 1986:55):

> When the Native American looks at nature, it isn't with the idea of training a glass upon it, or pushing it away so that he can focus upon it from a distance. In his mind, nature is not something apart from him. He conceives of it, rather, as an element in which he exists. He has existence within that element, much in the same way we think of having existence within the element of air.

Second, in many cultures, no sharp distinction or no distinction at all is made between the natural world and the supernatural world and the distinction by humans and animals is less clear than in the West. For example, the Tlingit believed that spirits inhabited all features of the environment—lakes, streams, trees, rocks, mountains, birds, fish, the sun, the moon, and so on. Humans could use these resources if they took care of them, respected the spirits that inhabited them, offered the appropriate prayers before hunting or fishing, and took only that which would be directly consumed. Failure to live by these rules and rituals could lead to punishment by the spirits in the future. In addition, Tlingit would interact with their environment through rigorous physical activity, fasting, meditation, and by deep thought about nature.

This example from the Tlingit points to a third major feature of non-Western conceptions—nature itself or all the spirits who inhabit and embody natural features control the environment. Humans, unlike in Western cultures, are permitted to exploit nature to meet their material needs but may do so only with the permission of supernatural forces and failure to follow proper rituals; the abuse of nature brings with it the risk of supernatural punishment.

A fourth and final feature is that most non-Western dualisms such as life-death or animate-inanimate do not always imply contradiction or exclusiveness as in the West. Instead, as discussed above, for many cultures like the Tlingit, the natural and supernatural are not seen as distinct entities. In many cultures, physical death and life are not distinct because the soul may live on—either on earth or in another world.

To give some sense of the complexity of ideas about the universe across cultures as well as variation across cultures, the following are summaries of the cosmological systems or some central aspects of these systems in four cultures—Chinese, Hopi, Iroquois, and San.

Chinese Cosmology

Traditional Chinese cosmology is one of, if not the most, complex set of ideas about the origin and structure of the universe. The system is so complex that most Chinese in pre-Communist China could not understand it and thus had to rely on ritual specialists for interpretation and applications in everyday life. In quite simplified form, four major elements of Chinese cosmology are Tao, Yin Yang, the Five Elements, and the Forces of Nature. Tao (also called the Way, Ch'i, and the Vital Force) is the force behind the physical universe and the source of all life forms. Tao exerts its influence through the two forces, or principles, of Yin and Yang. Yin is negative, passive, weak, destructive, dark, cold, humble, soft, and feminine. Yang is positive, strong, active, hot, light, dry, hard, and masculine. At a philosophical level, Yin and Yang are harmonious forces whose continual interaction produces the five elements—wood, fire, earth, metal, and water—whose interactions, in turn, produce all features of the universe. The outcomes of the interaction of the Five Elements are determined by two additional concepts. First are the laws of causality and opposition that influence the interaction of the Five Elements: ". . . Wood produces Fire, Fire produces Earth, Earth produces Metal, Metal produces Water, Water produces Wood, and second, that Fire opposes Metal, Metal opposes Wood, Wood

TABLE U-1   COMPONENTS ASSOCIATED WITH THE FIVE ELEMENTS IN CHINESE COSMOLOGY

Universe Feature	Wood	Fire	Earth	Metal	Water
Seasons	spring	summer	late summer	autumn	winter
Directions	east	south	center	west	north
Colors	green	red	yellow	white	black
Tastes	sour	bitter	sweet	acrid	salty
Virtues	benevolence	wisdom	faith	righteousness	decorum

opposes Earth, Earth opposes Water, and Water opposes Fire" (McCreary 1974:59). Second, each of the Five Elements is associated with components of the physical, social, and moral orders of the universe; Table U-1 lists examples of these (McCreary 1974:60).

Daily lie in traditional China was governed by the idea that human beings are a product of the forces of nature. Thus, seasons are governed by the "breath" or life force of nature, and people must locate their homes and burial places in accordance with natural forces reflected in the landscape. Making these decisions correctly took much knowledge and skill, and geomancers, men who could reckon the forces of "wind and water," were consulted for their expertise.

The Iroquois Cosmos

The Iroquois, who now live mainly on reservations in New York, Wisconsin, Oklahoma, and Ontario, were the inhabitants of what is now much of New York State and parts of Canada, Pennsylvania, and Ohio prior to European settlement. They subsisted through a combination of hunting, gathering, and farming. Their conception of the universe reflects these subsistence activities as well as being a clear example of the meshing of the natural and supernatural worlds that is common in non-Western cultures. The Iroquois cosmos contains three layers, with the spirit forces in each ascending layer having broader power and dominance over the forces in the layer below. Spirit forces in the same layer have relatively equal power (see Table U-2).

TABLE U-2   THREE LAYERS IN THE IROQUOIS COSMOLOGY

Spirit Forces beyond the Sky
Creator
Four Beings   Handsome Lake

Spirit Forces in the Sky
Wind   Thunderers   Sun   Moon   Stars

Spirit Forces on Earth
People   Earth   Grasses   Fruit   Trees   Water

While most of these spirit forces are self-explanatory in terms of the physical features of the universe they are part of, four require further clarification. The Four Beings (also called the Four Angels, Four Messengers, or Four People) are supernatural forces responsible for supervising the spirit forces of the sky. Handsome Lake refers to the Seneca prophet of that name who, in the years of dislocation in the early 1800s following the American Revolution, was central in stabilizing Seneca society through the Code of Handsome Lake. The Thunderers are spirits responsible for supervising activities on earth and for keeping the monsters contained beneath the earth.

Visually, the Iroquois cosmos can be depicted as a flat earth surrounded by a sky dome sitting on the back of a turtle with the Tree of Life above the sky dome.

The San Universe

The San are a mainly hunting and gathering people of southwestern Africa. The following cosmology is that of the G/wi San hunter-gatherers of Botswana. The G/wi believe that the world was created by the supreme being, N!adima, who also owns the earth and is free of control by other supernaturals or humans. Why N!adima created the world is unclear, although it was not for the benefit of humans. For the G/wi, the universe is a place of order, is a self-regulating system controlled by N!adima, and has three levels: Sky Country, Land, and the Underworld. Humans know little about the Sky Country and the Underworld other than that the former is occupied by supernatural forces and the latter by monsters and the spirits of the deceased. N!adima and his wife live in the upper reaches of the Sky Country. The G/wi live on the land, are alone in the universe, and derive security from the order created by N!adima and reliance on other G/wi. In general, however, it is up to

humans to use their own skills and knowledge to cope with the daily problems of living. In addition to the G/wi, other features of the human world are the land itself, other human beings, animals, and plants. The G/wi have little interest in the land beyond their immediate environment although they believe it is largely unchanging and stretches for some finite, though undetermined distance. The G/wi social world is centered on the individual with relationships conceptualized as a series of concentric rings of categories of individuals progressively more distant socially from the individual in the center of the circle. Animals are N!adima's creations so they must be respected and killed only for food or in self-defense. Plants are a lower form of life—without motion, thought, or sensation—and thus not entitled to the same treatment as animals.

The Hopi Universe

The Hopi are an agricultural people currently living on a reservation in northeast Arizona. They and their ancestors have continually inhabited the Southwest for several thousand years. The Hopi worldview rests on two basic principles—the bipartite universe and a system of correspondence among elements of the universe. The Hopi bipartite universe is based on a belief in a dual division of time and space and is reflected in dualisms of the upper world of the living-the lower world of the dead, light-dark, day-night, and east-west. These pairs, however, are not seen as being in opposition or as contradictory but as reverse elements in an ongoing system of alternation and continuity in the universe. The appearance of the sun in the east each morning, its movement across the sky, and disappearance in the west at night are the most obvious and predictable of this pattern of alternation and continuity in the universe. For the Hopi, the most important element in the universe is water, which, when combined with

Mother Earth, is the essence of all things. Virtually all Hopi rituals in some way are about rain. The Hopi world is ordered by a system of correspondences in which animals, plants, features of the weather, and so forth are ordered in accord with space, time, color, and numbers. This elaborate system serves as a guide in rituals, which are generally performed four or six times in accordance with the importance attached to the four cardinal directions (northwest, northeast, southwest, southeast) and the additional directions of above and below. Prayer is the primary means through which the Hopi move between the human and supernatural worlds with prayer seen as a form of reciprocity in which spirits are expected to respond by providing the asked-for assistance. In essence, the Hopi believe that if one feeds the spirits ritually, the spirits will feed the Hopi, generally by providing rain to make the corn grow.

See also COLOR; DIRECTION; EARTH, LAND, AND SOIL; FIRE, GEOMANCY; SEASONS; TIME; WATER.

Basso, Keith H. (1970) *The Cibecue Apache.*

Brennan, Richard P. (1992) *Dictionary of Scientific Literacy.*

Fenton, William N. (1962) "This Island, the World Is on the Turtle's Back." *Journal of American Folklore* 75:283–300.

Foster, Michael K. (1974) *From the Earth to beyond the Sky: An Ethnographic Approach to Four Longhouse Iroquois Speech Events.* National Museum of Man Mercury Series, paper no. 20.

Hieb, Louis A. (1979) "Hopi World View." In *Handbook of North American Indians. Volume 9. Southwest,* edited by Alfonso Ortiz, 577–580.

Jenness, Diamond. (1922) *The Life of the Copper Eskimos.*

Laguna, Frederica de. (1972) *Under Mount Saint Elias: The History and Culture of the Yakutat Tlingit.*

McCreary, John L. (1974) *The Symbolisms of Popular Taoist Magic.*

Malefijt, Annamarie de Wall. (1968) *Religion and Culture: An Introduction to the Anthropology of Religion.*

Rowe, David N., and Willmoore Kendall, eds. (1954) *China: An Area Manual.*

Silberbauer, George B. (1981) *Hunter and Habitat in the Central Kalahari Desert.*

Todd, Judith. (1986) *Earth Dwelling: The Hopi Environmental Ethos and Its Architectural Symbolism—A Model for the Deep Ecology Movement.*

Waters, Frank. (1963) *Book of the Hopi.*

mals, and plant life that provide food and material goods for peoples who live along lakes and oceans. Water is also the source of hydroelectric power when it is channeled to turn the turbines that produce electricity in hydroelectric power plants. Water also provides a quick and efficient transportation route for many peoples who live in regions with many rivers, streams, or canals. Water also plays a geopolitical function when water courses serve as boundaries between political units such as nations (the Rio Grande River between the United States and Mexico), states (the Hudson River between New York and New Jersey), cities (the Mississippi River between Minneapolis and St. Paul, Minnesota), and neighborhoods (the Rio Pueblo de Taos between the north and south sections of Taos Pueblo in New Mexico). The use of water as a boundary is related to its use in defense of territory—land and buildings such as castles or towns—through the use of moats. Water also has a ritual role in many cultures such as its symbolic use in baptism in some Christian denominations, its healing power in various Christian sects, and its use in purification rituals by Muslims and Jews. Water can also serve an aesthetic function as in the pleasure to the eye from a fountain in a garden or the soothing sound of a gently gurgling mountain stream.

For people in the industrialized world, ready and unlimited access to clean water is assumed. However, in much of the rest of the world, water is not readily available and much effort must be expended every day to acquire and store water. Additionally, the location of water is a major determinant of where people live across cultures. How much effort people must put into obtaining water and how important a determinant it is of where they live rests mainly on the extent of control they maintain over water sources. In industrialized societies, the building of dams, the creation of reservoirs, the diversion of rivers, and the building and maintenance of waterways has created abundant water systems

WATER

Water is one of the most ubiquitous and important features of human existence. Nearly three-quarters of the earth's surface is covered by water, all living organisms need water to survive, and all living organisms contain water—60 percent of human body weight is water. Water occurs in three physical states—liquid, gaseous (vapor or steam), and solid (ice). Water used by humans collects naturally in oceans, lakes, rivers, streams, canals, springs, and pools. Much water collects underground in water tables and is brought to the surface by humans through the digging of wells and mechanical devices such as windmills, pumps, and waterwheels. Water is also collected from rainfall and stored for future use in reservoirs, irrigation channels, cisterns, and containers.

Water is of major economic importance across cultures because it is needed to irrigate fields, making agriculture possible where it normally would not be possible otherwise, such as in deserts, and making agriculture more profitable elsewhere by prolonging the growing season. Water also houses fish, shellfish, sea mam-

that steadily supply large populations and industries. Thus, in these societies people do not need to locate settlements near water sources, nor do they need to relocate to find new water sources. Instead, industrialized technology allows the water to be brought directly to them. At the other extreme are some hunter-gatherer cultures who live in arid locales such as the Kalahari Desert in Africa or the interior of Australia where water is scarce at least part of the year and who have little control over the water supply. These cultures provide a vivid example of the importance of water to both individual human beings and entire societies and suggest that only quite recently in the human experience has water become something that humans can take for granted.

For the Dobe !Kung San of Botswana, obtaining water is a daily task and a major determinant in where the group lives at any given time. The availability of water also influences group size as a number of families may live together near a rich water source while in times of scarcity, the group must break up into smaller nuclear family units. The !Kung rely on five water sources: (1) permanent waterholes, (2) semipermanent waterholes that dry up in some years, (3) waterholes that have water only during the rainy season, (4) water that collects in the hollows of trees, and (5) the roots of water-holding plants. The !Kung try to always stay near one of the first three sources, although their search for food at least sometimes during the year makes them reliant on the last two sources. Water is collected each day—it is not stored—by women who haul it to camp in ostrich eggshell canteens, which hold about 1 liter of water each, in antelope stomach sacks, or in baobab tree pod canteens. In other areas of the Kalahari other San groups store water for use during the dry season in hundreds of ostrich shells buried in the sand where they remain cool. Modern industrial societies and hunter-gatherers like the San represent the two extremes regarding the control and utilization of water by cultures around the world. The manner in which a culture exploits water resources is known as its water system. As detailed below, such systems vary widely around the world. The common feature of all water systems is that people try to make maximum use of the sources of water closest to their settlements, regardless of the source of that water.

Water Systems

The Chipewyan Native Americans of Saskatchewan rely on the numerous lakes in their traditional territory. Thus, they locate their villages and hunting camps near the lakeshore, with no house being built within a quarter mile of the shore. During winter, holes are drilled in the ice for access to the water; during the rest of the year, water is taken from the lakes in buckets. Unfortunately, the lakes also serve for waste disposal and some are contaminated with bacteria as evidenced by the frequent occurrence of diarrhea, dysentery, and meningitis in some communities.

People in the West Bengali village of Gôndôgram rely on the 20 ponds in their village, 17 of which are small and unimportant and 3 large and the major source of water for the village. People draw drinking water from the ponds, rent fishing rights to others, bathe in the water, and wash clothes there as well. In some villages the ponds serve as a source of water for irrigation that allows a third annual crop of wet rice to be grown in the dry season.

On the island of Tikopia in Melanesia, the sources of drinking and bathing water are streams that run down to the beaches from low hills. These streams are directed into pools near the beach by aqueducts built from areca palm trunks. The pools are located near the houses of the chiefs and are technically owned by them, although they are used by the community for water and bathing and are an important location for social interaction in the morning and evening.

This house in Ethiopia in 1987 shows the effects of the prolonged drought.

The people of the island of Tonga in Polynesia, like those on Tikopia, also face the problem of having enough freshwater when surrounded by a sea of saltwater. In the past, the Tongans used water stored in cisterns for drinking and that stored in wells for bathing. The cistern water was mainly rainwater directed into 10-foot-deep cisterns by bamboo drains on the house roofs supplemented by water carried from springs. The wells were dug and used for bathing, with chiefs and women having their own bathing wells. More recently, innovations have been introduced including concrete-lined cisterns and pump wells. However, many pump wells have been contaminated by seawater drawn in by the pumping and have high chloride levels that restrict their use for drinking and limit their desirability for bathing.

Villages in rural Highland Scotland rely on a mix of water sources including rainwater, streams, springs, surface wells, and freshwater lochs (lakes). Rainwater is collected in a storage tank below the eves and then piped into the house. Lochs that serve as village water sources are located at a higher elevation than the village with the water drawn by gravity into the lower-lying buildings.

The Garifuna along the Caribbean coast in Belize get their wash water from communal wells and their drinking water from cisterns that fill during the rainy season and buckets set under their roofs. Large cisterns hold up to 50,000 gallons of water. The wells are dug 4 feet down and are lined with a metal bucket to keep the sand out; the wells are meant only for washing unless the water is first boiled. However, many people drink well water without boiling it first and "bad belly" is a common complaint.

Navajo farmers and sheepherders of New Mexico traditionally and today draw water from wells or springs and then haul it to their dwellings. Because of the difficulties involved in hauling water and the need for an adequate supply for their flocks, the availability of water was in the past a major factor in the location of houses. More recently, however, the use of trucks and metal barrels has meant that water can be hauled from as far as 40 miles away and dams, windmills, water tanks, diversion dikes, and better transportation have further eroded the importance of natural, local water sources in settlement planning.

The southern Turkana cattle herders of East Africa rely on two primary water sources—mineral springs and wells associated with drainage systems. They also recognize eleven types of water sources: (1) wells that produce year-round located in riverbeds, (2) wells that produce for a few months a year located in drainage channels, (3) wells that produce year-round that are dug in riverbeds, (4) a well dug in a drainage channel, (5) a small pool of water, (6) a mineral spring that pools on the surface, (7) flowing water, (8) an open pool, (9) water collected in holes in rocks, (10) small springs, and (11) collected water from flowing water that lasts only a few months. The Turkana concern with water and its various sources is based on their need to keep

Two human responses to water—a bridge over the Euphrates River and a waterwheel to bring the water to land for use

GE 170   155 2002

urnal of the American Statistical Association, 55,

hnic identity, and behavioral adjustment among
dolescence, 8, 57–68.
thnicity in the social identities of Mexicanos and
21–532.
and their implications for gender consciousness.

identity approach. London: Sage.
1). Rebels with a cause: group identification as a
Personality and Social Psychology Bulletin, 27,

in social psychology. In D. Gilbert, S. Fiske, &
chology, Vol. 1, 4th edn.. pp. 233–265). Boston, MA:
per & Row.

5). Self-esteem as an interpersonal monitor: the
chology, 68, 518–530.

. Salience of ethnicity in the spontaneous self-
ocial environment. *Journal of Personality and*

ge of the Internet: identity 'demarginalization'
l Social Psychology, 75, 681–694.
 (3rd edn.). Boston, MA: Allyn and Bacon.
cial class, and racial identity to depression in

their stock watered and to move to locations with the most abundant supplies of water. In general, they prefer to herd in regions with many wells and springs, a few wells, or rivers that flow most of the year. However, during the dry season, water sources often run out and wells must be dug, creating the issue of who owns the water. As with many other cultures, the Turkana live by the rule that naturally occurring water is an open resource and is available to all on a first-come basis while sources produced by humans such as dug wells are the property of those who dig them and others must first ask permission before using them.

Water Pollution

In the industrialized world and those parts of the nonindustrialized world affected by economic development, water pollution is a serious environmental and economic problem, rendering many bodies of water unsuitable for human use and damaging human, fish, animal, and plant life in and near the water sources. Such industrial-based pollution also removes from use vast quantities of water causing water shortages. While the forms of water contamination experienced traditionally by non-Western peoples are on a different scale than modern industrial-based pollution, they nonetheless have serious consequences for the local community. One major source of local water contamination is the use of a water source for multiple purposes such as drinking, bathing, and washing clothes. In most cultures, an attempt is made to keep drinking water separate from water used for other purposes or to boil water for drinking, but both of these measures are rarely used by all people and therefore some are afflicted by various intestinal disorders resulting from bacterial contamination. A second major source of contamination is the use of large bodies of water such as lakes or flowing bodies such as rivers for drinking water, bathing, clothes washing, human waste disposal, and the discard of garbage. For example,

one Chipewyan community in Saskatchewan so routinely used a lake, it led to the lake's contamination and the contamination of lakes 16 miles away. Another source of contamination is bacterial growth in standing water collected from rain in buckets or cisterns, a problem faced by the Tongans where open water in the hot climate becomes rapidly contaminated. A fourth source of contamination is natural caused by heavy rains that can make river water heavy with sediment or the mixing of seawater with freshwater on islands or along coasts. Finally, water can be ritually contaminated, as among some rural Taiwanese villagers who restrict bathing and swimming in the river because they believe that the souls of individuals who drowned there previously wait in the water to drown others so that those previously drowned might escape.

See also AGRICULTURE; FISHING; IRRIGATION; PRECIPITATION.

Bone, Robert M. (1973) *The Chipewyan of the Stony Rapids Region: A Study of Their Changing World with Special Attention Focused upon Caribou.*

Darling, Frank F. (1955) *West Highland Survey: An Essay in Human Ecology.*

Downs, James F. (1972) *The Navajo.*

Dyson-Hudson, Rada, and J. Terrence McCabe. (1985) *South Turkana Nomadism: Coping with an Unpredictably Varying Environment.*

Firth, Raymond W. (1936) *We, the Tikopia: A Sociological Study of Kinship in Primitive Polynesia.*

Gifford, Edward W. (1929) *Tongan Society.*

Hadel, Richard E. (1972) *Carib Folk Songs and Carib Culture.*

Kerns, Virginia. (1983) *Women and the Ancestors: Black Carib Kinship and Ritual.*

Klass, Morton. (1978) *From Field to Factory: Community Structure and Industrialization in West Bengal.*

Lee, Richard B. (1979) *The !Kung San: Men, Women, and Work in a Foraging Society.*

Thaman, Randolp R. (1975) *The Tongan Agricultural System: With Special Attention on Plant Assemblages.*

Wolf, Margery. (1968) *The House of Lim: A Study of a Chinese Family Farm.*

WEATHER CONTROL

The weather—and interest and efforts in predicting and controlling it—is a daily concern in all cultures. Across cultures, the feature of weather that is most often the object of both forecasting and control is rain. Considerable time and effort is devoted to predicting and taking action to ensure the right amounts of rain fall at the right times. Hunter-gatherers who live in dry regions need rain for drinking and for wild plant foods, horticulturalists and agriculturalists need rain for their crops during the growing season, and pastoralists need rain to water their herds and to support vegetation for grazing. Many peoples are also much concerned about predicting and controlling storms, ranging from heavy rains to tornadoes, all of which are a threat to human existence because they can destroy buildings, kill livestock, and decimate crops.

Forecasting

Curiosity and worry about what the weather will be—tomorrow, next week, during the growing season, and next year—seem to be a characteristic of peoples in all cultures. Thus, in most cultures, people have developed methods to help them predict the weather. These predictors fall into four general categories: (1) changes in nature, especially in animal behavior; (2) the appearance of features of the climate or the sky; (3) symbolic events such as the weather on the same day in the previous year; and (4) the behavior of humans. The Sarakatsani herders of Greece forecast the weather solely on the basis of animal behavior. Because sheep are so central to Sarakatsani life, sheep behavior is a prime predictor of the weather: bad weather is coming when on a sunny day sheep huddle together before noon; it will snow when sheep browse heavily; and a rain or a storm is likely when the sheep move down from higher elevations. Additionally, the Sarakatsani take the howling of wolves to be a harbinger of storms; an owl hooting while sitting in the shade on a sunny day is a predictor of bad weather while an owl hooting during a rainstorm while sitting in the open is a sign that the rain will soon end. Saami reindeer herders of Sweden forecast according to the sky and the climate. Strong northern lights tell them that snow is coming, northern lights moving across the sky from the southwest mean that it will be windy, and the lights on the northern horizon suggest a cold spell. The clouds, too, are helpful to the Lapps in predicting the weather. In the autumn, sinking red clouds mean a snowstorm but if the clouds rise and disperse, the weather will be fine. Finally, lightening in the winter means either snow or a warmer temperature while thunder moving across the sky to the northwest means a strong northwesterly wind. Serbian farmers of the Balkans rely heavily on certain auspicious days: the weather on Saint Michael's Day (November 21) will be the same as on Saint Luke's (October 31); every day of bad weather in February will bring a good day of weather in March and the reverse; and a mist on Saint George's Day means it will hail the following summer.

In other cultures, a mix of predictors are used. The Mountain Whites of Appalachia say that all the following are signs of rain: "a circle around the moon, lightning in the north, smoke settling on the ground, a dog howling, sun draw-ing water, a dove calling, a cow lying down in the morning, dreaming of the dead, rain on the first Sunday of the month means rain all the succeeding Sundays, warm weather in winter, a dog eating grass, for a fire in the stove to start quickly." The Iroquois of New York State also employed a wide range of predictors for a num-ber of different weather conditions:

Rain

Small explosions during the burning of hardwood

The call of a flying pileated woodpecker

A sturgeon flipping backwards in the water

Smoke blowing to one side

Cirrus clouds

Robin singing from the top of a tree

Horizontal new moon

Hearing copping or shouting at a far distance

Hens sitting on a fence or gate in daytime

Snow

Vertical new moon

Northern lights

Hooting of a horned owl

Cold Winter

Many husks on an ear of corn

Warm Weather

Meteor moving horizontally toward the north

Milky Way oriented north and south

Spring Thaw

Ice cracking

Mice tracks in the snow

Thunder in the early spring

Dry Weather

Whirlwinds

Cumulus clouds

Among the Iroquois, as with many other peoples, individuals often have their own predictors; the above list is a composite drawn from a number of individuals and not a list of predictors fol-lowed by all. The use of both individual weather predictors and customary ones suggests that weather prediction has a psychological as well as practical purpose. By predicting the weather, individuals feel some sense of control over it and thereby relieve some of the stress associated with unpredictable weather and its potentially harm-ful effects.

Control

While forecasting with some degree of accuracy (there is little information about how accurate these folk predictors are) can give some comfort to people whose well-being and even life is de-pendent on the weather, in some cultures people go a step further and actively seek to influence the weather to benefit themselves. In these cul-tures, efforts to control the weather often take the form of religious rites or prayer and often involve religious specialists because the weather is seen as either a supernatural force in and of itself or as being influenced by supernatural forces. Thus, the supernatural must be com-municated with and influenced to control the weather. In some cultures, such efforts are mini-mal or are left to individuals. For example, the San of Botswana do not attempt to control rain by prayer or ritual. Instead, in accord with their belief that the universe is created and controlled by N!adima, they act in ways that will not anger him and let him know that they appreciate the rain that is provided to them. The Mbuti Pygmies of central Africa may use ritual to make a storm move away quickly or to change its direction. Blowing on a magic pipe is used to indicate the direction in which the storm should move and a smoldering fire is used to alert the God of the Underground to "help his children."

In a significant number of cultures a ritual specialist is employed to control the weather. The Copper Inuit of northern Canada use shamans as "subduers of the weather" to end blizzards. One or two shamans, naked from the waist up except for a caribou-hair headband, run out into the blizzard to close the "weather's opening" through which the storm blows and then seal the opening with the headband. Western Shoshone shamans used a variety of techniques including dreaming of different weather conditions and building a snowman and removing a piece of ice from it to end a snowstorm. The Seminole of Oklahoma use ritual means to protect themselves from tornadoes, which they describe as a giant old woman riding a large broom. One method of control is to capture a part of the tornado. They attempt to do so by placing a turtle shell with the front aimed at the tornado. If any of the tornado enters the shell, the tornado becomes harmless. Homes are protected by placing four such shells around the home. Turtle shells are also broken into fragments, some of which are scattered on the ground and four of which are burned as the tornado approaches. As the burning shell crackles in the fire, the old woman is warned that she will cut her feet on the fragments on the ground and she stays away.

In other cultures such as the Central Thai, Shona, and Zulu, the ritual is more complex. These cultures tend to be ones with relatively large communities, centralized political organization, and a reliance on rainwater for their crops or herds. Cultures such as these not only use elaborate rites but also ritual specialists, either priests or specialized weather makers, to make rain or control the weather. The agricultural Central Thai use three rain-making rites as well as other folk rituals to divert storms. One ritual involves offering the spirits food and clay figures of people and animals. A second, sometimes combined with the first, is the Buddhist rite of merit making conducted by priests in the village. The third rite, also conducted by the priests, involves their asking the deity, Pra Pirum, for rain during the dry season. The Shona, a herding people of East Africa, conduct a *Mukwerere* ceremony each summer when drought approaches. The ceremony is conducted by a ritual specialist called the *svikiro*, a man of considerable status in the community whose hair is never cut, who wears only black and red clothing, and who must be obeyed. Upon his permission to conduct the *Mukwerere* ceremony, old women deposit tobacco and corn mush at the ceremonial spot. The next day the community gathers there and, led by the *svikiro*, sing and dance for rain that usually falls soon thereafter.

The ritual role of the weather maker is perhaps most elaborate among the Zulu of South Africa. The Zulu have ritual specialists responsible for making or controlling rain, hail, and lightning. The specialists' power derives from their closeness to the sky and the ancestors controlling it. They are seen as mediators who try to influence the sky to produce weather beneficial to humans. The effectiveness of hail and lightning specialists is based to a large extent on the degree to which they follow the rules of behavior specific to their positions. Rain makers, however, are judged more on the basis of their effectiveness. All weather controllers are trained by masters and undergo a rigorous training program and initiation rite including scarification of their bodies, food and social restrictions, sleeping outdoors, and confronting storms to prove their power. Hail and lightning controllers are charged with controlling these weather conditions, preventing them from causing harm, and correcting damage that is caused. Their work is carried out through the performance of protective rituals; the following of various sex, food, and social taboos; and the conduct of various rites to prevent storms or reverse their damage. Rain makers play a more active role and are responsible for bringing rain, a major responsibility during the dry season. Their activities and in some sense all rain making is controlled by the Zulu royalty, although individual rain makers might be beaten or killed if their efforts fail. To some extent, hail and lightning practitioners play a psychological role in Zulu culture by taking responsibility for the tension caused by the threat or occurrence of these dangerous weather conditions. Rain makers also serve a psychological function as targets for the anger and anxiety caused by the lack of rain.

See also PRECIPITATION; STORMS; THUNDER AND LIGHTNING.

Bernatzik, Hugo A. (1938) *Overland with the Nomad Lapps.*

Howard, James H., and Willie Lena. (1984) *Oklahoma Seminoles: Medicines, Magic, and Religion.*

Ingersoll, Jasper C. (1964) *The Priest and the Path: An Analysis of the Priest Role in a Central Thai Village.*

Kabbadias, Georgios B. (1965) *Mediterranean Pastoral Nomads: The Sarakatsani of Greece.*

Kileff, Peggy, and Clive Kileff, eds. (1970) *Shona Customs: Essays by African Writers.*

Pavlovic, Jeremija M. (1973) *Folk Life and Customs in the Kragujevac Region of the Jasenica in Sumadija.*

Rasmussen, Knud J. V. (1932) *Intellectual Culture of the Copper Eskimos.*

Raum, Otto F. (1973) *The Social Functions of Avoidances and Taboos among the Zulu.*

Sherman, Mandel, and Thomas R. Henry. (1933) *Hollow Folk.*

Silberbauer, George B. (1981) *Hunter and Habitat in the Central Kalahari Desert.*

Steward, Julian H. (1941) *Culture Element Distributions: XIII. Nevada Shoshoni.*

Turnbull, Colin M. (1965) *The Mbuti Pygmies: An Ethnographic Survey.*

Waugh, Frederick W. (1916) *Iroquois Foods and Food Preparation.*

WIND

The wind has a profound and readily observable effect on the climate and weather as well as the physical environment around the world. Some of these effects are for the better such as depositing a layer of rich soil over poor soil, bringing needed rain, or lowering the air temperature. Other effects are harmful such as the erosion of land, the destruction of crops, the blowing of ships off course, or the stirring of seawater. Some wind features such as speed, duration, direction, and temperature are predictable and often vary by the season in reaction to changes in the temperature of the earth; so too are storms with heavy winds such as hurricanes that hit the Caribbean and southern United States in the fall. Some well-known regionally limited winds are

Baguio (North America) or *burban* (Siberia)—a cold wind accompanied by driving snow

Chinook or *Santa Ana* (North America) or *foehn* (Alps)—a dry, hot wind flowing down a mountain across a flat plain below

Etesian or *meltemi* (Eastern Mediterranean)—a seasonal wind flowing from the north to the Sahara in the summer and reversing in the winter

Harmattan (Africa)—a constant, dry, dusty northeast wind

Khamsin (Egypt)—a hot, dry, dusty south or southeast wind

Mistral (Mediterranean)—a strong and cold wind blowing south from the Rhone Valley

Simoom (Africa and Asia)—a hot, dry, dusty desert wind

Sirocco (Mediterranean)—a hot, dusty wind from the Sahara

Twister (North America)—a tornado

Tramontana (Italy)—a brisk, cool wind blowing south from the Alps

Typhoon (West Pacific)—a tropical cyclone

Zephyr (Mediterranean)—a gentle breeze from the west

Not all winds, however, are predictable and even when they are, not all features can be predicted in advance such as direction or speed. Thus, wind is another aspect of the natural environment that potentially effects all peoples but can neither be predicted reliably nor controlled. Probably because it is unpredictable, in some cultures the effects of the wind are thought to go beyond changes in the environment and include causing harm to humans, especially disease and death. Not surprisingly, in many cultures people try to influence the wind, either to make it beneficial or to negate its possible harmful effects. The Serbs, Croats, and Bosnians of the Balkans were traditionally much concerned with the wind. Farmers knew that winds effected the weather and soil and in many communities special names were used for different types of winds. They also used the winds to predict the future and believed that a south or west wind before sunrise on the Day of the Epiphany meant a rich harvest, a north wind meant a lean year, and an east wind meant drought. But the greatest concern with the wind was as a source of disease and numerous diseases and disorders from skin rashes to arthritis to toothaches to smallpox were blamed on the wind and its supernatural powers. The Herzigovinian saying, "Keep the Devil's wind from me," sums up their attitude about the wind. Healers used incantations and rituals to counteract the influence of the wind:

Red Wind
Milica whined and moaned
When she met the Mother of Jesus.
What is it my daughter Milica?
The wind struck me. But then
Mileva the conjurer met me,
With a coal shovel to burn it,
She sent it to the Gypsies,
They dismantled it with iron bars,
Blew on it with bellows,
Sent it to the woods,
To the Siamese wood,
Under the hazelnut bark,
Where cocks do not crow.

The Yucatec Maya of Mexico are another culture with great concern about the potentially harmful effects of the wind. The Maya attribute nearly all diseases to the wind. The exact features of the wind that cause illness are not clear; different individuals describe them as small people or winds left by animals or evil spirits. Whirlwinds are especially feared because they are believed to be the Devil as are winds blowing from the north and west that are believed to cause fevers in children. The east and south winds are considered to be more benign. A central belief is that winds will more likely cause illness when an individual is already weak, ill, or tired and that children are especially susceptible. To protect them from the wind, children wear special bracelets, necklaces, and amulets, and illness is treated by blood-letting, herbal potions, and baths. People also try to follow all religious obligations to please the spirits and avoid the harmful effects of the wind.

The Senoi of Malaysia believe that a certain type of harmful wind is caused by people laughing at or making fun of animals or by eating snake meat. Such actions anger the Original Snake beneath the earth who through his nostrils blows a wind across the ground that is especially noticeable during thunderstorms and that will make people ill. The Senoi also have wind spirits who cause various illnesses, death, and calamities if humans come into contact with them.

However, not all peoples see the wind as harmful; some try to harness its valuable energy. Mongolian herders whistle for the wind in the summer when they want its breezes to keep the flies off their herds but do not whistle in the spring and winter for fear of bringing storms. Western Apache warriors would paint a wind sign on their moccasins to use "wind-power" to make themselves lighter.

In the absence of scientific explanations, some peoples have developed supernatural explanations for the wind. The Gosiute of the western United States believed that ghosts and spirits appear in whirlwinds and that ordering the whirlwind to stop and throwing dirt at it will control it. The Andaman Islanders in the Indian Ocean believe that the winds are controlled by two primary supernatural forces: Biliku who controls the northeast wind and Tarai who controls the southwest wind. The Toba of Argentina believe that the Mother-of-the-Winds has a large stomach that shrinks when the winds leave each evening and that enlarges when they return in the morning.

See also STORMS.

Goodwin, Grenville. (1971) *Western Apache Raiding and Warfare from the Notes of Grenville Goodwin*, edited by Keith H. Basso.

Howell, Signe. (1984) *Society and Cosmos: Chewong of Peninsular Malaya.*

Kemp, Phyllis. (1935) *Healing Ritual: Studies in the Technique and Tradition of the Southern Slaves.*

Lattimore, Owen. (1941) *Mongol Journeys.*

Malouf, Carling, and Elmer R. Smith. (1947) "Some Gosiute Mythological Characters and Concepts." *Utah Humanities Review* 1:369–377.

Metraux, Alfred. (1946) *Myths of the Toba and Pilaga Indians of the Gran Chaco.*

Pavlovic, Jeremija M. (1973) *Folk Life and Customs in the Kragujevac Region of the Jasenica in Sumadija.*

Radcliffe-Brown, Alfred R. (1922) *The Andaman Islanders: A Study in Social Anthropology.*

Redfield, Robert, and Alfonso Villa Rojas. (1934) *Chan Kom: A Maya Village.*

Villa Rojas, Alfonso. (1945) *The Maya of East Central Quintana Roo.*

Werner, Roland. (1975) *Jah-het of Malaysia: Art and Culture.*

BIBLIOGRAPHY

Abbink, Jon. (1993) "Famine, Gold, and Guns: The Suri of Southwestern Ethiopia, 1985–1991." *Disasters* 17:218–225.

Acheson, James M. (1975) "The Lobster Fiefs: Economic and Ecological Effects of Territoriality in the Maine Lobster Industry." *Human Ecology* 3:183–207.

———. (1980) "Anthropology of Fishing." *Annual Review of Anthropology* 10:275–316.

Adams, William Y. (1963) *Shonto: A Study of the Role of the Trader in a Modern Navaho Community.*

Alaiza, Carol Ann Harrington de. (1989) *Santa Grazi Pastorala: A Critical Study of the Basque Pastorale as Contemporary Tradition.*

Albert, Steven M., and Maria G. Cattell. (1994) *Old Age in Global Perspective.*

'Ali, 'Abdullah Yusaf. (1937) *The Holy Quran: Arabic Text with an English Translation and Commentary.*

Ammar, Hammed (1954) *Growing Up in an Egyptian Village: Silwa, Province of Aswan.*

Anderson, William. (1967) "A Journal of a Voyage made in His Majesty's Sloop *Resolution* May 16th, 1776." In *The Journals of Captain James Cook on His Voyage of Discovery*, edited by J. C. Beaglehole, 721–986.

Annandale, Nelson, and Herbert C. Robinson. (1903) *Fasciculi Malayenses.*

Aptekar, Lewis. (1994) *Environmental Disasters in Global Perspective.*

Ardrey, Robert. (1966) *The Territorial Imperative.*

Arensberg, Conrad M. (1937) *The Irish Countryman.*

Arterburn, Yvonne J. (1977) *The Silk Weavers of Kanchipruam: A Case Study of the Indian Cooperative Movement.*

Attagara, Kingkeo. (1968) *The Folk Religion of Ban Nai, a Hamlet in Central Thailand.*

Ayrout, Henry H. (1945) *The Fellaheen*, translated by Hilary Wayment.

Bahuchet, S. (1988) "Food Supply Uncertainty among the Aka Pygmies (Lobaye, Central African Republic)." In *Coping with Uncertainty in Food Supply*, edited by I. de Garine and G. A. Harrison, 118–149.

Bailey, R. C., and N. R. Peacock. (1988) "Efe Pygmies of Northeast Zaire: Strategies in the Ituri Forest." In *Coping with Uncertainty in Food Supply*, edited by I. de Garine and G. A. Harrison, 88–117.

Bailey, Robert C., et al., (1989) "Hunting and Gathering in Tropical Rain Forests: Is It Possible?" *American Anthropologist* 91:59–82.

Baksh, Michael, and Allen Johnson. (1990) "Insurance Policies among the Machiguenga: An Ethnographic Analysis of Risk Management in a Non-Western Society." In *Risk and Uncertainty in Tribal and Peasant Economies*, edited by Elizabeth Cashdan, 193–228.

Barnard, Alan. (1991) *Hunters and Herders: A Comparative Ethnography of Khoisan Peoples.*

Barnett, William K. (1971) *An Ethnographic Description of Sanlei Ts'un, Taiwan, with Emphasis on Women's Roles, Overcoming Research Problems Caused by the Presence of a Great Tradition.*

Barton, Roy F. (1919) *Ifugao Law.*

Bascom, William. (1969) *The Yoruba of Southwestern Nigeria.*

Basehart, Harry W. (1974) "Mescalero Apache Subsistence Patterns and Socio-Political Organization." In *Apache Indians XII.*

Basso, Keith H. (1970) *The Cibecue Apache.*

Becher, Hans. (1960) *The Surara and Pakidai, Two Yanoama Tribes in Northwest Brazil.*

Belshaw, Cyril S. (1951) "Social Consequences of the Mount Lamington Eruption." *Oceania* 21:241–252.

Bennett, John W. (1969) *Northern Plainsmen: Adaptive Strategy and Agrarian Life.*

Berlin, Brent, and Paul Kay. (1969*) Basic Color Terms: Their Universality and Evolution.*

Bernatzik, Hugo A. (1938) *Overland with the Nomad Lapps.*

———. (1947) *Akha and Miao: Problems of Applied Ethnography in Farther India.*

Berry, John W, Ype H. Poortinga, Marshall H. Segall, and Pierre R. Dasen. (1992) *Cross-Cultural Psychology: Research and Applications.*

Best, Günter. (1983) *Culture and Language of the Turkana, NW Kenya.*

Bhattacharya, Jogendra N. (1896) *Hindu Castes and Sects.*

Bicchieri, M., ed. (1972) *Hunters and Gatherers Today.*

Binford, Lewis R. (1980) "Willow Smoke and Dogs' Tails: Hunter-Gatherer Settlement Systems and Archaeological Site Formation." *American Antiquity* 45:4–20.

———. (1990) "Mobility, Housing, and Environment: A Comparative Study." *Journal of Anthropological Research* 46:119–152.

Bishop, Charles A. (1970) "The Emergence of Hunting Territories among the Northern Ojibwa." *Ethnology* 9:1–15.

Bishop, Kent A. (1986) *The Hmong of Central California: An Investigation and Analysis of the Changing Family Structure during Liminality, Acculturation, and Transition.*

Blackman, Winifred S. (1927) *The Fellahin of Upper Egypt, Their Religious, Social, and Industrial Life Today with Special Reference to Survivals from Ancient Times.*

Blong, R. J., and D. A. Radford. (1993) "Deaths in Natural Hazards in the Solomon Islands." *Disasters* 17:1–11.

Bogaras, Waldemar. (1904–1909) *The Chukchee.*

Bone, Robert M. (1973) *The Chipewyan of the Stony Rapids Region: A Study of Their Changing World with Special Attention Focused upon Caribou.*

Bornstein, Marc H. (1973) "The Psychophysiological Component of Cultural Difference in Color Naming and Illusion Susceptibility." *Behavior Science Research* 8:41–101.

Boserup, Elizabeth. (1965) *The Conditions of Agricultural Growth: The Economics of Agrarian Change under Population Pressure.*

Bourdillon, Michael F. C. (1976) *The Shona Peoples: An Ethnography of the Contemporary Shona with Special Reference to their Religion.*

Bouroncle Carreón, Alfonso. (1964) "Contribution to the Study of the Aymara." *América Indígena* 24:129–169, 233–269.

Boxberger, Daniel L. (1994) "Ethnicity and Labor in the Puget Sound Fishing Industry, 1880–1935." *Ethnology* 33:179–191.

Brennan, Richard P. (1992) *Dictionary of Scientific Literacy.*

Bromley, Ray. (1981) "Market Center and Market Place in Highland Ecuador: A Study of Organization, Regulation, and Ethnic Discrimination." In *Cultural Transformations and Ethnicity in Modern Ecuador*, edited by Norman E. Whitten, Jr., 233–259.

Brower, Barbara A. (1987) *Livestock and Landscape: The Sherpa Pastoral System in Sagarmatha (Mount Everest) National Park, Nepal.*

Brown, Barton M. (1987) "Population Estimation from Floor Area: A Restudy of 'Naroll's Constant.'" *Behavior Science Research* 21:1–49.

Building with Nature. (1992) September–October.

Bullock, Charles. (1950) *The Mashona and the Matabele.*

Bunzel, Ruth L. (1929–1930) "Introduction to Zuni Ceremonials." *U.S. Bureau of American Ethnology, Annual Report* 47.

Burdon, T. W., and M. L. Parry, eds. (1954) *Papers on Malay Fishing Methods.*

Button, John. (1988) *A Dictionary of Green Ideas.*

Buxton, D. R. (1949) "The Shoan Plateau and Its People: An Essay in Local Geography." *Geographical Record* 114:157–172.

Buxton, Leonard H. D. (1929) *China: The Land and the People: A Human Geography.*

Callicott, J. Baird. (1994) *Earth's Insights.*

Campbell, J. K. (1964) *Honour, Family, and Patronage: A Study of Institutions and Moral Values in a Greek Mountain Community.*

Casagrande, Joseph B. (1971) "The Indian and Ecuadorian Society" and "Indigenous Society." In *The Condor and the Bull: Tradition and Change in Andean Indian Culture*, edited by Peter T. Furst and Karen B. Reed, 337–489.

Cashdan, Elizabeth A. (1983) "Territoriality among Human Foragers: Ecological Models and an Application to Four Bushman Groups." *Current Anthropology* 24:47–66.

Cashdan, Elizabeth, ed. (1990) *Risk and Uncertainty in Tribal and Peasant Economies.*

Casimir, Michael J. (1992) "The Determinants of Rights to Pasture: Territorial Organisation and Ecological Constraints." In *Mobility and Territoriality: Social and Spatial Boundaries among Foragers, Fishers, Pastoralists, and Peripatetics*, edited by Michael J. Casimir and Aparana Rao, 153–177.

Casimir, Michael J., and Aparana Rao, eds. (1992) *Mobility and Territoriality: Social and Spatial Boundaries among Foragers, Fishers, Pastoralists, and Peripatetics.*

Caudill, Harry M. (1963) *Night Comes to the Cumberlands: A Biography of a Depressed Area.*

Chagnon, Napoleon A. (1968) *Yanomamö: The Fierce People.*

Chapman, Margaret D. (1987) "Women's Fishing in Oceania." *Human Ecology* 15:267–288.

Chen, Chung-min. (1983) *Ying-Ting: A Cultural-Ecological Study of a Chinese Mixed Cropping Village in Taiwan.*

Chen, Robert S., et al. (1990) *The Hunger Report.*

Child, Alice B., and Irvin L. Child. (1993) *Religion and Magic in the Life of Traditional Peoples.*

Christensen, Hanne, and Ole Mertz. (1993) "The Risk Avoidance Strategy of Traditional Shifting Cultivation in Borneo." *The Sarawak Museum Journal* 44:1–18.

Christensen, Karen. (1989) *Home Ecology: Making Your World a Better Place.*

Churchill, Ward, and Winona LaDuke. (1992) "Native North America: The Political Economy of Radioactive Colonialism." In *The State of Native America: Genocide, Colonization, and Resistance*, edited by M. Annette Jaimes, 241–266.

Cipriani, Lidio. (1966) *The Andaman Islanders*, edited and translated by D. Taylor Cox.

Clemmer, Richard O. (1973) *Directed Resistance to Acculturation: A Comparative Study of the Effects of Non-Indian Jurisdiction on Hopi and Western Shoshone Communities.*

Clutton-Brock, Juliet. (1981) *Domesticated Animals from Early Times.*

Cohen, Erik. (1976) "Environmental Orientations: A Multidimensional Approach to Social Ecology." *Current Anthropology* 17:49–70.

Cohen, Mark N. (1977) *The Food Crisis in Prehistory: Overpopulation and the Origins of Agriculture.*

Cohen, Ronald, and Elman R. Service, eds. (1978) *Origins of the State: The Anthropology of Political Evolution.*

Cohen, Yehudi. (1968) *Man in Adaptation: The Cultural Present.*

Colbacchini, Antonio, and Cesar Albisetti. (1942) *The Eastern Bororo Orarimogodogue of the Eastern Plateau of Mato Grosso.*

Cole, John T. (1969*) The Human Soul in the Aymara Culture of Pumasara: An Ethnographic Study in the Light of George Herbert Mead and Martin Buber.*

Coleman, Jack D. B. (1976*) Language Shift in a Bilingual Hebridean Crofting Community.*

Collinder, Bjorn. (1949) *The Lapps.*

Collocott, Ernest E. V. (1922) *Tongan Astronomy and Calendar.*

———. (1925) "Supplementary Tongan Vocabulary." *Polynesian Society Journal* 34:146–169, 193–213.

Colloredo-Mansfeld, Rudolf. (1994) "Architectural Conspicuous Consumption and Economic Change in the Andes." *American Anthropologist* 96:845–865.

Colson, Elizabeth. (1979) "In Good Years and in Bad: Food Strategies of Self-Reliant Societies." *Journal of Anthropological Research* 35:18–29.

Colton, Harold S. (1974) "Hopi History and Ethnobotany." In *Hopi Indians*, 279–386.

Conklin, Harold C. (1967) "Some Aspects of Ethnogaphic Research in Ifugao." *Transactions of the New York Academy of Sciences.* Series II, 30:99–121.

———. (1980) *Ethnographic Atlas of Ifugao.*

Courlander, Harold. (1960) *The Drum and the Hoe: Life and Lore of the Haitian People.*

Damas, David. (1984) "Copper Eskimo." In *Handbook of North American Indians. Volume 5. Arctic*, edited by David Damas, 397–414.

Darling, Frank F. (1955) *West Highland Survey: An Essay in Human Ecology.*

Dentan, Robert K. (1978) *The Semai: A Nonviolent People of Malaya.*

Desai, Meghnad. (1988) "The Economics of Famine." In *Famine*, edited by G. Ainsworth Harrison, 107–138.

Dewar, Robert E. (1984) "Environmental Productivity, Population Regulation, and Carrying Capacity." *American Anthropologist* 86:601–614.

Dewey, Alice G. (1962) *Peasant Marketing in Java.*

Dirks, Robert. (1993) "Starvation and Famine: Cross-Cultural Codes and Some Hypothesis Tests." *Cross-Cultural Research* 27:28–69.

Downs, James F. (1972) *The Navajo.*

D'Souza, Frances. (1988) "Famine: Social Security, and an Analyses of Vulnerability." In *Famine*, edited by G. Ainsworth Harrison, 1–56.

Dumont, Louis C. J. (1957) *A Subcaste of South India: Social Organization and Religion of the Pramalai Kallar.*

Duncan, James S. (1982) *Housing and Identity: Cross-Cultural Perspectives.*

Dyson-Hudson, Rada, and Eric A. Smith. (1978) "Human Territoriality: An Ecological Reassessment." *American Anthropologist* 80:21–41.

Dyson-Hudson, Rada, and J. Terrence McCabe. (1985) *South Turkana Nomadism: Coping with an Unpredictably Varying Environment.*

Dyson-Hudson, Rada, and Neville Dyson-Hudson. (1980) "Nomadic Pastoralism." *Annual Review of Anthropology* 9:15–61.

Ellis, Florence H. (1974) "The Hopi: Their History and Use of Lands." In *Hopi Indians*, 25–277.

Ember, Carol R. (1978) "Myths about Hunter-Gatherers." *Ethnology* 17:439–448.

Ember, Carol R., and Melvin Ember. (1990) *Anthropology.* 6th ed.

———. (1992) "Resource Unpredictability, Mistrust, and War." *Journal of Conflict Resolution* 36:242–262.

———. (1992) "Warfare, Aggression and Resource Problems: Cross-Cultural Codes." *Behavior Science Research* 26:169–226.

———. (1993) *Anthropology.* 7th ed.

Ember, Melvin. (1978) "Size of Color Lexicon: Interaction of Cultural and Biological Factors." *American Anthropologist* 80:364–367.

Evans, I. H. N. (1927) *Papers on the Ethnology and Archaeology of the Malay Peninsula.*

———. (1937) *The Negritos of Malaya.*

Evans-Pritchard, Edward E. (1940) *The Nuer.*

Ewers, John C. (1970) "Bodily Proportions as Guides to Lineal Measurements among the Blackfoot Indians." *American Anthropologist* 72:561–562.

———. (1971) *The Blackfoot: Raiders of the Northwestern Plains.*

Faegre, Torvald. (1979) *Tents: Architecture of the Nomads.*

Fei, Hsiao-tung. (1946) *Peasant Life in China: A Field Study of Country Life in the Yangtze Valley.*

Fenton, William N. (1962) "This Island, the World Is on the Turtle's Back." *Journal of American Folklore* 75:283–300.

Findley, Sally E. (1994) "Does Drought Increase Migration? A Study of Migration from Rural Mali during the 1983–1985 Drought." *International Migration Review* 28:539–553.

Firth, Raymond W. (1936) *We, the Tikopia: A Sociological Study of Kinship in Primitive Polynesia.*

———. (1946) *Malay Fisherman: Their Peasant Economy.*

———. (1959) *Economics of the New Zealand Maori.*

Fisher, James F. (1990) *Sherpas: Reflections on Change in Himalayan Nepal.*

Forbis, Richard G. (1978) "Some Facets of Communal Hunting." *Plains Anthropologist* 23:3–8.

Ford, Thomas R. (1962) *The Southern Appalachian Region: A Survey.*

Forde, C. Daryll. (1963) *Habitat, Economy, and Society.*

Forman, Shepard. (1980) "Cognition and Catch: The Location of Fishing Spots in a Brazilian Coastal Village." In *Maritime Adaptations: Essays on Contemporary Fishing Communities*, edited by Alexander Spoehr, 15–24.

Foster, Michael K. (1974) *From the Earth to Beyond the Sky: An Ethnographic Approach to Four Longhouse Iroquois Speech Events.* National Museum of Man Mercury Series, Paper no. 20.

Fraser, Douglas. (1968) *Village Planning in the Primitive World.*

Friedrich, Paul, and Norma Diamond, eds. (1994) *Encyclopedia of World Cultures. Volume 6. Russia/Eurasia and China.*

Frigout, Arlette. (1979) "Hopi Ceremonial Calendar." In *Handbook of North American Indians. Volume 9. Southwest*, edited by Alfonso Ortiz, 564–576.

———. (1979) "Hopi Ceremonial Organization." In *Handbook of North American Indians. Volume 9. Southwest*, edited by Alfonso Ortiz, 564–576.

Fürer-Haimendorf, Christoph von. (1975) *Himalayan Traders: Life in Highland Nepal.*

———. (1975) *The Sherpas of Nepal: Buddhist Highlanders.*

Gaffin, Dennis. (1993) "Landscape, Personhood, and Culture: Names of Places and People in the Faeroe Islands." *Ethnos* 58:53–72.

Galaty, John G., Dan Aronson, Philip C. Salzman, and Amy Chouinard, eds. (1980) *The Future of Pastoral Peoples.* Proceedings of a Conference Held in Nairobi, Kenya, August 4–8.

Gallin, Bernard. (1966) *Hsin Hsing, Taiwan: A Chinese Village in Change.*

Gannon, Martin J., and Associates. (1994) *Understanding Global Cultures: Metaphorical Journeys through 17 Countries.*

Garcilaso de la Vega (El Inca). (1869–1871) *First Part of the Royal Commentaries of the Incas*, translated and edited by Clements R. Markham.

Garine, I. de, and G. A. Harrison, eds. (1988) *Coping with Uncertainty in Food Supply.*

Gay, John, and Michael Cole. (1967) *The New Mathematics and an Old Culture: A Study of Learning among the Kpelle of Nigeria.*

Gelfand, Michael. (1959) *Shona Ritual with Special Reference to the Chaminuka Cult.*

Getty, Harry T. (1963) *The San Carlos Indian Cattle Industry.*

Gifford, Edward W. (1923) *Tongan Place Names.*

———. (1929) *Tongan Society.*

Gladwin, Thomas, and Seymour B. Sarason. (1953) *Truk: Man in Paradise.*

Godoy, Ricardo. (1985) "Mining: Anthropological Perspective." *Annual Review of Anthropology* 14:199–217.

Goodwin, Gary C. (1977) *Cherokees in Transition: A Study of Changing Culture and Environment Prior to 1775.*

Goodwin, Grenville. (1971) *Western Apache Raiding and Warfare from the Notes of Grenville Goodwin*, edited by Keith H. Basso.

Goody, Jack. (1993) *The Culture of Flowers.*

Gould-Martin, Katherine. (1977) *Women Asking Women: An Ethnography of Health Care in Rural Taiwan.*

Granskog, Jane E. (1979) *Efficiency in a Zapotec Indian Village.*

Greenberg, Joseph H. (1946) *The Influence of Islam on a Sudanese Religion.*

Grigson, Wilfrid V. (1949) *The Maria Gond of Bastar.*

Grinell, George B. (1962) *Blackfoot Lodge Tales: The Story of a Prairie People.*

Groot, Jan Jacob Maria de. (1912) *Religion in China: Universism. A Key to the Study of Taoism and Confucianism.*

Gurdon, Philip R. T. (1907) *The Khasis.*

Gutman, Robert. (1976) "The Social Function of the Built Environment." In *The Mutual Interaction of People and Their Built Environment*, edited by Amos Rapoport, 37–49.

Hadel, Richard E. (1972) *Carib Folk Songs and Carib Culture.*

Halpern, Joel M. (1958) *A Serbian Village.*

Halstead, Paul, and John O'Shea, eds. (1989) *Bad Year Economics: Cultural Responses to Risk and Uncertainty.*

Hamel, Paul B., and Mary U. Chiltoskey. (1975) *Cherokee Plants and Their Uses—A 400 Year History.*

Handy, Edward S. C. (1923) *The Native Cultures of the Marquesas.*

Hansen, Art. (1994) "The Illusion of Local Sustainability and Self-Sufficiency: Famine in a Border Area of Northwestern Zambia." *Human Organization* 53:11–20.

Hardin, G. (1968) "The Tragedy of the Commons." *Science* 162:1243–48.

Harrell, Clyde Stevan. (1983) *Belief and Unbelief in a Taiwan Village.*

Harrington, John P. (1907–1908) *The Ethnogeography of the Tewa Indians.*

Harrison, G. Ainsworth, ed. (1988) *Famine.*

Hart, David M. (1976) *The Aith Waryaghar of the Moroccan Rif.*

Hays, David G., Enid Margolis, Raoul Naroll, and Dale Revere Perkins. (1972) "Color Term Salience." *American Anthropologist* 74:1107–1121.

Headland, Thomas N., ed. (1992) *The Tasaday Controversy: Assessing the Evidence.*

Heiberg, Marianne. (1989) *The Making of the Basque Nation.*

Heiser, Charles B., Jr. (1990) *Seed to Civilization: The Story of Food.*

Hieb, Louis A. (1972) *The Hopi Ritual Clown: Life as It Should Not Be.*

———. (1979) "Hopi World View." In *Handbook of North American Indians. Volume 9. Southwest*, edited by Alfonso Ortiz, 577–580.

Hill, Kim, and M. Hurtado. (1989) "Hunter-Gatherers of the New World." *American Scientist* 77:436–443.

Hodge, Frederick W. (1959) *Handbook of American Indians North of Mexico.*

Homer-Dixon, Thomas F. (1994) "Environmental Scarcities and Violent Conflict: Evidence from Cases." *International Security* 19:5–40.

Homewood, K. M. (1988) "Pastoralism and Conservation." In *Tribal Peoples and Development Issues: A Global Overview*, edited by John H. Bodley, 310–320.

Hostetler, John A. (1980) *Amish Society.* 3rd ed.

Howard, James H., and Willie Lena. (1984) *Oklahoma Seminoles: Medicines, Magic, and Religion.*

Howell, Signe. (1984) *Society and Cosmos: Chewong of Peninsular Malaya.*

Hoyles, Martin. (1991) *The Story of Gardening.*

Hungry Wolf, Adolf. (1977) *The Blood People, a Division of the Blackfoot Confederacy: An Illustrated Interpretation of Old Ways.*

Hunn, Eugene. (1994) "Place-Names, Population Density, and the Magic Number 500." *Current Anthropology* 35:81–85.

Ingersoll, Jasper C. (1964) *The Priest and the Path: An Analysis of the Priest Role in a Central Thai Village.*

Ingold, Tim. (1980) *Hunters, Pastoralists, and Ranchers: Reindeer Economies and Their Transformations.*

Irvin, Michael T. T. (1985) *My Grandfathers Build the House: The Tlingit Potlatch as a System of Religious Belief.*

Itkonen, Toivo I. (1948) *The Lapps in Finland up to 1945.*

Jackson, Jean E. (1983) *The Fish People.*

Jacob-Pandian, Ebenezer T. (1972) *Dravidianization: A Tamil Revitalization Movement.*

Jellicoe, Sir Geoffrey, et al. (1986) *The Oxford Companion to Gardens.*

Jenness, Diamond. (1922) *The Life of the Copper Eskimo.*

Johannes, Robert. (1981) *Words of the Lagoon: Fishing and Marine Lore in the Palau District of Micronesia.*

Johnson, Allen, series ed. (1988-) *Cross-Cultural Studies in Time Allocation.*

Jorgensen, Joseph G. (1974) *The Sun Dance Religion: Power for the Powerless.*

Kabbadias, Georgios B. (1965*) Mediterranean Pastoral Nomads: The Sarakatsani of Greece.*

———. (1965) *Nomadic Shepherds of the Mediterranean.*

Keen, David. (1994) "In Africa, Planned Suffering." *The New York Times,* August 15, 1994:A15.

Kelly, Robert L. (1992) "Mobility-Sedentism: Concepts, Archaeological Measures, and Effects." *Annual Review of Anthropology* 21:43–66.

Kemp, Phyllis. (1935) *Healing Ritual: Studies in the Technique and Tradition of the Southern Slaves.*

Kent, Susan, ed. (1990) *Domestic Architecture and the Use of Space: An Interdisciplinary and Cross-Cultural Study.*

Kerns, Virginia. (1983) *Women and the Ancestors: Black Carib Kinship and Ritual.*

Kerr, John G. (1950) *A Naturalist in the Gran Chaco.*

Kileff, Peggy, and Clive Kileff, eds. (1970) *Shona Customs: Essays by African Writers.*

Kilpatrick, Jack F., and Anna G. Kilpatrick. (1967) *Run toward the Nightland: Magic of the Oklahoma Cherokee.*

Klass, Morton. (1978) *From Field to Factory: Community Structure and Industrialization in West Benegal.*

Knez, Eugene I. (1970) *Sam Jong Dong: A South Korean Village.*

Koyama, Shuzo, and David H. Thomas, eds. (1981) *Affluent Foragers.* Senri Ethnological Studies, no. 9.

Laguna, Frederica de. (1972) *Under Mount Saint Elias: The History and Culture of the Yakutat Tlingit.*

Lattimore, Owen. (1941) *Mongol Journeys.*

Laubin, Reginald, and Gladys Laubin. (1957) *The Indian Tipi: Its History, Construction, and Use.*

Laughlin, William S. (1980) *Aleuts: Survivors of the Bering Land Bridge.*

Lawrence, Denise L., and Setha M. Low. (1990) "The Built Environment and Spatial Form." *Annual Review of Anthropology* 19:453–505.

Leach, E. R. (1968) *Pul Eliya: A Village in Ceylon.*

Leacock, Eleanor. (1954) *The Montagnais "Hunting Territory" and the Fur Trade.* American Anthropological Association, Memoir 78.

Leaf, Murray J. (1984) *Song of Hope: The Green Revolution in a Punjab Village.*

LeBlanc, Steven. (1971) "An Addition to Naroll's Suggested Floor Area and Settlement Population Relationship." *American Antiquity* 36:210–211.

Lee, Richard B. (1979) *The !Kung San: Men, Women, and Work in a Foraging Society.*

Lee, Richard B., and Irven DeVore, eds. (1968) *Man the Hunter.*

Leeds, Anthony, and Andrew P. Vayda, eds. (1965*) Man, Culture, and Animals.*

Lees, Susan H. (1970) *Socio-Political Aspects of Canal Irrigation in the Valley of Oaxaca, Mexico.*

Lenski, Gerhard, and Jean Lenski. (1974) *Human Societies: An Introduction to Macrosociology.*

Lessa, William A., and Evon Z. Vogt, eds. (1965) *Reader in Comparative Religion: An Anthropological Approach.* 2d ed.

Levinson, David. (1994) *Aggression and Conflict: A Cross-Cultural Encyclopedia.*

———. (1994) *Ethnic Relations: A Cross-Cultural Encyclopedia.*

Levinson, David, ed. (1991–1995) *Encyclopedia of World Cultures.*

Levinson, David, and David Sherwood. (1993) *The Tribal Living Book.* 2d ed.

Levinson, David, and Martin J. Malone. (1980) *Toward Explaining Human Culture.*

Lewis, Henry. (1994) "Fire." In *The Encyclopedia of the Environment,* edited by Ruth A. Eblen and William R. Eblen, 248–250.

Leyburn, James G. (1966) *The Haitian People.*

Linton, Ralph. (1922) *The Thunder Ceremony of the Pawnee.*

Lorimer, Emily O. (1938) "The Burusho of Hunza." *Antiquity* 12:5–15.

Low, Bobbi S. (1990) "Human Responses to Environmental Extremeness and Uncertainty: A Cross-Cultural Perspective." In *Risk and Uncertainty in Tribal and Peasant Economies,* edited by Elizabeth Cashdan, 229–256.

Lustig-Arecco, Vera. (1975) *Technology: Strategies for Survival.*

MacCauley, Clay. (1884) *The Seminole Indians of Florida.*

McCoid, Catherine H. (1984) *Carrying Capacity of Nation-States.*

McCreary, John L. (1974) *The Symbolisms of Popular Taoist Magic.*

MacDougall, Robert D. (1971) *Domestic Architecture among the Kandyan Sinhalese.*

Malefijt, Annemarie de Wall. (1968) *Religion and Culture: An Introduction to the Anthropology of Religion.*

Malinowski, Bronislaw. (1935) *Coral Gardens and their Magic: A Study of the Methods of Tilling the Soil and Agricultural Rites in the Trobriand Islands.*

Malouf, Carling, and Elmer R. Smith. (1947) "Some Gosiute Mythological Characters and Concepts." *Utah Humanities Review* 1:369–377.

Man, Edward H. (1932) *On the Aboriginal Inhabitants of the Andaman Islands.*

Marshall, Mac. (1979) "Natural and Unnatural Disaster in the Mortlock Islands of Micronesia." *Human Organization* 38: 265–272.

Messing, Simon D. (1957) *The Highland-Plateau Amhara of Ethiopia.*

Metraux, Alfred. (1946) *Myths of the Toba and Pilaga Indians of the Gran Chaco.*

Mijatovich, Chedo. (1914) *Servia of the Servians.*

Minc, L., and K. Smith. (1989) "The Spirit of Survival: Cultural Responses to Resource Variability in Alaska." In *Bad Year Economics: Cultural Responses to Risk and Uncertainty,* edited by Paul Halstead and John O'Shea, 8–39.

Mirga, Andrzej. (1992) "Roma Territorial Behaviour and State Policy: The Case of the Socialist Countries of East Europe." In *Mobility and Territoriality: Social and Spatial Boundaries among Foragers, Fishers, Pastoralists, and Peripatetics,* edited by Michael J. Casimir and Aparana Rao, 259–278.

Mooney, James. (1982) *Myths of the Cherokee and Sacred Formulas of the Cherokees.*

Moore, John H. (1987) *The Cheyenne Nation: A Social and Demographic History.*

Morehouse, Goeffrey. (1972) *Calcutta.*

Moshen, Safia K. (1971) *The Quest for Order among Awlad Ali of the Western Desert of Egypt.*

Mukherjea, Charulal. (1962) *The Santals.*

Mullen, Patrick B. (1988) *I Heard the Old Fisherman Say: Folklore of the Texas Gulf Coast.*

Murdock, George P. (1981) *Atlas of World Cultures*.

Murdock, George P., and Caterina Provost. (1973) "Factors in the Division of Labor by Sex." *Ethnology* 12:203–225.

———. (1973) "Measurement of Cultural Complexity." *Ethnology* 12:379–392.

Murdock, George P., and Diana O. Morrow. (1970) "Subsistence Economy and Supportive Practices: Cross-Cultural Codes 1." *Ethnology* 9:302–330.

Murdock, George Peter, and Suzanne F. Wilson. (1972) "Settlement Patterns and Community Organization: Cross-Cultural Codes 3." *Ethnology* 11:254–295.

———. (1980) "Settlement Patterns and Community Organization: Cross-Cultural Codes III." In *Cross-Cultural Samples and Codes*, edited by Herbert Barry III and Alice Schlegel, 76–116.

Mushtaque, A., et al. (1993) "The Bangladesh Cyclone of 1991: Why So Many People Died." *Disasters* 17:291–304.

Naroll, Raoul. (1962) "Floor Area and Settlement Population." *American Antiquity* 27:587–589.

Nash, June C. (1970) *In the Eyes of the Ancestors: Belief and Behavior in a Maya Community*.

Needham, Rodney. (1973) *Right and Left: Essays on Dual Symbolic Classification*.

Netting, Robert McC. (1968) *Hill Farmers of Nigeria*.

Norbeck, Edward. (1954) *Takashima: A Japanese Fishing Community*.

———. (1959) *Pineapple Town Hawaii*.

Obermeyer, Gerald J. (1969) *Structure and Authority in a Bedouin Tribe: The 'Aishaibat of the Western Desert of Egypt*.

Oliver, Douglas L. (1989) *Oceania: The Native Cultures of Australia and the Pacific Islands*.

Oliver, Paul. (1987) *Dwellings: The House across the World*.

Olson, Paul A. (1989) *The Struggle for the Land: Indigenous Insight and Industrial Empire in the Semi-Arid World*.

O'Malley, Lewis S., ed. (1941) *Modern India and the West: A Study of the Interaction of Their Civilizations*.

Osgood, Ernest S. (1929) *The Day of the Cattleman*.

Östör, Akos. (1980) *The Play of the Gods: Locality, Ideology, Structure, and Time in the Festivals of a Bengali Town*.

Oswalt, Wendell H. (1976) *An Anthropological Analysis of Food-Getting Technology*.

Ott, Sandra. (1981) *The Circle of Mountains: A Basque Shepherding Community*.

Otterbein, Keith F. (1975) *Changing House Types on Long Bay Cays*.

Parrish, Lydia. (1942) *Slave Songs of the Georgia Sea Islands*.

Parry, William. (1992) *An Ethnographic Bibliography for South and Southeast Asian Hunters and Gatherers*.

Parsons, Elsie W. C. (1945) *Peguche, Canton of Otavalo, Province of Imbabura, Ecuador: A Study of Andean Indians*.

Pavlovic, Jeremija M. (1973) *Folk Life and Customs in the Kragujevac Region of the Jasenica in Sumadija*.

Pedersen, Lise Rishoj. (1982) "The Influence of the Spirit World on the Habitation of the Lao Song Dam, Thailand." In *The House in East and Southeast Asia*, edited by K. G. Izikowitz and P. Sorensen, 115–128.

Pelto, Pertti J. (1973) *The Snowmobile Revolution: Technology and Social Change in the Arctic*.

Peterson, Nicolas. (1975) "Hunter-Gatherer Territoriality: The Perspective from Australia." *American Anthropologist* 77:53–68.

Pfaffenberger, Bryan. (1992) "Social Anthropology of Technology." *Annual Review of Anthropology* 21:491–516.

Pitt-Rivers, J. A. (1961) *The People of the Sierra.*

Pittman, Anne M. (1972) *Recreation Activities Instrumental to Expressed Life Goals of San Carlos Teen-Age Apaches.*

Poggie, John J., Jr., ed. (1980) *Maritime Anthropology.* Special Issue of *Anthropological Quarterly* 53.

Pospisil, Leopold. (1964) *The Kapauku Papuans of West New Guinea.*

Radcliffe-Brown, Alfred R. (1922) *The Andaman Islanders: A Study in Social Anthropology.*

Rae, Edward. (1881) *The White Sea Peninsula: A Journey in Russian Lapland and Karelia.*

Rapoport, Amos. (1969) *House Form and Culture.*

———. (1994) "Spatial Organization and the Built Environment." In *Companion Encyclopedia of Anthropology*, edited by Tim Ingold, 460–500.

Rasmussen, Knud J. V. (1932) *Intellectual Culture of the Copper Eskimos.*

Raum, Otto F. (1973) *The Social Functions of Avoidances and Taboos among the Zulu.*

Reagan, Albert B. (1930) *Notes of the Indians of the Fort Apache Region.*

Redfield, Robert, and Alfonso Villa Rojas. (1934) *Chan Kom: A Maya Village.*

———. (1939) "Notes on the Ethnography of Tzeltal Communities of Chiapas." *Contributions to American Anthropology and History* 5:105–119.

Reid, John P. (1970) *A Law of Blood: The Primitive Law of the Cherokee Nation.*

Reno, Philip. (1963) *Taos Pueblo.*

Reynolds, Holly B. (1978) *To Keep the Tali Strong: Women's Rituals in Tamilnad, India.*

Riley, James N. (1973) *Family Organization and Population Dynamics in a Central Thai Village.*

Rivière, Peter. (1972) *The Forgotten Frontier: Ranchers of Northern Brazil.*

Robbins, Michael C. (1966) "House Types and Settlement Patterns." *Minnesota Archaeologist* 28:2–26.

Roland, Betty. (1973) "Farmers of the Australian Outback." In *Peoples of the Earth. Volume 1. Australia and Melanesia*, edited by Anthony Forge, 28–33.

Rowe, David N., and Willmoore Kendall, eds. (1954) *China: An Area Manual.*

Rowe, John H. (1946) "Inca Culture at the Time of the Spanish Conquest." In *Handbook of South American Indians, Volume 2*, edited by Julian H. Steward, 183–330.

Rubio Orbe, Gonzalo. (1956) *Punyaro.*

Ruddle, Kenneth, and Tommoya Akimichi, eds. (1984) *Maritime Institutions in the Western Pacific.* Senri Ethnological Studies, no. 17.

Russell, Scott C. (1983) *Factors Affecting Agricultural Production in a Western Navajo Community.*

Russell, W. M. S. (1977) "The Slash-and-Burn Technique." In *Man's Many Ways: The Natural History Reader in Anthropology*, edited by Richard A. Gould and *Natural History Magazine*, 71–76.

Sack, Robert D. (1986) *Human Territoriality.*

Sahrhage, Dietrich, and Johannes Lundbeck. (1992) *A History of Fishing.*

Salzman, Philip C. (1995) "Pastoralism." In *Encyclopedia of Cultural Anthropology*, edited by David Levinson and Melvin Ember.

Savage, Candace. (1994) *Aurora: The Mysterious Northern Lights.*

Scarre, Chris. (1993) *Smithsonian Timelines of the Ancient World: A Visual Chronology from the Origins of Life to A.D. 1500.*

Schryer, Frans J. (1980) *The Rancheros of Pisaflores.*

Schusky, Ernest L. (1989) *Culture and Agriculture: An Ecological Introduction to Traditional and Modern Farming Systems.*

Seavoy, Ronald E. (1986) *Famine in Peasant Societies.*

Sen, Amartya. (1981) *Poverty and Famines: An Essay on Entitlement and Deprivation.*

Shanklin, Eugenia. (1985) "Sustenance and Symbol: Anthropological Studies of Domesticated Animals." *Annual Review of Anthropology* 14:375–403.

Sheffer, Gabriel, ed. (1986) *Modern Diasporas in International Politics.*

Sherman, Mandel, and Thomas R. Henry. (1933) *Hollow Folk.*

Shorris, Earl. (1992) *Latinos: A Biography of the People.*

Silberbauer, George B. (1965) *Report to the Government of Bechuanaland on the Bushmen Survey.*

———. (1972) "The G/wi Bushmen." In *Hunters and Gatherers Today*, edited by Mario G. Bicchieri, 271–326.

———. (1981) *Hunter and Habitat in the Central Kalahari Desert.*

Sinclair, Peter R., ed. (1988) *A Question of Survival: The Fisheries and Newfoundland Society.*

Snyderman, George S. (1951) "Concept of Land Ownership among the Iroquois and Their Neighbors." In *Symposium on Local Diversity in Iroquois Culture*, edited by William N. Fenton, 13–34.

Sopher, David E. (1977) *The Sea Nomads: A Study of the Maritime Boat People of Southeast Asia.*

Spate, Oscar B. K. (1954) *India and Pakistan.*

Spencer, Walter B., and F. J. Gillen. (1927) *The Arunta: A Study of a Stone Age People.*

Spier, Robert F. G. (1970) *From the Hand of Man: Primitive and Preindustrial Technologies.*

Stegmiller, P. F. (1921) "The Religious Life of the Khasi." *Anthropos* 16:407–441.

Stern, Gerald M. (1976) *The Buffalo Creek Disaster: The Story of the Survivors' Unprecedented Lawsuit.*

Stern, Theodore. (1965) *The Klamath Tribe: A People and Their Reservation.*

Stevens, Stanley F. (1989) *Sherpa Settlement and Subsistence: Cultural Ecology and History in Highland Nepal.*

Steward, Julian H. (1941) *Culture Element Distributions: XIII. Nevada Shoshoni.*

Stewart, George R. (1970) *American Place Names.*

Stewart, Hilary. (1977) *Indian Fishing: Early Methods on the Northwest Coast.*

Stewart, Kenneth M. (1983) "Mohave." In *Handbook of North American Indians. Volume 10. Southwest,* edited by Alfonso Ortiz, 55–70.

Strickon, Arnold. (1965) "The Euro-American Ranching Complex." In *Man, Culture, and Animals: The Role of Animals in Human Ecological Adjustments,* edited by Anthony Leeds and Andrew P. Vayda, 229–258.

Tanaka, Jiro. (1980) *The San Hunter-Gatherers of the Kalahari: A Study in Ecological Anthropology.*

Taylor, Ralph B. (1988) *Human Territorial Functioning.*

Textor, Robert B. (1973) *Roster of the Gods: An Ethnography of the Supernatural in a Thai Village.*

Thaman, Randolph R. (1975) *The Tongan Agricultural System: With Special Attention on Plant Assemblages.*

Tindale, Norman B. (1974) *Aboriginal Tribes of Australia: Their Terrain, Environmental Controls, Distribution, Limits, and Proper Names.*

Tobe, John H. (1960) *Hunza: Adventure in a Land of Paradise.*

Todd, Judith. (1986) *Earth Dwelling: The Hopi Environmental Ethos and Its Architectural Symbolism—A Model for the Deep Ecology Movement.*

Tollefson, Kenneth. (1976) *The Cultural Foundations of Political Revitalization among the Tlingit.*

Tonkinson, Robert. (1978) *The Mardudjara Aborigines: Living the Dream in Australia's Desert.*

Tooker, Elizabeth, and Harold C. Conklin, eds. (1984) *Naming Systems.*

Torry, William I. (1978a) "Bureaucracy, Community, and Natural Disasters." *Human Organization* 37:302–308.

———. (1978b) "Natural Disasters, Social Structure, and Change in Traditional Societies." *Journal of Asian and African Studies* 13:167–183.

———. (1979) "Anthropology and Disaster Research." *Disasters* 3:43–52.

Trager, Felicia H. (1968) *Picuris Pueblo, New Mexico: An "Ethnolinguistic" Salvage Survey.*

Trepp, Leo. (1980) *The Complete Book of Jewish Observance.*

Tschopik, Harry, Jr. (1951) *The Aymara of Chucuito, Peru: 1. Magic.*

Turnbull, Colin M. (1965) *The Mbuti Pygmies: An Ethnographic Survey.*

Turner, B. L., II, and Stephen B. Brush, eds. (1987) *Comparative Farming Systems.*

Turner, Victor W. (1952) *The Lozi Peoples of North-Western Rhodesia.*

Underhill, Muriel M. (1921) *The Hindu Religious Year.*

Upton, Dell, ed. (1986) *America's Architectural Roots: Ethnic Groups That Built America.*

Vayda, Andrew P. (1976) *War in Ecological Perspective.*

Villa Rojas, Alfonso. (1945) *The Maya of East Central Quintana Roo.*

———. (1969) "The Tzeltal." In *Handbook of Middle American Indians, Volume 7,* edited by Robert Wauchope, 195–225.

Viviani, Nancy. (1970) *Nauru: Phosphate and Political Progress.*

Waddell, Eric. (1975) "How the Enga Cope with Frost: Responses to Climatic Perturbations in the Central Highlands of New Guinea." *Human Ecology* 3:249–273.

Walker, Anthony R. (1986) *The Toda of South India: A New Look.*

Wallace, William. (1978) "Northern Valley Yokuts." In *Handbook of North American Indians. Volume 8. California,* edited by Robert F. Heizer, 462–470.

Wang, Hsing-ju (1948) *The Miao People of Hainan Island.*

Waters, Frank. (1963) *Book of the Hopi.*

Waugh, Frederick W. (1916) *Iroquois Foods and Food Preparation.*

Weiss, Jerome. (1978) *Folk Psychology of the Javanese of Ponorogo.*

Weissleder, Wolfgang. (1978) *The Nomadic Alternative: Modes and Models of Interaction in the African-Asian Deserts and Steppes.*

Weissner, Polly. (1974) "A Functional Estimation of Population from Floor Area." *American Antiquity* 39:343–350.

Weltfish, Gene. (1965) *The Lost Universe: With a Closing Chapter on "The Universe Regained."*

Werner, Roland. (1975) *Jah-het of Malaysia: Art and Culture*

Westermann, Diedrich H. (1921) *The Kpelle: A Negro Tribe in Liberia.*

White, Benjamin N. F. (1976) *Production and Reproduction in a Javanese Village.*

Whiting, Alfred F. (1939) *Ethnobotany of the Hopi.*

Whiting, John W. M., and Barbara Ayres. (1968) "Inferences from the Shape of Dwellings." In *Settlement Archaeology*, edited by K. C. Chang, 117–133.

Wilbert, Johannes. (1967) "Secular and Sacred Functions of the Fire among the Warao." *Anthropologica* 19:3–23.

Williams, Paula J. (1983) *The Social Organization of Firewood Procurement and Use in Africa: A Study of the Division of Labor by Sex.*

Wilmer, Frankie. (1993) *The Indigenous Voice in World Politics: Since Time Immemorial.*

Wilmsen, Edwin. (1989) *Land Filled with Flies: A Political Economy of the Kalahari.*

Wilson, Paul B. (1972) *Farming and Ranching on the Wind River Indian Reservation, Wyoming.*

Winterhalder, Bruce, and Eric A. Smith, eds. (1981) *Hunter-Gatherer Foraging Strategies: Ethnographic and Archeological Analyses.*

Wissler, Clark. (1910) *Material Culture of the Blackfoot Indians.*

Wittfogel, Karl. (1957) *Oriental Despotism: A Comparative Study of Total Power.*

Wolf, Margery. (1968) *The House of Lim: A Study of a Chinese Family Farm.*

Young, Allan L. (1970) *Medical Beliefs and Practices of the Begemder Amhara.*

Young, John E. (1992) "Mining the Earth." In *State of the World*, 100–118.

Zirakzadeh, Cyrus E. (1989) *Popular Politics in the Basque Region of Spain: A Study in Political Anthropology.*

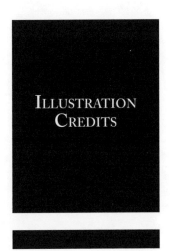

ILLUSTRATION CREDITS

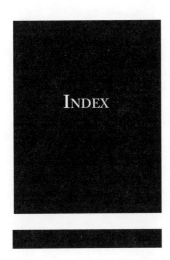

INDEX